3

SECOND EDITION

STEP FORWARD

STANDARDS-BASED LANGUAGE LEARNING
FOR WORK AND ACADEMIC READINESS

SERIES DIRECTOR
Jayme Adelson-Goldstein

Lesson Plans

OXFORD
UNIVERSITY PRESS

198 Madison Avenue
New York, NY 10016 USA

Great Clarendon Street, Oxford, OX2 6DP, United Kingdom

Oxford University Press is a department of the University of Oxford.
It furthers the University's objective of excellence in research, scholarship,
and education by publishing worldwide. Oxford is a registered trade
mark of Oxford University Press in the UK and in certain other countries

First published in 2018

2022 2021 2020 2019 2018

10 9 8 7 6 5 4 3 2 1

ISBN: 978 0 19 474833 9

Printed in China

This book is printed on paper from certified and well-managed sources

ACKNOWLEDGMENTS

Back cover photograph: Oxford University Press building/David Fisher

CONTENTS

The First Step

Lesson Overview	Lesson Notes

MULTILEVEL OBJECTIVES

Pre-, On-, and Higher-level: Meet classmates, alphabetize names, and review parts of speech

LANGUAGE FOCUS

Grammar: Parts of speech (noun, adjective, verb, adverb)

Vocabulary: Words for introducing, parts of speech, classroom items

For vocabulary support, see these **Oxford Picture Dictionary** topics: Meeting and Greeting, pages 2–3; Prepositions, page 25

READINESS CONNECTION

In this lesson, students explore parts of speech and the alphabet and communicate greetings.

PACING

To compress this lesson: Conduct 3A and 3C as whole-class activities. Have students practice 1B with just one partner.

To extend this lesson: Have students practice adjectives and adverbs. (See end of lesson.)

And/or have students complete **Multilevel Activities 3 Pre-unit pages 13–16.**

CORRELATIONS

CCRS: SL.2.B Determine the main ideas and supporting details of a text read aloud or information presented in diverse media and formats, including visually, quantitatively, and orally.

L.1.A (e.) Use verbs to convey a sense of past, present and future. (j.) Use frequently occurring prepositions.

L.1.B (b.) Explain the function of nouns, pronouns, verbs, adjectives, and adverbs in general and their functions in particular sentences. (l.) Produce simple, compound and complex sentences.

L.2.A (b.) Capitalize dates and names of people.

RF.4.B (a.) Read grade-level text with purpose and understanding.

ELPS: 8. An ELL can determine the meaning of words and phrases in oral presentations and literary and informational text. 9. An ELL can create clear and coherent level-appropriate speech and text. 10. An ELL can demonstrate command of the conventions of standard English to communicate in level-appropriate speech and writing.

Warm-up and Review
10–15 minutes (books closed)

Write information about yourself on the board—for example, your name, the city you live in, the city (or state or country) where you are from, your marital status, how many children you have. Elicit the question to go with each piece of information. For example: *What's your name? Where do you live?* Have students repeat the questions. Elicit any other questions they have about you.

Introduction
5 minutes

1. Say: *Now you know something about me. It's time for us to get to know each other.*

2. State the objective: *Today we're going to get to know each other and review alphabetizing and the parts of speech.*

1 Introducing yourself to your classmates

Presentation I
15–20 minutes

A 🔊 1-02 1. Direct students to look at the picture. Ask: *Who are these people? What are they doing?*

2. Read the instructions aloud. Direct students to read the conversation silently and underline the examples of the past, present, and future. Call on volunteers for the answers.

3. Play the audio. Ask students to listen and repeat the conversation.

4. Elicit different completions for *I want to improve my _____.* Write students' ideas on the board.

Answers
Present: Answers will vary.
Past: I studied
Future: I'm going to

Guided Communicative Practice I
15–20 minutes

B 1. Model the conversation with a volunteer. Switch roles and model with a different volunteer.

2. Direct students to walk around the room and practice the conversation with five different partners. Tell them to remember the first names of their classmates. Participate in the exercise and provide feedback.

C Ask students to write the names of the classmates they met. Encourage them to ask each other for help with spelling. Elicit and write this question on the board: *Excuse me, how do you spell your name?*

2 Alphabetize a list

Guided Communicative Practice II
15–20 minutes

A 1. Introduce the new topic: *Now we're going to practice alphabetizing.* Write *alphabetize = put in alphabetical order* on the board. Ask students why this skill is important in English class. [for organizing vocabulary lists and looking up words in the dictionary]

2. Direct students to look at the list of names and mark the sentences *T* (true), *F* (false), or *NI* (no information). Go over the answers as a class.

3. Point out that Maki, Maria, and Miguel all begin with the same letter. Elicit the process for alphabetizing words that start with the same letter.

Answers
1. F
2. T
3. F
4. NI

B Have students refer to their lists and call out the name they think should come first on the list. Working together, create an alphabetized list of the students' names on the board.

3 Review parts of speech

Presentation II
15–20 minutes

A 1. Introduce the new topic: *Now we're going to review the parts of speech.* Write *Noun, Adjective, Verb,* and *Adverb* on the board as column heads. Elicit an example of each and write the words in the correct column.

2. Direct students' attention to the chart. Read the information about nouns and the example sentences. Elicit a few more nouns and write them in the Noun column on the board. Test each noun in the list with this question: Does this word tell us who, what, or where? Repeat the process with each part of speech. When you elicit examples of verbs, ask students to say them in different forms.

3. Direct students to work individually to label each of the words below the chart. Go over the answers as a class. Use the questions from the chart to clarify any confusion. Elicit a sample sentence for each word.

Answers	
1. n	6. n
2. v	7. adj
3. adj	8. adv
4. adv	9. v
5. v	

Guided Practice
10–15 minutes

 1. Add *Preposition* to your chart on the board and write the words from the box in the new column. Direct students to look back at the picture in 1A. Read the sample sentences aloud and elicit another sentence from a volunteer.

2. Have students work with a partner to talk about the picture. Monitor their practice and provide feedback. Ask volunteers to say one of their sentences for the class.

Communicative Practice
15–20 minutes

 1. Read the instructions and the sample sentences aloud. Elicit the parts of speech.

2. Have students work with a group of three or four students. Tell them to take turns thinking up sentences. After the first student says a sentence, have all group members write the sentence down. Then have the next student say a sentence and the group members write it down. Model the exercise with a volunteer group.

3. Assign a time limit (five minutes) and tell students to take turns saying sentences until "time" is called. Call "time." Ask volunteers to read their sentences aloud.

MULTILEVEL STRATEGIES

Provide a simpler and more challenging means of completing 3C and tell students to use whichever method they feel comfortable with. Explain that you will be watching and listening to them so that you can determine their levels and target your instruction to their individual needs.

• **Pre-level** Provide fill-in-the-blank sentences with different parts of speech missing.
The _____ is next to the door. The students are speaking _____. The teacher's desk is _____. The exit sign is _____ the door.
Write these sentences on the board. Tell students that if it's difficult for them to come up with their own sentences for 3C, they can use the sentences on the board.

• **Higher-level** Tell students who want a challenge to try using an adjective or an adverb in each sentence and to write sentences in different tenses.

Monitor student practice and make a note of which students will need extra help or extra challenges.

Evaluation
10–15 minutes

Dictate several sentences about the classroom. *Three students are sitting next to the bookcase. Tom always comes to class early. Maria is writing carefully in her new notebook.* Ask students to write the sentences and then label the nouns, verbs, adjectives, adverbs, and prepositions. Collect and correct their writing.

EXTENSION ACTIVITY

Practice Adjectives and Adverbs

Brainstorm adjective-noun and verb-adverb combinations. Write sentence frames on the board. *Mia is a(n) _____ woman. Joseph speaks very _____. Brian likes _____ food. That was a(n) _____ movie.* Tell students to work with a partner to brainstorm completions. Have volunteers take turns writing their ideas on the board.

Unit Overview

This unit explores study skills and the U.S. educational system with a range of employability skills and contextualizes present and past tense verb structures.

KEY OBJECTIVES	
Lesson 1	Discuss study skills and the U.S. educational system
Lesson 2	Write a paragraph describing your feelings the first day of class
Lesson 3	Use present and past tense to describe study habits and learning
Lesson 4	Talk about career choices and your strengths and weaknesses
Lesson 5	Identify educational resources
At Work	Show that you are listening
Teamwork & Language Review	Review unit language

UNIT FEATURES	
Academic Vocabulary	*accurately, challenge, revise, research, schedule*
Employability Skills	• Locate information • Infer information • Analyze information • Determine how to talk with classmates as a new student • Work independently • Understand teamwork • Communicate verbally • Listen actively • Use writing skills • Comprehend written material • Analyze information

Resources	**Class Audio** CD1, Tracks 03–13
	Workbook Unit 1, pages 2–8
	Teacher Resource Center
	    Multilevel Activities 3 Unit 1
	    Multilevel Grammar Exercises 3 Unit 1
	    Unit 1 Test
	Oxford Picture Dictionary Schools and Subjects, Succeeding in School, Career Planning

| Lesson Overview | Lesson Notes |

MULTILEVEL OBJECTIVES

On-level: Identify study skills and study habits and describe the educational system

Pre-level: Identify study skills, study habits, and educational-system vocabulary

Higher-level: Talk and write about study skills and study habits and explain the educational system

LANGUAGE FOCUS

Grammar: Simple present tense (*Sometimes I make an outline.*)

Vocabulary: Study skills and study habits, the educational system

For vocabulary support, see this **Oxford Picture Dictionary** topic: Schools and Subjects, pages 200–201

STRATEGY FOCUS

Pool knowledge with team members to maximize vocabulary learning.

READINESS CONNECTION

In this lesson, students explore and communicate information about study skills, study habits, and the U.S. educational system.

PACING

To compress this lesson: Conduct 1C as a whole-class activity.

To extend this lesson: Have students talk about school systems. (See end of lesson.)

And/or have students complete **Workbook 3 page 2** and **Multilevel Activities 3 Unit 1 pages 18–19**.

CORRELATIONS

CCRS: SL.1.A (a.) Follow agreed-upon rules for discussions.

SL.4.B Report on a topic or text, tell a story, or recount an experience with appropriate facts and relevant, descriptive details, speaking clearly at an understandable pace.

R.5.A Know and use various text features to locate key facts or information in a text.

W.7.A Participate in shared research and writing projects.

L.1.B (l.) Produce simple, compound and complex sentences.

L.4.B (e.) Use glossaries and beginning dictionaries, both print and digital, to determine or clarify the meaning of words and phrases.

RF.4.B (a.) Read grade-level text with purpose and understanding.

ELPS: 8. An ELL can determine the meaning of words and phrases in oral presentations and literary and informational text.

Warm-up and Review
10–15 minutes (books closed)

Write *In bed, At the library,* and *At the kitchen table* on the board. Ask: *Which of these is the best place to study?* Elicit the advantages and disadvantages of each place. Use the students' ideas to come to a class consensus on the qualities of an ideal study place (quiet, comfortable, good light, materials at hand, etc.).

Introduction
3 minutes

1. Say: *We've talked about where to study; now let's talk about how to study. What should you do when you study?* Elicit students' ideas.

2. State the objective: *Today we're going to talk about study skills, study habits, and the U.S. educational system.*

1 Identify study skills and habits

Presentation I
20–25 minutes

A 1. Write *Study skills* on the board and elicit one example from the whole class. Have students work together to brainstorm in a group. Make a list on the board of the ways to learn and practice English that your students identify.

2. Have students identify the most essential study skills and habits. Elicit ideas and put a checkmark next to the five skills and habits students feel are essential, encouraging them to explain their reasons.

B 1. Direct students to look at the pictures. Say: *This is David. Where is he studying? Do you think David is a good student?*

2. Group students and assign roles: manager, researcher, administrative assistant, and reporter. Explain that students work with their groups to match the words and pictures. Verify students' understanding of the roles.

3. Set a time limit (three minutes). As students work together, copy the wordlist onto the board.

4. Call "time." Have reporters take turns giving their answers. Write each group's answer on the board next to the words.

Answers	
3 (do) research	8 memorize words
2 find a quiet place	5 search online
7 make a study schedule	6 organize materials
9 make an outline	4 take a break
	1 take notes

TIP

When setting up task-based activities, verify that students understand their roles using physical commands. For example: *If you report on your team's work, stand up* [reporter]. *If you keep the team on task, point to the clock* [manager]. *If you write the team's responses, raise your hand* [administrative assistant]. *If you help the team research, point to your book* [researcher].

MULTILEVEL STRATEGIES

After the group comprehension check in 1B, call on individuals and tailor your questions to the level of your students.

- **Pre-level** Ask *or* questions. *In picture 1, are they taking notes or searching online?* [taking notes]
- **On-level** Ask information questions. *In picture 5, what is he doing?* [searching online]
- **Higher-level** Ask these students to compare the pictures to their own study methods. *What is the best place for you to study? Why? How do you organize your materials?*

C 🔊 1-03 1. To prepare students for listening, say: *We're going to hear about David's study habits.* Ask students to listen and check their answers.

2. Have students check the wordlist on the board and then write the correct numbers in their books.

3. Pair students. Set a time limit (three minutes). Monitor pair practice to identify pronunciation issues.

4. Call "time" and work with the pronunciation of any troublesome words or phrases.

Guided Practice I
10–15 minutes

D 1. Model the conversation with a volunteer. Model it again using other information from 1B.

2. Set a time limit (three minutes). Direct students to practice with a partner.

3. Call on volunteers to present one of their conversations for the class.

2 Learn about the U.S. educational system

Presentation II
15–20 minutes

A 1. Direct students to look at the brochure. Introduce the new topic by asking: *What is this brochure about?*

2. Ask students to work individually to complete the brochure. Call on volunteers to read the completed sentences aloud. Write the answers on the board.

3. Check comprehension. Ask: *What school do seventh graders attend? What do you need to attend a university or community college?*

4. Draw students' attention to the photos. Prompt students to use vocabulary not labeled in the art. Ask: *What do you see in the pictures that is the same as schools in your country? What is different?*

Answers	
elementary school 1. middle school 2. high school 3. adult school	4. community college/ university 5. university/ community college 6. vocational school

Guided Practice II
10–15 minutes

B 1. Model the conversation with a volunteer. Model it again using different words from 2A.

2. Set a time limit (three minutes). Direct students to practice with a partner.

3. Call on volunteers to present one of their conversations for the class.

Communicative Practice and Application
20–25 minutes

C 1. If students will use the Internet for this task, establish what device(s) they'll use: a class computer, tablets, or smartphones. Alternatively, print information from the Internet before class and distribute to groups.

2. Write the question from 2C on the board. Explain that students will work in teams to research and report on this question. Ask: *Which search terms or questions can you use to find the information you need?* ["elementary school" + your city] *What information will you scan for?* [names, addresses] How will you record the information you find? [table, checklist, index cards] Remind students to bookmark or record sites so they can find or cite them in the future.

3. Group students and assign roles: manager, administrative assistant, IT support, and reporter. Verify students' understanding of the roles.

4. Give managers the time limit for researching question 1 (ten minutes). Direct the IT support to begin the online research or pick up the printed materials for each team. Direct the administrative assistant to record information for the team using a table, a checklist, or index cards.

5. Give a two-minute warning. Call "time."

D 1. Copy the sentence stem on the board.

2. Direct teams to help their administrative assistant use the sentence stem to record the team's findings. Direct the reporter to use the recorded information to report the team's findings to the class or another team.

Evaluation
10–15 minutes (books closed)

TEST YOURSELF

Read the instructions aloud. Model the activity with a volunteer. Have students do the task. Circulate and monitor.

MULTILEVEL STRATEGIES

Target the *Test Yourself* to the level of your students.

• **Pre-level** Have these students do the activity the first time with the option to look at the answers if needed. Then have them do the activity a second time without looking at the answers.

• **Higher-level** Have these students say a sentence about their own study habits that uses the words as they point to each picture.

TIP

To provide further practice of the vocabulary:

1. Direct students to work individually to write a list of at least ten words from the lesson. Assign a time limit (three minutes). Call "time" and direct students to work with a partner to combine their lists and put the words in alphabetical order. Circulate and monitor students' progress.

2. Ask a volunteer pair to write its list on the board. Ask other students to add words to the list on the board.

EXTENSION ACTIVITY

Talk about School Systems

Explore students' questions about the U.S. school system in general or about your local school system in particular. Have students work with a partner to brainstorm two or three questions they have about the U.S. school system or about your local schools. Elicit questions and discuss them as a class. Write down any unanswered questions. Suggest where students can look for the answers, or find the answers yourself and share them with the class.

Lesson Overview	Lesson Notes

MULTILEVEL OBJECTIVES

On- and Higher-level: Analyze, write, and edit a journal entry about a life lesson

Pre-level: Read a journal entry and write about a life lesson

LANGUAGE FOCUS

Grammar: Simple past tense (*The students worked in groups.*)

Vocabulary: *Journal entry, nervous, embarrassed, worried, whispered*

For vocabulary support, see this **Oxford Picture Dictionary** topic: Succeeding in School, page 10

STRATEGY FOCUS

When writing, make sure the sentences in a paragraph are about the same idea.

READINESS CONNECTION

In this lesson, students listen actively, read, and write about things that are done in English class.

PACING

To compress this lesson: Assign the *Test Yourself* and/or 3C for homework.

To extend this lesson: Have students discuss overcoming challenges. (See end of lesson.)

And/or have students complete **Workbook 3 page 3** and **Multilevel Activities 3 Unit 1 page 20**.

CORRELATIONS

CCRS: SL.1.A (a.) follow agreed-upon rules for discussions.

R.1.B Ask and answer such questions as who, what, where, when, why, and how to demonstrate understanding of key details in a text.

R.5.A Know and use various text features to locate key facts or information in a text.

R.7.A Use the illustrations and details in a text to describe its key ideas.

W.3.A Write narratives in which they recount two or more appropriately sequenced events, include some details regarding what happened, use temporal words to signal event order, and provide some sense of closure.

W.5.B With guidance and support from peers and others, develop and strengthen writing as needed by planning, revising and editing.

L.1.B (l.) Produce simple, compound and complex sentences.

L.2.B (h.) Use conventional spelling for high-frequency and other studied words and for adding suffixes to base words.

L.4.B (c.) Use a known root word as a clue to the meaning of an unknown word with the same root.

L.6.B Acquire and use accurately level-appropriate conversational, general academic, and domain-specific words and phrases, including those that signal spatial and temporal relationships.

RF.3.B (c.) Identify and know the meaning of the most common prefixes and derivational suffixes.

RF.4.B (a.) Read grade-level text with purpose and understanding.

ELPS: 6. An ELL can analyze and critique the arguments of others orally and in writing. 9. An ELL can create clear and coherent level-appropriate speech and text.

Warm-up and Review
10–15 minutes (books closed)

Think of four to six activities that your students do in class—for example, *Talk in groups, Work with a partner, Write new words in a notebook, Read the textbook, Do grammar exercises, Listen to conversations,* etc. Make a sign for each activity and post the signs around the room. Direct students to stand next to the activity they like to do most. Ask students to tell a partner what they like about the activity they chose.

Introduction
5 minutes

1. Briefly explain why all of the activities you discussed in the *Warm-up* are important. Tell students that today they will focus on writing.

2. State the objective: *Today we'll read and write about the things we do in English class.*

1 Prepare to write

Presentation
20–25 minutes

A 1. Build students' schema by asking questions about the picture and the last paragraph of the journal entry. Ask: *Who are these people? Where are they?*

2. Give students one minute to tell a partner their responses to questions 1 and 2. Elicit responses from the class.

B 🔊 **1-04** 1. Introduce the model journal entry and its purpose: *You're going to read a journal entry about a student's first day of class. As you read, look for the purpose of the journal entry: Why is the student writing?* Have students read the journal entry silently.

2. Check comprehension. Ask: *What was the first assignment?* [to tell the group why they were studying English] *Who is nervous?* [everyone] *What helped them overcome their fear?* [joking about it]

3. Play the audio. Have students read along silently.

Guided Practice I
10 minutes

C 1. Have students work independently to underline the answers to the questions in the journal entry.

2. Point out the *Writer's Note* and ask students to annotate the information they underlined with the phrases "challenge" for question 1, "overcame the challenge" for question 2, and "lesson learned" for question 3. Have pairs compare answers. Have volunteers call out answers and write them on the board for the class to check.

> **Possible Answers**
> 1. I was nervous at first because I usually like to work alone.
>   I was afraid I might make a mistake and feel embarrassed.
>   I was worried about my pronunciation.
> 2. We all laughed a lot.
>   The joke helped us overcome our fear.
> 3. I want to work in groups again tomorrow because it gives me the chance to really practice my English.
>   I know that everything will be fine in the end.
>   Humor makes English learning more enjoyable.

> **MULTILEVEL STRATEGIES**
>
> Seat pre-level students together for 1C.
>
> • **Pre-level** While other students are working on 1C, ask these students *yes/no* and *or* questions about the reading. *Was the English class interesting? Was the writer relaxed or nervous? Did she have a lot to say or nothing to say? Did she finally relax?* Allow these students to copy the answers to 1C from the board.
>
> • **On- and Higher-level** After these students complete 1C, ask them to circle the adjectives the writer uses to describe the class and her feelings.

2 Plan and write

Guided Practice II
15–20 minutes

A 1. Read the questions aloud. Elicit students' answers.

2. Write students' ideas for question 2 on the board so they can refer to them while they write.

B Read through the journal entry template. Elicit ideas that could go in each paragraph. Have students write their journal entries individually.

Adapt 2B to the level of your students.

- **Pre-level** Work with these students to write a group journal entry. Read through the template. At each ellipsis, stop and elicit completions. Decide as a group what to write. Have these learners copy the group journal entry into their notebooks.

- **Higher-level** Ask these students to add a fourth paragraph that answers these questions: *What was another activity you did when you started English classes? Was it challenging? Why or why not?*

3 Get feedback and revise

Guided Practice III
5 minutes

A Direct students to check their writing using the editing checklist. Tell them to read each item in the list and check their papers before moving on to the next item. Explain that students should not edit their writing at this stage. They should just use the checklist to check their work and mark any areas they want to revise.

Communicative Practice
15 minutes

B 1. Read the instructions and the sample sentences aloud. Emphasize to students that they are responding to their partners' work, not correcting it.

2. Use the journal entry in 1B to model the exercise. *I think the part about the students whispering to each other is interesting. I'd like to ask this writer what else he did on the first day of class.*

3. Direct students to exchange papers with a partner and follow the instructions.

C Allow students time to edit and revise their writing as necessary, using the editing checklist from 3A and their partner's feedback from 3B. If necessary, students could complete this task as homework.

TIP

Suggest to students that they keep a learning journal. They can write a paragraph or two at the end of every week and talk about how they have learned something difficult, what their learning difficulties are, a plan for the next week, etc.

Application and Evaluation
10 minutes

TEST YOURSELF

1. Review the instructions aloud. Assign a time limit (five minutes) and have students work independently.

2. Before collecting student work, invite two or three volunteers to share their sentences. Ask students to raise their hands if they wrote similar answers.

EXTENSION ACTIVITY

Talk about Challenges

Write a list of classroom activities on the board. Share your thoughts about the purpose of each one. Ask students which activities are challenging and why. Come to a class consensus about how to overcome the challenge of each activity.

Lesson Overview	Lesson Notes

MULTILEVEL OBJECTIVES

On- and Higher-level: Use present and past verb forms to describe study habits and learning and listen for simple past, simple present, and present continuous

Pre-level: Recognize present and past verb forms and answer *yes/no* questions in present and past tense in order to talk about study habits and learning

LANGUAGE FOCUS

Grammar: Simple present tense (*He studies every day.*); present continuous tense (*He is studying.*); simple past tense (*He studied last night.*)

Vocabulary: *Assignment, memorize*

For vocabulary support, see this **Oxford Picture Dictionary** topic: Succeeding in School, page 10

READINESS CONNECTION

In this lesson, students review present and past verb forms to talk about study habits and other activities.

PACING

To compress this lesson: Conduct 1C as a whole-class activity.

To extend this lesson: Have students practice talking about study habits. (See end of lesson.)

And/or have students complete **Workbook 3 pages 4–5, Multilevel Activities 3 Unit 1 pages 21–22**, and **Multilevel Grammar Exercises 3 Unit 1**.

CORRELATIONS

CCRS: R.1.B Ask and answer such questions as who, what, where, when, why, and how to demonstrate understanding of key details in a text.

R.7.A Use the illustrations and details in a text to describe its key ideas.

L.1.B (b.) Explain the function of nouns, pronouns, verbs, adjectives, and adverbs in general and their functions in particular sentences. (h.) Form and use the simple verb tenses. (l.) Produce simple, compound and complex sentences.

L.2.B (c.) Use commas in greetings and closings of letters. (h.) Use conventional spelling for high-frequency and other studied words and for adding suffixes to base words.

L.4.B (c.) Use a known root word as a clue to the meaning of an unknown word with the same root.

RF.3.B (c.) Identify and know the meaning of the most common prefixes and derivational suffixes.

RF.4.B (a.) Read grade-level text with purpose and understanding.

ELPS: 7. An ELL can adapt language choices to purpose, task, and audience when speaking and writing. 10. An ELL can demonstrate command of the conventions of standard English to communicate in level-appropriate speech and writing.

Warm-up and Review
10–15 minutes (books closed)

Write *Yesterday, Every day*, and *Now* as column heads on the board. Ask: *What did you do yesterday? What do you do every day? What are you doing right now?* As students answer, write the base forms of the verbs they use to the right of the columns. Leave these on the board.

Introduction
5–10 minutes

1. Elicit the names of the tenses that are represented on the board and write *Simple past* above *Yesterday*, *Present continuous* above *Now*, and *Simple present* above *Every day*. Tell students: *When we are speaking and writing in English, we use these tenses all the time.*

2. State the objective: *Today we're going to review present and past verb forms so that we can talk about our study habits and other activities.*

1 Review present and past verb forms

Presentation I
20–25 minutes

 1. Direct students to look at the notebook page. Ask: *What is on the notebook page? Do you write your assignments in your notebook?*

2. Read the instructions aloud. Ask students to read the paragraph and notebook page silently and answer the questions.

3. Read the first question aloud. Call on a volunteer for the answer. Ask the volunteer where in the conversation he or she found the answer. Read the rest of the questions aloud, calling on a different volunteer for each answer.

Answers
1. Every day
2. Monday night
3. He is memorizing this week's new words and preparing for tomorrow's class.
4. He was eating dinner.

B 1. Demonstrate how to read the grammar charts. Read the charts through sentence by sentence. Then read them again and have students repeat after you.

2. Ask students to substitute a new verb into each chart—for example, *memorize*.

3. Direct students to underline one example of each tense in the paragraph in 1A. Go over the answers as a class.

4. Talk about the form and meaning of each verb in the paragraph. Ask: *Where is the writer right now? How do you know? How do you form the present continuous? Why does the writer use simple present for "learn new words"?*

5. Assess students' understanding of the verb tenses. Refer to the verbs from the *Warm-up*. Elicit the correct verb forms for each "time" column (*Yesterday, Every day, Now*) in complete sentences.

Possible Answers
Simple present: write, learn, memorize, forget
Present continuous: am memorizing, am preparing
Simple past: wrote, answered
Past continuous: was eating

Guided Practice I
10–15 minutes

 1. Tell students they will collaborate to complete the description of the grammar point. Model collaboration by working with the class to complete the first sentence. Encourage students to look at 1A and 1B to help them complete the blanks.

2. Pair students and have them work together to complete the description.

3. Project or write the completed definition on the board and have pairs verify the accuracy of their responses. Ask volunteers which sentences confused them and discuss.

Answers
simple present
present continuous
simple past
past continuous

Guided Practice II
15–20 minutes

 1. Direct students' attention to Danny's schedule and have students take turns reading it aloud. Then read the instructions aloud and model the conversation with a volunteer.

2. Write the question stems on the board. Have volunteers come to the board and write a question for each one. Point to the verb in each sentence and have the class identify the tense and why it is used in that question.

3. Have students do the task in pairs. Circulate and monitor.

MULTILEVEL STRATEGIES
Group same-level students together.
• **Pre-level** Sit with these students and write questions together. Take turns with them asking and answering questions.
• **Higher-level** Challenge these students to substitute different activities into Danny's schedule and do the activity again.

2 Ask and answer present and past *yes/no* questions

Presentation II
20–25 minutes

 1. Introduce the new topic: *Now we're going to practice asking present and past tense questions about studying.*

2. Read each question and short answer in the chart aloud. Ask students to identify the two parts of each verb.

3. Check comprehension. Say several different questions without time clues and ask students to call out the time frame (right now, usually, in the past). *Are you working?* [right now] *Did you sleep well?* [in the past] *Does she work?* [usually] *Do you go to the library?* [usually]

Guided Practice III
20–25 minutes

 1. Read the instructions aloud. Direct students to circle the correct words in the sentences first and then match the questions and answers. Ask volunteers to read the questions and answers aloud.

2. Have pairs compare answers before going over answers as a class.

3. Set a time limit (five minutes) and have pairs practice asking and answering new questions. Circulate and monitor. After you call "time," have students write one of their additional questions on the board. Have another student answer it.

Answers	
1. Did, f	4. Did, c
2. Are, a	5. Is, e
3. Do, d	6. Do, b

TIP
As you circulate, make notes of any common problems students have and go over them as a class.

 1. Elicit the importance of accuracy. Tell students they will be building their accuracy in this task.

2. Organize students into groups. Demonstrate how to correct the sentence using the first example.

3. Have team members work together to correct the sentences. Circulate and monitor teamwork.

4. Project or write the corrected sentences on the board and have teams check their work.

5. Address questions and any issues you noted during your observation.

Answers
1. Paulo isn't taking notes now.
2. Yan memorizes words every day.
3. We are taking a break now.
4. I didn't take notes yesterday.

3 Listen for the tenses to determine the meaning

Guided Practice IV
15–20 minutes

 1-05 1. Say: *We've been talking about our study habits—what we usually do, what we did yesterday, and what we're doing right now. Now we're going to listen to sentences about different people and decide what tense the sentence is in.*

2. Direct students to look at the chart. Elicit an example sentence for each row.

3. Play the audio. Ask students to check the correct box.

4. Call on volunteers for the answers.

Answers	
1. Present continuous	6. Present continuous
2. Simple past	7. Past continuous
3. Past continuous	8. Simple present
4. Simple past	9. Simple present
5. Simple present	10. Past continuous

MULTILEVEL STRATEGIES
Replay the audio to challenge on- and higher-level students while allowing pre-level students to catch up.

• **Pre-level** Have these students listen again to complete the exercise.

• **On- and Higher-level** Ask these students to write the verb they hear. When you elicit the answers to 3A, call on these students to state the verb and pre-level students to state the tense.

4 Use present and past verb forms

Communicative Practice and Application
20–25 minutes

 1. Direct students to look at the illustration. Read the instructions aloud and model the sample conversation with a volunteer.

2. Have groups of three or four take turns asking and answering questions about the illustration. Circulate and monitor.

3. Have students share their conversations with the class.

MULTILEVEL STRATEGIES

- **Pre-level** Work with these students and guide them in writing questions. Suggest verbs and question words they can use based on the picture and help them put the verb in the correct tense.
- **Higher-level** Have these students change the time on the clock in the illustration and ask and answer at least two questions for each tense in the chart in 2A.

Evaluation
10–15 minutes

TEST YOURSELF

Ask students to write the sentences independently. Collect and correct their writing.

EXTENSION ACTIVITY

Ask about Study Habits

Have students practice speaking in the third person.

1. Direct students to use the questions in 2B and take turns asking and answering with a partner.

2. Direct students to stand up and find a new partner. Have them tell their new partners what they learned about their previous partners. Tell them to move on to another partner when they have finished speaking. They should tell that person about their previous partner.

3. As students are talking, participate in the activity, or monitor and provide feedback.

Lesson Overview	Lesson Notes
MULTILEVEL OBJECTIVES	
Pre-, On-, and Higher-level: Talk about career possibilities and listen for information about career preparation	
LANGUAGE FOCUS	
Grammar: Adjectives and adverbs (*He's a careful worker. He works carefully.*) **Vocabulary:** Career words For vocabulary support, see this **Oxford Picture Dictionary** topic: Career Planning, pages 174–175	
STRATEGY FOCUS	
Use adjectives to describe nouns and adverbs to give information about verbs.	
READINESS CONNECTION	
In this lesson, students verbally communicate about careers and career choices.	
PACING	
To compress this lesson: Skip 4A and do 5C as a whole-class activity. **To extend this lesson:** Have students write a story. (See end of lesson.) And/or have students complete **Workbook 3 page 6** and **Multilevel Activities 3 Unit 1 page 23**.	

CORRELATIONS

CCRS: SL.1.B (d.) Explain their own ideas and understanding in light of the discussion.

SL.2.B Determine the main ideas and supporting details of a text read aloud or information presented in diverse media and formats, including visually, quantitatively, and orally.

SL.4.B Report on a topic or text, tell a story, or recount an experience with appropriate facts and relevant, descriptive details, speaking clearly at an understandable pace.

SL.6.B Speak in complete sentences when appropriate to task and situation in order to provide requested detail or clarification.

L.1.B (l.) Produce simple, compound and complex sentences.

RF.2.A (g.) Isolate and pronounce initial, medial vowel, and final sounds (phonemes) in spoken single-syllable words.

RF.4.B (a.) Read grade-level text with purpose and understanding.

ELPS: 2. An ELL can participate in level-appropriate oral and written exchanges of information, ideas, and analyses, in various social and academic contexts, responding to peer, audience, or reader comments and questions. 9. An ELL can create clear and coherent level-appropriate speech and text.

Warm-up and Review
10–15 minutes (books closed)

Review job titles. Write the alphabet on the board and have volunteers come up and write one job title on the board for each letter. When students have run out of ideas, help them come up with something for the missing letters or allow them to check *The Oxford Picture Dictionary* or another picture dictionary.

Introduction
5 minutes

1. Say: *There are many different careers and many different things to think about when you're choosing one. What kind of person are you? What do you like to do? What type of training do you need for different jobs? How many jobs are available? A school counselor will have the answers to many of these questions.*

2. State the objective: *Today we're going to learn how to talk about careers and career choices.*

1 Learn ways to talk about careers

Presentation I
10 minutes

 1-06 1. Direct students to look at the picture. Ask students to talk about who each person is and what they are doing. Read the question aloud.

2. Read the instructions aloud. Play the audio. Give students a minute to answer the question. Go over the answer as a class.

Answer
She volunteered at the junior high school.

Guided Practice I
20–25 minutes

 1-06 1. Read the instructions and the questions aloud. Play the audio. Ask students to listen for the answer to each question.

2. Ask students to compare their answers with a partner. Circulate and monitor to ensure students understand the audio.

Answers
1. Volunteering at the junior high school last year, working part-time in a hotel after school, and business class
2. He suggested a career in education or hotel management.
3. Her part-time job at a hotel

 1-07 1. Read the instructions. Have students copy the sentence frames in their notebooks. Play the audio and have students listen silently.

2. Play the audio again. Have students write their answers individually before comparing answers in pairs. Check answers as a class.

Answers
1. just not
2. to choose
3. hard to

2 Practice your pronunciation

Pronunciation Extension
10–15 minutes

 1-08 1. Write *Which job should she choose?* on the board. Say the sentence and ask

students to repeat it. Underline *sh, ch,* and *j* and repeat each sound. Say: *Now we're going to focus on pronunciation of these three sounds.*

2. Play the audio. Direct students to listen for the pronunciation of *sh, ch,* and *j.*

3. Ask: *Which letters make the* sh *sound?* [*sh* and *su*] Make a sound and ask students to read you the sentence(s) with that sound.

 1-09 1. Have students write the sentences in their notebooks. Play the audio. Ask students to listen and write the missing words in the sentences.

2. Have volunteers write the sentences on the board to check answers.

Answers
1. just, sure
2. choices
3. should, education

C **1-09** 1. Read the instructions aloud. Play the audio again and have students do the task individually.

2. Write the chart on the board and have students come to the board and fill it in.

Answers
sh: sure, should, education
ch: choices
j: just, education

3 Use adjectives and adverbs to describe your skills

Presentation II and Guided Practice II
10–15 minutes

A 1. Introduce the new topic. Write *The students are quiet* and *The students worked quietly* on the board. Ask: *What does* quiet *describe in the first sentence? What kind of word is* students? *What does* quietly *describe in the second sentence? What kind of word is* worked? Say: Quiet *is an adjective. It describes the students.* Students *is a noun. Adjectives describe nouns.* Quietly *is an adverb. It describes the way students work. Adverbs describe verbs.*

2. Read the sentences in the charts aloud. Draw students' attention to the *Grammar Notes* and have volunteers take turns reading them aloud.

Communicative Practice
10–15 minutes

 1. Read the instructions. Read the sentence frame aloud and ask students for words to fill in the blanks.

2. Have pairs do the task. Circulate and monitor.

3. Have students tell the class about their partner.

4 Building conversation skills

Guided Practice III
15–20 minutes

A Direct students to look at the picture and skim the conversation in 4B. Have them work with partners to identify the purpose of the conversation. Elicit responses and ask: *How do you know?* or *Why do you say that?* to encourage students to state their reasoning.

Answer
They are talking about Carlos's career plans. Carlos is visiting a career advisor and is thinking about his future.

B **1-10** 1. Ask students to read the instructions and tell you what they are going to do [listen and read and respond to the question]. Play the audio and then elicit the answer to the question.

2. Ask students to read the conversation with a partner. Circulate and monitor pronunciation. Model and have students repeat difficult words or phrases.

3. Ask: *In what other situation could you use this conversation?* Point out a few phrases that are not specific to talking about a career. Ask volunteers to point out others.

Answer
Carlos wants to work with people.

Communicative Practice and Application I
15–20 minutes

C 1. Pair students and have them read the instructions silently. Check their comprehension of the exercise. Ask: *What are the two roles? Is the conversation at home or school?*

2. Model and have students repeat the expressions in the *In Other Words* box in 4B. Explain that they should use these expressions in their conversations.

3. Draw a T-chart on the board. Label the left column *Student* and the right column *School counselor*. Elicit examples of what each person might say and take notes in the chart.

4. Set a time limit (five minutes). Have students act out the role-play. Call "time" and have students switch roles.

5. Ask three volunteer pairs to act out their role-play for the class. Tell students who are listening to make a simple table with four rows and two columns. Use the top row to label the columns *Interests* and *Career goals*. Have students take notes in the chart for each role-play.

> **MULTILEVEL STRATEGIES**
>
> Seat same-level students together.
>
> • **Pre-level** Work with these students and guide them in writing their new conversation.
>
> • **Higher-level** Challenge students to use their imaginations and use silly or far-fetched interests and experiences in their conversations.

5 Focus on listening for details

Presentation III and Guided Practice IV
15–20 minutes

A 1. Read the questions and statement aloud and model a discussion with a volunteer. Ask: *Do you think every good career requires a good education? Why? / Why not? I agree because… / I disagree because…*

2. Pair students and tell them to discuss their own answers to the questions. Circulate and monitor.

> **TIP**
>
> Make sure students know to be respectful of each other's ideas and opinions and that showing anger and frustration is not appropriate classroom behavior.

B Direct students to read the sentences before they listen to the interview. Ask what kind of information they'll be writing in the blanks. Ask volunteers for predictions. If students struggle, start by offering your own prediction: *I think we will hear how the speaker became a carpenter.*

C ◆)) 1-11 1. Play the audio. Ask students to listen and write the correct answers.

2. Pair students and have them compare answers. If a pair has different answers, have the class vote on the correct answer with a show of hands.

Answers
1. apply
2. real
3. academic
4. working

6 Discuss

Communicative Practice and Application II
15–20 minutes

A 1. Read the instructions aloud. Draw a sample chart on the board with space for jobs on one side and skills on the other. Call on volunteers to complete the sentence stems in 6A. Fill in the chart for a teacher, writing *Tutoring children* and *Patience*. Explain that students will make a chart like this one based on their own discussions.

2. Put students into teams of three and assign roles: manager, administrative assistant, and reporter. Verify students' understanding of the roles. Encourage students to use the phrases in the *Speaking Note* during their discussions.

3. Set a time limit for the discussions (ten minutes). Write the sentence frame from 6B on the board. Then circulate and monitor.

B Call "time." Ask the reporter for each team to report the results of the team's discussion using the sentence frame on the board.

Evaluation
5 minutes

TEST YOURSELF

1. Ask students to complete the checkboxes individually.

2. Tell students that you are going to read each of the items in the checklist aloud. If they are not at all confident with that skill, they should hold up a closed fist. If they are not very confident, they should hold up one finger. If they are somewhat confident, two fingers; confident, three fingers; very confident, four

fingers. If they think they could teach the skill, they should hold up five fingers. Read each item in the checklist and identify students who may need further support.

Lesson Overview	Lesson Notes

MULTILEVEL OBJECTIVES

Pre-, On-, and Higher-level: Read about and discuss educational resources

LANGUAGE FOCUS

Grammar: Simple present tense and simple past tense (*I read the newspaper every day. I read the newspaper yesterday.*)

Vocabulary: *Check out, librarian*

For vocabulary support, see this **Oxford Picture Dictionary** topic: Succeeding in School, page 10

STRATEGY FOCUS

Read with a purpose by asking: *What do I want from this text?*

READINESS CONNECTION

In this lesson, students verbally communicate information about educational resources.

PACING

To compress this lesson: Assign 2A for homework.

To extend this lesson: Have students write and answer advice column letters. (See end of lesson.)

And/or have students complete **Workbook 3 page 7** and **Multilevel Activities 3 Unit 1 pages 24–25**.

CORRELATIONS

CCRS: SL.1.B (d.) Explain their own ideas and understanding in light of the discussion.

SL.2.B Determine the main ideas and supporting details of a text read aloud or information presented in diverse media and formats, including visually, quantitatively, and orally.

R.1.B Ask and answer such questions as who, what, where, when, why, and how to demonstrate understanding of key details in a text.

R.2.A Identify the main topic and retell key details of a text.

R.7.C Interpret information presented visually, orally, or quantitatively and explain how the information contributes to an understanding of the text in which it appears.

L.1.B (l.) Produce simple, compound and complex sentences.

L.4.B (b.) Determine the meaning of the new word formed when a known prefix is added to a known word.

RF.3.B (c.) Identify and know the meaning of the most common prefixes and derivational suffixes.

RF.4.B (a.) Read grade-level text with purpose and understanding.

ELPS: 1. An ELL can construct meaning from oral presentations and literary and informational text through level-appropriate listening, reading, and viewing. 3. An ELL can speak and write about level-appropriate complex literary and informational texts and topics.

Warm-up and Review
10–15 minutes (books closed)

Make an idea map on the board with *Library* in the central circle. Add branching circles with *Library services, What you find at the library*, and *What you can do at the library*. Have the class brainstorm words and phrases to go with each of the branches. Leave the idea map on the board.

Introduction
5 minutes

1. Read the words on the board aloud and answer any questions. Say: *You can find more than books at your library.*

2. State the objective: *Today we're going to read and talk about some educational resources.*

1 Read

Presentation
10–20 minutes

A Read the questions aloud. Call on volunteers to share their ideas and use ideas from the *Introduction* to help guide discussion.

B Read the words and definitions. Elicit sample sentences using the words.

Pre-reading

C Read the instructions aloud and confirm that students understand what an advice column is. Have students answer the question individually and then check answers as a class. If any students answer incorrectly, ask them to support their answer using the bulleted headings. Establish the correct answer.

Answer
a. Allison gives advice to her readers in the newspaper.

Guided Practice: While Reading
20–30 minutes

D 1. Direct students' attention to the *Reader's Note* and read the information aloud. Ask students to read the article silently and answer the question.

2. Check answers as a class.

3. Check comprehension. Ask: *What is* Sad Student's *problem?* [He's bored in the car.] *What's* Looking in Laredo's *problem?* [He needs to research career choices.] *What's* Frustrated Father's *problem?* [His son's homework is difficult.] Ask students if Allison mentions any library services, items, or activities that were missed during the warm-up. Add them to the idea map on the board.

Possible Answers
Check out audio books from the library.
Research jobs at the library.
Ask the librarian for help with homework.

> **TIP**
>
> Preview any unfamiliar vocabulary: *running, available, download, access, over my head, frustrated,* etc. Write these words (and any others that may be new to students) on the board and ask volunteers for definitions or examples. Alternatively, let students read the letters and guess the definitions from context. Confirm their answers.

> **MULTILEVEL STRATEGIES**
>
> For 2D, adapt your comprehension questions to the level of your students.
>
> • **Pre-level** Ask these students short-answer information questions. *What does* Sad Student *have in his car?* [a radio]
>
> • **On-level** Ask these students information questions that will elicit longer responses. *Why does* Looking in Laredo *need a computer?* [He needs to research career choices.]
>
> • **Higher-level** Ask these students inference questions. *Why do you think* Frustrated Father *dislikes computers?*

Guided Practice: Rereading
10–15 minutes

E 1. Provide an opportunity for students to extract evidence from the text. Have students reread the article and underline any words or phrases that indicate that Allison is encouraging her readers to succeed.

2. Pair students and tell them to compare the words they underlined and report anything they disagree on. Discuss and clarify as needed.

Answers
Yes. Underlined text may include:
No need to worry.
It's easy.
You can do it!
Anyone can do it!

> **TIP**
>
> Have students go online to find other advice columns that they might enjoy while practicing their reading skills at the same time. Provide them with the website addresses of any that you know, or give them some search terms that they can use for their own research (e.g., "advice" + "pet care"; "advice" + "relationships"; "advice" + "home repairs").

F 1. Have students work individually to mark the answers *T* (true), *F* (false), and *NI* (no information). They should then write the line numbers where they found the true and false answers. Write the answers on the board.

2. Elicit and discuss any additional questions about the reading. You could introduce new questions for class discussion: *Do you have different advice for anyone in the column? Which letter had the easiest/most difficult problem to fix? Why?*

Answers	
1. T, lines 9–11	4. T, line 23
2. T, lines 24–25	5. F, line 36
3. T, line 22	6. NI

MULTILEVEL STRATEGIES

Call on individuals and tailor your questions to the level of your students.

• **Pre-level** Ask *yes/no* questions. *Can you get CDs from the library?* [yes]

• **On-level** Ask information questions. *How can you get audio books from the library?* [on CD or digital download]

• **Higher-level** Ask critical-thinking questions. *Are libraries an important part of a community? Why or why not?*

2 Word study

Guided Practice: Post-reading
15–20 minutes

A 1. Direct students to look at the chart and identify the topic (the prefix *dis-*). Have students read the chart.

2. Read the first two sentences in the chart and the example for *dislike.* Elicit sentences for the other words in the chart.

3. Have students repeat after you as you say each word with natural intonation, rhythm, and stress.

4. Direct students to complete the sentences and then compare answers with a partner. Read the correct answers and have students check their work.

Answers	
1. dishonest	5. dislikes
2. disagree	6. disarmed
3. disorganized	7. disable
4. disobey	

MULTILEVEL STRATEGIES

After 2A, give on- and pre-level students more time to work with the words in 2A while you challenge higher-level students.

• **Pre- and On-level** Have these students work together to write sentences for some of the words in the chart. Provide sentence frames. *My _____ (family member) and I agree about _____. I like _____. I dislike _____. _____ (famous person) is honest. _____ (famous person) is dishonest.* Ask volunteers to complete the sentences on the board.

• **Higher-level** Have these students look in their dictionaries for words beginning with *dis-*. Ask them to look for words that have a base word that they already know. Tell them to write sentences with the words they find.

B 1. Read the prompts aloud. Give students a few minutes to think of their answers.

2. Set a time limit (ten minutes). Have groups of three or four discuss the prompts. Circulate and help as needed.

3. Have students share their responses with the class.

3 Talk it over

Guided Practice
15–20 minutes

A Have students look at the graph and read the note and *Reader's Note.* Point out that they need to use the information from the graph and the note to complete the sentences and answer the question. Set a time limit (ten minutes). Have students work in pairs to complete the task. Ask volunteers to share their answers with the class.

Answers
1. Active
2. Live practicing, dramatic presentations, role plays, tutoring
3. 70
4. Giving a talk, multimedia programs, group discussions
5. Passive (seeing and hearing)

Communicative Practice
15–20 minutes

B 1. Read the information and instructions aloud.

2. Set a time limit (ten minutes) for pairs to write more ideas in the chart.

C While students are doing the activity in 3B, write the chart on the board. Have pairs share their answers with the class and write them in the chart. Have students add any new ideas to their charts. Have a class discussion about which of the ideas students have actually used with success.

Application
5–10 minutes

BRING IT TO LIFE

Read the instructions aloud. Write the name, address, and directions to the local library on the board. If transportation is a problem, help students make arrangements for a car pool.

> **TIP**
>
> If you have access to computers, have your students check out the local library's website. Ask them to find the library hours and the list of services. Provide students with the name of a book and demonstrate how to search for the book in the online catalog.

EXTENSION ACTIVITY

Advice Column

Have students write letters asking for and giving advice.

1. Put students in groups and provide them with a large sheet of paper. Fold the paper in half. Tell the groups to use the top of the paper to write a "Dear Allison" letter about a problem with studying English or with reading. Encourage them to sign the letter with a nickname.

2. When each group finishes the letter, pass it to a new group. Have the new group write "Allison's" advice letter in response.

3. Post the letters and the answers in the front of the room. Have two reporters from each group come to the front to read the letter they received and the advice they wrote.

Warm-up and Review
10–15 minutes

Begin the lesson by discussing the *Bring It to Life* assignment from Lesson 5. Ask volunteers to describe their library experiences. As each volunteer speaks, make eye contact, nod, tilt your head to the side, and interject with comments to show you are listening. Say: *Really? Hmm. Go on.*

Introduction
10 minutes

1. Ask: *What do you do when you listen to someone talking?*

2. State the objective: *Today we're going to talk about showing that you are listening.*

Presentation
5 minutes

 A **1-12** Read the instructions aloud. Play the audio. Give students a minute to think about the question. Elicit responses from the class.

Answer
Two

Guided Practice
10–15 minutes

 B **1-12** 1. Read the activities aloud. Play the audio and have students do the exercise individually.

2. Have pairs compare answers. Play the audio again for the class to check answers.

Answers
Checked:
search online
take a break
make an outline
make a schedule
take notes in meeting
memorize a code
find a quiet place

Presentation and Communicative Practice
15–20 minutes

 C 1. Direct students' attention to the *Do/Say* chart and ask students to identify the lesson's soft skill [showing that you are listening]. Ask the class which column has examples of language [right] and which has examples of activities [left].

2. Say a phrase from the left column and act it out. Say it again and have the class act it out with you. Say it a third time and have the class act it out for you. To confirm understanding, combine phrases: *Lean forward and nod your head slowly.*

3. Model the sentences/phrases from the right column using authentic intonation. Have students practice imitating your inflection.

4. Put students in teams of four and assign each team a question. Assign roles: manager, administrative assistant, researcher, and reporter. Researchers will ask you questions on behalf of the team. Verify understanding of the roles. Set a time limit (five minutes) and monitor.

5. Write sentence frames on the board that teams can use to summarize their response. (*Our team discussed the following question: _____ We decided _____ because _____.*)

6. Call "time" and let reporters rehearse their report for one minute. Direct each reporter to present to three other teams.

Communicative Practice and Application
20–25 minutes

 D 1. Put students in teams of three. Tell students that they are going to be discussing their favorite ways to practice English out of the classroom and use the phrases and gestures from C. Read the instructions for each team member aloud. Have students write the chart in their notebook.

2. Model the activity with two volunteers and then check understanding of the activity: *What does Speaker A do?* [Ask Speaker B about how they practice English.] *What does Speaker B do?* [Answer Speaker A.] *What does the Observer do?* [Mark the chart.]

3. As students carry out the role-play, circulate and monitor. Make sure they switch roles so each team member has a chance to do each task. Provide global feedback once the activity ends.

MULTILEVEL STRATEGIES

Seat same-level students together.

• **Pre- and On-level** Work with these students and write a conversation they can use for practice.

• **Higher-level** Challenge these students to use each of the actions and phrases in their conversations.

TEAMWORK & LANGUAGE REVIEW

Lesson Overview

Lesson Notes

MULTILEVEL OBJECTIVES

Pre-, On-, and Higher-level: Review unit language

LANGUAGE FOCUS

Grammar: Simple present and past; present and past continuous questions and answers (*Where do you like to study? I like to study in the library. Are you taking other classes? No, I'm not.*)

Vocabulary: Classroom activities

For vocabulary support, see these **Oxford Picture Dictionary** topics: Succeeding in School, page 10; Schools and Subjects, pages 200–201

READINESS CONNECTION

In this review, students work in a team to talk about learning English.

PACING

To extend this review: Have students complete **Workbook 3 page 8**, **Multilevel Activities 3 Unit 1 page 26**, and **Multilevel Grammar Exercises 3 Unit 1**.

CORRELATIONS

CCRS: SL.1.B (d.) Explain their own ideas and understanding in light of the discussion.

SL.4.B Report on a topic or text, tell a story, or recount an experience with appropriate facts and relevant, descriptive details, speaking clearly at an understandable pace.

R.2.A Identify the main topic and retell key details of a text.

W.3.B Write narratives in which they recount a well-elaborated event or short sequence of events, include details to describe actions, thoughts, and feelings, use temporal words to signal event order, and provide a sense of closure.

W.4.B Produce writing in which the development and organization are appropriate to task and purpose.

L.1.B (b.) Explain the function of nouns, pronouns, verbs, adjectives, and adverbs in general and their functions in particular sentences. (h.) Form and use the simple verb tenses. (l.) Produce simple, compound and complex sentences.

RF.4.B (a.) Read grade-level text with purpose and understanding.

ELPS: 5. An ELL can conduct research and evaluate and communicate findings to answer questions or solve problems. 6. An ELL can analyze and critique the arguments of others orally and in writing.

Warm-up and Review
10–15 minutes (books closed)

1. Review *At Work* activity D.

2. Ask students to share the good, not-so-good, and interesting things that happened during the role-play. As students speak, write their responses in a chart on the board.

Introduction and Presentation
5 minutes

1. Pair students and direct them to look at the picture in their book. Ask them to describe what they see to their partner.

2. Ask volunteer pairs to share their ideas with the class.

3. State the objective: *Today we're going to review how to talk about learning English.*

Guided Practice
20–25 minutes

A 1. Direct students to work in groups of three or four and look at the picture. Read the instructions aloud and model the conversation with a volunteer.

2. Set a time limit (ten minutes) for groups to write conversations. Circulate and monitor.

3. Have each group say one conversation for the class.

> **TIP**
> Take one or two of the conversations and write them on the board but with some mistakes. Have the class correct the mistakes.

B 1. Read the instructions aloud and have students work in the same teams from A to complete the task. Circulate and monitor.

> **Possible Answers**
> How is the teacher?
> Did you attend this class last year?
> What were you studying last year?
> Are you enjoying class?

C Pair the teams from A and have them ask each other their questions from B. Circulate and monitor.

Communicative Practice
30–45 minutes

D 1. Group students and assign roles: manager, administrative assistant, and reporter. Explain that students are going to work with their teams to write a paragraph about the picture. Verify students' understanding of the roles.

2. Check comprehension of the task: *What is the first thing you should do?* [Decide what you will write.] *Will you write a list or a paragraph?* [a paragraph]

3. Set a time limit (ten minutes) to complete the exercise. Circulate and answer any questions.

4. Have the reporter from each team read the team's paragraph to another team.

> **TIP**
> Provide students with a little guidance about what/how to write. Tell them how many sentences to write, write a sample beginning sentence on the board, remind them to indent the first sentence, etc.

E 1. Have students walk around the room to conduct the interviews. To get students moving, tell them to interview three people who were not on their team for D.

2. Set a time limit (five minutes) to complete the exercise.

3. Tell students to make a note of their classmates' answers but not to worry about writing complete sentences.

> **MULTILEVEL STRATEGIES**
> Adapt the mixer in E to the level of your students.
> • **Pre- and On-level** Pair these students and have them interview other pairs together.
> • **Higher-level** Have these students ask an additional question and write all answers in complete sentences.

F 1. Call on individuals to report what they learned about their classmates. Keep a running tally on the board for each question, marking where students like to study, if they are taking other classes, if they studied English before this class, and what they were doing today at 7:30 a.m.

2. Use your tally for question 1 to create a pie chart on the board. Instruct students to draw pie charts for questions 2, 3, and 4 in their notebooks. Circulate and answer any questions.

PROBLEM SOLVING
10–15 minutes

A 1. Ask: *Were you nervous the first day of English class? Do you like meeting new people, or are you shy?* Tell students they will read a story about a woman who has a problem in her English class. Direct students to read Teresa's story silently.

2. Play the audio and have students read along silently again.

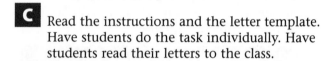

B 1. Elicit answers to question 1. Guide students to a class consensus on the answer.

2. As a class, brainstorm answers to question 2. Ask students if they know someone who has this problem and has overcome it or what they have done themselves to overcome the same problem. Have students share their responses and write them on the board for students to refer to in the next activity.

Answers
1. She started class late and doesn't know anyone.
2. Answers will vary.

C Read the instructions and the letter template. Have students do the task individually. Have students read their letters to the class.

Evaluation
20–25 minutes

To test students' understanding of the unit language and content, have them take the Unit 1 Test, available on the Teacher Resource Center.

2 Ready for Fun

Unit Overview

This unit explores recreational activities with a range of employability skills and contextualizes structures to talk about the future.

KEY OBJECTIVES	
Lesson 1	Identify and locate places to go for fun
Lesson 2	Write an email asking for information to plan a party
Lesson 3	Use future tense to talk about future plans
Lesson 4	Express preferences
Lesson 5	Identify the benefits of walking in the park
At Work	Check your understanding
Teamwork & Language Review	Review unit language

UNIT FEATURES	
Academic Vocabulary	*physical, relaxing, prediction, resolution, stress, security*
Employability Skills	• Use inference to match words with pictures • Match words with their definitions • Determine categories of information for a request • Determine the purpose of statements • Determine how to compromise to agree on plans • Work independently • Understand teamwork • Locate information • Communicate verbally • Listen actively • Use writing skills • Comprehend written material • Analyze information

Resources	**Class Audio** CD1, Tracks 14–24
	Workbook Unit 2, pages 9–15
	Teacher Resource Center
	    Multilevel Activities 3 Unit 2
	    Multilevel Grammar Exercises 3 Unit 2
	    Unit 2 Test
	Oxford Picture Dictionary Taking Care of Your Health, The Park and Playground, Entertainment

LESSON **1** VOCABULARY

Lesson Overview	Lesson Notes

MULTILEVEL OBJECTIVES

On-level: Identify and describe recreational activities, places, and events

Pre-level: Identify recreational activities, places, and events

Higher-level: Talk and write about recreational activities, places, and events

LANGUAGE FOCUS

Grammar: Gerunds (*bowling, dancing*)

Vocabulary: Recreational places and activities

For vocabulary support, see this **Oxford Picture Dictionary** topic: Places to Go, pages 228–229

STRATEGY FOCUS

Pool knowledge with team members to maximize vocabulary learning.

READINESS CONNECTION

In this lesson, students explore and communicate information about places to go for fun.

PACING

To compress this lesson: Conduct 1C as a whole-class activity.

To extend this lesson: Have students play a game with adjectives. (See end of lesson.)

And/or have students complete **Workbook 3 page 9** and **Multilevel Activities 3 Unit 2 pages 28–29**.

CORRELATIONS

CCRS: SL.1.A (a.) Follow agreed-upon rules for discussions.

SL.4.B Report on a topic or text, tell a story, or recount an experience with appropriate facts and relevant, descriptive details, speaking clearly at an understandable pace.

R.5.A Know and use various text features to locate key facts or information in a text.

W.7.A Participate in shared research and writing projects.

L.1.A (f.) Use frequently occurring adjectives.

L.1.B (b.) Explain the function of nouns, pronouns, verbs, adjectives, and adverbs in general and their functions in particular sentences. (l.) Produce simple, compound and complex sentences.

L.4.B (e.) Use glossaries and beginning dictionaries, both print and digital, to determine or clarify the meaning of words and phrases.

RF.4.B (a.) Read grade-level text with purpose and understanding.

ELPS: 8. An ELL can determine the meaning of words and phrases in oral presentations and literary and informational text.

Warm-up and Review
10–15 minutes (books closed)

Bring in items from games, sports, and free-time activities and pass them around the room. Elicit the name of an activity, sport, or game with which each item may belong. Write the words on the board. Items could include dice, sports equipment, entertainment listings, etc.

Introduction
3 minutes

1. Write *Fun* on the board. Say: *What do you like to do for fun? Do you think our (community/town/city) has a lot of places to go for fun or to relax?*

2. State the objective: *Today we're going to learn ways to identify and locate places to go for fun.*

1 Identify places to go for fun

Presentation I
20–25 minutes

A 1. Write *Recreation* on the board. Explain that *recreation* means the things you do during free time that are fun or relaxing. Elicit one example of a fun place to go or event from the whole class. Have students work together to brainstorm in a group. Make a list on the board of the recreational places and events your students identify.

2. Have students identify the recreational activities that are good for families, for single people, or for both. Elicit ideas and for each idea write *S* (single), *F* (family), or *B* (both). Have students explain their reasons.

B 1. Copy the first two rows of the chart onto the board.

2. Model the task by "thinking aloud" about the first location in the chart and marking the first column appropriately. Work with a volunteer to demonstrate completing the second and third columns.

3. Direct students to review the vocabulary independently, marking the first column of the chart in their books.

4. Pair students and ask them to complete the second and third columns of the chart together.

C 1. Elicit any words that pairs did not know and write them on the board. Ask volunteers to explain any of the words they know.

2. Direct students to look up any remaining unknown words in their dictionaries. Discuss those words in relation to the lesson. (Note: 1D and 1E will confirm students' understanding of the target vocabulary.)

Guided Practice I
15–20 minutes

D 1. Direct students to look at the first item. Then read definition 2 aloud. Ask if there are any words in the definition that are similar to the vocabulary from 1B. Elicit the answer.

2. Set a time limit (five minutes). Direct students to complete the activity individually. Do not check the answers as a class yet.

Answers	
1. d	6. h
2. c	7. g
3. a	8. i
4. f	9. b
5. e	

E 🔊 1-14 1. Prepare students to listen by saying: *Now we're going to listen to someone presenting plans for new recreational facilities at a town meeting. While you listen, check your work in 1D.*

2. Play the audio. Ask students to circle any of their answers in 1D that don't match the audio. Elicit those items and play them again, focusing on clues to meaning in the 1D sentences.

3. Work with the pronunciation of any troublesome words or phrases.

2 Learn to describe recreational activities

Presentation II
10–15 minutes

A 1. Direct students to look at the flyer. Introduce the new topic: *We've talked about places and activities. Now we're going to learn how to describe those places and activities.*

2. Say and have students repeat the places and activities in the brochure.

3. Ask students to work individually to match the adjectives to the activities they describe. Write the number-letter matches on the board. Call on volunteers to read the matching activities and adjectives aloud.

4. Check comprehension. Ask: *Is going to the dentist exciting? Is taking a hot shower relaxing? Is washing the dishes boring?*

Answers	
1. e	4. c
2. f	5. d
3. a	6. b

MULTILEVEL STRATEGIES

Provide a challenge for higher-level students.

• **Higher-level** After these students finish 2A, direct them to look up synonyms for *exciting*, *entertaining*, and *boring*. Help them with pronunciation and example sentences.

Guided Practice II
10–15 minutes

B 1. Read the *Language Note* aloud. Model asking and answering the first question with a volunteer.

2. Set a time limit (three minutes). Direct students to ask and answer the questions with a partner.

3. Call on volunteer pairs to present one of their conversations for the class.

Communicative Practice and Application
10–15 minutes

C 1. If students will use the Internet for this task, establish what device(s) they'll use: a class computer, tablets, or smartphones. Alternatively, print information from the Internet before class and distribute to groups.

2. Write the information types from 2C on the board. Explain that students will work in teams to research and report on this information. Ask: *Which search terms or questions can you use to find the information you need?* ["nightclub" + city name or "amusement park" + city name] *What information will you scan for?* [name, address, hours of operation, cost, things to do] *How will you record the information you find?* [table, checklist, index cards] Remind students to bookmark or record sites so they can find or cite them in the future.

3. Group students and assign roles: manager, administrative assistant, IT support, and reporter. Verify students' understanding of the roles.

TIP

When setting up task-based activities, verify that students understand their roles using physical commands. For example: *If you report on your team's work, stand up* [reporter]. *If you keep the team on task, point to the clock* [manager]. *If you write the team's responses, raise your hand* [administrative assistant]. *If you help the team research, hold up your smartphone/tablet* [IT support].

4. Give managers the time limit for researching the question (ten minutes). Direct the IT support to begin the online research or pick up the printed materials for each team. Direct the administrative assistant to record information for the team using a table, a checklist, or index cards.

5. Give a two-minute warning. Call "time."

D 1. Copy the sentence frames on the board.

2. Direct teams to help their administrative assistant use the sentence frames to record the team's findings. Direct the reporter to use the recorded information to report the team's findings to the class or another team.

Evaluation
10–15 minutes (books closed)

TEST YOURSELF

1. Direct Partner A to read prompts 1–5 from 1D on page 20 to Partner B. Partner B should close his or her book and write the vocabulary words in his or her notebook. When finished, students switch roles. Partner B reads prompts 6–9 from 1D.

2. Direct both partners to open their books and check their answers and spelling when they finish.

MULTILEVEL STRATEGIES

Target the *Test Yourself* to the level of your students.

• **Pre-level** Have these students do the activity the first time with the option to look at the answers if needed. Then have them do the activity a second time without looking at the answers.

• **Higher-level** Have these students write three to five sentences using vocabulary words from 1B.

TIP

To provide further practice of the vocabulary:

1. Direct students to work individually to write a list of at least ten words from the lesson. Assign a time limit (three minutes). Call "time" and direct students to work with a partner to combine their lists and put the words in alphabetical order. Circulate and monitor students' progress.

2. Ask a volunteer pair to write its list on the board. Ask other students to add words to the list on the board.

EXTENSION ACTIVITY

Play a Game

Play a "round-table" game using the adjectives from this unit. Put students in mixed-level groups and give each group a piece of paper. Write an adjective on the board. Have each student write one place or activity on the paper that can be described by that adjective. After the first student writes, he/she passes the paper to the person to the left. Members of the group can help each other with ideas, but everyone must write. Call "time" after two minutes. Ask groups how many places/ activities they have written. Ask a reporter from the group with the most ideas to read the group's paper aloud. Play again with a different adjective.

Lesson Overview	Lesson Notes

MULTILEVEL OBJECTIVES

On- and Higher-level: Analyze, write, and edit an email asking for information to plan a party

Pre-level: Read and write an email asking for information to plan a party

LANGUAGE FOCUS

Grammar: Verbs + infinitives (*I need to plan a party.*)

Vocabulary: Party-planning vocabulary

For vocabulary support, see this **Oxford Picture Dictionary** topic: Places to Go, pages 228–229

STRATEGY FOCUS

Understand that business emails are usually brief and bullet points identify important information for the reader.

READINESS CONNECTION

In this lesson, students listen actively to, read, and write an email asking for information to plan a party.

PACING

To compress this lesson: Assign the *Test Yourself* and/or 3C for homework.

To extend this lesson: Have students practice party planning. (See end of lesson.)

And/or have students complete **Workbook 3 page 10** and **Multilevel Activities 3 Unit 2 page 30**.

CORRELATIONS

CCRS: SL.1.A (a.) follow agreed-upon rules for discussions (e.g., listening to others with care, speaking one at a time about the topics and texts under discussion).

R.1.B Ask and answer such questions as who, what, where, when, why, and how to demonstrate understanding of key details in a text.

R.5.A Know and use various text features to locate key facts or information in a text.

W.2.A Write informative/explanatory texts in which they name a topic, supply some facts about the topic, and provide some sense of closure.

W.5.B With guidance and support from peers and others, develop and strengthen writing as needed by planning, revising and editing.

L.1.B (l.) Produce simple, compound and complex sentences.

L.2.B (c.) Use commas in greetings and closings of letters. (h.) Use conventional spelling for high-frequency and other studied words and for adding suffixes to base words.

L.4.B (c.) Use a known root word as a clue to the meaning of an unknown word with the same root.

RF.3.B (c.) Identify and know the meaning of the most common prefixes and derivational suffixes.

RF.4.B (a.) Read grade-level text with purpose and understanding.

ELPS: 6. An ELL can analyze and critique the arguments of others orally and in writing. 9. An ELL can create clear and coherent level-appropriate speech and text.

Warm-up and Review
10–15 minutes (books closed)

Review verbs + infinitives. Ask: *What information do you need to plan a party?* Write students' ideas on the board. After you have a list of eight to ten ideas, have students say complete sentences using a verb + an infinitive: *I need to know how many people will come. To plan a party I want to know how much food to buy.*

Introduction
5 minutes

1. Ask students how many of them use email to communicate with their friends or co-workers when they plan a party or other event.

2. State the objective: *Today we're going to learn how to write an email asking for information to plan a party.*

1 Prepare to write

Presentation
20–25 minutes

 1. Build students' schema by asking questions about the survey and the Subject line of the email. Ask: *What information does the survey ask for? What activity choices are there? How many people want to go to each activity? Which activity would you choose to do?*

2. Give students one minute to tell a partner their responses to questions 1 and 2. Elicit responses from the class.

Answers
1. Summer employee bowling party. Most people surveyed voted for a bowling and pizza party. 2. Answers will vary.

 1-15 1. Introduce the model email and its purpose: *Now we're going to read an email about a party. As you read, look for the purpose of the email: Why is she writing?* Have students read the email silently.

2. Check comprehension. Ask: *Who is writing?* [Marta, an employee of Clark Electronics] *Why is she writing?* [to get information to plan a bowling party] *Who is asking Marta to get information?* [her supervisor] *What is the name of the bowling alley?* [Family Bowl] *When does Marta need the information?* [before May 16]

3. Play the audio. Have students read along silently.

Guided Practice I
10 minutes

 1. Have students work independently to underline the answers to the questions in the email.

2. Point out the *Writer's Note* and read the information aloud. Ask students to annotate the information they underlined with the words/phrases "# of people" for question 1, "purpose" for question 2, "quick reply" for question 3, and "additional information" for question 4. Have pairs compare answers. Have volunteers call out answers and write them on the board for the class to check.

Answers
1. 15 2. I am writing to inquire about your prices for the following items. 3. Would you please send me this information at your earliest convenience? I look forward to hearing from you soon. 4. I need to complete my budget by May 16.

TIP

Ask students to identify the greeting and the closing. Elicit other greetings and closings. Talk about the level of formality of each greeting. Point out that when friends email each other, they often do not use a closing, but in a formal email, you need to have a formal closing and contact information.

MULTILEVEL STRATEGIES

Seat pre-level students together for 1C.

• **Pre-level** While other students are working on 1C, ask these students *yes/no* and *or* questions about the reading. *Are there 50 employees going? Does Marta want the rental for 1 hour or 3 hours?* Allow these students to copy the answers to 1C from the board.

• **On- and Higher-level** After these students complete 1C, ask them to individually write three questions about the email. Then have them close their books and work with a partner to take turns asking and answering questions to see how much they remember.

2 Plan and write

Guided Practice II
15–20 minutes

 1. Read the question aloud. Elicit students' answers and write them on the board.

MULTILEVEL STRATEGIES

Adapt 2A to the level of your students.

• **Pre-level** Work with these students to brainstorm answers to the question in 2A. Give students time to answer in complete sentences before moving on to the next question.

• **Higher-level** Ask these students to add two or three more specific pieces of information that they will need.

B 1. Direct students to look back at the model email in 1B. Focus their attention on the bullet points. Ask them to look through the email quickly and make a note of what information is asked for. Ask what other information they might need to ask for in their own emails.

2. Read through the email template and *Need help?* box. Elicit ideas that could go in each blank. Have students write their emails individually.

3 Get feedback and revise

Guided Practice III
5 minutes

A Direct students to check their writing using the editing checklist. Tell them to read each item in the list and check their papers before moving on to the next item. Explain that students should not edit their writing at this stage. They should just use the checklist to check their work and mark any areas they want to revise.

Communicative Practice
15 minutes

B 1. Read the instructions and the sample sentences aloud. Emphasize to students that they are responding to their partners' work, not correcting it.

2. Use the email in 1B to model the exercise. *I agree that a bowling alley is a great place for a party. I think Marta might need to plan for more food for 15 people.*

3. Direct students to exchange papers with a partner and follow the instructions.

C Allow students time to edit and revise their writing as necessary, using the editing checklist from 3A and their partner's feedback from 3B. If necessary, students could complete this task as homework.

TIP

Suggest to students that they start thinking about ideas for a class party that they can have at the end of term. Alternatively, they can think about planning once-a-week gatherings for the class to have some fun together.

Application and Evaluation
10 minutes

TEST YOURSELF

1. Review the instructions aloud. Assign a time limit (five minutes) and have students work independently.

2. Before collecting student work, invite two or three volunteers to share their sentences. Ask students to raise their hands if they wrote similar answers.

MULTILEVEL STRATEGIES

Adapt the *Test Yourself* to the level of your students.

• **Pre-level** Write questions for these students to answer in writing. *Was today's writing assignment difficult or easy? How do you feel about writing?*

EXTENSION ACTIVITY

Practice Party Planning

Have students practice asking for information. Put students in small groups and have them plan a class party. Write sentences/sentence frames for asking for information on the board. *How much is _____? How many people will come? How many _____ do I need?* Have groups plan the party, including plans for food, drinks, location, day, and time. Have groups present their party ideas to the class. If time allows, choose a plan and have the party!

Lesson Overview	Lesson Notes

MULTILEVEL OBJECTIVES

On- and Higher-level: Use *be going to* and *will* to talk about future plans

Pre-level: Recognize *be going to* and *will* to understand future plans

LANGUAGE FOCUS

Grammar: *Be going to* (*I'm going to go bowling.*); *will* (*I'll call you.*)

Vocabulary: Recreational activities; *plan, promise, prediction*

For vocabulary support, see this **Oxford Picture Dictionary** topic: The Park and Playground, page 230

STRATEGY FOCUS

Use *think* or *probably* with *will* to make predictions about the future.

READINESS CONNECTION

In this lesson, students learn the difference between *be going to* and *will.*

PACING

To compress this lesson: Conduct 1C and/or 1D as a whole-class activity.

To extend this lesson: Have students predict the future. (See end of lesson.)

And/or have students complete **Workbook 3 pages 11–12, Multilevel Activities 3 Unit 2 pages 31–32,** and **Multilevel Grammar Exercises 3 Unit 2.**

CORRELATIONS

CCRS: SL.1.B (d.) Explain their own ideas and understanding in light of the discussion.

R.1.B Ask and answer such questions as who, what, where, when, why, and how to demonstrate understanding of key details in a text.

L.1.B (b.) Explain the function of nouns, pronouns, verbs, adjectives, and adverbs in general and their functions in particular sentences. (h.) Form and use the simple verb tenses. (l.) Produce simple, compound and complex sentences.

L.2.B (h.) Use conventional spelling for high-frequency and other studied words and for adding suffixes to base words.

L.4.B (c.) Use a known root word as a clue to the meaning of an unknown word with the same root.

RF.3.B (c.) Identify and know the meaning of the most common prefixes and derivational suffixes.

RF.4.B (a.) Read grade-level text with purpose and understanding.

ELPS: 7. An ELL can adapt language choices to purpose, task, and audience when speaking and writing. 10. An ELL can demonstrate command of the conventions of standard English to communicate in level-appropriate speech and writing.

Warm-up and Review
10–15 minutes (books closed)

Review the differences in form between *will* and *be going to*. Write first-person sentences on the board. *I'm going to call my mother tonight. I'll call you around 6:00. I'm going to go to the mall this weekend. I'll buy something for you.* Say and have students repeat the sentences. Ask volunteers to change the sentences to third person. Point out that the verb *be* changes in *be going to* but that the *will* form is the same for all subjects. Leave the sentences on the board.

Introduction
5–10 minutes

1. Tell students that all of the sentences on the board refer to future time but that *will* and *be going to* are not used in exactly the same way.

2. State the objective: *Today we're going to learn the difference between* be going to *and* will.

1 Review *be going to* and *will*

Presentation I
20–25 minutes

 1. Direct students to look at the picture. Ask: *Are they talking about something serious or fun?*

2. Read the instructions aloud. Ask students to read the conversation silently and answer the questions.

3. Read the first question aloud. Call on a volunteer for the answer. Ask the volunteer where in the conversation they found the answer. Read the rest of the questions aloud, calling on a different volunteer for each answer.

Answers
1. He is going to study all day.
2. They won't stay late at the pool.
3. He decides to go to the pool and study tomorrow night.

B 1. Demonstrate how to read the grammar chart.

2. Ask students to substitute a new verb into each sentence—for example, *read a book*.

3. Direct students to underline the examples of *will* and circle the examples of *be going to* in 1A. Go over the answers as a class.

4. Talk about form and meaning. Ask: *When Ken says, "I'm going to study," is it his plan or a promise? Why does he say* I'll go *when he agrees to go to the pool?*

5. Assess students' understanding of the chart. Ask: *Which sentences on the board from the Warm-up are plans and which are promises? Why?*

Answers
Underline:
We'll
We won't
I'll go
I'll see you
Circle:
What are you going to do
I'm going to study all day.

Guided Practice I
10–15 minutes

C 1. Tell students they will collaborate to complete the description of the grammar point. Model collaboration by working with the class to complete the first sentence. Encourage students to look at 1A and 1B to help them determine the tense.

2. Pair students and have them work together to complete the description.

3. Project or write the completed definition on the board and have pairs verify the accuracy of their responses. Ask volunteers which sentences confused them and discuss.

Answers	
be going to	is
be	will
am	

Guided Practice II
30–35 minutes

 1. Ask students to work individually to complete the conversations. Make sure they understand to use the words in brackets as a guide.

2. Have pairs compare answers. Have volunteers read the completed conversations aloud for the class to check answers.

Answers
1. **A:** What time <u>are</u> you <u>going to</u> get up?
B: I <u>am going to</u> get up very early tomorrow.
A: I <u>will</u> call you at 9:15.
2. **A:** When <u>are</u> you <u>going to</u> reply to Tom's email?
B: I <u>am going to</u> reply to it soon.
A: When? Tomorrow <u>will</u> be too late.
B: I <u>will</u> respond this afternoon.
A: Are you sure? It's very important.
B: I <u>won't</u> forget. He <u>will</u> have my response by the end of the day.
3. **A:** <u>Are</u> you <u>going to</u> come in on Saturday?
B: No, I'm not. My kids and I <u>are going to</u> go to the zoo.
A: Have fun. I <u>will</u> talk to you next week.

MULTILEVEL STRATEGIES
For 1D, group same-level students together.
• **Pre-level** Sit with these students and complete the exercise together. Take turns with them to read each part of the conversations.
• **Higher-level** Challenge these students to add one more exchange to one of the conversations.

 1. Elicit the importance of accuracy. Tell students they will be building their accuracy in this task.

2. Organize students into groups. Demonstrate how to correct the sentence using the first example.

3. Have team members work together to correct the sentences. Circulate and monitor teamwork.

4. Project or write the corrected sentences on the board and have teams check their work.

5. Address questions and any issues you noted during your observation.

Answers

1. I will **call** you later today.
2. We **are** going to go to class next week.
3. She **is** going to work tomorrow.
4. They're **going to** study tonight.

F

1. Read the instructions and the sample sentences aloud. Set a time limit (five minutes) and have pairs do the activity.

2. Have students share their partner's sentences with the class.

MULTILEVEL STRATEGIES

Group same-level students together.

• **Pre-level** Provide these students with phrases to use in their sentences: *study every night, use a dictionary, watch TV in English for 30 minutes*, etc.

• **Higher-level** Challenge these students to make sentences about a weekly plan. *On Mondays, I will _____. On Tuesday nights, I will _____*, etc.

2 Learn about future predictions

Presentation II and Guided Practice III
20–25 minutes

TIP

Students may ask about making predictions with *be going to* (as in *It's going to rain.*). Explain that we often use *be going to* for predictions that are strongly connected to the present. (*It's cloudy. Therefore, it's going to rain.*)

1. Introduce the new topic. Say: *Now we're going to talk about predictions. A prediction is something we think will happen in the future. For example: Someday we'll drive flying cars. I think it's true, but it's not my plan!*

2. Read the first sentence in the chart aloud and write it on the board. Underline *will*. Say: *When I use* will, *it means that I am saying what I think can happen in the future.*

3. Underline *have*. Point out that after *will*, the verb is always in the base form. Ask students to make predictions about something that will happen after class.

4. Read the *Grammar Note* aloud. Explain that *probably* and *think* are used when you are reasonably sure something will happen, but maybe not 100% sure. Write the sentences from the *Grammar Note* on the board. Underline *think* and *probably* and point out the position of each: Think *comes after the subject, and* probably *comes after* will. *It can also come directly before* will.

5. Check comprehension. Have volunteers say sentences predicting what they will do after class, tomorrow, or over the weekend, using the sentences on the board as a guide.

6. Set a time limit (five minutes) and have students complete the sentences below the chart. Have students compare answers with a partner before checking answers as a class.

Answers

1. will build
2. will employ
3. will take
4. will cost
5. will benefit

TIP

After 2, provide more practice with predictions. Make a list or show pictures of items for students to make predictions about—for example, a computer, a car, a hospital, a TV, a house, etc. Put students in groups. Write the names of the items on large sheets of paper and give a different one to each group. Tell the students in each group to write one prediction about its group's item and then pass the paper to another group. Direct that group to make a different prediction. Continue passing the papers until every group has had a chance to make a prediction about each item. Go over students' ideas as a class.

Alternatively, show a video clip from a futuristic movie and have students make predictions based on what they saw.

3 Identify the difference between plans, promises, and predictions

Guided Practice IV
15–20 minutes

A 🔊 1-16 1. Say: *We've been talking about plans, promises, and predictions. Now we're going to listen to sentences with different people speaking and decide what kind of sentence each is.*

2. Direct students to read the first set of statements and then play the first exchange and have them check the correct boxes in the chart.

3. Elicit answers from the class. If students answered incorrectly, play the audio again, providing a listening clue (for example, *listen for whether the speaker is talking about something they will definitely do, something they will do for someone else, or something they think will happen*).

4. Repeat for numbers 2–6.

Answers	
1. *be going to* / Plan	4. *will* / Prediction
2. *will* / Promise	5. *will* / Promise
3. *be going to* / Plan	6. *will* / Prediction

B 🔊 1-16 Play the audio again and have students compare answers with a partner. Go over answers as a class.

4 State predictions

Communicative Practice and Application
20–25 minutes

A 1. Direct students to look at the photos. Read the instructions aloud and have volunteers read the sample sentences.

2. Put students in pairs. Direct pairs to work together to make three predictions.

3. Check comprehension of the exercise. Ask: *How many years in the future will you predict?* [50] *Will your prediction be about family life or work life?* [work life]

4. Have students share their predictions with the class.

B 1. Have pairs merge to form teams of four. Read the instructions aloud and model the sample conversation with a volunteer.

2. Set a time limit (five minutes). Have groups work together to write five questions about the future. Circulate and monitor.

3. Have students from each group take turns asking their questions to the whole class. Have volunteers answer, but if the same students keep answering, call on different students to answer the questions.

Evaluation
10–15 minutes

TEST YOURSELF

Ask students to write the sentences independently. Collect and correct their writing.

MULTILEVEL STRATEGIES

Target the *Test Yourself* to the level of your students.

• **Pre-level** Provide sentence frames for these students to complete. *1. This year, I plan to _____ and _____. 2. I will try to _____ and _____. 3. In five years, I think I will _____. 4. In ten years, I think I will _____.*

• **Higher-level** Have these students write a paragraph in response to this prompt: *Write a paragraph about your future plans. Include two predictions and two resolutions.*

EXTENSION ACTIVITY

Predict the Future

For more prediction practice, have students write and read fortunes. Write *fortune cookie* on the board and ask a student to explain what it is (or bring a fortune cookie to class). Tell students that everyone in the class has a fantastic future ahead of them, and you want them to write predictions for each other. The predictions can be wild or funny, but they must be happy predictions (no bad news!). Give students small slips of paper and have them write one prediction each. Collect all of the predictions and put them in a hat. Have students pull their "fortune" out of the hat and read it to the class.

Lesson Overview	Lesson Notes

MULTILEVEL OBJECTIVES

Pre-, On-, and Higher-level: Ask about and express preferences and listen for information about an event

LANGUAGE FOCUS

Grammar: *Would rather* + simple verb (*I'd rather go to the park.*)

Vocabulary: Free time activities, *event*

For vocabulary support, see these **Oxford Picture Dictionary** topics: The Park and Playground, page 230; Entertainment, pages 242–243

STRATEGY FOCUS

Use *would rather* + verb to talk about preferences.

READINESS CONNECTION

In this lesson, students verbally communicate about preferences.

PACING

To compress this lesson: Do 6A as a whole-class activity and skip 6B.

To extend this lesson: Have students make a flyer. (See end of lesson.)

And/or have students complete **Workbook 3 page 13** and **Multilevel Activities 3 Unit 2 page 33**.

CORRELATIONS

CCRS: SL.1.B (d.) Explain their own ideas and understanding in light of the discussion.

SL.2.B Determine the main ideas and supporting details of a text read aloud or information presented in diverse media and formats, including visually, quantitatively, and orally.

SL.4.B Report on a topic or text, tell a story, or recount an experience with appropriate facts and relevant, descriptive details, speaking clearly at an understandable pace.

SL.6.B Speak in complete sentences when appropriate to task and situation in order to provide requested detail or clarification.

L.1.B (l.) Produce simple, compound and complex sentences.

L.1.C (d.) Use modal auxiliaries to convey various conditions.

L.3.B (b.) Recognize and observe differences between the conventions of spoken and written standard English.

RF.4.B (a.) Read grade-level text with purpose and understanding.

ELPS: 2. An ELL can participate in level-appropriate oral and written exchanges of information, ideas, and analyses, in various social and academic contexts, responding to peer, audience, or reader comments and questions. 9. An ELL can create clear and coherent level-appropriate speech and text.

Warm-up and Review
10–15 minutes (books closed)

Write these newspaper categories on the board: *Arts, Nightlife, Family events, Festivals, Concerts.* Ask students if they can name any recent examples of these in your area.

Introduction
5 minutes

1. Ask students which kind of event they would like to attend. Say: *Most people like to do some things more than other things. They have preferences.*

2. State the objective: *Today we're going to learn how to talk about our preferences.*

1 Learn to talk about preferences

Presentation I
10–15 minutes

 A ((•)) **1-17** 1. Direct students to look at the pictures. Ask students to talk about who the people are and what they are each talking about.

2. Read the questions aloud. Play the audio. Give students a minute to answer the question. Go over the answer as a class.

Answer
They decide to go to a movie Wednesday and to the mall on Friday night.

Guided Practice I
20–25 minutes

B ((•)) **1-17** 1. Read the instructions and the questions aloud. Play the audio. Ask students to listen for the answer to each question.

2. Ask students to compare their answers with a partner. Circulate and monitor to ensure students understand the audio.

Answers
1. Watch a movie
2. Going to the mall
3. The man (Jack) decides the Wednesday plan and the woman (Diana) decides what to do on Friday.
4. Decide in the moment

C ((•)) **1-18** Read the instructions aloud. Explain that students are going to hear the audio one more time. They should write the words they hear to complete the sentences. Play the audio. Call on volunteers to elicit the answers.

Answers	
1. want to get together	4. rather
2. your pick	5. up to
3. play it by ear	

2 Practice your pronunciation

Pronunciation Extension
10–15 minutes

 A ((•)) **1-19** 1. Write *Would you like to eat your lunch in the park?* on the board. Say the sentence with relaxed pronunciation and ask students to repeat it. Draw a line to connect the final *d* in *would* and the final *t* in *eat* with

the *y* in *you* and *your*. Say: *Now we're going to focus on the* j *and* ch *sounds that we make when we connect these sounds.*

2. Play the audio. Direct students to listen for the linking sound made in *would + you* and in *meet + you.* Ask several students to say the two sentences, pronouncing the linking sound.

B ((•)) **1-20** 1. Play the audio. Have students work individually to underline the letters.

2. Call on volunteers to read the sentences aloud and say what letters they underlined. Ask: *What letters make the* j *sound? What letters make the* ch *sound?*

Answers
1. <u>Could you</u> call me tomorrow?
2. I'll <u>get you</u> two tickets for the game.
3. <u>Would you</u> like to go out?
4. What <u>did you</u> do last Saturday night?
5. What <u>should you</u> do when you're sick?
6. I <u>bought you</u> a present.

C ((•)) **1-20** Ask students to take turns reading the sentences in 2B with a partner. Play the audio again for students to check their pronunciation. Monitor and provide feedback.

3 Use modals to express preferences

Presentation II
10–15 minutes

A 1. Introduce the new topic. Say: *Now we're going to look at questions and answers with* would rather.

2. Read the conversations in the chart aloud. Give students a few moments to underline the verbs. Ask what form they're in.

3. Draw students' attention to the *Grammar Note.* Point out that *would* is pronounced clearly in the question but is usually contracted in the statement.

Answers
see, see, stay, go

Guided Practice II
10–15 minutes

B 1. Read the instructions aloud.

2. Have pairs do the task individually. Circulate and monitor.

3. Have pairs take turns asking and answering their questions. Have students share their partner's answers with the class.

Answers
1. Would you rather work indoors or outdoors?
2. Would you rather study online or in a classroom?
3. Possible response: Would you rather walk or take the bus?

MULTILEVEL STRATEGIES

• **Pre-level** Have these students work together to complete the questions. If necessary, brainstorm ways to fill in question 3 as a group.

• **Higher-level** Have these students write one or two more questions using their own ideas.

4 Building conversation skills

Guided Practice III
15–20 minutes

A Direct students to look at the calendar. Have them work with partners to identify what the men are planning. Elicit responses and ask: *How do you know?* or *Why do you say that?* to encourage students to state their reasoning.

Answer
They are planning what to do that night.

B 1. Ask students to read the instructions and tell you what they are going to do [listen and read and respond to the question]. Play the audio and then elicit the answer to the question.

2. Ask students to read the conversation with a partner. Circulate and monitor pronunciation. Model and have students repeat difficult words or phrases.

3. Ask: *In what other situations could you use this conversation?* Point out a few phrases that are not specific to a conversation about making plans for that night. Ask volunteers to point out others.

Answer
Bo is feeling very tired.

Communicative Practice and Application I
20–25 minutes

C 1. Pair students and have them read the instructions silently. Check their comprehension of the exercise. Ask: *What are the two roles? Is the conversation at home or work?*

2. Model and have students repeat the expressions in the *In Other Words* box in 4B. Explain that they should use these expressions in their conversations.

3. Draw a T-chart on the board. Label the left column *Co-worker 1* and the right column *Co-worker 2*. Elicit examples of what each person might say and make notes in the chart.

4. Set a time limit (three minutes). Have students act out the role-play. Call time and have students switch roles.

5. Ask three volunteer pairs to act out their role-play for the class. Tell students who are listening to make a simple table with four rows and two columns. Use the top row to label the columns *Exciting and fun* and *Relaxing*. Have students take notes in the chart for each role-play.

MULTILEVEL STRATEGIES

Seat same-level students together.

• **Pre-level** Work with these students and guide them in writing their new conversation.

• **Higher-level** You can challenge students to use their imaginations and use silly or far-fetched ideas in their conversations.

5 Focus on listening for details

Presentation III and Guided Practice IV
15–20 minutes

A 1. Read the questions aloud. Set a time limit (five minutes) and have pairs discuss their ideas.

2. Have students share their partner's responses with the class. Encourage students to respond to one another's ideas. After one student speaks, ask other students if they have ever been to that venue and why.

TIP

Make sure students know to be patient while other students are speaking and not interrupt or talk over each other. One way to ensure this is to make a habit of asking a student to repeat back what another student said.

B 🔊 **1-22** 1. Direct students to read the questions before they listen to the interview. Ask what kind of information they'll be writing in the blanks.

2. Play the audio and have students take notes on the questions individually.

Answers
1. 1
2. Employment opportunities
3. Greenville fries, snacks, and drinks
4. ushering, ticket takers, or information personnel

MULTILEVEL STRATEGIES

Seat same-level students together.

• **Pre-level** After playing the audio through once, play it again, but stop the audio after each item for students to write their answer.

• **Higher-level** Have these students write the answers after listening once. When you play the audio again, have them write another question about what they hear. Then have them take turns asking and answering their questions with a partner.

C 🔊 **1-22** Pair students and have them compare answers. If a pair has different answers, have the class vote on the correct answer with a show of hands.

6 Discuss

Communicative Practice and Application II
15–20 minutes

A 1. Read the instructions and questions aloud. Confirm that students understand the jobs/vocabulary. Draw a sample chart on the board, with the headings *Event coordinator*, *Concessions*, *Director*, *Guest relations*, *Year-round*, and *Only at events*. Call on volunteers to read the sample conversation in 6A. Make a tally mark under *Concessions* to show how that matches the answer in the sample conversation. Explain that students will make a chart like this one based on their own discussions.

2. Put students into teams of three and assign roles: manager, administrative assistant, and reporter. Verify students' understanding of the roles. Encourage students to use the phrases in the *Speaking Note* during their discussions.

3. Set a time limit for the discussions (ten minutes). Write the sentence frames from 6B on the board. Then circulate and monitor.

B Call "time." Ask the reporter for each team to report the results of the team's discussion using the sentence frames on the board.

TIP

Extend the discussion in 6B. Ask: *What job needs the most training/skills? What job is the most difficult? What other jobs are there at a large venue? Would you prefer any of these jobs?*

Evaluation
5 minutes

TEST YOURSELF

1. Ask students to complete the checkboxes individually.

2. Tell students that you are going to read each of the items in the checklist aloud. If they are not at all confident with that skill, they should hold up a closed fist. If they are not very confident, they should hold up one finger. If they are somewhat confident, two fingers; confident, three fingers; very confident, four fingers. If they think they could teach the skill, they should hold up five fingers. Read each item in the checklist and identify students who may need further support.

EXTENSION ACTIVITY

Make a Flyer

Have students make a flyer of fun events.

1. Put students in groups. Tell each group to make a flyer for their city, which has three wonderful events planned this weekend. Direct students to include the day, the time, the price of the events, who can attend, and a short description.

2. Have a reporter from each group share his or her group's flyer. Have the class decide which event they'd rather attend.

Lesson Overview	Lesson Notes
MULTILEVEL OBJECTIVES	

MULTILEVEL OBJECTIVES

Pre-, On-, and Higher-level: Read about and discuss the benefits of walking in the park

LANGUAGE FOCUS

Grammar: Simple present (*The park offers walking paths.*)

Vocabulary: *Immune system, strengthen, outdoors, stress*

For vocabulary support, see this **Oxford Picture Dictionary** topic: The Park and Playground, page 230

STRATEGY FOCUS

Read text near a chart to understand the chart's labels.

READINESS CONNECTION

In this lesson, students verbally communicate information about how parks help people and communities stay healthy.

PACING

To compress this lesson: Assign 1F and/or 3B for homework.

To extend this lesson: Have students talk about time off. (See end of lesson.)

And/or have students complete **Workbook 3 page 14** and **Multilevel Activities 3 Unit 2 pages 34–35**.

CORRELATIONS

CCRS: SL.1.B (d.) Explain their own ideas and understanding in light of the discussion.

SL.2.B Determine the main ideas and supporting details of a text read aloud or information presented in diverse media and formats, including visually, quantitatively, and orally.

R.1.B Ask and answer such questions as who, what, where, when, why, and how to demonstrate understanding of key details in a text.

R.2.A Identify the main topic and retell key details of a text.

R.5.A Know and use various text features to locate key facts or information in a text.

R.7.C Interpret information presented visually, orally, or quantitatively and explain how the information contributes to an understanding of the text in which it appears.

L.4.B (c.) Use a known root word as a clue to the meaning of an unknown word with the same root. (e.) Use glossaries and beginning dictionaries, both print and digital, to determine or clarify the meaning of words and phrases.

RF.3.B (c.) Identify and know the meaning of the most common prefixes and derivational suffixes.

RF.4.B (a.) Read grade-level text with purpose and understanding.

ELPS: 1. An ELL can construct meaning from oral presentations and literary and informational text through level-appropriate listening, reading, and viewing. 3. An ELL can speak and write about level-appropriate complex literary and informational texts and topics.

Warm-up and Review
10–15 minutes (books closed)

Make a transparency of a local map. Ask students to identify the parks on the map. Ask them if they ever go to the parks, how big the various parks are, and what you can find there.

Introduction
5 minutes

1. Ask how much people usually pay for activities at the park. Say: *Parks have a lot to offer, and their services are usually either free or very low priced.* Ask: *Why is it important for park activities to be free?*

2. State the objective: *Today we're going to talk about how parks help people and communities stay healthy.*

1 Read

Presentation
10–20 minutes

 A Read the questions aloud. Use ideas from the *Warm-up* and *Introduction* to help guide discussion.

B Read the words and definitions. Elicit sample sentences for each word, or supply them if the students can't.

Pre-reading

 C 1. Review how to scan a text. Say: *When you scan a text, you look for specific information. You don't read the text word for word. In this article, you will read for numbers.*

2. Read the instructions aloud and have students scan the text for numbers. Have students complete the sentences individually and then check answers as a class. If any students answer incorrectly, ask them to support their answer using the article. Establish the correct answer.

Answers
1. 21
2. 89
3. 24

Guided Practice: While Reading
20–30 minutes

D 1. Direct students' attention to the *Reader's Note* and read the information aloud. Ask students to read the article silently and answer the question.

2. Check answers as a class.

3. Check comprehension. Ask: *How do parks help your physical health?* [Being outside helps your immune system; exercise is healthy.] *How do parks help mental health?* [Spending time outdoors lowers stress.] *How do parks help the community?* [They provide healthy activities for children and teenagers.]

Answer
Strengthen immune system, add minutes to your life, lower stress, increase happiness

TIP

Preview any unfamiliar vocabulary: *stress, afterschool program, working parents, out of trouble,* etc. Write these words (and any others that may be new to students) on the board and ask volunteers for definitions or examples. Alternatively, let students read the article and guess the definitions from context. Confirm their answers.

MULTILEVEL STRATEGIES

Adapt 2D to the level of your students.

• **Pre-level** Provide these students with an outline of the ideas in the reading. *1. Exercise helps you stay healthy. Parks are a good, free place to exercise. 2. Stress is bad for you. Relaxing outdoors lowers stress. 3. Many parks have afterschool programs for children and teenagers. These programs teach kids to share and work in teams.* Direct them to read the outline while other students are reading 1B.

• **Higher-level** Have these students identify the topic sentence in each paragraph.

Guided Practice: Rereading
15–20 minutes

 E 1. Provide an opportunity for students to extract evidence from the text. Have students reread the article and underline any words or phrases that support the idea that walking in a park is healthy.

2. Pair students and tell them to compare the words they underlined and report anything they disagree on. Discuss and clarify as needed.

Possible Answers
Strengthen immune system, add minutes to your life, get healthy, lower stress, increase happiness, keep teenagers out of trouble; underlines will vary.

TIP

Have students go online to find other advice on lowering stress. Provide them with the website addresses of any that you know, or give them some search terms that they can use for their own research (e.g., "advice" + "reduce stress"; "advice" + "boost immune system").

F 1. Have students work individually to mark the answers *T* (true), *F* (false), and *NI* (no information). They should then write the line numbers where they found the true and false answers. Write the answers on the board.

2. Elicit and discuss any additional questions about the reading. You could introduce new questions for class discussion: *What is the most interesting fact for you? Do you already walk in the park? If not, does this article convince you to do it? Why or why not?*

Answers
1. T, lines 5–8
2. F, lines 12–13
3. T, line 23
4. NI
5. NI

MULTILEVEL STRATEGIES

After 2F, adapt further comprehension questions to the level of your students.

• **Pre-level** Ask these students short-answer information questions. *How long can a walk in the park boost your immune system?* [48 hours]

• **On-level** Ask these students information questions that will elicit longer responses. *Why are parks excellent places to stay healthy?* [They are free, and when you walk in the park you boost your immune system.]

• **Higher-level** Ask these students inference questions. *Why does nature help people with stress?*

2 Word study

Guided Practice: Post-reading
20–25 minutes

 1. Direct students to look at the chart and identify the topic (the suffix *-ful*). Have students read the chart.

2. Read the first two sentences in the chart and the examples for *stress* and *stressful*. Elicit sentences for the other words in the chart.

3. Have students repeat after you as you say each word with natural intonation, rhythm, and stress.

4. Direct students to complete the sentences and then compare answers with a partner. Read the correct answers and have students check their work.

Answers	
1. beautiful	3. stressful
2. colorful	4. helpful

MULTILEVEL STRATEGIES

After 2A, give on- and pre-level students more time to work with the words in 2A while you challenge higher-level students.

• **Pre- and On-level** Have these students work together to write sentences for some of the words in the chart. Provide sentence frames. _____ *is stressful to me. I try to* _____ *to have less stress. The* _____ *is the most beautiful place I know. My favorite color is* _____., *etc.* Ask volunteers to complete the sentences on the board.

• **Higher-level** Have these students look in their dictionaries or research online lists for words ending with *-ful*. Ask them to look for words that have a base word that they already know. Tell them to write sentences with the words they find.

 1. Read the prompts aloud. Give students a few minutes to think of their answers.

2. Set a time limit (ten minutes). Have groups of three or four discuss the prompts. Circulate and help as needed.

3. Have students share their responses with the class.

3 Talk it over

Guided Practice
15–20 minutes

 Have students look at the pie chart and the text and read the *Reader's Note*. Point out that they need to use the information from the pie chart and the text to answer the questions. Set a time limit (ten minutes). Have students work in pairs to complete the task. Ask volunteers to share their answers with the class.

Answers
1. Workload
2. Lack of job security
3. Lack of job security
4. Answers will vary.

Communicative Practice
15–20 minutes

B Read the questions aloud. Set a time limit (ten minutes). Tell students to copy the chart in their notebooks and complete it with their answers to the questions.

C While students are doing the activity in 3B, write the chart on the board. Have volunteers share their answers with the class and write them in the chart. Have students add any new ideas to the charts in their notebooks. Have a class discussion about students' ideas.

Application
15–20 minutes

BRING IT TO LIFE

Have students tell the class where they are going to look for information. Try to vary the information students will find by having different students go to different places or look in different sources.

EXTENSION ACTIVITY

Write a Letter

1. Use student responses from 3B as the basis for writing a letter to an HR department of a company. Elicit their suggestions for new programs for employee stress reduction that they would like to see offered by the company. Help them articulate arguments for the new programs. Ask: *How would this program benefit the employees and the company?*

2. As a class, choose one idea and compose a letter. The letter should include a greeting and a closing, a suggestion for the new program, and at least one argument in favor of the program. Have a volunteer copy the letter neatly or type it on the computer.

AT WORK

Warm-up and Review
10–15 minutes

1. Review the *Bring It to Life* assignment from Lesson 5. Have students who did the exercise discuss what they learned.

2. As students describe what they found, ask questions that demonstrate checking understanding. For example: *So if I understand you correctly, the class is for children with their parents? Are you saying that you have to register the week before the class starts?*

Introduction
5 minutes

1. Ask students questions about how they check their understanding. *What can you say or do to make sure you understand what someone is saying?*

2. State the objective: *Today we're going to review ways to check your understanding when listening.*

Presentation
5 minutes

A 🔊 **1-23** Read the instructions aloud. Play the audio. Give students a minute to think about the question. Elicit responses from the class.

Answer
She wants to take some time off.

Guided Practice
10–15 minutes

B 🔊 **1-23** Read the question aloud. Play the audio again and have students write the three reasons in their notebooks. Set a time limit (five minutes) for students to discuss their answers with a partner. Circulate to monitor.

Answer
Her daughter is getting married; her son was sick; it is a national holiday.

C Read the information in the chart aloud. Have students check the boxes in the chart in their books or draw a new chart in their notebooks.

2. While students are doing the activity, write the chart on the board.

3. Have students compare answers with a partner. Then have students take turns sharing their answers and mark them on the board for the class to check.

Answers
Taking a trip to Las Vegas: Vacation
Getting the flu (you): Sick Leave
Caring for a sick family member: Family Leave
Attending a wedding: Vacation
Celebrating a national holiday: Holiday (Paid)
Having a baby: Family Leave
Going camping: Vacation
Breaking your leg: Sick Leave
Celebrating a birthday: Vacation

Presentation and Communicative Practice
15–20 minutes

D 1. Direct students' attention to the *Do/Say* chart and ask students to identify the lesson's soft skill [checking your understanding]. Ask the class which column has examples of language [right] and which has examples of behaviors [left].

2. Say a phrase from the left column and act it out. Say it again and have the class act it out with you. Say it a third time and have the class act it out for you. To confirm understanding, combine phrases: *Raise your finger and make eye contact with the speaker.*

3. Model the sentence frames from the right column using authentic intonation. Have students practice imitating your inflection.

4. Put students in teams of four and assign each team a question. Assign roles: manager, administrative assistant, researcher, and reporter. Researchers will ask you questions on behalf of the team. Verify understanding of the roles. Set a time limit (five minutes) and monitor.

5. Write sentence frames on the board that teams can use to summarize their response. (*Our team discussed the following question: _____ We decided _____ because _____.*)

6. Call "time" and let reporters rehearse their report for one minute. Direct each reporter to present to three other teams.

Communicative Practice and Application
10–15 minutes

 1. Have students form pairs. Tell students that they are going to be role-playing a conversation between a supervisor and an employee using appropriate body language. Read the situation in the chart aloud.

2. Direct pairs to take turns doing each role.

3. As students carry out the conversation, circulate and monitor. Provide global feedback once the activity ends.

Lesson Overview	Lesson Notes

MULTILEVEL OBJECTIVES

Pre-, On-, and Higher-level: Review unit language

LANGUAGE FOCUS

Grammar: *Be going to* (*We're going to go to the park.*); *will* (*I think I'll take a vacation this summer.*)

Vocabulary: Vocabulary for making plans to do something fun and ask for time off

For vocabulary support, see this **Oxford Picture Dictionary** topic: Taking Care of Your Health, pages 116–117

READINESS CONNECTION

In this review, students work in a team to use *be going to* and *will* to write an email requesting time off.

PACING

To extend this review: Have students complete **Workbook 3 page 15**, **Multilevel Activities 3 Unit 2 page 36**, and **Multilevel Grammar Exercises 3 Unit 2**.

CORRELATIONS

CCRS: SL.1.B. (a.) Come to discussions prepared, having read or studied required material; explicitly draw on that preparation and other information known about the topic to explore ideas under discussion. (b.) Follow agreed-upon rules for discussions. (c.) Ask questions to check understanding of information presented, stay on topic, and link their comments to the remarks of others. (d.) Explain their own ideas and understanding in light of the discussion.

SL.2.B Determine the main ideas and supporting details of a text read aloud or information presented in diverse media and formats, including visually, quantitatively, and orally.

SL.4.B Report on a topic or text, tell a story, or recount an experience with appropriate facts and relevant, descriptive details, speaking clearly at an understandable pace.

R.2.A Identify the main topic and retell key details of a text.

W.3.B Write narratives in which they recount a well-elaborated event or short sequence of events, include details to describe actions, thoughts, and feelings, use temporal words to signal event order, and provide a sense of closure.

W.4.B Produce writing in which the development and organization are appropriate to task and purpose.

L.1.B (h.) Form and use the simple verb tenses. (l.) Produce simple, compound and complex sentences.

RF.4.B (a.) Read grade-level text with purpose and understanding.

ELPS: 5. An ELL can conduct research and evaluate and communicate findings to answer questions or solve problems. 6. An ELL can analyze and critique the arguments of others orally and in writing.

Warm-up and Review
10–15 minutes (books closed)

1. Review *At Work* activity E.

2. Ask students to share the good, not-so-good, and interesting things that happened during the role-play. As students speak, write their responses in a chart on the board.

Introduction and Presentation
5 minutes

1. Pair students and direct them to look at the picture in their book. Ask them to describe what they see to their partner.

2. Ask volunteer pairs to share their ideas with the class.

Guided Practice

10–15 minutes

 A 1. Direct students to work in groups of three or four and look at the picture. Have students take turns reading the sentences aloud.

2. Set a time limit (five minutes) for groups to complete the task. Circulate and monitor.

3. Check answers as a class.

Answers	
1. g	4. b
2. e	5. c
3. f	6. a

B 1. Read the instructions aloud and have students work in the same teams from A to complete the task. Circulate and monitor.

2. Check answers as a class.

Answers
Plan: 2, 4
Promise: 1, 4, 6
Prediction: 3, 5

Communicative Practice

30–45 minutes

 C 1. Group students and assign roles: manager, writer, editor, and presenter. Explain that students are going to work with their teams to write an email asking for time off using the reasons list. Editors will review the email and offer suggestions for changes. Verify students' understanding of the roles.

2. Check comprehension of the task. *What details will you include in your email?* [reason for time off and specific dates] *What grammar will you use in the sentences?* [the verbs tenses from Lesson 3, exercise 1B]

3. Set a time limit (ten minutes) to complete the exercise. Circulate and answer any questions.

4. Have presenters from each team read their team's paragraph to another team.

MULTILEVEL STRATEGIES
• **Pre-level** Assign these students the role of writer.
• **On-level** Assign these students the role of presenter or manager.
• **Higher-level** Assign these students the role of manager or editor.

D 1. Have students walk around the room to conduct the interviews. To get students moving, tell them to interview three people who were not on their team for C.

2. Set a time limit (five minutes) to complete the exercise.

3. Tell students to make a note of their classmates' answers but not to worry about writing complete sentences.

MULTILEVEL STRATEGIES
Adapt the mixer in D to the level of your students.
• **Pre- and On-level** Pair these students and have them interview other pairs together.
• **Higher-level** Have these students ask an additional question and write all answers in complete sentences.

E 1. Call on individuals to report what they learned about their classmates using the sentence frame. Keep a running tally on the board for each question, marking the kind of event or class, the benefits of the class, and whether they would do it again.

2. Use your tally for question 1 to create a pie chart on the board. Instruct students to choose a question and draw a pie chart. Circulate and answer any questions.

PROBLEM SOLVING

10–15 minutes

A 1. Ask: *Do your friends and family like to spend their free time the same way that you do? Do you have to compromise a lot?* Tell students they will read a story about two friends who have a disagreement about free time. Direct students to read Juanita and Anna's story silently.

2. Play the audio and have students read along silently again.

B 1. Elicit answers to question 1. Guide students to a class consensus on the answer.

2. As a class, brainstorm answers to question 2. Ask students if they know someone who has this problem and has overcome it or what they have done themselves to overcome the same problem. Have students share their responses and write them on the board for students to refer to in the next activity.

Answers
1. They have different interests for the weekend.
2. Answers will vary.

C Read the instructions and the note template. Have students do the task individually. Have students read their letters to the class.

Evaluation
20–25 minutes

To test students' understanding of the unit language and content, have them take the Unit 2 Test, available on the Teacher Resource Center.

Unit Overview

This unit explores the work environment with a range of employability skills and contextualizes structures using comparisons and superlatives.

KEY OBJECTIVES	
Lesson 1	Identify computer and office vocabulary
Lesson 2	Identify workplace problems and write an email describing the rules
Lesson 3	Use comparisons to choose the best product to buy
Lesson 4	Respond to negative feedback
Lesson 5	Learn about work-based training and education
At Work	Ask for clarification
Teamwork & Language Review	Review unit language

UNIT FEATURES	
Academic Vocabulary	*evaluation, range, subsidize, policy, flexible, medical, benefits*
Employability Skills	• Decide which meaning of a word is appropriate • Decide on the seriousness of bad behavior at work • Decide which factors are most important in accepting a job • Work independently • Work with others • Locate information • Listen actively • Use writing skills • Comprehend written materials • Analyze information

Resources	**Class Audio** CD1, Tracks 25–35
	Workbook Unit 3, pages 16–22
	Teacher Resource Center
	    Multilevel Activities 3 Unit 3
	    Multilevel Grammar Exercises 3 Unit 3
	    Unit 3 Test
	Oxford Picture Dictionary Describing Things, The Workplace, Career Planning, Information Technology (IT)

Lesson Overview	Lesson Notes

MULTILEVEL OBJECTIVES

On-level: Identify and describe computer equipment, problems, and jobs

Pre-level: Identify computer equipment, problems, and jobs

Higher-level: Talk and write about computer equipment, problems, and jobs

LANGUAGE FOCUS

Grammar: Simple present tense sentences with *when* (*When computers crash, documents are lost.*)

Vocabulary: Computer and office vocabulary

For vocabulary support, see these **Oxford Picture Dictionary** topics: The Workplace, pages 182–183; Information Technology (IT), pages 190–191

STRATEGY FOCUS

Pool knowledge with team members to maximize vocabulary learning.

READINESS CONNECTION

In this lesson, students explore and communicate information about computers and office vocabulary.

PACING

To compress this lesson: Conduct 1B as a whole-class activity.

To extend this lesson: Have students label a picture. (See end of lesson.)

And/or have students complete **Workbook 3 page 16** and **Multilevel Activities 3 Unit 3 pages 38–39**.

CORRELATIONS

CCRS: SL.1.B (d.) Explain their own ideas and understanding in light of the discussion.

SL.4.B Report on a topic or text, tell a story, or recount an experience with appropriate facts and relevant, descriptive details, speaking clearly at an understandable pace.

W.7.A Participate in shared research and writing projects (e.g., explore a number of "how-to" books on a given topic and use them to write a sequence of instructions).

L.1.B (l.) Produce simple, compound and complex sentences.

L.4.B (e.) Use glossaries and beginning dictionaries, both print and digital, to determine or clarify the meaning of words and phrases.

RF.4.B (a.) Read grade-level text with purpose and understanding.

ELPS: 8. An ELL can determine the meaning of words and phrases in oral presentations and literary and informational text.

Warm-up and Review
10–15 minutes (books closed)

Put up one sign on each wall: *I don't know anything; I know a little; I know an average amount; I know a lot.* Tell students the topic is computers. Ask them to stand next to the sign that best represents their knowledge of computers. As a class, discuss the pros and cons of computers as part of everyday life: how they help us and how they might get in the way.

Introduction
3 minutes

1. Call on individuals to talk about their experience with computers. Elicit the names of some jobs in which people use computers.

2. State the objective: *Today we're going to learn some computer and office vocabulary.*

1 Identify computer and office vocabulary

Presentation I
15–20 minutes

 1. Direct students to look at the picture. Ask: *Do you think this is a typical office? Have you worked in an office like this one?*

2. Have students work together to brainstorm in a group to answer the question. Make a list on the board of the advantages and disadvantages your students identify.

Guided Practice I
15–20 minutes

 🔊 1-25 1. Model the task by "thinking aloud" about the word that goes in the first sentence: *I know that when a computer is broken, I need a person to fix it. When I look at the picture, I see a man with tools in front of a computer. The label is* computer technician, *so this is the word that goes in the blank.*

2. Have students complete the task individually. Have pairs compare answers and then play the audio for students to check their answers.

Answers	
1. computer technician	6. monitor
2. CPU	7. keyboard
3. digital camera	8. office manager
4. headset	9. photographer
5. graphic designer	10. cubicle

MULTILEVEL STRATEGIES

After the group comprehension check in 1B, call on individuals and tailor your questions to the level of your students.

• **Pre-level** Ask *or* questions. *Does an office manager fix computers or help everyone in the office?* [helps everyone in the office]

• **On-level** Ask information questions. *What part of the computer is under a monitor?* [a keyboard]

• **Higher-level** Ask these students to give their opinion about the office. *Which person in the office needs the quietest workspace? Should everyone in an office work in a cubicle?*

C 1. Read the questions aloud. Set a time limit (five minutes) and have pairs discuss the questions.

2. Have students share their partner's answers with the class.

2 Learn more computer vocabulary

Presentation II
10–15 minutes

 1. Direct students to look at the pictures. Introduce the new topic: *Now we're going to learn more computer words. All of these words have a computer and a "non-computer" meaning.*

2. Ask students to work individually to check the words they know.

3. Go through the words. Ask students to give examples of the "non-computer" and the computer meanings. *The flu is a dangerous virus. It makes people sick. Computer viruses cause computers not to work properly.* Provide examples for the words students don't know.

4. Say and have students repeat the words.

5. Check comprehension. Ask: *What do you call a secret program that makes your computer not work properly?* [a virus]

Guided Practice II
10–15 minutes

 Have students work independently to complete the sentences. Go over the answers as a class.

Answers
1. crash
2. mouse
3. desktop
4. virus
5. window

Communicative Practice and Application
25–30 minutes

 1. If students will use the Internet for this task, establish what device(s) they'll use: a class computer, tablets, or smartphones. Alternatively, print information from the Internet before class and distribute to groups.

2. Write the questions from 2C on the board. Explain that students will work in teams to research and report on these questions. Ask: *Which question should you research first?* [1] *Which search terms or questions can you use to find the information you need?* ["computer

training" + your city] Point to the *Need help?* box and suggest students use the ideas in their searches. Then ask: *What information will you scan for?* [names of class and locations/ addresses of class, dates of classes, cost of classes] *How will you record the information you find?* [table, checklist, index cards] Remind students to bookmark or record sites so they can find or cite them in the future.

3. Group students and assign roles: manager, administrative assistant, reporter, and IT support. Verify students' understanding of the roles.

4. Give managers the time limit for researching the questions (fifteen minutes). Direct the IT support to begin the online research or pick up the printed materials for each team. Direct the administrative assistant to record information for the team using a table, a checklist, or index cards.

5. Give a two-minute warning. Call "time."

TIP

When setting up task-based activities, verify that students understand their roles using physical commands. For example: *If you report on your team's work, stand up* [reporter]. *If you keep the team on task, point to the clock* [manager]. *If you write the team's responses, raise your hand* [administrative assistant]. *If you help the team research, hold up your smartphone/tablet* [IT support].

D 1. Copy the sentence frames on the board.

2. Direct teams to help their administrative assistant use the sentence frames to record the team's findings. Direct the reporter to use the recorded information to report the team's findings to the class or another team.

Evaluation
10–15 minutes (books closed)

TEST YOURSELF

1. Make a three-column chart on the board with the headings *Computer parts and equipment*, *Computer problems*, and *Jobs*. Have students close their books and give you an example for each column.

2. Have students copy the chart into their notebooks.

3. Give students five to ten minutes to test themselves by writing the words they recall from the lesson.

4. Call "time" and have students check their spelling in a dictionary. Circulate and monitor.

5. Direct students to share their work with a partner and add additional words to their charts.

MULTILEVEL STRATEGIES

Target the *Test Yourself* to the level of your students.

• **Pre-level** Have these students do the activity the first time with the option to look in their books. Then have them do the activity a second time without looking at their books.

• **Higher-level** Have these students complete the chart and then write a sentence with one word from each column. Challenge them to write sentences that illustrate the meaning of the words.

TIP

To provide further practice of the vocabulary:

1. Direct students to work with a partner to combine their lists from the *Test Yourself* and put the words in alphabetical order. Circulate and monitor students' progress.

2. Ask a volunteer pair to write its list on the board. Ask other students to check that the words are in alphabetical order and fix any errors.

EXTENSION ACTIVITY
Label a Picture

Have groups practice or extend their computer vocabulary. Put students in groups of three or four. Direct them to draw a picture of a computer and label its parts. For the class discussion, have each group member name a part of the computer. If some of the students are knowledgeable about computers, ask them to talk about what the various parts do or are used for.

Lesson Overview	Lesson Notes
MULTILEVEL OBJECTIVES	

MULTILEVEL OBJECTIVES

On- and Higher-level: Analyze, write, and edit an email describing the rules

Pre-level: Read and write an email describing the rules

LANGUAGE FOCUS

Grammar: Present continuous tense (*Employees are taking longer breaks.*)

Vocabulary: *Policies, break, employee handbook*

For vocabulary support, see these **Oxford Picture Dictionary** topics: The Workplace, pages 182–183; Information Technology (IT), pages 190–191

STRATEGY FOCUS

Use the subject line to write a short but clear title for your email that describes the content of your message.

READINESS CONNECTION

In this lesson, students listen actively to, read, and write an email about employees not following rules.

PACING

To compress this lesson: Assign the *Test Yourself* and/or 3C for homework.

To extend this lesson: Have students write a policy email. (See end of lesson.)

And/or have students complete **Workbook 3 page 17** and **Multilevel Activities 3 Unit 3 page 40**.

CORRELATIONS

CCRS: SL.1.B (d.) Explain their own ideas and understanding in light of the discussion.

R.1.B Ask and answer such questions as who, what, where, when, why, and how to demonstrate understanding of key details in a text.

R.5.A Know and use various text features to locate key facts or information in a text.

W.2.A Write informative/explanatory texts in which they name a topic, supply some facts about the topic, and provide some sense of closure.

W.4.B Produce writing in which the development and organization are appropriate to task and purpose.

W.5.B With guidance and support from peers and others, develop and strengthen writing as needed by planning, revising and editing.

L.1.B (l.) Produce simple, compound and complex sentences.

L.2.B (c.) use commas in greetings and closings of letters.

RF.4.B (a.) Read grade-level text with purpose and understanding.

ELPS: 6. An ELL can analyze and critique the arguments of others orally and in writing. 9. An ELL can create clear and coherent level-appropriate speech and text.

Warm-up and Review
10–15 minutes (books closed)

Write *Home, School*, and *Work* on the board. Ask: *What are some things children do when they're not following their parents' rules?* Write their ideas under *Home*. Ask the same question about students and employees and write their ideas in the correct columns.

Introduction
5 minutes

1. Refer to the problems on the board from the *Warm-up* and say: *When people don't follow the rules, there may be problems at home, at work, or at school. Another word for* rule *is* policy.

2. State the objective: *Today we're going to read and write an email about some employees who aren't following the rules.*

1 Prepare to write

Presentation
20–25 minutes

A 1. Build students' schema by asking questions about the pictures. Ask: *Are the same people in the pictures? Where are the pictures taking place? Do you think the situations are common?*

2. Give students one minute to tell a partner their responses to questions 1 and 2. Elicit responses from the class.

Answers
1. Workers are late; they are taking long breaks; workers are spilling drinks on their keyboards.
2. Answers will vary.

B 🔊 1-26 1. Introduce the model email and its purpose: *You're going to read an email about situations in an office. As you read, look for the purpose of the email: Why is the person writing?* Have students read the email silently.

2. Check comprehension. Ask: *Who is writing?* [the president of a company] *How many problems are there?* [3] *Does the writer want people to follow rules?* [yes] *How do you know?* [He says that people not following the rules are "problems."] *Does he want employees to contact him?* [no]

3. Play the audio. Have students read along silently.

Guided Practice I
10 minutes

C 1. Have students work independently to answer the questions.

2. Point out the *Writer's Note* and explain how the model email's subject line describes the email's content.

3. Have pairs compare answers. Have volunteers call out answers and write them on the board for the class to check.

Answers
1. Company policy
2. Employees are not coming to work on time; some employees are taking longer and longer breaks; coffee and water spills are hurting computer keyboards.
3. The employee handbook
4. Their office manager

MULTILEVEL STRATEGIES

Seat pre-level students together for 1C.

• **Pre-level** While other students are working on 1C, ask these students *yes/no* and *or* questions about the reading. *Are employees coming to work on time? Are employees taking longer or shorter breaks? Should employees be at work by 9 a.m. or 10 a.m.?* Allow these students to copy the answers to 1C from the board.

• **On- and Higher-level** Write questions on the board for these students to answer after they finish 1C. *Do you think this email will be effective? Why or why not?* After allowing students to work individually to answer the questions, ask volunteers to share their opinions with the class.

2 Plan and write

Guided Practice II
15–20 minutes

A 1. Read the questions aloud. Elicit students' answers and encourage them to take notes to use in 2B.

2. Write students' ideas for question 1 on the board so they can refer to them while they write.

B 1. Direct students to look back at the model in 1B. Focus their attention on the different sections. Ask them to look through the email quickly and put brackets around the different sections of the email. Elicit student responses and discuss any questions.

2. Read through email template. Elicit ideas that could go in each section. Have students write their email individually.

MULTILEVEL STRATEGIES

Adapt 2B to the level of your students.

• **Pre-level** Work with these students to write a group email. Go through the template together. Decide as a group what to write.

• **Higher-level** Ask these students to include an additional problem and an additional policy.

3 Get feedback and revise

Guided Practice III
5 minutes

 Direct students to check their writing using the editing checklist. Tell them to read each item in the list and check their papers before moving on to the next item. Explain that students should not edit their writing at this stage. They should just use the checklist to check their work and mark any areas they want to revise.

Communicative Practice
15 minutes

 1. Read the instructions and the sample sentences aloud. Emphasize to students that they are responding to their partners' work, not correcting it.

2. Use the email in 1B to model the exercise. *I think this is a good description of the problem. People are late for many different reasons.*

3. Direct students to exchange papers with a partner and follow the instructions.

 Allow students time to edit and revise their writing as necessary, using the editing checklist from 3A and their partner's feedback from 3B. If necessary, students could complete this task as homework.

TIP
Suggest to students that they keep a copy of their Lesson 2 writings in a notebook or binder. After two or three weeks, they can go back to a piece of writing and see if they would change anything based on what they have learned since they first wrote it.

Application and Evaluation
10 minutes

TEST YOURSELF

1. Review the instructions aloud. Assign a time limit (five minutes) and have students work independently.

2. Before collecting student work, invite two or three volunteers to share their sentences. Ask students to raise their hands if they wrote similar answers.

MULTILEVEL STRATEGIES

Adapt the *Test Yourself* to the level of your students.

• **Pre-level** Write questions for these students to answer in writing. *Was today's writing assignment difficult or easy? Do you think you will have to write an email like this at work or in another part of your life?*

EXTENSION ACTIVITY
Write a Policy Email

Have some fun with problems and policies. Tell students that even though we don't write policy emails in our personal lives, sometimes we might want to. Have students work in pairs or groups and brainstorm problems and policies for "An Email to My Children/Husband/ Wife/Boyfriend/Girlfriend/Friend." Have pairs come to the board and write one problem and its corresponding policy.

Lesson Overview

Lesson Notes

MULTILEVEL OBJECTIVES

On- and Higher-level: Use comparisons and superlatives to choose the best product to buy

Pre-level: Recognize comparisons and superlatives when choosing the best product to buy

LANGUAGE FOCUS

Grammar: Comparisons (*The 580 laptop is more expensive than the 480 laptop.*); superlatives (*The 250Z laptop is the most expensive.*)

Vocabulary: Adjectives

For vocabulary support, see these **Oxford Picture Dictionary** topics: Describing Things, page 23; Information Technology (IT), pages 190–191

STRATEGY FOCUS

Learn spelling rules for comparative adjectives.

READINESS CONNECTION

In this lesson, students practice comparing products and stores and how to talk about which ones are best.

PACING

To compress this lesson: Conduct 4C as a whole-class activity.

To extend this lesson: Have students make an ad. (See end of lesson.)

And/or have students complete **Workbook 3 pages 18–19, Multilevel Activities 3 Unit 3 pages 41–42,** and **Multilevel Grammar Exercises 3 Unit 3**.

CORRELATIONS

CCRS: SL.1.B (d.) Explain their own ideas and understanding in light of the discussion.

SL.2.B Determine the main ideas and supporting details of a text read aloud or information presented in diverse media and formats, including visually, quantitatively, and orally.

SL.6.B Speak in complete sentences when appropriate to task and situation in order to provide requested detail or clarification.

R.1.B Ask and answer such questions as who, what, where, when, why, and how to demonstrate understanding of key details in a text.

R.7.A Use the illustrations and details in a text to describe its key ideas.

L.1.B (b.) Explain the function of nouns, pronouns, verbs, adjectives, and adverbs in general and their functions in particular sentences. (h.) Form and use the simple verb tenses. (j.) Form and use comparative and superlative adjectives and adverbs, and choose between them depending on what is to be modified. (l.) Produce simple, compound and complex sentences.

RF.4.B (a.) Read grade-level text with purpose and understanding.

ELPS: 7. An ELL can adapt language choices to purpose, task, and audience when speaking and writing. 10. An ELL can demonstrate command of the conventions of standard English to communicate in level-appropriate speech and writing.

Warm-up and Review
10–15 minutes (books closed)

Review the comparative form. Put up a series of nouns on one side of the board: *sofa, refrigerator, laptop, cell phone, printer, car*. Put up adjectives on the other side: *small, modern, expensive, comfortable, attractive, durable*. Ask volunteers to match adjectives with nouns (accept any logical combination). Ask more advanced students to use a comparative form of the adjective. *Cell phones are smaller than cameras. Sofas are more comfortable than cars.* Call on volunteers to write their sentences on the board.

Introduction
5–10 minutes

1. Ask: *When you shop for expensive products, do you compare stores and brands?*

2. State the objective: *Today we're going to learn how to compare products and stores and how to talk about which ones are best.*

1 Use comparisons

Presentation I
20–25 minutes

 Direct students to look at the ads and the paragraph. Ask: *What are the ads for?* Establish that they are ads for computers at different stores.

2. Read the instructions aloud. Ask students to read the paragraph and the ads silently, answer the question, and underline their reasons.

3. Have pairs compare their answers. Call on volunteers to share their partner's answer and reasons.

 1. Demonstrate how to read the grammar chart. Read each sentence and check for comprehension. Say: *The 580 is as heavy as the 680. Does that mean they are the same or different?*

2. Direct students to underline the examples of comparisons in the paragraph in 1A. Go over the answers as a class.

3. Ask questions about the paragraph in 1A. *Is the 580 laptop the same price as the 680 laptop? Is the 580 laptop or the 680 laptop heavier?*

4. Assess students' understanding of the chart. Read the *Grammar Notes*. Elicit comparisons for the words on the board from the *Warm-up*. Use

this exercise to demonstrate that *as...as* can be used with all adjectives but that *more/less than* are not used with one-syllable adjectives.

Answers	
as...as *not as...as*	The 580 is as heavy as the 680 it doesn't have as much memory as the 680 aren't as experienced as
-er than	The 680 is faster than the 580
less...than	The 580 laptop is less expensive than the 680.
more...than	it's more expensive than the 580

Guided Practice I
10–15 minutes

 1. Tell students they will collaborate to complete the description of the grammar point. Model collaboration by working with the class to complete the first sentence. Encourage students to look at 1A to help them determine the correct word for the blank.

2. Pair students and have them work together to complete the description.

3. Project or write the completed definition on the board and have pairs verify the accuracy of their responses. Ask volunteers which sentences confused them and discuss.

Answers	
the same 1 *-er*	2 more

Guided Practice II
15–20 minutes

1. Model the questions and answers with a volunteer.

2. Ask students to practice the questions and answers with their partners using information from the computer ads in 1A and their own ideas.

3. Have pairs merge to form teams of four and then take turns demonstrating questions and answers. Set a time limit (four minutes) and monitor the practice, identifying any issues.

4. Provide clarification or feedback to the whole class as needed.

2 Use superlatives

Presentation II
20–25 minutes

 1. Introduce the new topic. Say: *When you are comparing two things, you use a comparative. But when you are saying that one thing in a group is the most or least in some quality, you use a superlative.*

2. Direct students to read the ad. Demonstrate how to read the grammar chart. Read each sentence and check for comprehension. Put the same adjectives and nouns on the board that you used during the *Warm-up*. Write on the board: *Cell phones are (small) of these items. Cars are (expensive).* Ask volunteers to come to the board and fill in the blanks with the adjective in the parentheses. Check comprehension for form. Ask: *What is the superlative form of* more? [*most*] *What is the superlative form of* less? [*least*] *Can I use these with one-syllable adjectives?* [no]

3. Read the questions and sample answer aloud. Direct students to answer the questions individually. Ask volunteers to read the completed sentences aloud.

Answers
1. The 750XL is the most expensive.
2. The 180Z is the most popular.
3. The 250Z is the newest.
4. The 750XL is the most powerful.
5. The 750XL is the largest.

Guided Practice III
10–15 minutes

 1. Elicit the importance of accuracy. Tell students they will be building their accuracy in this task.

2. Organize students into groups. Demonstrate how to correct the sentence using the first example.

3. Have team members work together to correct the sentences. Circulate and monitor teamwork.

4. Project or write the corrected sentences on the board and have teams check their work.

5. Address questions and any issues you noted during your observation.

Answers
1. The 100X is the least expensive camera.
2. Summer solstice is the longest day.
3. My teacher is the smartest teacher I've ever had.
4. The cheapest prices are online.

 1. Model the first question and answer with a volunteer.

2. Ask students to ask and answer the questions with their partners using their own ideas.

3. Have pairs merge to form teams of four and then take turns demonstrating questions and answers. Set a time limit (four minutes) and monitor the practice, identifying any issues.

4. Provide clarification or feedback to the whole class as needed.

3 Listen for comparisons

Guided Practice IV
15–20 minutes

🔊 **1-27** 1. Say: *We've been talking about making comparisons between two or more things. Now we're going to listen to an office manager discussing her rationale for buying office supplies at different businesses.*

2. Direct students to read the first set of statements. Then play the first item and have students circle the correct statement.

3. Elicit answers from the class. If students answered incorrectly, play the audio again, providing a listening clue (for example, *listen for less* or *more*).

4. Repeat for numbers 2–6.

Answers	
1. a	4. a
2. a	5. b
3. b	6. a

4 Use comparisons to talk about your life experience

Communicative Practice and Application
20–25 minutes

A 1. Direct students to work independently to answer the questions with their own ideas. Review clothing vocabulary and brainstorm local stores. Write responses on the board for students to refer to.

2. Call on volunteers to share their sentences, correcting grammar as necessary. Establish the correct grammar for each sentence.

B Direct students to work with a partner to write two more questions to complete the sentence stems.

C 1. Have pairs merge to form teams of four. Model the exercise by "joining" one of the teams. Each pair takes a turn asking and answering questions while the class listens.

2. Check comprehension of the exercise. Ask: *Who asks questions?* [everyone] *Who answers questions?* [everyone]

3. Ask volunteers to share something interesting they learned about their classmates.

TIP

For more practice with comparisons and superlatives, have students compare information from ads.

1. Put students in groups. Give each group sales flyers from several different stores that sell the same products—for example, grocery stores, clothing stores, or furniture stores—or print out pages from online stores selling similar items.

2. Tell the groups to look through the ads and write three comparative or superlative sentences based on the information they find. Have a reporter from each group read the group's sentences to the class.

Evaluation

10–15 minutes

TEST YOURSELF

Ask students to write the sentences independently. Collect and correct their writing.

MULTILEVEL STRATEGIES

Target the *Test Yourself* to the level of your students.

• **Pre-level** Provide sentence frames for these students to complete. *1. _____ is not as expensive as _____. 2. _____ is more crowded than _____.*
3. _____ is the most expensive store in this area.
4. _____ is the least expensive store in this area.

• **On- and Higher-level** Have these students write a paragraph in response to these questions: *Where do you usually shop? Why? Compare your favorite store to other stores.*

EXTENSION ACTIVITY

Make an Ad

Have students create a short TV ad for a store.

1. Put students in groups. Ask each group to choose a store (or invent one) and write a short ad for it.

2. Have a reporter from each group read the ad to the class. Have the class decide which group had the most convincing ad.

Lesson Overview

Lesson Notes

MULTILEVEL OBJECTIVES

On- and Higher-level: Learn how to give and respond to feedback and listen for information in a job evaluation

Pre-level: Identify ways to give and respond to feedback and listen for information in a job evaluation

LANGUAGE FOCUS

Grammar: Superlatives (*She's the friendliest person in the office.*)

Vocabulary: *Experienced, friendly, kind, careful*

For vocabulary support, see this **Oxford Picture Dictionary** topic: The Workplace, pages 182–183

STRATEGY FOCUS

Practice listening for details.

READINESS CONNECTION

In this lesson, students verbally communicate about and practice how to describe people's qualities and how to give feedback and accept correction.

PACING

To compress this lesson: Skip 4A and do 6A as a class activity.

To extend this lesson: Have students do a self-evaluation. (See end of lesson.)

And/or have students complete **Workbook 3 page 20** and **Multilevel Activities 3 Unit 3 page 43**.

CORRELATIONS

CCRS: SL.1.B (d.) Explain their own ideas and understanding in light of the discussion.

SL.2.B Determine the main ideas and supporting details of a text read aloud or information presented in diverse media and formats, including visually, quantitatively, and orally.

SL.4.B Report on a topic or text, tell a story, or recount an experience with appropriate facts and relevant, descriptive details, speaking clearly at an understandable pace.

SL.6.B Speak in complete sentences when appropriate to task and situation in order to provide requested detail or clarification.

R.7.B Use information gained from illustrations and the words in a text to demonstrate understanding of the text.

L.1.B (h.) Form and use the simple verb tenses. (j.) Form and use comparative and superlative adjectives and adverbs, and choose between them depending on what is to be modified. (l.) Produce simple, compound and complex sentences.

RF.2.A (g.) Isolate and pronounce initial, medial vowel, and final sounds (phonemes) in spoken single-syllable words.

RF.4.B (a.) Read grade-level text with purpose and understanding.

ELPS: 2. An ELL can participate in level-appropriate oral and written exchanges of information, ideas, and analyses, in various social and academic contexts, responding to peer, audience, or reader comments and questions. 9. An ELL can create clear and coherent level-appropriate speech and text.

Warm-up and Review
10–15 minutes (books closed)

Review adjectives for describing people. Say: *My best friend is friendly, helpful, and talkative.* Write the adjectives on the board and ask: *How would you describe your best friend?* Write students' ideas on the board.

Introduction
5 minutes

1. Ask students which of the adjectives on the board from the *Warm-up* are important for an employee. Leave those adjectives on the board for students to refer to later.

2. State the objective: *Today we're going to learn how to describe people's qualities and how to respond to negative feedback.*

1 Learn ways to respond to negative feedback

Presentation I
10 minutes

 A 🔊 **1-28** 1. Direct students to look at the picture. Ask students to talk about who each person is and what she is doing.

2. Read the instructions aloud. Play the audio. Give students a minute to answer the question. Go over the answer as a class.

Answer
Some of Vicki's bad work habits

Guided Practice I
20–25 minutes

 B 🔊 **1-28** 1. Read the instructions and the questions aloud. Play the audio. Ask students to listen for the answer to each question.

2. Ask students to compare their answers with a partner. Circulate and monitor to ensure students understand the audio.

Answers
1. She is late, and she talks on the phone too much.
2. No
3. She won't let it happen again.

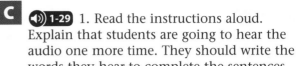 **C** 🔊 **1-29** 1. Read the instructions aloud. Explain that students are going to hear the audio one more time. They should write the words they hear to complete the sentences. Play the audio. Call on volunteers to elicit the answers.

Answers
1. to do better
2. have to tell me
3. letting me know

2 Practice your pronunciation

Pronunciation Extension
10–15 minutes

 A 🔊 **1-30** 1. Write *Vince is a terrific boss* on the board. Say the sentence and ask students to repeat it. Underline *V, f,* and *b* and repeat each sound. Say: *Now we're going to focus on pronunciation of these three sounds.*

2. Play the audio. Direct students to listen for the *v, b,* and *f* sounds.

3. Say the words with the bolded sounds and direct students to look at your mouth. Ask them which sound uses a different mouth position [/b/].

B 🔊 **1-31** Play the audio. Have students work individually to circle the sounds they hear.

Answers	
1. v	4. b
2. b	5. f
3. f	6. v

TIP

Students from some language backgrounds, such as Korean and Vietnamese, also have trouble distinguishing /p/ from /f/. If your students have that difficulty, have them practice these sentences: *I saw Paul fall down the stairs. Pam pricked her fourth finger with a pin.*

If your students are having difficulty with the difference between the /b/ and /v/ lip positions, encourage them to look in a mirror as they practice. (Ask them to bring small mirrors to class or use the camera on their smartphone for pronunciation practice.)

C 🔊 **1-31** 1. Play the audio again. Have students check their answers to 2B. Call on volunteers to repeat the names.

TIP

For more practice with these sounds after 2C, write these tongue twisters on the board and have students practice saying them with a partner: *Becky and Brandon are the best bosses in the business. Farrah finally found five file folders for her efficient friend.*

3 Use superlatives to describe employees

Presentation II and Guided Practice II
10–15 minutes

A 1. Introduce the new topic. Write *1. Bob is a good employee. 2. Carla is a better employee. 3. Jan is _____ employee.* on the board. Ask a volunteer to fill in the blank. Say: *Now we are going to use superlatives to describe employees.* Point to the adjectives on the board from the *Introduction.* Ask students if they can think of any other adjectives that can be used to describe an employee. Write them on the board.

2. Draw students' attention to the chart and have them circle the basic adjective individually.

3. Check comprehension of the grammar in the chart. Refer students to the adjectives on the board from the *Introduction.* Ask volunteers to make superlatives of each one.

Answers
circled: kind, happi, big, patient

B 1. Read the instructions aloud. Point out the sample answer.

2. Read the adjectives aloud and have students repeat. Answer any questions about vocabulary.

3. Have students do the task individually and then compare answers with a partner. Check answers as a class.

Answers			
2	angry	1	kind
2	happy	3	flat
2	friendly	4	comfortable
3	big	4	organized
3	hot	4	patient
1	fast	1	great
4	efficient	3	thin

C 1. Read the instructions. Read the sample sentence aloud and ask a few volunteers to substitute the superlative adjective to make a new sentence.

2. Have students do the task individually. Circulate and monitor. Have students share their sentences with the class.

4 Building conversation skills

Guided Practice III
15–20 minutes

A Direct students to look at the picture and skim the conversation in 4B. Have them work with partners to identify the purpose of the conversation. Elicit responses and ask: *How do you know?* or *Why do you say that?* to encourage students to state their reasoning.

Answers
They are discussing bad work habits; answers will vary.

B 🔊 **1-32** 1. Ask students to read the instructions and tell you what they are going to do [listen and read and respond to the question]. Play the audio and then elicit the answer to the question.

2. Ask students to read the conversation with a partner. Circulate and monitor pronunciation. Model and have students repeat difficult words or phrases.

3. Ask: *In what other situation could you use this conversation?* Point out a few phrases that are not specific to a conversation with a supervisor. Ask volunteers to point out others.

Answer
Be more organized

Communicative Practice and Application I
20–25 minutes

C 1. Pair students and have them read the instructions silently. Check their comprehension of the exercise. Ask: *What are the two roles? Is the conversation at school?*

2. Model and have students repeat the expressions in the *In Other Words* box in 4B. Explain that they should use these expressions in their conversations.

3. Draw a T-chart on the board. Label the left column *School principal* and the right column *Secretary*. Elicit examples of what each person might say and make notes in the chart.

4. Set a time limit (three minutes). Have students act out the role-play. Call "time" and have students switch roles.

5. Ask three volunteer pairs to act out their role-play for the class. Tell students who are listening to make a simple table with four rows and two columns. Use the top row to label the columns *Feedback* and *Response*. Have students take notes in the chart for each role-play.

MULTILEVEL STRATEGIES

Seat same-level students together.

• **Pre-level** Work with these students and guide them in writing their new conversation.

• **Higher-level** Challenge these students to use their imaginations to think of silly or far-fetched excuses for the secretary to use for being on the phone.

5 Focus on listening for details

Presentation III and Guided Practice IV
15–20 minutes

A 1. Read the questions and statement aloud and model a discussion with a volunteer. Ask: *Do you think there are other ways to improve employee performance? Why? / Why not? I agree because… / I disagree because…*

2. Pair students and tell them to discuss their own answers to the questions. Circulate and monitor.

B Direct students to read the workers' names and list of skills before they listen to the interview. Ask what kind of information they'll be checking. Ask volunteers for predictions. If students struggle, start by offering your own prediction: *I think we will hear about how one of the workers is not as good as the others.*

C 🔊 **1-33** 1. Play the audio. Ask students to listen and make checks next to the correct answers.

2. Pair students and have them compare answers. If a pair has different answers, have the class vote on the correct answer with a show of hands.

Answers
1. Elizabeth is organized and creative.
2. Ben is helpful and reliable.
3. Habib is careful and confident.

MULTILEVEL STRATEGIES

Replay the audio to challenge on- and higher-level students while allowing pre-level students to catch up.

• **Pre-level** Have these students listen again to complete 5C.

• **On- and Higher-level** Write questions on the board and ask these students to write short answers. *Which workers does he describe with superlatives? What does he say?* Ask volunteers to share their answers after you have gone over the answers to 5C.

D 🔊 **1-33** Read the instructions aloud. Play the audio again and have students complete the sentences individually. Check answers as a class.

Answers
1. be on time
2. be more organized
3. be more helpful

6 Discuss

Communicative Practice and Application II
15–20 minutes

A 1. Read the instructions aloud. Call on volunteers to read the list of bad work habits. Confirm understanding of the task. Ask: *What number will you give to the bad habit that is most likely to get someone fired?* [1]

2. Put students into teams of three and assign roles: manager, administrative assistant, and reporter. Verify students' understanding of the roles.

3. Set a time limit for the discussions (ten minutes). Write the sentence frame from 6B on the board. Then circulate and monitor.

B Call "time." Ask the reporter for each team to report the results of the team's discussion using the sentence frame on the board.

Evaluation
5 minutes

TEST YOURSELF

1. Ask students to complete the checkboxes individually.

2. Tell students that you are going to read each of the items in the checklist aloud. If they are not at all confident with that skill, they should hold up a closed fist. If they are not very confident, they should hold up one finger. If they are somewhat confident, two fingers; confident, three fingers; very confident, four fingers. If they think they could teach the skill, they should hold up five fingers. Read each item in the checklist and identify students who may need further support.

EXTENSION ACTIVITY

Do a Self-evaluation

Have students conduct self-evaluations.

1. Tell students that supervisors often ask employees to evaluate themselves. Ask them to choose one of their roles in life (worker, parent, student, etc.) and write a self-evaluation for that role. Tell them they must include at least one piece of positive feedback and one area in which they could improve. Write your own self-evaluation (for one of your life roles) on the board as a model.

2. Don't require students to share their self-evaluations. Allow them to read them with a partner or turn them in only if they want to.

Lesson Overview	Lesson Notes
MULTILEVEL OBJECTIVES	
Pre-, On-, and Higher-level: Read about and discuss work-based training and education	
LANGUAGE FOCUS	
Grammar: Simple present (*Workplace training helps employees and companies.*) **Vocabulary:** *Training, range, literacy, subsidized* For vocabulary support, see this **Oxford Picture Dictionary** topic: Career Planning, pages 174–175	
STRATEGY FOCUS	
Pay attention to bold headings above the sections of a text as they usually summarize the main ideas.	
READINESS CONNECTION	
In this lesson, students verbally communicate information about ways that companies help their workers learn new skills.	
PACING	
To compress this lesson: Assign 2A for homework. **To extend this lesson:** Have students research different jobs and salaries. (See end of lesson.) And/or have students complete **Workbook 3 page 21** and **Multilevel Activities 3 Unit 3 pages 44–45**.	

CORRELATIONS

CCRS: SL.1.B (d.) Explain their own ideas and understanding in light of the discussion.

SL.2.B Determine the main ideas and supporting details of a text read aloud or information presented in diverse media and formats, including visually, quantitatively, and orally.

R.1.B Ask and answer such questions as who, what, where, when, why, and how to demonstrate understanding of key details in a text.

R.2.A Identify the main topic and retell key details of a text.

R.5.A Know and use various text features to locate key facts or information in a text.

R.7.C Interpret information presented visually, orally, or quantitatively and explain how the information contributes to an understanding of the text in which it appears.

W.7.A Participate in shared research and writing projects.

L.2.B (h.) Use conventional spelling for high-frequency and other studied words and for adding suffixes to base words.

L.4.B (c.) Use a known root word as a clue to the meaning of an unknown word with the same root. (e.) Use glossaries and beginning dictionaries, both print and digital, to determine or clarify the meaning of words and phrases.

RF.3.B (c.) Identify and know the meaning of the most common prefixes and derivational suffixes.

RF.4.B (a.) Read grade-level text with purpose and understanding.

ELPS: 1. An ELL can construct meaning from oral presentations and literary and informational text through level-appropriate listening, reading, and viewing. 3. An ELL can speak and write about level-appropriate complex literary and informational texts and topics.

Warm-up and Review
10–15 minutes (books closed)

Write *Hospital, Factory,* and *Office* on the board. Ask students to brainstorm names of items people use in those work locations. Then ask which items have changed in the past 20 years.

Introduction
5 minutes

1. Say: *Did you ever learn to use a new technology or do a new job? Who taught you? How did you feel about it?* Call on volunteers to share their experiences.

2. State the objective: *Today we're going to read and talk about ways that companies help their workers learn new skills.*

1 Read

Presentation
10–20 minutes

A Read the questions aloud. Use ideas from the *Introduction* to help guide discussion.

B Read the words and definitions. Elicit sample sentences for each word, or supply them if the students can't. Ask students to identify how each of the words relates to the words from the *Warm-up*. Ask students what kind of job training they have received, if any.

Pre-reading

C Read the instructions aloud and have students look at the title and bolded headings. Have students answer the question individually and then check answers as a class. If any students answer incorrectly, ask them to support their answer using the title and bolded headings. Establish the correct answer.

Answer
b. The value of work-based training and two examples.

Guided Practice: While Reading
20–30 minutes

D 1. Ask students to read the article silently and answer the question.

2. Check answers as a class.

3. Check comprehension. Ask: *How many workers report that they receive training?* [one-quarter] *How do employers benefit from employees getting training?* [Employees become more productive.] *How many successful programs are there?* [two]

Possible Answers
Many companies train workers on the job. Both workers and their employers benefit from workplace training. Workers will earn more money and will be more productive.

> **TIP**
>
> Preview any unfamiliar vocabulary: *on the job, participation, ranges from, earn, apprenticeship,* etc. Write these words (and any others that may be new to students) on the board and ask volunteers for definitions or examples. Alternatively, let students guess the definitions from context. Confirm their answers.

MULTILEVEL STRATEGIES

For 1D, adapt your comprehension questions to the level of your students.

• **Pre-level** Ask these students short-answer information questions. *Where does most training in the U.S. take place?* [in the workplace]

• **On-level** Ask these students information questions that will elicit longer responses. *Why do workers benefit from training?* [They can get paid more.]

• **Higher-level** Ask these students inference questions. *Why do people need job training after they've been hired for a job?*

Guided Practice: Rereading
10–15 minutes

E 1. Provide an opportunity for students to extract evidence from the text. Have students reread the article and underline the words that support their answer.

2. Pair students and tell them to compare the words they underlined and report anything they disagree on. Discuss and clarify as needed.

Answer
Positive; <u>benefit from workplace training</u>

F 1. Have students work individually to mark the answers *T* (true), *F* (false), and *NI* (no information). They should then write the line numbers where they found the true and false answers. Write the answers on the board.

2. Elicit and discuss any additional questions about the reading. You could introduce new questions for class discussion: *Which type of training program would you prefer to learn a new job skill? How do you think it makes an employee feel to learn a new job skill?*

Answers
1. T, lines 1–2
2. F, lines 4–5
3. T, lines 8–10
4. F, line 14–15
5. F, lines 24–25

2 Word study

Guided Practice: Postreading
15–20 minutes

A 1. Direct students to look at the chart and identify the topic (the suffix *-tion*). Have students read the chart.

2. Read the first two sentences in the chart and the examples for *produce* and *production*. Elicit sentences for the other words in the chart.

3. Have students repeat after you as you say each word with natural intonation, rhythm, and stress.

4. Direct students to complete the sentences and then compare answers with a partner. Read the correct answers and have students check their work.

Answers
1. education
2. produces
3. description
4. Addition
5. dictate

MULTILEVEL STRATEGIES

After 2A, give on- and pre-level students more time to work with the words in 2A while you challenge higher-level students.

• **Pre- and On-level** Direct these students to write sentences with three of the nouns from the chart.

• **Higher-level** Have these students look in their dictionaries or an online list for words ending in *-tion*. Ask them to look for words that have a base word that they already know. Tell them to write sentences with the words they find.

B 1. Read the questions aloud. Give students a few minutes to think of their answers.

2. Set a time limit (ten minutes). Have groups of three or four discuss the questions. Circulate and help as needed.

3. Have students share their responses with the class.

C Read the instructions and the sample sentence aloud. Have students do the task individually. Circulate and monitor.

3 Talk it over

Guided Practice
15–20 minutes

A Have students look at the chart and read the note and *Reader's Note*. Point out that they need to use the information from the chart and the note to complete the sentences and answer the question. Set a time limit (ten minutes). Have students work in pairs to complete the task. Ask volunteers to share their answers with the class.

Answers
1. $668
2. $1,249
3. Men

Communicative Practice
10–15 minutes

B Read the questions aloud. Set a time limit (ten minutes). Tell students to copy the chart in their notebooks and complete it with their answers to the questions.

C Ask volunteers to share their ideas with the class. Have a class discussion about which of the ideas students agree or disagree with.

Application
15–20 minutes

BRING IT TO LIFE

Have students decide where they are going to look for the information. Provide URLs or locations of career-counseling offices.

EXTENSION ACTIVITY
Jobs and Salaries
Have students research different jobs and the average salary for each job. Then have them research which degrees or specialized training is needed for that job. To prevent duplicate research, write several jobs on the board (surgeon, dentist, computer programmer, vet tech, plumber, etc.) and assign one to each student. Have students share their findings with the class.

Warm-up and Review
10–15 minutes

1. Review the *Bring It to Life* assignment from Lesson 5. Have students who did the exercise discuss what they learned. Tell students who didn't do the assignment to ask their classmates questions about what they learned about local degree programs.

2. As volunteers describe their experiences, model asking clarifying questions. Ask: *What was that? Could you repeat that slowly?*

Introduction
5 minutes

1. Ask: *What do you do when you don't understand what someone is saying? Does it make you nervous?*

2. State the objective: *Today we're going to review how to indicate that you didn't hear something.*

Presentation
5 minutes

 1-34 Read the instructions aloud. Play the audio. Give students a minute to think about the question. Elicit responses from the class.

Answer
An orientation at the first day of a new job

Guided Practice
10–15 minutes

 1-34 Play the audio again. Direct students to listen for each item listed and put a check next to any that they hear mentioned.

Answers
Checked: locker combination break times how to get into the storage room

C **1-34** Read the instructions aloud. Play the audio again, encouraging students to take notes in their notebooks. Set a time limit (five minutes) for students to discuss their answers with a partner. Circulate to monitor.

Answers
I'm sorry, I missed that. Could you repeat that slowly? Did you say 15 minutes? What was that? It's locked all the time? Excuse me? Did you mean if Tony is not here?

Presentation and Communicative Practice
10–15 minutes

D 1. Direct students' attention to the *Do/Say* chart and ask students to identify the lesson's soft skill [showing that you don't understand]. Ask the class which column has examples of language [right] and which has examples of behaviors [left].

2. Say a phrase from the left column and act it out. Say it again and have the class act it out with you. Say it a third time and have the class act it out for you. To confirm understanding, combine phrases: *Make eye contact and raise your hand.*

3. Model the phrases from the right column using authentic intonation. Have students practice imitating your inflection.

4. Put students in teams of four and assign each team a question. Assign roles: manager, administrative assistant, reporter, and researcher. Researchers will ask you questions on behalf of the team. Verify understanding of the roles. Set a time limit (five minutes) and monitor.

5. Write sentence frames on the board that teams can use to summarize their response. (*Our team discussed the following question: _____ We decided _____ because _____.)*

6. Call "time" and let reporters rehearse their report for one minute. Direct each reporter to present to three other teams.

Communicative Practice and Application
10–15 minutes

 1. Have students work in the same teams as D. Tell students that they are going to have a conversation about someone's first day at a new job.

2. Direct groups to take turns doing each role and observing and marking the listening behaviors that they see.

3. As students carry out the conversation and observation, circulate and monitor. Provide global feedback once the activity ends.

MULTILEVEL STRATEGIES

Seat same-level students together.

• **Pre- and On-level** Work with these students and write a conversation they can use for practice.

• **Higher-level** Challenge these students to use each of the actions and phrases in their conversations.

TEAMWORK & LANGUAGE REVIEW

Lesson Overview	Lesson Notes
MULTILEVEL OBJECTIVES	
Pre-, On-, and Higher-level: Review unit language	
LANGUAGE FOCUS	
Grammar: Comparisons **Vocabulary:** Adjectives and sports For vocabulary support, see this **Oxford Picture Dictionary** topic: Describing Things, page 23	
READINESS CONNECTION	
In this review, students work in a team to use superlatives and comparisons to describe sports and people.	
PACING	
To extend this review: Have students complete **Workbook 3 page 22**, **Multilevel Activities 3 Unit 3 page 46**, and **Multilevel Grammar Exercises 3 Unit 3**.	

CORRELATIONS

CCRS: SL.1.B (a.) Come to discussions prepared, having read or studied required material; explicitly draw on that preparation and other information known about the topic to explore ideas under discussion. (b.) Follow agreed-upon rules for discussions. (c.) Ask questions to check understanding of information presented, stay on topic, and link their comments to the remarks of others. (d.) Explain their own ideas and understanding in light of the discussion.

SL.2.B Determine the main ideas and supporting details of a text read aloud or information presented in diverse media and formats, including visually, quantitatively, and orally.

SL.4.B Report on a topic or text, tell a story, or recount an experience with appropriate facts and relevant, descriptive details, speaking clearly at an understandable pace.

R.2.A Identify the main topic and retell key details of a text.

W.4.B Produce writing in which the development and organization are appropriate to task and purpose.

L.1.B (h.) Form and use the simple verb tenses. (l.) Produce simple, compound and complex sentences.

RF.4.B (a.) Read grade-level text with purpose and understanding.

ELPS: 5. An ELL can conduct research and evaluate and communicate findings to answer questions or solve problems. 6. An ELL can analyze and critique the arguments of others orally and in writing.

Warm-up and Review
10–15 minutes (books closed)

1. Review *At Work* activity E.

2. Ask students to share the good, not-so-good, and interesting things that happened during the conversation. As students speak, write their responses in a chart on the board.

Introduction and Presentation
5 minutes

1. Pair students and direct them to look at the pictures in their book. Ask them to describe what they see to their partner and to talk about which of the sports they have tried and which ones they would like to try.

2. Ask volunteer pairs to share their ideas with the class.

Guided Practice
15–20 minutes

A 1. Direct students to work in groups of three or four and look at the pictures. Read the instructions aloud and model writing a question.

2. Set a time limit (ten minutes) for groups to write questions. Circulate and monitor.

Possible Answers
What sport is more challenging than tennis? Which sport is the least hard to learn?

B Have students work in the same teams as in A and take turns asking and answering their questions to each other. Circulate and monitor.

C 1. Read the instructions aloud and have students work in the same teams from A to complete the task. Circulate and monitor.

2. Have students read their sentences to the class and correct any mistakes.

Communicative Practice
30–45 minutes

D Have teams take turns describing each other using superlatives. Circulate and monitor.

E 1. Group students and assign roles: manager, writer, editor, and presenter. Explain that students are going to work with their teams to write an advertisement for a product from the choices in the box. Editors will review the advertisement and offer suggestions for changes. Verify students' understanding of the roles.

2. Tell students to review the example advertisement. Check comprehension of the task. *What will you write about in your advertisement?* [why the product is great] *What grammar will you use in the sentences?* [comparisons and superlatives]

3. Set a time limit (ten minutes) to complete the exercise. Circulate and answer any questions.

4. Have presenters from each team read their team's advertisement to another team.

F 1. Have students walk around the room to conduct the interviews. To get students moving, tell them to interview three people who were not on their team for E.

2. Set a time limit (five minutes) to complete the exercise.

3. Tell students to make a note of their classmates' answers but not to worry about writing complete sentences.

MULTILEVEL STRATEGIES
Adapt the mixer in F to the level of your students.   • **Pre- and On-level** Pair these students and have them interview other pairs together.   • **Higher-level** Have these students ask an additional question and write all answers in complete sentences.

G 1. Call on individuals to report what they learned about their classmates. Keep a running tally on the board for each question, marking the most difficult thing about learning English, the least difficult thing, and which language is easier to speak than English.

2. Use your tally for question 1 to create a pie chart on the board. Instruct students to choose a question and draw a pie chart. Circulate and answer any questions.

PROBLEM SOLVING
10–15 minutes

A 🔊 1-35 1. Ask: *What are the most important things for you about a job? Money? Commute? Benefits? Co-workers?* Tell students they will read a story about a man who has a problem about choosing a job. Direct students to read Omar's story silently.

2. Play the audio and have students read along silently.

B 1. Elicit answers to question 1. Guide students to a class consensus on the answer.

2. As a class, brainstorm answers to question 2. Ask students if they know someone who has this problem and has overcome it or what they have done themselves to overcome the same problem. Have students share their responses and write them on the board for students to refer to in the next activity.

Answers
1. He is having trouble deciding between two different job offers.   2. Answers will vary.

Evaluation
20–25 minutes

To test students' understanding of the unit language and content, have them take the Unit 3 Test, available on the Teacher Resource Center.

Unit Overview

This unit explores job searches with a range of employability skills and contextualizes present perfect tense structures.

KEY OBJECTIVES	
Lesson 1	Identify job interview vocabulary
Lesson 2	Write a thank-you letter after a job interview
Lesson 3	Use the present perfect to talk about past events
Lesson 4	Interview for a promotion
Lesson 5	Identify ways to get a promotion
At Work	Show a willingness to learn
Teamwork & Language Review	Review unit language

UNIT FEATURES	
Academic Vocabulary	*network, promotion, creative, team, promoted, automatically, interact, intermediate*
Employability Skills	• Decide whether you agree or disagree with statements about jobs • Discuss good and bad things to do at a job interview • Answer questions about yourself for a job interview • Decide what to do when you're not prepared for an upcoming job interview • Work independently • Understand teamwork • Locate information • Communicate verbally • Listen actively • Use writing skills • Comprehend written material • Analyze information

Resources	**Class Audio** CD1 Tracks 36–46
	Workbook Unit 4, pages 23–29
	Teacher Resource Center
	    Multilevel Activities 3 Unit 4
	    Multilevel Grammar Exercises 3 Unit 4
	    Unit 4 Test
	Oxford Picture Dictionary Jobs and Occupations, Job Skills, Career Planning, Job Search, Interview Skills

Lesson Overview	Lesson Notes

MULTILEVEL OBJECTIVES

On-level: Identify job interview dos and don'ts and describe personal strengths

Pre-level: Identify job interview and personal strength vocabulary

Higher-level: Talk and write about work using job interview and personal strength vocabulary

LANGUAGE FOCUS

Grammar: Simple present tense (*A team player works well with other people.*)

Vocabulary: Job interview and personal strength vocabulary

For vocabulary support, see these **Oxford Picture Dictionary** topics: Job Search, pages 168–169; Interview Skills, page 179

STRATEGY FOCUS

Pool knowledge with team members to maximize vocabulary learning.

READINESS CONNECTION

In this lesson, students explore and communicate information about what to do and say at job interviews.

PACING

To compress this lesson: Conduct 1B as a whole-class activity.

To extend this lesson: Have students role-play an interview. (See end of lesson.)

And/or have students complete **Workbook 3 page 23** and **Multilevel Activities 3 Unit 4 pages 48–49**.

CORRELATIONS

CCRS: SL.1.B (d.) Explain their own ideas and understanding in light of the discussion.

SL.4.B Report on a topic or text, tell a story, or recount an experience with appropriate facts and relevant, descriptive details, speaking clearly at an understandable pace.

W.7.A Participate in shared research and writing projects.

L.1.B (l.) Produce simple, compound and complex sentences.

L.4.B (e.) Use glossaries and beginning dictionaries, both print and digital, to determine or clarify the meaning of words and phrases.

RF.4.B (a.) Read grade-level text with purpose and understanding.

ELPS: 8. An ELL can determine the meaning of words and phrases in oral presentations and literary and informational text.

Warm-up and Review
10–15 minutes (books closed)

Find out how many of your students have been on a job interview. Ask them to share their experiences. For students who have not had a job interview, ask about other interviewing experiences. Elicit details. *How long did the interview take? How did you feel? Did you have to wait a long time for the results?*

Introduction
3 minutes

1. Say: *If your friend is going for an interview, what advice would you give him or her? How can your friend make the job interview successful?* Call on volunteers to share their ideas.

2. State the objective: *Today we're going to learn about what to do and say at job interviews.*

1 Identify job interview vocabulary

Presentation I
20–25 minutes

A 1. Write *Employer* and *Job applicant* on the board. Explain that an *applicant* is someone who is trying to get a particular job and that the verb form is *to apply*. Elicit an example question an employer might ask and write it under *Employer*. Elicit something a job applicant might do to prepare for an interview and write it under *Job applicant*.

2. Have students work together to brainstorm in a group to do the tasks. List the interview questions and ways to prepare that your students identify under the correct headings on the board. Have students explain their reasons for their ideas in task 2.

3. Tell students to copy the questions and ways to prepare from the board into their notebooks for use in Lesson 4.

Possible Answers
1. Why do you want to work here? How are you qualified for this job? Tell me about your previous experience. 2. Get a good night's sleep. Practice answering questions. Dress well.

B 1. Direct students to look at the pictures. Ask: *Who is going to have a successful interview: the first applicant or the second applicant?*

2. Group students and assign roles: manager, researcher, administrative assistant, and reporter. Verify students' understanding of the roles.

3. Explain that students work with their groups to match the phrases and the numbers in the pictures. Set a time limit (five minutes). As students work together, copy the phrases onto the board.

4. Call "time." Have reporters take turns giving their answers. Write each group's answers on the board next to the phrases.

Answers	
5 arrive on time	6 greet the interviewer
3 (don't) dress inappropriately	9 bring your resume
7 look confident	2 (don't) look nervous
8 dress professionally	1 (don't) be late
4 (don't) use your cell phone	

TIP

When setting up task-based activities, verify that students understand their roles using physical commands. For example: *If you report on your team's work, stand up* [reporter]. *If you keep the team on task, point to the clock* [manager]. *If you write the team's responses, raise your hand* [administrative assistant]. *If you help the team research, point to your book* [researcher].

C 🔊 1-36 1. To prepare students for listening, say: *We're going to listen to some advice about what to do and what not to do at job interviews. As you listen, look at the pictures and check your answers.* Play the audio.

2. Have students check the phrases on the board and then write the correct numbers in their books.

3. Pair students. Set a time limit (three minutes). Monitor pair practice to identify pronunciation issues.

4. Call "time" and work with the pronunciation of any troublesome words or phrases.

Guided Practice I
15–20 minutes

 1. Model the conversation with a volunteer. Model it again using other information from 1B.

2. Set a time limit (three minutes). Direct students to practice with a partner. Ask volunteers to repeat one of their conversations for the class.

2 Learn to describe your personal strengths

Presentation II
10–20 minutes

 1. Direct students to look at the chart. Introduce the new topic: *We've talked about dos and don'ts of having an interview. Now we're going to talk about how you can describe your good qualities, or strengths, that will make you a good person for a job.*

2. Discuss the meaning of each word in the first column. Elicit examples of classroom behaviors that demonstrate each type of worker. For example, a problem-solver could be a student who figures out a better way to distribute classroom materials or arrange the seating; a team player could be a student who is always helpful in the group without dominating it. Apply the words to your students: *Maria always gets her books out and starts reviewing yesterday's work before the class begins. Which word could describe her?* [self-

starter or go-getter] *Hong always helps the other students at his table. How could we describe him?* [a team player]

3. Ask students to work individually to check the strengths they have.

4. Call on volunteers to say which strengths they checked and why. Encourage them to give examples of their own behaviors that illustrate those strengths.

5. Check comprehension. Ask: *What type of worker is someone with great ideas?* [a creative thinker] For further practice with critical vocabulary, ask students to think of different jobs and what strengths are needed for each job and why. Alternatively, ask them to think of famous people who are examples of those strengths in their jobs.

Guided Practice II
10–15 minutes

 1. Model a conversation with a volunteer. Model it again using a different word from 2A.

2. Set a time limit (three minutes). Direct students to practice with a partner.

3. Call on volunteers to repeat one of their conversations for the class.

Communicative Practice and Application
25–30 minutes

 1. If students will use the Internet for this task, establish what device(s) they'll use: a class computer, tablets, or smartphones. Alternatively, print information from the Internet before class and distribute to groups.

2. Write the information types from 2C on the board. Explain that students will work in teams to research and report on this information. Ask: *Which search terms or questions can you use to find the information you need?* ["job search assistance" + city name, "resume examples" + type of job, "interview tips"] *How will you record the information you find?* [table, checklist, index cards] Remind students to bookmark or record sites so they can find or cite them in the future.

3. Group students and assign roles: manager, administrative assistant, IT support, and reporter. Verify students' understanding of their roles.

4. Give managers the time limit for researching the question (ten minutes). Direct the IT support to begin the online research or pick up the printed materials for each team. Direct the recorder to record information for the team using a table, a checklist, or index cards.

5. Give a two-minute warning. Call "time."

D 1. Read the sentence stem aloud.

2. Direct teams to help their administrative assistant use the sentence stem to record the team's findings. Direct the reporter to use the recorded information to report the team's findings to the class or another team.

Evaluation
10–15 minutes (books closed)

TEST YOURSELF

1. Make a three-column chart on the board with the headings *Interview dos, Interview don'ts*, and *Personal strengths*. Have students close their books and give you an example for each column.

2. Have students copy the chart into their notebooks.

3. Give students five to ten minutes to test themselves by writing the words they recall from the lesson.

4. Call "time" and have students check their spelling in a dictionary. Circulate and monitor students' progress.

5. Direct students to share their work with a partner and add additional words to their charts.

MULTILEVEL STRATEGIES

Target the *Test Yourself* to the level of your students.

• **Pre-level** Have these students do the activity the first time with the option to look in their books. Then have them do the activity a second time without looking at their books.

• **Higher-level** Have these students complete the chart and then write a sentence with one word from each column. Challenge them to write sentences that illustrate the meaning of the words.

EXTENSION ACTIVITY

Role-play an Interview

Have students act out interviews. Group students and have the groups write a short job interview with two or three question-answer exchanges. Have two members from each group perform their interview for the class. After each pair has performed, ask the class to say what good interview behaviors they saw.

Lesson Overview

Lesson Notes

MULTILEVEL OBJECTIVES

On- and Higher-level: Analyze, write, and edit a thank-you letter after a job interview

Pre-level: Read and write a thank-you letter after a job interview

LANGUAGE FOCUS

Grammar: Verb + gerund or infinitive (*I hope to have the chance to use my computer skills. I enjoyed learning more about your company.*)

Vocabulary: Business-letter vocabulary, job-skills vocabulary, *colon*

For vocabulary support, see this **Oxford Picture Dictionary** topic: Interview Skills, page 179

STRATEGY FOCUS

Use a colon (:) after the greeting in a formal business letter.

READINESS CONNECTION

In this lesson, students listen actively to, read, and write a thank-you letter appropriate for after a job interview.

PACING

To compress this lesson: Assign the *Test Yourself* and/or 3C for homework.

To extend this lesson: Have students practice thank-you notes. (See end of lesson.)

And/or have students complete **Workbook 3 page 24** and **Multilevel Activities 3 Unit 4 page 50**.

CORRELATIONS

CCRS: SL.1.B (d.) Explain their own ideas and understanding in light of the discussion.

SL.2.B Determine the main ideas and supporting details of a text read aloud or information presented in diverse media and formats, including visually, quantitatively, and orally.

R.1.B Ask and answer such questions as who, what, where, when, why, and how to demonstrate understanding of key details in a text.

W.2.A Write informative/explanatory texts in which they name a topic, supply some facts about the topic, and provide some sense of closure.

W.4.B Produce writing in which the development and organization are appropriate to task and purpose.

W.5.B With guidance and support from peers and others, develop and strengthen writing as needed by planning, revising and editing.

L.1.B (l.) Produce simple, compound and complex sentences.

L.2.B (c.) use commas in greetings and closings of letters.

RF.4.B (a.) Read grade-level text with purpose and understanding.

ELPS: 6. An ELL can analyze and critique the arguments of others orally and in writing. 9. An ELL can create clear and coherent level-appropriate speech and text.

Warm-up and Review
10–15 minutes (books closed)

Review job titles. Elicit places that students have worked and write the words on the board—for example, restaurant, factory, hospital, and office. Ask volunteers to come to the board and write job titles of people who work in those places.

Introduction
5 minutes

1. Ask who has ever interviewed for any of the jobs on the board. Say: *One final step in the job-interview process is to write a thank-you letter after the interview.*

2. State the objective: *Today we're going to read and write a thank-you letter that you would write after a job interview.*

1 Prepare to write

Presentation
20–25 minutes

 1. Build students' schema by asking questions about the picture and the signature. Ask: *What is the man doing?*

2. Give students one minute to tell a partner their responses to questions 1 and 2. Elicit responses from the class. Encourage students to respond to each other's ideas. After one student speaks, ask other students their opinions. *Do you agree or disagree with what he/she just said? Why?*

Answers
1. Tom Ling
2. It demonstrates that you appreciate the interviewer's time; it shows you are interested in the job.

B 1. Introduce the explanation above the letter. Ask: *Is an interview thank-you letter a formal letter or an informal letter?* Point out the formal letter convention of writing the address above the greeting. Introduce the model letter and its purpose: *Now we're going to read a thank-you letter. As you read, look for the purpose of the letter: why is he writing?* Have students read the letter silently.

2. Check comprehension. Ask: *Who is writing?* [Tom Ling] *Who is he writing to?* [Paulina Reyes] *What job did he interview for?* [sales manager] *What kind of business is it?* [auto sales] *What experience does he have?* [sales experience]

3. Play the audio. Have students read along silently.

Guided Practice I
10 minutes

C 1. Have students work independently to answer the questions.

2. Point out the *Writer's Note* and read the information aloud. Say: *For letters to friends, use a comma after the greeting. For business letters, use a colon after the greeting.* Point out that thank-you letters can be emailed.

3. Have pairs compare answers. Have volunteers call out answers and write them on the board for the class to check.

Answers
1. For the interview he was given
2. To use his communication skills and sales experience at Sherman's
3. At his email address

TIP

After you go over 1C, have the class brainstorm additional sentences using *I enjoyed* and *I hope to*: *I enjoyed talking with you. I enjoyed visiting your company. I hope to hear from you soon. I hope to speak with you again soon.* Write the ideas on the board and have students copy them for possible use in a writing assignment for 2B.

2 Plan and write

Guided Practice II
15–20 minutes

A 1. Read the questions aloud. Elicit students' answers.

2. Write students' ideas for question 3 on the board so they can reference them while they write.

MULTILEVEL STRATEGIES

Adapt 2A to the level of your students.

• **Pre-level** Work with these students to brainstorm answers to the questions in 2A. Give students time to answer in complete sentences before moving on to the next question.

• **Higher-level** Ask these students to add two or three specific personal strengths that make them a good candidate for that job to include in their answer to question 3.

B Read through the letter template. Elicit ideas that could go in each paragraph. Have students write their letters individually. Remind them to refer to their ideas from 1A in Lesson 1 and the *Tip* from 1C in this lesson.

Adapt 2B to the level of your students.

• **Pre-level** Work with these students to go through the letter template sentence by sentence. Elicit students' ideas and write them on the board. Have students complete the letter with the ideas from the board.

• **Higher-level** Ask these students to include one additional sentence to remind the interviewer of why they are a perfect match for the job.

3 Get feedback and revise

Guided Practice III
5 minutes

 Direct students to check their writing using the editing checklist. Tell them to read each item in the list and check their papers before moving on to the next item. Explain that students should not edit their writing at this stage. They should just use the checklist to check their work and mark any areas they want to revise.

Communicative Practice
15 minutes

B 1. Read the instructions and the sample sentences aloud. Emphasize to students that they are responding to their partners' work, not correcting it.

2. Use the letter in 1B to model the exercise. *Your third sentence makes it sound like you're perfect for the job.*

3. Direct students to exchange papers with a partner and follow the instructions.

C Allow students time to edit and revise their writing as necessary, using the editing checklist from 3A and their partner's feedback from 3B. If necessary, students could complete this task as homework.

TIP

Students may be interested in more information about available jobs at your school. Ask your personnel office for job descriptions, requirements, and starting salaries. You can use this kind of information to demonstrate to students how continuing education can improve economic prospects.

Application and Evaluation
10 minutes

TEST YOURSELF

1. Review the instructions aloud. Assign a time limit (five minutes) and have students work independently.

2. Before collecting student work, invite two or three volunteers to share their sentences. Ask students to raise their hands if they wrote similar answers.

Adapt the *Test Yourself* to the level of your students.

• **Pre-level** Write questions for these students to answer in writing. *Was today's writing assignment difficult or easy? Is it more difficult to write a formal letter or an email?*

EXTENSION ACTIVITY

Practice Thank-you Notes

Have students write a different kind of thank-you letter. Brainstorm a list of other situations in which students might want to write a thank-you note (after receiving a gift, after being a guest at someone's house, after someone helps them, etc.). As a class, come up with appropriate expressions for these kinds of thank-you notes. Point out that *Thank you for...* is followed by either a noun phrase or a gerund: *Thank you for the lovely gift. Thank you for being so patient.* Have students compose a short thank-you note. Ask volunteers to read their notes to the class.

Lesson Overview	Lesson Notes

MULTILEVEL OBJECTIVES

On- and Higher-level: Use the present perfect to talk about life and work events and experience and listen for information about work events

Pre-level: Recognize the present perfect in sentences about life and work events and experience

LANGUAGE FOCUS

Grammar: Present perfect (*He has worked in an office.*)

Vocabulary: Past participles, *apply for, supply*

For vocabulary support, see these **Oxford Picture Dictionary** topics: Job Search, pages 168–169; Career Planning, pages 174–175

STRATEGY FOCUS

Use the present perfect to describe activities that began in the past and continue to the present.

READINESS CONNECTION

In this lesson, students practice using the present perfect to talk about life and work events and experience.

PACING

To compress this lesson: Conduct 1C and/or 1D as a whole-class activity.

To extend this lesson: Have students play the "liar" game. (See end of lesson.)

And/or have students complete **Workbook 3 pages 25–26, Multilevel Activities 3 Unit 4 pages 51–52**, and **Multilevel Grammar Exercises 3 Unit 4**.

CORRELATIONS

CCRS: SL.2.B Determine the main ideas and supporting details of a text read aloud or information presented in diverse media and formats, including visually, quantitatively, and orally.

SL.6.B Speak in complete sentences when appropriate to task and situation in order to provide requested detail or clarification.

R.1.B Ask and answer such questions as who, what, where, when, why, and how to demonstrate understanding of key details in a text.

L.1.B (b.) Explain the function of nouns, pronouns, verbs, adjectives, and adverbs in general and their functions in particular sentences. (l.) Produce simple, compound and complex sentences.

L.1.C (e.) Form and use the perfect verb tenses.

RF.4.B (a.) Read grade-level text with purpose and understanding.

ELPS: 7. An ELL can adapt language choices to purpose, task, and audience when speaking and writing. 10. An ELL can demonstrate command of the conventions of standard English to communicate in level-appropriate speech and writing.

Warm-up and Review
10–15 minutes (books closed)

Write on the board: *Work here* and the year you started your current position, a year after that, *Today*, and *Tomorrow*. Say: *I worked here in 2015. I worked here in 2016. I am working here today. I will work here tomorrow.* Write *Live here* on the board and have a few volunteers say true sentences similar to yours.

Introduction
5–10 minutes

1. Write on the board: *be married, live here, be sick.* Say: *These are examples of some events that can start in the past and continue into the present and the future.*

2. State the objective: *Today we're going to use the present perfect to talk about life and work events and experience.*

1 Use the present perfect

Presentation I
20–25 minutes

1. Direct students to look at Jafar's job application. Ask: *What is Jafar's most recent job?*

2. Read the instructions aloud. Ask students to read the paragraph and the job application silently and answer the questions.

3. Read the first question aloud. Call on a volunteer for the answer. Ask the volunteer where in the conversation they found the answer. Read the rest of the questions aloud, calling on a different volunteer for each answer.

Answers
1. July 2013
2. Yes
3. Assistant manager at an automotive supply store
4. He doesn't know yet.

B 1. Write a sentence about yourself on the board. *I have worked in an office.* Ask: *Do I work in an office now?* [no] *So I'm talking about the past. Do you know when I worked in an office?* [no] Write another sentence on the board using the simple past and a date. *I worked in an office from 1995 to 1998.* Ask: *Now do you know when I worked in an office?* Ask students to identify the verb and the tense in the simple past sentence [*worked*]. Underline the verb. Draw students' attention back to the present perfect sentence. Ask students to

identify the verb and underline both parts [*have worked*]. Elicit the difference between the two sentences. Say: *The sentence without the date uses a present perfect verb form. We use the present perfect when we talk about events in the past but don't say when they happened.*

2. Demonstrate how to read the grammar chart. Point out that the past participle of *worked* is the same as the simple past. Read and have students repeat the irregular verbs in the *Need help?* box.

3. Direct students to circle the four examples of the present perfect in 1A. Go over the answers as a class.

4. Assess students' understanding of the chart. Write these sentence frames on the board: *1. I _____ to college. 2. I _____ to college from 2000 to 2004.* Tell students to hold up one or two fingers to indicate which sentence the verb belongs in. Say: *have gone.* Repeat with different sample sentences.

Answers
Circled:
he has also worked as a sales representative
He has completed high school
but he hasn't finished college
the manager hasn't called him back yet

Guided Practice I
10–15 minutes

1. Tell students they will collaborate to complete the description of the grammar point. Model collaboration by working with the class to complete the first sentence. Encourage students to look at 1A and 1B to help them determine the correct words.

2. Pair students and have them work together to complete the description.

3. Project or write the completed definition on the board and have pairs verify the accuracy of their responses. Ask volunteers which sentences confused them and discuss.

Answers
past
present
past
regular

Before moving on to 1D, play "memory" on the overhead projector to help students learn the present perfect. Write the following words in random order in a 4 x 4 grid on a transparency: *read, has read, did, has done, went, has gone, called, has called, heard, has heard, gave, has given, wrote, has written, knew, has known.* Cover each word with a slip of paper. Divide the class into two teams. Ask a student from Team 1 to uncover two words. Have the students repeat both words. Ask: *Do they match?* If they don't match, cover them up again. When students get a match, give the team a point and leave the words uncovered. Ask a student from Team 2 to uncover two words. Continue until all of the words are uncovered. Then say the pairs and have students repeat them.

Guided Practice II
10–15 minutes

 1. Ask students to work individually to complete the sentences. Make sure they understand to use the words in parentheses.

2. Have pairs compare answers. Have students read the sentences aloud for the class to check answers.

Answers
1. has completed
2. has interviewed
3. has written
4. has had

MULTILEVEL STRATEGIES

For 1D, group same-level students together.

• **Pre-level** Sit with these students and complete the exercise together. Take turns with them to read each sentence.

• **Higher-level** Challenge these students to add two more sentences in the present perfect using verbs from the *Need help?* box.

2 Use *for* and *since* with the present perfect

Presentation II
15–25 minutes

 1. Introduce the new topic. Say: *Now we're going to learn how to use* for *and* since *with the present perfect to talk about life events and experiences.*

2. Draw a time line on the board with *today* at the far right end. Write: *She has gone to college.* Mark *gone to college* as a point on the time line labeled 2005. Ask: *Is she still going to college?* [no] Write: *She has gone to college since 2005. She has gone to college for _____ years.* Mark the time period on the time line, showing that it continues to the present. Ask: *Is she still going college?* [yes] Say: *Using* for + *period of time or* since + *a date with the present perfect tells us that an action is continuing.*

3. Read and have students repeat the sentences in the chart. Use the time line to illustrate the sentences. Have students identify both parts of the verb in each sentence.

4. Read the *Grammar Note* aloud and check comprehension. Direct students to look back at the chart in 1B and have volunteers say the sentences using a specific time in the past.

5. Direct students to look at the time line and read Carlos's life events. Have students work individually to mark the statements *T* (true) or *F* (false). Go over the answers as a class.

Answers
1. F
2. T
3. F
4. T

Guided Practice III
20–25 minutes

 1. Before moving on, confirm and consolidate students' understanding of how to use *for* and *since* with time phrases in the present perfect. Write *Monday, three weeks, last month, January, July 4, 1991, last summer,* and *ten days* on the board. Write *For* and *Since* as column heads and have students tell you which words belong in which column. Write an incomplete sentence: *I have had my car _____.* Call on students to complete the sentence with the expressions on the board, using *for* or *since* appropriately.

2. Have students work individually to complete the sentences. Go over the answers as a class.

Answers

1. since	5. since
2. for	6. for
3. since	7. since
4. for	8. for

C

1. Elicit the importance of accuracy. Tell students they will be building their accuracy in this task.

2. Organize students into groups. Demonstrate how to correct the sentence using the first example.

3. Have team members work together to correct the sentences. Circulate and monitor teamwork.

4. Project or write the corrected sentences on the board and have teams check their work.

5. Address questions and any issues you noted during your observation.

Answers

1. Dennis has been sick for a week.
2. Carlos has worked in an office for three years.
3. They have driven here since 2004.
4. Eric has been promoted five times since 2009.

MULTILEVEL STRATEGIES

After 2C, provide pre-level students with more practice with participles while you challenge on- and higher-level students.

• **Pre-level** Direct these students to "test" their partners on the participles in the *Need help?* box on page 56. Tell one partner to work with the book closed while the other partner reads aloud the base form. The partner whose book is closed should respond with the simple past and past participle forms. When they feel confident with saying the forms, tell them to try writing the forms rather than saying them.

• **On- and Higher-level** Write a time line of your important life events on the board (when you started teaching, got married, had children, began working at this school, etc.). Have these students work in groups to write simple past and present perfect sentences about you. Have volunteers write their sentences on the board. Correct them together.

3 Listen for the present perfect

Guided Practice IV
15–20 minutes

🔊 **1-38** 1. Say: *We're going to listen to a story that uses the present perfect to tell about Sasha and her friends at work. Circle the correct statement based on what you hear.*

2. Direct students to read the sets of statements to preview what they will listen for. Ask: *What information will you listen for in the first set of sentences?* [if Sasha has or hasn't worked there for a long time] Repeat for numbers 2–5.

3. Play the audio and have students do the task individually.

4. Elicit answers from the class. If students answered incorrectly, play the audio again, reminding them what to listen for.

Answers

1. Sasha hasn't worked for J & J Shipping for very long.
2. She has made some great friends.
3. Julie and Jenna have worked for J & J for 12 years.
4. Julie and Jenna have been in the same department since they started.
5. Julie has helped Sasha prepare orders.

MULTILEVEL STRATEGIES

Replay the audio to challenge on- and higher-level students while allowing pre-level students to catch up.

• **Pre-level** Have these students listen again to complete the exercise.

• **On- and Higher-level** Ask these students to write any other information they can from the story. When you elicit the answers, call on these students to state what other information they heard.

4 Use the present perfect to talk about your life

Communicative Practice and Application
20–25 minutes

A 1. Direct students to look at the time line. Ask a few volunteers: *When did you move to this city? Move to your current address?*

2. Ask students to write the appropriate dates on their time lines.

B 1. Direct students to work independently to complete the questions using the verb in parentheses.

2. Call on volunteers to share their questions, correcting grammar as necessary. Establish the correct grammar for each sentence.

Answers
1. have you lived
2. have you studied
3. have you attended

C Direct students to work with a partner to write two more questions using the present perfect. Brainstorm other verbs to use, if necessary.

D 1. Have pairs merge to form teams of four. Model the exercise by "joining" one of the teams. Each pair takes a turn asking and answering questions while the other pair listens. Make sure that students are taking notes on their teammates' answers.

2. Ask volunteers to share something interesting they learned about their classmates.

Evaluation
10–15 minutes

TEST YOURSELF

Ask students to write the sentences independently. Collect and correct their writing.

MULTILEVEL STRATEGIES

Target the *Test Yourself* to the level of your students.

• **Pre-level** Provide four sentence frames for these students to complete. *1. _____ has lived in this city for _____. 2. _____ has lived at his/her current address since _____. 3. _____ has studied English since _____. 4. _____ has attended this class for _____.*

• **Higher-level** Have these students write a paragraph in response to this prompt: *Contrast your own information with your partner's. I have lived in this city for _____, but Flor has lived here for _____.*

EXTENSION ACTIVITY

Play the "Liar" Game

1. Direct students to write three sentences about themselves using the present perfect. Two sentences should be true and one should be false. Encourage students to include at least one sentence with *since* or *for*.

2. Put students in mixed-level groups. Direct each student to read his/her sentences to the group. Encourage the group to ask follow-up questions to help them decide if a statement is true or false. Have group members guess which statements are false. Have each group tell the class which person fooled the most people.

Lesson Overview	Lesson Notes

MULTILEVEL OBJECTIVES

On- and Higher-level: Interview for a promotion and listen for information in a job history

Pre-level: Answer basic interview questions and listen for information in a job history

LANGUAGE FOCUS

Grammar: Present perfect (*I've been a salesperson for five years.*)

Vocabulary: Occupations, past participles

For vocabulary support, see these **Oxford Picture Dictionary** topics: Job Skills, pages 168–169; Career Planning, pages 174–175

STRATEGY FOCUS

Understand that when using the present perfect, *'s* can mean *has*. *'s* can also mean *is* in the present tense.

READINESS CONNECTION

In this lesson, students verbally communicate about and practice how to interview for promotions.

PACING

To compress this lesson: Do 6A as a class activity and skip 6B.

To extend this lesson: Have students speak and write about job experiences. (See end of lesson.)

And/or have students complete **Workbook 3 page 27** and **Multilevel Activities 3 Unit 4 page 53**.

CORRELATIONS

CCRS: SL.1.B (d.) Explain their own ideas and understanding in light of the discussion.

SL.2.B Determine the main ideas and supporting details of a text read aloud or information presented in diverse media and formats, including visually, quantitatively, and orally.

SL.4.B Report on a topic or text, tell a story, or recount an experience with appropriate facts and relevant, descriptive details, speaking clearly at an understandable pace.

SL.6.B Speak in complete sentences when appropriate to task and situation in order to provide requested detail or clarification.

R.7.B Use information gained from illustrations and the words in a text to demonstrate understanding of the text.

L.1.B (h.) Form and use the simple verb tenses. (l.) Produce simple, compound and complex sentences.

L.1.C (e.) Form and use the perfect verb tenses.

L.2.B (f.) Use an apostrophe to form contractions and frequently occurring possessives.

RF.2.A (g.) Isolate and pronounce initial, medial vowel, and final sounds (phonemes) in spoken single-syllable words.

RF.4.B (a.) Read grade-level text with purpose and understanding.

ELPS: 2. An ELL can participate in level-appropriate oral and written exchanges of information, ideas, and analyses, in various social and academic contexts, responding to peer, audience, or reader comments and questions. 9. An ELL can create clear and coherent level-appropriate speech and text.

Warm-up and Review
10–15 minutes (books closed)

Write the following sentence frames on the board: *I have gone to _____. I have had _____. I have studied _____. I have worked _____.* Use the sentences to tell students about yourself. Then call on volunteers to complete the sentences about themselves.

Introduction
3 minutes

1. Say: *We often use these present perfect forms in a job interview when we talk about our experience.*

2. State the objective: *Today we're going to learn how to interview for promotions.*

1 Learn ways to interview for a promotion

Presentation I
10 minutes

 A ◀») **1-39** 1. Direct students to look at the picture and the caption. Ask: *What job does the woman have?* [server] *When did she do this job?* [2009–2011] Elicit the present perfect sentence from a volunteer. [*She has been a server since 2009/for three years.*]

2. Read the instructions aloud. Play the audio. Give students a minute to answer the question. Go over the answer as a class.

Answer
Ms. Ortiz's qualifications to be the new assistant chef

Guided Practice I
20–25 minutes

 B ◀») **1-39** 1. Read the instructions and the questions aloud. Play the audio. Ask students to listen for the answer to each question.

2. Ask students to compare their answers with a partner. Circulate and monitor to ensure students understand the audio.

Answers
1. Server
2. Assistant chef
3. She wants to learn how to create delicious food.

 C ◀») **1-40** Read the instructions aloud. Explain that students are going to hear the audio one more time. They should write the words they hear to complete the sentences. Play the audio. Call on volunteers to elicit the answers.

Answers
1. I'm
2. can do it
3. working
4. fast

2 Practice your pronunciation

Pronunciation Extension
10–15 minutes

A ◀») **1-41** 1. Write: *They've always wanted to work at this company* on the board. Say the sentence and ask students to repeat it. Underline the two instances of *th* and repeat *they've* and *this*. Say: *Now we're going to focus on* th *sounds.*

2. Play the audio. Direct students to listen for the pronunciation of *th*.

3. Say and have students repeat *think* and *that's*.

TIP

Change the sentence on the board to read: *They've always wanted to work at this theater.* Say the sentence and underline the *th* in *theater*. Ask students if it sounds the same as the other *th* sounds. Elicit more examples of the unvoiced *th* sound—for example, *think, with, fifth, birthday.* Show students that the mouth position is the same in both sounds, but they need to use their voices to produce the sound in *this*, whereas the sound in *think* is produced with air.

B ◀») **1-42** Play the audio. Have students work individually to write the missing words.

Answers
1. The
2. There
3. the
4. Thank
5. three

C 🔊 **1-42** 1. Play the audio again. Have students check their answers to 2B. Call on volunteers to read the completed sentences aloud. Ask: *Is the* th *voiced or unvoiced?*

2. Ask students to take turns reading the sentences in 2B with a partner. Monitor and provide feedback.

3 Use contractions with the present perfect

Presentation II and Guided Practice II
15–20 minutes

A 1. Introduce the new topic: *In everyday speech, we usually use contractions with the present perfect. Now we're going to work on present perfect contractions.*

2. Read the sentences in the chart and go over the *Grammar Note*.

3. Check comprehension of the grammar in the chart. Ask: *How do you contract* she has? *How do you contract* have not?

4. Have students underline the contractions individually. Read the sentences again and have students repeat them. Then have them read the sentences with a partner.

Answers
Underlined: I've, She's, hasn't, haven't

B 1. Read the instructions aloud. Have students do the task individually.

2. Have pairs compare answers before checking answers as a class.

Answers
1. They've 2. He's 3. We 4. hasn't 5. She's

TIP

For additional practice with contractions, dictate a few sentences. Pronounce the contracted form, but ask students to write the sentence with the full form of the verb. *She's worked here for a long time. She's a good employee. I've read that book three times. He's a very creative thinker.* Have volunteers write the sentences on the board.

4 Building conversation skills

Guided Practice III
15–20 minutes

A Direct students to look at the picture and skim the conversation in 4B. Have them work with partners to identify what the woman is thinking. Elicit responses and ask: *How do you know?* or *Why do you say that?* to encourage students to state their reasoning.

Answer
She wants to be the head chef.

B 1. Ask students to read the instructions and tell you what they are going to do [listen and read and respond to the question]. Play the audio and then elicit the answer to the question.

2. Ask students to read the conversation with a partner. Circulate and monitor pronunciation. Model and have students repeat difficult words or phrases.

3. Ask: *In what other situations could you use this conversation?* Point out a few phrases that are not specific to an interview for a promotion. Ask volunteers to point out others.

Answer
She wants to continue to create delicious new dishes for Henri's customers.

Communicative Practice and Application I
20–25 minutes

C 1. Pair students and have them read the instructions silently. Check their comprehension of the exercise. Ask: *What are the two roles? Is the conversation at home or work?*

2. Model and have students repeat the expressions in the *In Other Words* box in 4B. Explain that they should use these expressions in their conversations.

3. Draw a T-chart on the board. Label the left column *Manager* and the right column *Salesperson*. Elicit examples of what each person might say and make notes in the chart.

4. Set a time limit (three minutes). Have students act out the role-play. Call "time" and have students switch roles.

5. Ask three volunteer pairs to act out their role-play for the class. Tell students who are listening to make a simple table with four rows and two columns. Use the top row to label the columns *Skills* and *Experience*. Have students take notes in the chart for each role-play.

MULTILEVEL STRATEGIES

Seat same-level students together.

• **Pre-level** Work with these students and guide them in writing their new conversation or provide a simplified conversation for these students to practice.

A: *How long have you been a salesperson?*

B: *I've been a salesperson for five years.*

A: *Why should you be the assistant manager?*

B: *I want to teach other employees what I have learned.*

• **Higher-level** You can challenge students to talk about the personal strengths that they possess that make them good at the job.

---

5 Focus on listening for details

Presentation III and Guided Practice IV
20–25 minutes

A 1. Read the questions and statement aloud and model a discussion with a volunteer. Ask: *Do you think everyone should be promoted? Why? / Why not? I agree because… / I disagree because…*

2. Pair students and tell them to discuss their own answers to the questions. Circulate and monitor.

TIP

Make sure students know to be patient while other students are speaking and not interrupt or talk over each other. One way to ensure this is to make a habit of asking a student to repeat back what another student said.

B Direct students to read the sentences before they listen to the interview. Ask what kind of information they'll be writing in the blanks. Ask volunteers for predictions. If students struggle, start by offering your own prediction: *I think we will hear why Miguel wants to change jobs.*

C 🔊 1-44 1. Play the audio. Ask students to listen and write the correct answers.

2. Pair students and have them compare answers. If a pair has different answers, have the class vote on the correct answer with a show of hands.

Answers
1. education
2. worked
3. job
4. drive
5. hospital

6 Discuss

Communicative Practice and Application II
15–20 minutes

A 1. Read the instructions aloud. Call on volunteers to read the list of interview questions. Confirm understanding of the task. Ask: *What number will you give to the most difficult question?* [1]

2. Put students into teams of three and assign roles: manager, administrative assistant, and reporter. Verify students' understanding of the roles.

3. Set a time limit for the discussions (ten minutes). Write the sentence frame from 6B on the board. Then circulate and monitor.

B Call "time." Ask the reporter for each team to report the results of the team's discussion using the sentence frame on the board.

Evaluation
5 minutes

TEST YOURSELF

1. Ask students to complete the checkboxes individually.

2. Tell students that you are going to read each of the items in the checklist aloud. If they are not at all confident with that skill, they should hold up a closed fist. If they are not very confident, they should hold up one finger. If they are somewhat confident, two fingers; confident, three fingers; very confident, four fingers. If they think they could teach the skill, they should hold up five fingers. Read each item in the checklist and identify students who may need further support.

Lesson Overview

| Lesson Notes |

MULTILEVEL OBJECTIVES

Pre-, On-, and Higher-level: Read about and discuss getting a promotion

LANGUAGE FOCUS

Grammar: Imperatives (*Take classes or study at home.*)

Vocabulary: *Honest, interpersonal skills, market, network*

For vocabulary support, see this **Oxford Picture Dictionary** topic: Career Planning, pages 174–175

STRATEGY FOCUS

Read an inset for additional information on a topic.

READINESS CONNECTION

In this lesson, students verbally communicate information about ways to get a promotion.

PACING

To compress this lesson: Assign 1F and/or 2C for homework.

To extend this lesson: Have students write about top qualities. (See end of lesson.)

And/or have students complete **Workbook 3 page 28** and **Multilevel Activities 3 Unit 4 pages 54–55**.

CORRELATIONS

CCRS: SL.1.B (d.) Explain their own ideas and understanding in light of the discussion.

SL.2.B Determine the main ideas and supporting details of a text read aloud or information presented in diverse media and formats, including visually, quantitatively, and orally.

R.1.B Ask and answer such questions as who, what, where, when, why, and how to demonstrate understanding of key details in a text.

R.2.A Identify the main topic and retell key details of a text.

R.5.B Know and use various text features to locate key facts or information in a text efficiently.

R.7.C Interpret information presented visually, orally, or quantitatively and explain how the information contributes to an understanding of the text in which it appears.

L.1.B (h.) Form and use the simple verb tenses. (l.) Produce simple, compound and complex sentences.

L.4.B (b.) Determine the meaning of the new word formed when a known prefix is added to a known word. (e.) Use glossaries and beginning dictionaries, both print and digital, to determine or clarify the meaning of words and phrases.

RF.3.B (c.) Identify and know the meaning of the most common prefixes and derivational suffixes.

RF.4.B (a.) Read grade-level text with purpose and understanding.

ELPS: 1. An ELL can construct meaning from oral presentations and literary and informational text through level-appropriate listening, reading, and viewing. 3. An ELL can speak and write about level-appropriate complex literary and informational texts and topics.

Warm-up and Review
10–15 minutes (books closed)

Write the words *Description* and *Behavior* on the board. Elicit words that describe a good employee—for example, *self-starter, go-getter*, etc. Write them under *Description*. Elicit what a person who fits that description does and write it under *Behavior: works without supervision, comes to work on time.*

Introduction
5 minutes

1. Use students' ideas from the *Warm-up* to talk about good employees. Ask: *Which of these behaviors do you think are most important to help you get a promotion? Is a promotion always a good thing?*

2. State the objective: *Today we're going to read about and discuss ways to get a promotion.*

1 Read

Presentation
10–20 minutes

A Read the questions aloud. Use ideas from the *Introduction* to help guide discussion.

B Read the words and definitions. Elicit sample sentences for the words or supply them if the students can't. Students may use the more common noun form of *market* and *network*. Show them how these words can be used as verbs. *He put up a website to market his skills. She tries to network with other employees because meeting new people might help her find a better job.* Ask students to identify how each of the words relates to getting a promotion.

Pre-reading

C Read the instructions aloud and confirm that students understand where the bulleted headings are. Have students answer the question individually and then check answers as a class. If any students answer incorrectly, ask them to support their answer using the bulleted headings. Establish the correct answer.

Answer
b. You need to work for your promotion.

Guided Practice: While Reading
20–30 minutes

D 1. Direct students' attention to the *Reader's Note* and read the information aloud. Ask students to read the article silently and answer the question.

2. Check answers as a class.

3. Check comprehension. Ask: *What is one way you can you improve your skills?* [take a class] *Why is how you dress important?* [It can make a difference in how your supervisor sees you.] *What is one way to network?* [attend company events]

Possible Answers
Take classes
Dress for success
Network
Have a positive attitude
Strengthen your skills

MULTILEVEL STRATEGIES

Adapt 1D to the level of your students.

• **Pre-level** Provide these students with a summary of the reading. *There are three important ways to get a promotion. 1. Take classes or do extra jobs at work to learn new skills. 2. Market yourself. Dress nicely for work so you look serious. Try to meet other employees. 3. Know your strengths. Some important strengths are: speak and write well, be honest, be friendly, work well in teams, and be flexible.*

Direct these students to read the summary while other students are reading 1D.

Guided Practice: Rereading
10–15 minutes

E 1. Provide an opportunity for students to extract evidence from the text. Have students reread the article and underline the words that support who the author believes is the most responsible for getting a promotion.

2. Pair students and tell them to compare the words they underlined and report anything they disagree on. Discuss and clarify as needed.

Answers
You are most responsible; underlines will vary.

F

1. Have students work individually to mark the answers *T* (true), *F* (false), and *NI* (no information). They should then write the line numbers where they found the true and false answers. Write the answers on the board.

2. Elicit and discuss any additional questions about the reading. You could introduce new questions for class discussion: *Have you followed any of the advice in the article? What is the hardest piece of advice to follow? What is the easiest?*

Answers
1. T, line 6
2. F, line 18
3. NI
4. F, line 9
5. NI

2 Word study

Guided Practice: Post-reading
10–15 minutes

1. Direct students to look at the chart and identify the topic (the prefix *inter-*). Have students read the chart.

2. Read the first two sentences in the chart and the examples for *act* and *interact*. Elicit sentences for the other words in the chart.

3. Have students repeat after you as you say each word with natural intonation, rhythm, and stress.

4. Direct students to complete the sentences and then compare answers with a partner. Read the correct answers and have students check their work.

Answers	
1. international	4. view
2. interview	5. national
3. intermediate	6. interacted

B

1. Read the prompts aloud. Give students a few minutes to think of their answers.

2. Set a time limit (ten minutes). Have groups of three or four discuss the prompts. Circulate and help as needed.

3. Have students share their responses with the class.

C

Direct students to work individually to write a sentence that includes each underlined word in 2B. Ask volunteers to write their sentences on the board. Have the rest of the class suggest grammar and spelling edits as needed.

3 Talk it over

Guided Practice
15–20 minutes

 A Have students look at the flow chart and read the note and *Reader's Note*. Point out that they need to use the information from the flow chart and the note to complete the sentences. Set a time limit (ten minutes). Have students work in pairs to complete the task. Ask volunteers to share their answers with the class.

Answers
1. 10
2. 15
3. Store manager
4. Cashier supervisor
5. Three

Communicative Practice
15–20 minutes

B Read the questions aloud. Set a time limit (ten minutes). Tell students to copy the chart in their notebooks and complete it with their answers to the questions.

C While students are doing the activity in 3B, write the chart on the board. Have volunteers share their answers with the class and write them in the chart. Have students add any new ideas to their charts. Have a class discussion about which of the ideas students have actually used with success.

Application
15–20 minutes

BRING IT TO LIFE

Help make the assignment more concrete by asking students whom they will talk to. Have everyone write down the name of the person they plan on asking.

EXTENSION ACTIVITY

Write about Top Qualities

Have students write examples of behaviors that demonstrate the "top qualities" from the article in 1D.

1. Put students in pairs or small groups. Have each pair come up with a specific example of a behavior that demonstrates each quality. Tell them to use their own actions or the actions of people they know as an example. Good communication skills: I have successfully taught my co-workers how to use the cash register.

2. Have volunteers read their sentences aloud. Congratulate correct usage of the present perfect. As a class, decide which examples would be most persuasive for an employer.

Warm-up and Review
10–15 minutes

Review the *Bring It to Life* assignment from Lesson 5. Ask students for examples of job skills they don't have but might like to learn. List students' ideas on the board.

Introduction
5 minutes

1. Refer to the list of job skills on the board from the *Warm-up*. Ask: *Do you enjoy learning new things? What things at your job or school do you need to learn?*

4. State the objective: *Today we're going to learn how to express a willingness to learn new things.*

Presentation
5 minutes

 A **1-45** Read the instructions aloud. Play the audio. Give students a minute to think about the question. Elicit responses from the class.

Answer
An interview

Guided Practice
10–15 minutes

 B **1-45** Play the audio again. Direct students to listen for each thing Mary is going to learn to do and put a check next to any that they hear mentioned.

Answers
Checked:
draw blood
put in IVs
visit the website

C **1-45** Read the instructions aloud. Play the audio again, encouraging students to take notes in their notebooks. Set a time limit (five minutes) for students to discuss their answers with a partner. Circulate to monitor.

Answers
I can't draw blood but want to learn how.
I'm a fast learner.
Are there any classes I can attend to better prepare me for this job?
Does that mean I'm hired?
Where would you suggest I start?

Presentation and Communicative Practice
15–20 minutes

D 1. Direct students' attention to the *Do/Say* chart and ask students to identify the lesson's soft skill [showing a willingness to learn]. Ask the class which column has examples of language [right] and which has examples of activities [left].

2. As a class, brainstorm ways to complete the first two sentences in the right column. Write students' ideas on the board.

3. Model the sentences from the right column using authentic intonation. Have students practice imitating your inflection.

4. Put students in teams of four and assign each team a question. Assign roles: manager, administrative assistant, researcher, and reporter. Researchers will ask you questions on behalf of the team. Verify understanding of the roles. Set a time limit (five minutes) and monitor.

5. Write sentence frames on the board that teams can use to summarize their response. (*Our team discussed the following question: _____ We decided _____ because _____.*)

6. Call "time" and let reporters rehearse their report for one minute. Direct each reporter to present to three other teams.

Communicative Practice and Application
10–15 minutes

E 1. Tell students that they are going to work in pairs and have a conversation about learning new skills using the sentences in D. Model the conversation with a volunteer.

2. Direct pairs to take turns doing each role.

3. As students carry out the conversation, circulate and monitor. Provide global feedback once the activity ends.

MULTILEVEL STRATEGIES

Divide the class into same-level groups and have the discussion separately.

• **Pre- and On-level** Work with these students to write a conversation they can use for practice.

• **Higher-level** Challenge these students to give advice for how to learn each of the skills.

Lesson Overview

MULTILEVEL OBJECTIVES

Pre-, On-, and Higher-level: Review unit language

LANGUAGE FOCUS

Grammar: Present perfect (*We've been here for 20 minutes.*)

Vocabulary: interview vocabulary

For vocabulary support, see this **Oxford Picture Dictionary** topic: Interview Skills, page 179

READINESS CONNECTION

In this review, students work in a team to use irregular past participles and the present perfect to talk about experience.

PACING

To extend this review: Have students complete **Workbook 3 page 29**, **Multilevel Activities 3 page 56**, and **Multilevel Grammar Exercises 3 Unit 4**.

Lesson Notes

CORRELATIONS

CCRS: SL.1.B (a.) Come to discussions prepared, having read or studied required material; explicitly draw on that preparation and other information known about the topic to explore ideas under discussion. (b.) Follow agreed-upon rules for discussions. (c.) Ask questions to check understanding of information presented, stay on topic, and link their comments to the remarks of others. (d.) Explain their own ideas and understanding in light of the discussion.

SL.2.B Determine the main ideas and supporting details of a text read aloud or information presented in diverse media and formats, including visually, quantitatively, and orally.

SL.4.B Report on a topic or text, tell a story, or recount an experience with appropriate facts and relevant, descriptive details, speaking clearly at an understandable pace.

R.2.A Identify the main topic and retell key details of a text.

W.3.B Write narratives in which they recount a well-elaborated event or short sequence of events, include details to describe actions, thoughts, and feelings, use temporal words to signal event order, and provide a sense of closure.

W.4.B Produce writing in which the development and organization are appropriate to task and purpose.

L.1.B (h.) Form and use the simple verb tenses. (l.) Produce simple, compound and complex sentences.

L.1.C (e.) Form and use the perfect verb tenses.

RF.4.B (a.) Read grade-level text with purpose and understanding.

ELPS: 5. An ELL can conduct research and evaluate and communicate findings to answer questions or solve problems. 6. An ELL can analyze and critique the arguments of others orally and in writing.

Warm-up and Review
10–15 minutes (books closed)

1. Review *At Work* activity E.

2. Ask students to share the good, not-so-good, and interesting things that happened during the conversation. As students speak, write their responses in a chart on the board.

Introduction and Presentation
5 minutes

1. Ask students a few questions using the present perfect. *Anna, how long have you studied English? Kyung Hee, have you been to Kansas?* Write their answers on the board in the third person. *Anna has studied English for four years. Kyung Hee hasn't been to Kansas.*

2. Ask volunteers to come to the board and underline the verb in each sentence. Pointing to the sentences to make your meaning clear, ask other volunteers to tell you the name of the form, the auxiliary used, and the form of the main verb.

3. Discuss the meaning of each sentence on the board. *Is Anna still studying English?* [yes] *When did Kyung Hee go to Kansas?* [never] *Is it possible she'll go in the future?* [yes]

4. State the objective: *Today we're going to learn more irregular past participles and review using the present perfect to talk about our experience.*

Guided Practice
15–20 minutes

A 1. Direct students to work in pairs to look at the picture.

2. Set a time limit (five minutes) for pairs to complete the task. Check answers as a class.

3. Have pairs practice the conversation. Circulate and monitor.

Answers	
1. have, worked	4. 've supervised
2. 've worked	5. Have, had
3. have, supervised	6. 've had

B 1. Read the instructions aloud and have students work in teams to complete the task. Circulate and monitor.

2. Have volunteers share their questions with the class.

C 1. Read the instructions aloud. Have each student in the team write two or three sentences in the present perfect using contractions. Circulate and monitor.

2. Have students take turns saying their sentences aloud and calling out the verb in the contraction.

Communicative Practice
30–45 minutes

D 1. Group students and assign roles: manager, writer, editor, and presenter. Explain that students are going to work with their teams to write a thank-you note for after an interview. Editors will review the thank-you note and offer suggestions for changes.

2. Read steps 2–5 of the activity aloud. Check comprehension of the task. *What will you think about first?* [a job] *Who will you write the letter to?* [the interviewer for the job] *What will you tell him/her?* [why you're writing and what you hope for]

3. Set a time limit (ten minutes) to complete the exercise. Circulate and answer any questions.

4. Have presenters from each team read their team's thank-you note to another team.

MULTILEVEL STRATEGIES

• **Pre-level** Assign these students the role of presenter.

• **On-level** Assign these students the role of writer or manager.

• **Higher-level** Assign these students the role of manager or editor.

E 1. Have students walk around the room to conduct the interviews. To get students moving, tell them to interview three people who were not on their team for D.

2. Set a time limit (five minutes) to complete the exercise.

3. Tell students to make a note of their classmates' answers but not to worry about writing complete sentences.

MULTILEVEL STRATEGIES

Adapt the mixer in E to the level of your students.

• **Pre- and On-level** Pair these students and have them interview other pairs together.

• **Higher-level** Have these students ask an additional question and write all answers in complete sentences.

F 1. Call on individuals to report what they learned about their classmates. Keep a running tally on the board for each question, marking if students have interviewed for a job and what it was like, how they heard about the job, and what they brought to the interview.

2. Use your tally for question 1 to create a pie chart on the board. Instruct students to choose a question and draw a pie chart. Circulate and answer any questions.

PROBLEM SOLVING
10–15 minutes

A ◄))) 1-46 1. Ask: *Do you think it's difficult to prepare for an interview? How much time do you think it takes to prepare?* Tell students they will read a story about a man who has a job interview in the morning. Direct students to read Hector's story silently.

2. Ask: *What did Hector do today? What did he not do today?*

3. Play the audio and have students read along silently.

B 1. Elicit answers to question 1. Guide students to a class consensus on the answer.

2. As a class, brainstorm answers to question 2. Ask students if they know someone who has this problem and has overcome it or what they have done themselves to overcome the same problem.

Answers
1. He hasn't had time to prepare for his job interview.
2. Answers will vary.

Evaluation
20–25 minutes

To test students' understanding of the unit language and content, have them take the Unit 4 Test, available on the Teacher Resource Center.

Unit Overview

This unit explores community resources, concerns, and volunteering opportunities with a range of employability skills and contextualizes present perfect grammar structures.

KEY OBJECTIVES

Lesson 1	Identify and locate community resources
Lesson 2	Identify community problems and write an email asking for assistance
Lesson 3	Use *yes/no* questions in the present perfect to ask about personal, work, and academic experiences
Lesson 4	Express interest in volunteering
Lesson 5	Identify ways to reduce trash and protect the environment
At Work	Give a helpful suggestion
Teamwork & Language Review	Review unit language

UNIT FEATURES

Academic Vocabulary	*consequences, community, job, behalf, contractor, environment, resources*
Employability Skills	• Choose solutions to workplace problems • Determine what makes a job safe or unsafe • Decide what steps to take to find volunteer opportunities • Work independently • Understand teamwork • Locate information • Communicate verbally • Listen actively • Use writing skills • Comprehend written material • Analyze information

Resources	**Class Audio** CD2, Tracks 02–12
	Workbook Unit 5, pages 30–36
	Teacher Resource Center
	    Multilevel Activities 3 Unit 5
	    Multilevel Grammar Exercises 3 Unit 5
	    Unit 5 Test
	Oxford Picture Dictionary Everyday Conversation, Downtown, Civic Engagement, Public Safety, Energy and the Environment

Lesson Overview	Lesson Notes

MULTILEVEL OBJECTIVES

On-level: Identify community resources and describe services

Pre-level: Identify community resources and services

Higher-level: Talk and write about community resources and services

LANGUAGE FOCUS

Grammar: *Should (You should go to the job fair.)*

Vocabulary: Community resources and services

For vocabulary support, see this **Oxford Picture Dictionary** topic: Downtown, pages 126–127

STRATEGY FOCUS

Pool knowledge with team members to maximize vocabulary learning.

READINESS CONNECTION

In this lesson, students explore and communicate information about community places and services.

PACING

To compress this lesson: Conduct 1B as a whole-class activity.

To extend this lesson: Have students write and role-play a conversation about community services. (See end of lesson.)

And/or have students complete **Workbook 3 page 30** and **Multilevel Activities 3 Unit 5 pages 58–59.**

CORRELATIONS

CCRS: SL.1.B (d.) Explain their own ideas and understanding in light of the discussion.

SL.2.B Determine the main ideas and supporting details of a text read aloud or information presented in diverse media and formats, including visually, quantitatively, and orally.

SL.4.B Report on a topic or text, tell a story, or recount an experience with appropriate facts and relevant, descriptive details, speaking clearly at an understandable pace.

R.1.B Ask and answer such questions as who, what, where, when, why, and how to demonstrate understanding of key details in a text.

R.5.A-Know and use various text features to locate key facts or information in a text.

W.7.A Participate in shared research and writing projects.

L.1.B (l.) Produce simple, compound and complex sentences.

L.4.B (e.) Use glossaries and beginning dictionaries, both print and digital, to determine or clarify the meaning of words and phrases.

RF.4.B (a.) Read grade-level text with purpose and understanding.

ELPS: 8. An ELL can determine the meaning of words and phrases in oral presentations and literary and informational text.

Warm-up and Review
10–15 minutes (books closed)

Draw a dollar sign ($) on the board and ask students to guess what community place it represents [a bank]. Direct students to come up with a quick drawing that represents a community place. Ask volunteers to draw their pictures on the board. Have the class guess what the pictures represent.

Introduction
5 minutes

1. Refer to the drawings on the board from the *Warm-up*. Say: *Identify the places where we buy things. Identify the places people go for recreation. Name the places that provide help.*

2. State the objective: *Today we're going to learn more vocabulary for community places and community services.*

1 Identify community resources

Presentation I
20–25 minutes

A 1. Write *Government services/offices* on the board and elicit one example from the whole class. Have students work together to brainstorm in a group. Make a list on the board of the services your students identify.

2. Have students identify the most essential office or service. Elicit ideas and put a checkmark next to the services students feel are essential, encouraging them to explain their reasons.

B 1. Copy the first two rows of the chart onto the board.

2. Model the task by "thinking aloud" about the first word in the chart and marking the first column appropriately. Work with a volunteer to demonstrate completing the second and third columns.

3. Direct students to review the vocabulary independently, marking the first column of the chart in their books.

4. Pair students and ask them to complete the second and third columns of the chart together.

C 1. Elicit any words that pairs did not know and write them on the board. Ask volunteers to explain any of the words they know.

2. Direct students to look up any remaining unknown words in their dictionaries. Discuss those words in relation to the lesson. (Note: 1D and 1E will confirm students' understanding of the target vocabulary.)

Guided Practice I
10–20 minutes

D 1. Direct students to look at the first item. Then read question 2 aloud. If students struggle to answer, direct their attention to the *Vocabulary Note*. Ask if there are any words in the question that are similar to the vocabulary from 1B. Elicit the answer.

2. Set a time limit (five minutes). Direct students to complete the activity individually and then check their answers in pairs. Do not check the answers as a class yet.

Answers	
1. b	5. a
2. g	6. e
3. h	7. f
4. c	8. d

E (◄)) **2-02** 1. Prepare students to listen by saying: *Now we're going to listen to speakers describe each of the community places we've been studying. While you listen, check your work in 1D.*

2. Play the audio. Ask students to circle any of their answers in 1D that don't match the audio. Elicit those items and play them again, focusing on clues to meaning in the 1D sentences.

3. Work with the pronunciation of any troublesome words or phrases.

2 Learn about community services

Presentation II
10–20 minutes

A 1. Direct students to look at the website. Introduce the new topic: *We've talked about places. Now we're going to talk about services those places provide.*

2. Elicit the names of the places students see on the website.

3. Ask students to work individually to make a chart like the one below the website. Go over the answers as a class.

4. Check comprehension. Ask: *Where can I take a fitness class?* [at the recreation center] *Where can I get a wellness checkup?* [at the community clinic]

5. Draw students' attention to the menu on the website and establish their familiarity with web page navigation. Ask: *What do I click to go to the homepage?* [the home icon] *How do I return to the previous page?* [click the back button]

Answers	
Location	**Service**
Employment Agency	job fair
Community Clinic	wellness checkups
Senior Center	volunteer program
City Hall	open house
Recreation Center	fitness classes
Animal Shelter	pet adoption day

Guided Practice II
10–15 minutes

 1. Model the conversation with a volunteer. Model it again using other information from 2A.

2. Set a time limit (three minutes). Direct students to practice with a partner.

3. Call on volunteers to present their version of the conversation for the class.

MULTILEVEL STRATEGIES

Adapt 2B to the level of your students.

• **Pre- and On-level** Pair pre- and on-level students for 2B. Assign pre-level students part A for the first round and then have them switch roles.

• **Higher-level** Pair students and direct them to create a conversation based on the structure provided in the Extension Activity.

Communicative Practice and Application
20–25 minutes

 1. If students will use the Internet for this task, establish what device(s) they'll use: a class computer, tablets, or smartphones. Alternatively, print information from the Internet before class and distribute to groups.

2. Write the questions from 2C on the board. Explain that students will work in teams to research and report on these questions. Ask: *Which question requires research?* [1] *Which search terms or questions can you use to find the information you need?* ["community services" + your city, "community events" + your city] *What information will you scan for?* [names, addresses of services; names, dates of events] *How will you record the information you find?* [table, checklist, index cards] Remind students to bookmark or record sites so they can find or cite them in the future.

3. Group students and assign roles: manager, administrative assistant, IT support, and reporter. Verify students' understanding of the roles.

4. Give managers the time limit for researching question 1 (ten minutes). Direct the IT support to begin the online research or pick up the printed materials for each team. Direct the administrative assistant to record information for the team using a table, a checklist, or index cards.

5. Give a two-minute warning. Call "time." Tell reporters to first answer and then ask each member of the team question 2.

TIP

When setting up task-based activities, verify that students understand their roles using physical commands. For example: *If you report on your team's work, stand up* [reporter]. *If you keep the team on task, point to the clock* [manager]. *If you write the team's responses, raise your hand* [administrative assistant]. *If you help the team research, hold up your smartphone/tablet* [IT support].

D 1. Copy the sentence frames on the board.

2. Direct teams to help their administrative assistant use the sentence frames to record the team's findings. Direct the reporter to use the recorded information to report the team's findings to the class or another team.

Evaluation
10–15 minutes

TEST YOURSELF

1. Direct Partner A to read questions 1–4 from 1D on page 68 to Partner B. Partner B should close his or her book and write the answers in his or her notebook. When finished, students switch roles. Partner B reads questions 5–8 from 1D.

2. Direct both partners to open their books and check their spelling when they finish.

EXTENSION ACTIVITY

Community Service Role-play

1. Put students in pairs. Instruct them to write a short conversation between someone who needs a community service and someone who can provide the information the person needs.

2. Provide this structure on the board for pairs to follow:

A: *Explain your problem/need to B.*

B: *Tell what service will help.*

A: *Ask where to go for that service.*

B: *Tell A where and when to go.*

Lesson Overview	Lesson Notes

MULTILEVEL OBJECTIVES

On- and Higher-level: Analyze, write, and edit an email asking for assistance

Pre-level: Read and write an email asking for assistance

LANGUAGE FOCUS

Grammar: Adjectives (*The parking lot is dangerous.*)

Vocabulary: *On behalf of, sincerely*

For vocabulary support, see this **Oxford Picture Dictionary** topic: Public Safety, page 146

STRATEGY FOCUS

When you are writing, focus each paragraph on a clear purpose or main idea.

READINESS CONNECTION

In this lesson, students listen actively, read, and write about seeing a problem in the community and possible solutions.

PACING

To compress this lesson: Assign the *Test Yourself* for homework.

To extend this lesson: Role-play a conversation with a school board member. (See end of lesson.)

And/or have students complete **Workbook 3 page 31** and **Multilevel Activities 3 Unit 5 page 60.**

CORRELATIONS

CCRS: SL.1.B (d.) Explain their own ideas and understanding in light of the discussion.

SL.2.B Determine the main ideas and supporting details of a text read aloud or information presented in diverse media and formats, including visually, quantitatively, and orally.

R.1.B Ask and answer such questions as who, what, where, when, why, and how to demonstrate understanding of key details in a text.

R.2.A Identify the main topic and retell key details of a text.

W.2.A Write informative/explanatory texts in which they name a topic, supply some facts about the topic, and provide some sense of closure.

W.4.B Produce writing in which the development and organization are appropriate to task and purpose.

W.5.B With guidance and support from peers and others, develop and strengthen writing as needed by planning, revising and editing.

L.1.B (l.) Produce simple, compound and complex sentences.

L.2.B (c.) use commas in greetings and closings of letters.

RF.4.B (a.) Read grade-level text with purpose and understanding.

ELPS: 6. An ELL can analyze and critique the arguments of others orally and in writing. 9. An ELL can create clear and coherent level-appropriate speech and text.

Warm-up and Review
10–15 minutes (books closed)

Write *Safety* on the board. Tell students that all communities have some safety problems. Give them an example from your neighborhood—for example, uneven sidewalks, trees with branches that get knocked down in the wind, blind corners. Ask students to brainstorm other safety problems that they have encountered. Write their ideas on the board.

Introduction
5 minutes

1. Refer to the problems on the board from the *Warm-up* and ask: *What do you do when you encounter these problems? Where can you go for help?*

2. State the objective: *Today we're going to read and write about seeing a problem in the community and asking for a solution.*

1 Prepare to write

Presentation
20–25 minutes

A 1. Build students' schema by asking questions about the picture and the email. Ask: *Who are these people? How do they look? Who is the email to? What is the subject?*

2. Give students one minute to tell a partner their responses to questions 1 and 2. Elicit responses from the class.

Answers
1. No lights in the parking lot
2. Answers will vary.

B 🔊 2-03 1. Introduce the model email and its purpose: *You're going to read an email from a student to a school board member. As you read, look for the purpose of the email: Why is she writing?* Have students read the email silently.

2. Check comprehension. Ask: *Who is Marta?* [a student at Mid-City community center] *Is the email offering help or asking for help?* [asking for help] *Is the email formal or informal?* [formal] *How do you know?* [it includes formal language: "Dear," "Sincerely"]

3. Play the audio. Have students read along silently.

Guided Practice I
10 minutes

C 1. Have students work independently to underline the answers to the questions in the email.

2. Point out the *Writer's Note* and ask students to annotate the information they underlined with the phrases "reason for writing" for question 1, "description of the problem" for question 2, and "request" for question 3.

Answers
Underlined:
1. I am writing to you on behalf of the students in my English class at Mid-City community center. ...we are worried about a safety issue.
2. The problem is that there are no lights in the parking lot.
3. Will you help us get these lights?

2 Plan and write

Guided Practice II
15–20 minutes

A 1. Read question 1. Elicit school problems and write them on the board. Demonstrate how to create a cluster diagram by drawing a circle and writing one of the school problems in the center. Draw "spokes" with circles at the end and ask volunteers for one or two answers to fill them in. Have students select another one of the problems and create their own cluster diagram of possible solutions. Have students share their diagrams with partners.

2. Read question 2. Ask volunteers to report on the problem and solution they focused on.

B Read through the email template. Elicit ideas that could go in each paragraph. Have students write their emails individually.

> **TIP**
>
> For 2B, if you don't know the name of a school board member, make one up as a place holder. Another option is to use *To Whom It May Concern* rather than an actual person's name.

> **MULTILEVEL STRATEGIES**
>
> Adapt 2B to the level of your students.
>
> • **Pre-level** Work with these students to write a group email. Read through the template. At each blank, stop and elicit completions. Decide as a group what to write. Have these learners copy the group email into their notebooks.
>
> • **Higher-level** Encourage these students to include an example of something specific that happened or might happen because of the safety problem. Provide sentence frames: *As a result of this situation, _____. Our class is concerned that _____ could _____ as a result of the situation.*

3 Get feedback and revise

Guided Practice III
5 minutes

 Direct students to check their writing using the editing checklist. Tell them to read each item in the list and check their papers before moving on to the next item. Explain that students should not edit their writing at this stage. They should just use the checklist to check their work and mark any areas they want to revise.

Communicative Practice
15 minutes

 1. Read the instructions aloud. Emphasize to students that they are responding to their partners' work, not correcting it.

2. Use the letter in 1B to model the exercise. *I think the sentence that says, "There are no lights in the parking lot" describes the problem clearly. I'm not sure I understand the sentence…*

3. Direct students to exchange papers with a partner and follow the instructions.

C Allow students time to edit and revise their writing as necessary, using the editing checklist from 3A and their partner's feedback from 3B. If necessary, students could complete this task as homework.

> **TIP**
>
> After completing 3C, hold a "school board meeting" in class. Ask for volunteers to come to the front of the room and explain their problems and proposed solutions. All non-volunteers are "board members." Ask the board members to listen and take notes. Tell them they need to prioritize the problems. Have the board come to a consensus about which problem they should deal with first.

Application and Evaluation
10 minutes

TEST YOURSELF

1. Review the instructions aloud. Assign a time limit (five minutes) and have students work independently.

2. Before collecting student work, invite two or three volunteers to share their sentences. Ask students to raise their hands if they wrote similar sentences.

EXTENSION ACTIVITY

School board Role-play

1. Put students in pairs. Partner A is a school board member, and Partner B is a concerned student.

2. Put a structure on the board for the pairs to follow:

A: *What's the problem?*

B: *At our school, [describe problem].*

A: *Do you want us to [describe solution]?*

B: *That would be great.*

A: *OK. We'll talk about it at the next meeting.*

3. Have pairs take turns demonstrating their role-plays to each other.

Lesson Overview

MULTILEVEL OBJECTIVES

On- and Higher-level: Use the present perfect to ask questions about personal, work, and academic experiences and listen for information about community involvement

Pre-level: Recognize the present perfect in questions about personal, work, and academic experiences

LANGUAGE FOCUS

Grammar: Present perfect questions (*Has the contractor pulled all the permits?*)

Vocabulary: *Ever, yet, already*

For vocabulary support, see this **Oxford Picture Dictionary** topic: Downtown, pages 126–127

READINESS CONNECTION

In this lesson, students practice the present perfect and talk about being involved in the community.

PACING

To compress this lesson: Conduct 2B and 2C as whole-class activities.

To extend this lesson: Have students talk about a community event calendar. (See end of lesson.)

And/or have students complete **Workbook 3 pages 32–33, Multilevel Activities 3 Unit 5 pages 61–62,** and **Multilevel Grammar Exercises 3 Unit 5.**

Lesson Notes

CORRELATIONS

CCRS: SL.2.B Determine the main ideas and supporting details of a text read aloud or information presented in diverse media and formats, including visually, quantitatively, and orally.

SL.6.B Speak in complete sentences when appropriate to task and situation in order to provide requested detail or clarification.

R.1.B Ask and answer such questions as who, what, where, when, why, and how to demonstrate understanding of key details in a text.

L.1.B (b.) Explain the function of nouns, pronouns, verbs, adjectives, and adverbs in general and their functions in particular sentences. (l.) Produce simple, compound and complex sentences.

L.1.C (e.) Form and use the perfect verb tenses.

RF.4.B (a.) Read grade-level text with purpose and understanding.

ELPS: 7. An ELL can adapt language choices to purpose, task, and audience when speaking and writing. 10. An ELL can demonstrate command of the conventions of standard English to communicate in level-appropriate speech and writing.

Warm-up and Review
10–15 minutes (books closed)

Ask students to brainstorm jobs or errands they do every week or every day—for example, make dinner, go grocery shopping, go to work. Write their ideas on the board.

Introduction
5–10 minutes

1. Tell students which of the jobs on the board you have already done or haven't done yet this week (or today). *I haven't made dinner today. I'm going to make it tonight. I've already taken the kids to school. I took them at 8:00 this morning.*

2. State the objective: *Today we're going to learn how to ask questions in the present perfect and how to use* already, ever, *and* yet *to talk about being involved in the community.*

1 Use *yes/no* questions with the present perfect

Presentation I
20–25 minutes

1. Direct students to look at the picture and conversation. Ask: *Who are these people? What are they doing?* Establish that an official is someone who is in charge. An aide helps people in charge with their work.

2. Read the instructions aloud. Ask students to read the conversation silently and answer the questions.

3. Read the first question aloud. Call on a volunteer for the answer. Ask the volunteer where in the conversation he or she found the answer. Read the rest of the questions aloud, calling on a different volunteer for each answer.

Answers	
1. Next week	3. No
2. No	4. No

B 1. Demonstrate how to read the grammar chart.

2. Direct students to underline the present perfect questions in the conversation in 1A. Write the questions on the board.

3. Ask: *Are these questions about the past? Do they state a specific time?* Say: *We use the present perfect to mean before now. We don't use it to say when something happened.*

4. Ask students to identify the two parts of the verb in the questions.

5. Pair students and direct them to read the chart aloud to each other. (One partner reads the questions, and the other responds with the answers.) Then read the chart aloud as students follow along.

6. Assess students' understanding of the chart. Elicit the past participles of the verbs from the *Warm-up*. Then elicit questions with those verbs in the present perfect. Provide your own short answers.

Answers
Underlined:
Has the contractor pulled all the permits?
Have you been to the school?
Have the workers finished the job?

Guided Practice I
15–20 minutes

1. Tell students they will collaborate to complete the description of the grammar point. Model collaboration by working with the class to complete the first sentence. Encourage students to look at 1A and 1B to see if the time is specific or non-specific.

2. Pair students and have them work together to complete the description.

3. Project or write the completed definition on the board and have pairs verify the accuracy of their responses. Ask volunteers which sentences confused them and discuss.

Answers	
non-specific	repeat
past	future

Guided Practice II
5–10 minutes

1. Model the questions and answers with a volunteer. Go over the words in the *Senior Center Project Report*.

2. Ask students to practice the questions and answers with their partners using information from the *Senior Center Project Report* and their own ideas.

3. Have pairs merge to form teams of four and then take turns demonstrating questions and answers. Set a time limit (four minutes) and monitor the practice, identifying any issues.

4. Provide clarification or feedback to the whole class as needed.

2 Use *ever, already,* and *yet* with the present perfect

Presentation II
20–25 minutes

1. Introduce the new topic: *Now we're going to learn some words that we often use with the present perfect:* ever, yet, *and* already.

2. Read the question with *ever* in the chart aloud and write it on the board. Underline *ever*. Say: *When I use* ever, *it means at any time before now—maybe yesterday, maybe last year, maybe 20 years ago. We usually use* ever

in questions. Sometimes we use ever *in negative statements.* Read the sentence with *haven't ever* aloud, and write it on the board. Ask: *Can you tell me another way to say this sentence?* Write the answer on the board [*I have never volunteered before.*].

3. Read the question with *already* aloud and write it on the board. Say: Already *also means before now, but we use it to talk about recent events. When I say* He's already repaired the stove, *I'm referring to a recent event.*

4. Write the question with *yet* on the board. Say: *When I ask a question with* yet, *I want to know if something I expected has happened. When I say* Have you finished yet? *I expect you to have finished or to be finished soon. When I use* yet *with a negative, it means something I expected hasn't happened, but I expect it to.* Write: *I haven't finished yet, but I will soon.*

5. Draw students' attention to the positions of *ever*, *already*, and *yet* in the sentences and questions.

6. Use the verbs from the *Warm-up* to check comprehension. Write *Have you washed the dishes?* on the board. Ask students whether they would use *ever*, *already*, or *yet* in this question and where they would put it. [*Ever* isn't likely because almost everyone has washed the dishes at some point in life; *already* and *yet* are both possible, but they take different positions in the sentence.] Practice with more verbs and phrases from the *Warm-up*.

7. Direct students to circle the correct words to complete the sentences. Ask volunteers to read the completed sentences aloud.

Answers	
1. ever	3. yet
2. ever	4. already

Guided Practice III
10–15 minutes

B Ask students to work individually to match the questions and answers and then compare their answers with a partner. Ask volunteer pairs to read their matching questions and answers aloud. Write the letter-number match on the board.

Answers	
1. d	3. b
2. c	4. a

MULTILEVEL STRATEGIES

Seat same-level students together for 2B.

• **Pre-level** Work with these students to help them recognize the difference between simple past and present perfect. Read each question aloud, and call on a volunteer for the answer. Discuss the tense of each answer.

• **On- and Higher-level** Direct these students to complete 2B and then ask and answer the questions with a partner. Have them write two or three original questions and answers with *ever*, *already*, and *yet*. Ask volunteers to read their questions and answers to the class.

C 1. Elicit the importance of accuracy. Tell students they will be building their accuracy in this task.

2. Organize students into groups. Demonstrate how to correct the sentence using the first example.

3. Have team members work together to correct the sentences. Circulate and monitor teamwork.

4. Project or write the corrected sentences on the board and have teams check their work.

5. Address questions and any issues you noted during your observation.

Answers
1. Marisol hasn't **ever** volunteered.
2. I haven't done my homework **yet**. I'll do it tonight.
3. Natasha went to the DMV **already**. She got her license last week.
4. Michael has **never** been to a job fair. Maybe he'll go next week.

3 Listen for the present perfect to determine the meaning

Guided Practice IV
10–15 minutes

🔊 **2-04** 1. Say: *We're going to listen to different people use the present perfect to ask and answer questions. You will hear the first speaker ask a question about volunteering and the second speaker answer. Circle the statement that has the same meaning as the second speaker's answer.*

2. Direct students to read the first set of statements. Then play the first exchange and have them circle the correct statement.

---

3. Elicit answers from the class. If students answered incorrectly, play the audio again, providing a listening clue (for example, *listen for has been* or *hasn't been*).

4. Repeat for numbers 2–6.

Answers	
1. a	4. b
2. a	5. a
3. b	6. b

4 Use the present perfect to talk about your life experience

Communicative Practice and Application
20–25 minutes

A 1. Direct students to work independently to complete the questions with their own ideas. Brainstorm several places for number 1 as an example.

2. Call on volunteers to share their sentences, correcting grammar as necessary. Establish the correct grammar for each sentence. *Have you ever read… Have you ever visited/used… Have you eaten…*

Possible Answers
1. Have you ever been to the Grand Canyon?
2. Have you ever read *The Old Man and the Sea*?
3. Have you ever been to the library?
4. Have you eaten lunch yet today?

B Direct students to work with a partner to write two more questions using the present perfect.

C 1. Have pairs merge to form teams of four. Model the exercise by "joining" one of the teams. Each pair takes a turn asking and answering questions while the class listens.

2. Check comprehension of the exercise. Ask: *Who asks questions?* [everyone] *Who answers questions?* [everyone]

3. Ask volunteers to share something interesting they learned about their classmates.

MULTILEVEL STRATEGIES

After 4C, provide more practice with *ever, yet,* and *already* for all levels.

• **Pre-level** Have these students use each sentence frame twice to write six sentences: *I have already _____ today. I haven't _____ yet this week. Have you ever _____?*

• **On-level** Have these students write one question with *ever, already,* and *yet*. Direct them to ask each other their questions and write their partners' short answers.

• **Higher-level** Have these students write one question with *ever, already,* and *yet*. Direct them to ask one follow-up question for each *yes/no* question. *When? Where? Why?* Direct them to take notes on their partners' answers.

Have volunteers from each group share their work with the class.

Evaluation
10–15 minutes

TEST YOURSELF

Ask students to write the sentences independently. Collect and correct their writing.

MULTILEVEL STRATEGIES

Target the *Test Yourself* to the level of your students.

• **Pre-level** Provide sentence frames for these students to complete.
1. _____ (name) hasn't ever read _____.
2. _____ (name) has been to _____.
3. _____ (name) has visited _____.
4. _____ (name) hasn't _____ yet today.

• **Higher-level** Have these students write eight sentences about their classmates.

EXTENSION ACTIVITY

Community Event Calendar

1. Provide students with a copy of a current community event calendar—for example, from the local library or from your community's parks and recreation department.

2. Seat students in mixed-level groups. Have the highest-level student in the group ask the rest questions about the calendar using *already* and *yet*: *Have the preschool classes started yet?* Direct the rest of the group to answer with short answers.

3. Discuss any events of interest on the calendar.

Lesson Overview

Lesson Notes

MULTILEVEL OBJECTIVES

Pre-, On-, and Higher-level: Talk about expressing interest in volunteering and listen for information about volunteering

LANGUAGE FOCUS

Grammar: Present perfect versus simple past (*He worked last night. He has worked here for two years.*)

Vocabulary: *Volunteer*

For vocabulary support, see this **Oxford Picture Dictionary** topic: Energy and the Environment, pages 224–225

STRATEGY FOCUS

Practice language to build on other's ideas.

READINESS CONNECTION

In this lesson, students verbally communicate about and practice how to express interest in volunteering.

PACING

To compress this lesson: Conduct *Discuss* as a whole-class activity.

To extend this lesson: Have students start a petition. (See end of lesson.)

And/or have students complete **Workbook 3 page 34** and **Multilevel Activities 3 Unit 5 page 63**.

CORRELATIONS

CCRS: SL.1.B (d.) Explain their own ideas and understanding in light of the discussion.

SL.2.B Determine the main ideas and supporting details of a text read aloud or information presented in diverse media and formats, including visually, quantitatively, and orally.

SL.4.B Report on a topic or text, tell a story, or recount an experience with appropriate facts and relevant, descriptive details, speaking clearly at an understandable pace.

SL.6.B Speak in complete sentences when appropriate to task and situation in order to provide requested detail or clarification.

R.7.B Use information gained from illustrations and the words in a text to demonstrate understanding of the text.

L.1.B (h.) Form and use the simple verb tenses. (l.) Produce simple, compound and complex sentences.

L.1.C (e.) Form and use the perfect verb tenses.

RF.2.A (g.) Isolate and pronounce initial, medial vowel, and final sounds (phonemes) in spoken single-syllable words.

RF.4.B (a.) Read grade-level text with purpose and understanding.

ELPS: 2. An ELL can participate in level-appropriate oral and written exchanges of information, ideas, and analyses, in various social and academic contexts, responding to peer, audience, or reader comments and questions. 9. An ELL can create clear and coherent level-appropriate speech and text.

Warm-up and Review
10–15 minutes (books closed)

Elicit some of the problems in the school and the community that the class talked about in Lesson 2. Write them on the board under the headings *Community* and *School*.

Introduction
5 minutes

1. Say: *In Lesson 2, we practiced writing emails to the school board. Whom do you write to if the problem is in your neighborhood?* Tell students that giving your time to help solve a problem in your community is called *volunteering*.

2. State the objective: *Today we're going to talk about how to express interest in volunteering.*

1 Learn ways to express interest in volunteering

Presentation I
10–20 minutes

 A 🔊 **2-05** 1. Direct students to look at the website. Ask: *How are these volunteers helping?*

2. Read the instructions aloud. Play the audio. Give students a minute to answer the question. Go over the answer as a class.

Answer
Complete a training session

Guided Practice I
20–25 minutes

 B 🔊 **2-05** 1. Read the instructions aloud. Play the audio. Ask students to listen for the answers to each question.

2. Ask students to compare their answers with a partner. Circulate and monitor to ensure students understand the audio.

Answers
1. Possible answers: helping during emergencies, setting up and staffing shelters, rescuing people, teaching community members how to prepare for weather emergencies, showing people how to prepare an emergency kit, telling people how they can make their homes safer
2. Teaching
3. An application and more information

C 🔊 **2-06** Read the instructions aloud. Explain that students are going to hear the audio one more time. They should write the words they hear to complete the sentences. Play the audio. Call on volunteers to elicit the answers.

Answers
1. I'm interested in
2. I'd love to
3. Sign me up

2 Practice your pronunciation

Pronunciation Extension
10–15 minutes

 A 🔊 **2-07** 1. Write: *I'm, I'd,* and *I'll* on the board. Say the sentence frames and ask students to repeat them. Underline *m, d,* and *ll.* Say: *Now we're going to focus on the* m, d, *and* l *sounds.*

2. Play the audio. Direct students to listen for the *m, d,* and *l* sounds.

B 🔊 **2-08** Play the audio. Have students work individually to write the missing words.

Answers	
1. I'd like to volunteer	4. I'm interested in
2. I'm putting together	5. I'd love
3. I'll help	

 C 🔊 **2-08** 1. Play the audio again. Have students check their answers to 2B. Call on volunteers to read the completed sentences aloud.

2. Ask students to take turns reading the sentences in 2B with a partner. Monitor and provide feedback.

3 Review the simple past and the present perfect

Presentation II and Guided Practice II
10–15 minutes

A 1. Introduce the new topic. Write a present perfect sentence and a simple past sentence on the board. *He has volunteered a lot. He volunteered last week.* Ask students to identify the verb and elicit the tense of each sentence. Ask: *Why is the second sentence past tense? In the first sentence, do we know when he volunteered?*

2. Read the information and the sample sentences in the chart and go over the *Grammar Note.* Ask volunteers to identify the time reference in each sentence. Establish that the simple past tense sentences give a specific time, while the present perfect sentences give a non-specific time.

3. Check comprehension of the grammar in the chart. Elicit a question and a short answer for each of the situations written on the board. *Has he volunteered a lot? Yes, he has. Did he volunteer last week? Yes, he did.*

Answers
last night, last month, for many years, before

B 1. Have students work individually to circle the verbs in the sentences. Go over the answers as a class.

2. Set a time limit (five minutes). Ask students to practice asking and answering the questions with several partners. Call on individuals to share their answers with the class.

Answers	
1. volunteered	3. hasn't gone
2. work	4. has been

4 Building conversational skills

Guided Practice III
15–20 minutes

A Direct students to look at the picture and skim the phone conversation in 4B. Have them work with partners to identify the purpose of the phone call. Elicit responses and ask: *How do you know?* or *Why do you say that?* to encourage students to state their reasoning.

Answers
Volunteering opportunities at a pet shelter. The caller asks if there are any volunteering opportunities at the shelter.

B **2-09** 1. Ask students to read the instructions and tell you what they are going to do [listen and read and respond to the question]. Play the audio and then elicit the answer to the question.

2. Ask students to read the conversation with a partner. Circulate and monitor pronunciation. Model and have students repeat difficult words or phrases.

3. Ask: *In what other situation could you use this conversation?* Point out a few phrases that are not specific to volunteering at an animal shelter. Ask volunteers to point out others.

Answer
She loves animals but can't have pets in her apartment.

Communicative Practice and Application I
15–20 minutes

C 1. Pair students and have them read the instructions silently. Check their comprehension of the exercise. Ask: *What are the two roles? Is the conversation at an animal shelter?*

2. Model and have students repeat the expressions in the *In Other Words* box in 4B. Explain that they should use these expressions in their conversations.

3. Draw a T-chart on the board. Label the left column *Receptionist* and the right column *Caller*. Elicit examples of what each person might say and make notes in the chart.

4. Set a time limit (three minutes). Have students act out the role-play. Call "time" and have students switch roles.

5. Ask three volunteer pairs to act out their role-play for the class. Tell students who are listening to make a simple table with four rows and three columns. Use the top row to label the columns *Location, Opportunities,* and *Preferences.* Have students take notes in the chart for each role-play.

MULTILEVEL STRATEGIES

For 4C, adapt the role-play to the level of your students.

• **Pre-level** Provide these students with a simplified role-play. *Receptionist: Linwood Senior Center. How can I help you? Caller: I'm interested in volunteering. Receptionist: Have you ever volunteered before? Caller: No, I haven't. Receptionist: I'll send you some materials.*

---

5 Focus on listening for details

Presentation III and Guided Practice IV
20–25 minutes

A 1. Read the questions and statement aloud and model a discussion with a volunteer. Ask: *Do you think there are many benefits to volunteering? Why? / Why not? I agree because… / I disagree because…*

2. Pair students and tell them to discuss their own answers to the questions. Circulate and monitor.

B Direct students to read the sentences before they listen to the interview. Ask what kind of information they'll be writing in the blanks. Ask volunteers for predictions. If students struggle, start by offering your own prediction: *I think we will hear that one of every four Americans volunteers for an organization.*

C 🔊 2-10 1. Play the audio. Ask students to listen and write the correct answers.

2. Pair students and have them compare answers. If a pair has different answers, have the class vote on the correct answer with a show of hands.

Answers	
1. four	4. making and serving food
2. Two-thirds	
3. fundraising	5. more likely

6 Discuss

Communicative Practice and Application II
15–20 minutes

A 1. Read the instructions aloud. Draw a sample chart on the board with space for activities on one side and skills on the other. Call on volunteers to read the sample sentences in 6A. Fill in the chart, writing *Tutoring children* and *Serving food* on the left and *Patient* and *Get along with people* on the right. Explain that students will make a chart like this one based on their own discussions.

2. Put students into teams of three and assign roles: manager, administrative assistant, and reporter. Verify students' understanding of the roles. Encourage students to use the phrases in the *Speaking Note* during their discussions.

3. Set a time limit for the discussions (ten minutes). Write the sentence frame from 6B on the board. Then circulate and monitor.

B Call "time." Ask the reporter for each team to report the results of the team's discussion using the sentence frame on the board.

Evaluation
5 minutes

TEST YOURSELF

1. Ask students to complete the checkboxes individually.

2. Tell students that you are going to read each of the items in the checklist aloud. If they are not at all confident with that skill, they should hold up a closed fist. If they are not very confident, they should hold up one finger. If they are somewhat confident, two fingers; confident, three fingers; very confident, four fingers. If they think they could teach the skill, they should hold up five fingers. Read each item in the checklist and identify students who may need further support.

EXTENSION ACTIVITY

Start a Petition

Explain that one way to work for change in a community is to start a petition. A petition is a request someone writes and asks others to sign in a show of support.

1. Put students into groups. Tell them to brainstorm ideas for a petition to change something at the school. Ask them to describe what they want in three or four sentences.

2. When they finish, tell them it's time to collect signatures. Each group should present its petition, and students should select which petitions they want to support and sign them.

3. Have students return to their groups, count their signatures, and determine which petition got the most signatures.

Lesson Overview

MULTILEVEL OBJECTIVES

Pre-, On-, and Higher-level: Read about and discuss reducing trash and protecting the environment

LANGUAGE FOCUS

Grammar: Adjectives *(Dirty water is unhealthy.)*

Vocabulary: *Environment, natural resources, pollution, litter*

For vocabulary support, see this **Oxford Picture Dictionary** topic: Energy and the Environment, pages 224-225

READINESS CONNECTION

In this lesson, students verbally communicate information about ways to protect the environment.

PACING

To compress this lesson: Conduct the word study in 2A as a whole-class activity.

To extend this lesson: Have students make predictions about the environment. (See end of lesson.)

And/or have students complete **Workbook 3 page 35** and **Multilevel Activities 3 Unit 5 pages 64–65**.

Lesson Notes

CORRELATIONS

CCRS: SL.1.B (a.) Come to discussions prepared, having read or studied required material; explicitly draw on that preparation and other information known about the topic to explore ideas under discussion. (b.) Follow agreed-upon rules for discussions. (c.) Ask questions to check understanding of information presented, stay on topic, and link their comments to the remarks of others. (d.) Explain their own ideas and understanding in light of the discussion.

SL.2.B Determine the main ideas and supporting details of a text read aloud or information presented in diverse media and formats, including visually, quantitatively, and orally.

R.1.B Ask and answer such questions as who, what, where, when, why, and how to demonstrate understanding of key details in a text.

R.2.A Identify the main topic and retell key details of a text.

R.6.B Identify the main purpose of a text, including what the author wants to answer, explain, or describe.

R.5.B Know and use various text features to locate key facts or information in a text efficiently.

R.7.C Interpret information presented visually, orally, or quantitatively and explain how the information contributes to an understanding of the text in which it appears.

L.1.B (h.) Form and use the simple verb tenses. (l.) Produce simple, compound and complex sentences.

L.4.B (b.) Determine the meaning of the new word formed when a known prefix is added to a known word. (e.) Use glossaries and beginning dictionaries, both print and digital, to determine or clarify the meaning of words and phrases.

RF.3.B (c.) Identify and know the meaning of the most common prefixes and derivational suffixes.

RF.4.B (a.) Read grade-level text with purpose and understanding.

ELPS: 1. An ELL can construct meaning from oral presentations and literary and informational text through level-appropriate listening, reading, and viewing. 3. An ELL can speak and write about level-appropriate complex literary and informational texts and topics.

Warm-up and Review
10–15 minutes (books closed)

Draw a cluster diagram on the board. Write *Nature* in the center circle. Ask students to brainstorm words they associate with nature. Categorize their words on the board into branches for water, land, plants, and animals.

Introduction
5 minutes

1. Use students' ideas from the *Warm-up* to talk about things that have changed in the past 100 years.

2. State the objective: *Today we're going to read about and discuss how to protect the environment.*

1 Read

Presentation
10–20 minutes

A Read the questions aloud. Use ideas from the *Introduction* to help guide discussion.

B Read the words and definitions. Elicit sample sentences for each word, or supply them if the students can't. Ask students to identify the natural resources that are on the board from the *Warm-up* (water, trees, etc.). Elicit other natural resources and examples of pollution. Ask students where they have seen "no littering" signs.

Pre-reading

C Read the instructions aloud. Have students answer the question individually and then check answers as a class. If any students answer incorrectly, ask them to support their answer using the bulleted headings. Establish the correct answer.

Answer
b. Earth Day is celebrated in many countries.

Guided Practice: While Reading
20–30 minutes

D 1. Ask students to read the article silently and answer the question.

2. Check answers as a class.

3. Check comprehension. Ask: *Where did Earth Day begin?* [the United States] *What were the people who started Earth Day worried about?* [pollution]

Possible Answers
collect litter, plant trees, teach about the environment, plan ways to take care of the earth

MULTILEVEL STRATEGIES
Adapt 1D to the level of your students.   • **Pre-level** Read the text aloud to these students as they follow along.   • **On- and Higher-level** Pair students and have them read the article aloud to each other, taking turns to read each paragraph.

Guided Practice: Rereading
10–15 minutes

E 1. Provide an opportunity for students to extract evidence from the text. Have students reread the article and underline any words or phrases that indicate the author's attitude toward Earth Day.

2. Pair students and tell them to compare the words they underlined and report anything they disagree on. Discuss and clarify as needed.

Answer
Positive; underlines will vary.

TIP
Have students go online to find out about Earth Day activities in your area. Decide which device(s) students will use and elicit search terms ("Earth Day" + your city).

F 1. Have students work individually to mark the answers *T* (true), *F* (false), and *NI* (no information). They should then write the line numbers where they found the true and false answers. Write the answers on the board.

2. Elicit and discuss any additional questions about the reading. You could introduce new questions for class discussion: *Which of the activities in the article create a cleaner Earth? What makes the three events in the article success stories?*

Answers
1. T, line 13   2. NI   3. F, line 14   4. T, lines 25–27   5. T, lines 28–32

MULTILEVEL STRATEGIES
For 1F, work with pre-level students.   • **Pre-level** Ask these students *yes/no* and short-answer information questions about the reading while other students are completing 1F. *Where did people pick up 700 bags of litter?* [the Ohio River] *Did they plant hundreds of trees in Canada?* [no—thousands] Have these students copy the answers to 1F from the board.

2 Word study

Guided Practice: Post-reading
10 minutes

 A 1. Direct students to look at the chart and identify the topic (the prefix *un-*). Have students read the chart.

2. Read the first two sentences in the chart and the examples for *clean* and *unclean*. Elicit sentences for the other words in the chart.

3. Have students repeat after you as you say each word with natural intonation, rhythm, and stress.

4. Direct students to complete the sentences and then compare answers with a partner. Read the correct answers and have students check their work.

Answers
1. clean
2. unclean, unsafe, and unhealthy
3. unhappy
4. important
5. healthy

B Direct students to work individually to write a sentence for each topic that includes the underlined word. Ask volunteers to write their sentences on the board. Have the rest of the class suggest grammar and spelling edits as needed.

3 Talk it over

Guided Practice
15–20 minutes

A Have students look at the graph and read the note and *Reader's Note*. Point out that they need to use the information from the graph and the note to complete the sentences and answer the questions. Set a time limit (ten minutes). Have students work in pairs to complete the task. Ask volunteers to share their answers with the class.

Answers
1. 2013
2. 1975
3. 19
4. 25
5. Americans recycled 34.3% of their trash in 2013
6. The average American throws away 4.4 pounds of trash every day. That means a family of four throws away 6,424 pounds of trash every year.

Communicative Practice
20 minutes

B Read the questions aloud. Set a time limit (ten minutes). Tell students to copy the chart in their notebooks and complete it with their answers to the questions.

C Ask volunteers to share their ideas with the class.

Application
5–10 minutes

BRING IT TO LIFE

Ask students to brainstorm about green improvements they could make in your school. Ask volunteers to share their ideas. Have the class choose one of the ideas and brainstorm a plan for putting it into action.

EXTENSION ACTIVITY

Make Environmental Predictions

1. Write several topics related to the environment on the board: *water, air, food production, energy.*

2. Put students into groups. Remind students that during the *Warm-up* they talked about how the environment is today compared to 100 years ago. Tell them that now they're going to think about 100 years in the future. Ask the groups to come up with predictions for each of the topics. Tell them to write sentences with *will. Water in the future will be cleaner/dirtier because _____.*

3. Have a reporter from each group share the group's ideas with the class.

AT WORK

Warm-up and Review
10–15 minutes (books closed)

Begin the lesson by exaggeratedly complaining about an imaginary problem in the staff room. Ask students for their suggestions on how to solve the issue. Discuss consequences for each solution.

Introduction
5 minutes

State the objective: *Today we're going to talk about problems and solutions in the workplace.*

Presentation
5 minutes

 2-11 Read the instructions aloud. Play the audio. Give students a minute to think about the question. Elicit responses from the class.

Answer
Problems in the office

Guided Practice
10–15 minutes

 2-11 Play the audio again. Direct students to listen for each problem and put a check next to any that they hear mentioned.

Answers
Checked: staff throwing away paper too dark in the stairwell

 2-11 Read the instructions aloud. Play the audio again, encouraging students to take notes in their notebooks. Set a time limit (five minutes) for students to discuss their answers with a partner. Circulate to monitor.

Answers
Problem: Some staff throwing away paper. Solution: Put recycling cans near the copier. Consequence: They might fill up quickly. Problem: It's too dark in the stairwell. Solution: Put in new, brighter lighting. Consequence: It will cost a lot.

Presentation and Communicative Practice
10 minutes

 1. Direct students' attention to the *Do/Say* chart and ask students to identify the lesson's soft skill [making suggestions]. Ask the class which column has examples of language [right] and which has examples of behaviors [left].

2. Say a phrase from the left column and act it out. Say it again and have the class act it out with you. Say it a third time and have the class act it out for you. To confirm understanding, combine phrases: *Make eye contact and lean toward me.*

3. Model the sentence frames from the right column using authentic intonation. Have students practice imitating your inflection.

4. Put students in teams of four and assign each team a question. Assign roles: manager, administrative assistant, researcher, and reporter. Researchers will ask you questions on behalf of the team. Verify understanding of the roles. Set a time limit (five minutes) and monitor.

5. Write sentence frames on the board that teams can use to summarize their response. *(Our team discussed the following question: _____ We decided _____ because _____.*

6. Call "time" and let reporters rehearse their report for one minute. Direct each reporter to present to three other teams.

Communicative Practice and Application
20–25 minutes

E 1. Direct students to work in pairs to match problems with suggestions and come up with further suggestions.

2. Invite volunteers to share their suggestions.

F 1. Have pairs merge to form teams of four. Tell students that they are going to be role-playing a staff meeting where they will suggest solutions to problems at work.

2. Direct groups to come up with three problems and three solutions. Each group should select a manager to run the meeting. The other three members should each choose a problem to bring up.

3. As students carry out the role-play, circulate and monitor. Provide global feedback once the activity ends.

TEAMWORK & LANGUAGE REVIEW

Lesson Overview

Lesson Notes

MULTILEVEL OBJECTIVES

Pre-, On-, and Higher-level: Review unit language

LANGUAGE FOCUS

Grammar: Present perfect questions and answers (*Have they called her yet? No, they haven't.*)

Vocabulary: Community and environment

For vocabulary support, see this **Oxford Picture Dictionary** topic: Civic Engagement, pages 142–143

READINESS CONNECTION

In this review, students work in a team to use the present perfect and discuss community resources and volunteering.

PACING

To extend this review: Have students complete **Workbook 3 page 36, Multilevel Activities 3 Unit 5 page 66, and Multilevel Grammar Exercises 3 Unit 5.**

CORRELATIONS

CCRS: SL.1.B (d.) Explain their own ideas and understanding in light of the discussion.

SL.2.B Determine the main ideas and supporting details of a text read aloud or information presented in diverse media and formats, including visually, quantitatively, and orally.

SL.4.B Report on a topic or text, tell a story, or recount an experience with appropriate facts and relevant, descriptive details, speaking clearly at an understandable pace.

SL.6.B Speak in complete sentences when appropriate to task and situation in order to provide requested detail or clarification.

R.2.A Identify the main topic and retell key details of a text.

L.1.B (h.) Form and use the simple verb tenses. (l.) Produce simple, compound and complex sentences.

L.1.C (e.) Form and use the perfect verb tenses.

RF.4.B (a.) Read grade-level text with purpose and understanding.

ELPS: 5. An ELL can conduct research and evaluate and communicate findings to answer questions or solve problems. 6. An ELL can analyze and critique the arguments of others orally and in writing.

Warm-up and Review
10–15 minutes (books closed)

1. Review *At Work* activity F.

2. Ask students to share the good, not-so-good, and interesting things that happened during the role-play. As students speak, write their responses in a chart on the board.

Introduction and Presentation
5 minutes

1. Pair students and direct them to look at the picture in their book. Ask them to describe what they see to their partner.

2. Ask volunteer pairs to share their ideas with the class.

Guided Practice
15–20 minutes

A 1. Group students and assign roles: manager, administrative assistant, researcher, and reporter. Explain that students are going to work with their groups to look at the picture and match the sentence parts. Verify students' understanding of the roles. Set a time limit (five minutes).

2. Call "time." Have reporters take turns giving their answers.

Answers	
1. e	4. c
2. f	5. a
3. d	6. b

B 1. Read the instructions aloud and have students work in the same teams from A to complete the task. Circulate and monitor.

2. Have students read their questions to the class and correct any mistakes.

Communicative Practice
30–40 minutes

C Have teams ask their questions to another team. Circulate and monitor.

D 1. Put students in groups of three to five and have them read the instructions silently. Check their comprehension of the exercise. Ask: *What are the roles? Where does the conversation take place?*

2. Model and have students repeat the expressions from Lesson 4, exercise 4B. Explain that they should use these expressions in their conversations.

3. Draw a T-chart on the board. Label the left column *Student* and the right column *Librarian*. Elicit examples of what each person might say and make notes in the chart.

4. Set a time limit (five minutes). Have students act out the role-play. Call "time" and have students switch roles.

E Have groups perform their role-plays from D for the class.

F 1. Have students walk around the room to conduct the interviews. To get students moving, tell them to interview four people who were not on their team for B.

2. Set a time limit (five minutes) to complete the exercise.

3. Tell students to make a note of their classmates' answers but not to worry about writing complete sentences.

MULTILEVEL STRATEGIES

Adapt the mixer in F to the level of your students.

• **Pre- and On-level** Pair these students and have them interview other pairs together.

• **Higher-level** Have these students ask an additional question and write all answers in complete sentences.

G 1. Call on individuals to report what they learned about their classmates. Keep a running tally on the board for each question, marking how many students have/have not helped with a neighborhood project, seen a problem in their neighborhood, or gone to a town or neighborhood meeting.

2. Have students work in small groups and use the class results on the board to make a poster. Display the posters in the classroom.

PROBLEM SOLVING
10–15 minutes

A 🔊 2-12 1. Ask: *Have you ever volunteered somewhere?* Tell students they will read a story about a woman who just moved into a new neighborhood and wants to volunteer. Direct students to read Paulina's story silently.

2. Ask: *How long has Paulina lived in Lake City? Why does she want to volunteer?*

3. Play the audio and have students read along silently.

B 1. Elicit answers to question 1. Come to a class consensus on the answer.

2. As a class, brainstorm places Paulina might go to answer question 2. Ask students if they know where to find these places in your area.

Answers
1. She wants to starting volunteering but doesn't know what to do.
2. Answers will vary.

Evaluation
20–25 minutes

To test students' understanding of the unit language and content, have them take the Unit 5 Test, available on the Teacher Resource Center.

6 What's Cooking?

Unit Overview

This unit explores recipes and cooking with a range of employability skills and contextualizes separable and inseparable verb structures and possessive pronouns.

KEY OBJECTIVES	
Lesson 1	Identify kitchen vocabulary
Lesson 2	Describe the steps to cook a favorite recipe
Lesson 3	Use separable phrasal verbs
Lesson 4	Express uncertainty
Lesson 5	Identify ways to protect yourself from food poisoning
At Work	Interrupt someone to ask a question
Teamwork & Language Review	Review unit language

UNIT FEATURES	
Academic Vocabulary	*sequencing, assistant*
Employability Skills	• Determine how much to tip in different situations • Use inferences to match pictures and words • Decide how much to tip • Work independently • Understand teamwork • Locate information • Communicate verbally • Listen actively • Use writing skills • Comprehend written material • Analyze information

Resources	**Class Audio** CD2, Tracks 13–23
	Workbook Unit 6, pages 37–43
	Teacher Resource Center
	   Multilevel Activities 3 Unit 6
	   Multilevel Grammar Exercises 3 Unit 6
	   Unit 6 Test
	Oxford Picture Dictionary Food Preparation and Safety, A Restaurant

LESSON **1** VOCABULARY

Lesson Overview	Lesson Notes

MULTILEVEL OBJECTIVES

On-level: Identify things in the kitchen and describe kitchen activities

Pre-level: Identify things in the kitchen and kitchen activities

Higher-level: Talk and write about the kitchen using words for utensils, foods, and cooking

LANGUAGE FOCUS

Grammar: *Is/are + -ing* (*She's peeling a carrot. The vegetables are steaming.*)

Vocabulary: Kitchen utensils, food items, and cooking

For vocabulary support, see this **Oxford Picture Dictionary** topic: Food Preparation and Safety, pages 76–77

STRATEGY FOCUS

Pool knowledge with team members to maximize vocabulary learning.

READINESS CONNECTION

In this lesson, students explore and communicate information about cooking.

PACING

To compress this lesson: Conduct 1E as a whole-class activity.

To extend this lesson: Have students learn more kitchen utensils. (See end of lesson.)

And/or have students complete **Workbook 3 page 37** and **Multilevel Activities 3 Unit 6 pages 68–69**.

CORRELATIONS

CCRS: SL.1.B (d.) Explain their own ideas and understanding in light of the discussion.

SL.2.B Determine the main ideas and supporting details of a text read aloud or information presented in diverse media and formats, including visually, quantitatively, and orally.

R.1.B Ask and answer such questions as who, what, where, when, why, and how to demonstrate understanding of key details in a text.

R.4.B Determine the meaning of general academic and domain-specific words and phrases in a text relevant to a topic or subject area.

L.1.B (b.) Explain the function of nouns, pronouns, verbs, adjectives, and adverbs in general and their functions in particular sentences. (l.) Produce simple, compound and complex sentences.

L.4.B (a.) Use sentence-level context as a clue to the meaning of a word or phrase. (e.) Use glossaries and beginning dictionaries, both print and digital, to determine or clarify the meaning of words and phrases.

RF.4.B (a.) Read grade-level text with purpose and understanding.

ELPS: 8. An ELL can determine the meaning of words and phrases in oral presentations and literary and informational text.

Warm-up and Review
10–15 minutes (books closed)

Write *Vegetables* on the board. Have volunteers come to the board and take turns writing the name of a vegetable. Allow them to help each other, but have a different student write each word. When the class runs out of ideas or you have at least ten words on the board, pronounce the words together and elicit any questions.

Introduction
3 minutes

1. Call on volunteers and ask if they eat one of the foods on the board. Ask how often they eat it and whether they cook it.

2. State the objective: *Today we're going to learn words for cooking.*

1 Identify kitchen vocabulary

Presentation I
15–20 minutes

 1. Write *Cooking* and *Utensils* on the board. Ask: *Do you think cooking is easy or hard? Is it relaxing or stressful? If you cook, do you use many utensils? What are the utensils you use the most?*

2. Read the instructions and the questions aloud. Put students in groups of three or four and have them take turns reading the paragraphs in the text to each other. Circulate and answer any questions about vocabulary. Have students work together to answer the questions based on the picture and the text.

Answers
1. seven
2. Possible answers: it hurts, there are always emergencies, health department can shut you down

B 1. Read the instructions aloud. Model the task by "thinking aloud" about the word *famous*: *TV chefs have many people watch them, so I think* famous *means that many people know about a person.*

2. Set a time limit (three minutes) and direct students to do the task individually and then compare their answers with a partner.

3. Have students share their partner's answers with the class.

Guided Practice I
20–25 minutes

C **2-13** 1. Direct students to look at the words in the picture in 1A. Elicit any words that students do not know and write them on the board. Ask volunteers to explain any of the words they know.

2. Direct students to look up any remaining unknown words in their dictionaries. Discuss those words in relation to the lesson.

3. Set a time limit (five minutes) and have students do the task individually.

4. Play the audio for students to check their answers.

Answers	
1. chop, knife	5. pot
2. pouring	6. utensils
3. stir	7. plate
4. cook, pan	8. glass

D **2-13** 1. To prepare students for listening, say: *Now we're going to listen again to the sentences using the words from the picture in 1A. As you listen, make a note of the pieces of kitchen equipment you hear.*

2. Play the audio and have students do the task.

3. Check answers. Play the audio again, stopping after each sentence. Have volunteers say what kitchen equipment is mentioned in the sentence.

Answer
Six

MULTILEVEL STRATEGIES

After the group comprehension check in 1D, call on volunteers and tailor your questions to the level of your students.

- **Pre-level** Ask *or* questions. *Do you chop or stir with a spoon?* [stir]

- **On-level** Ask information questions. *What can you do with a knife?* [chop]

- **Higher-level** Ask these students to compare the picture with their own kitchen. *What things do you have in your own kitchen? How is this kitchen different from yours?*

Communicative Practice and Application I
10–15 minutes

 1. Read the instructions aloud and model by asking and answering the first question with a volunteer.

2. Set a time limit (five minutes). Direct students to ask and answer the questions with a partner. Ask volunteer pairs to repeat one of their conversations for the class.

2 Learn more kitchen vocabulary

Presentation II
10–20 minutes

 1. Direct students to look at the pictures. Introduce the new topic: *Now we're going to learn more words for cooking.*

2. Say and have students repeat each of the words. After each word, elicit other foods or items that one can peel, steam, grate, and so on.

3. Read the sample sentences aloud. Have pairs take turns practicing making statements. Circulate and monitor.

4. Ask students about their cooking habits. *How do you cook broccoli?*

Guided Practice II
10–15 minutes

 1. Read the information in the *Need help?* box aloud. Provide this example, being sure to stress the *-er* ending: *I teach, so I am a teacher.* Hold up a stapler. *What's this? What does it do?* [staple] Point to a pencil sharpener. *What does that do?* [sharpen] *What is it?*

2. Have students work individually to do the task. Ask volunteers to read the completed sentences aloud.

Answers	
1. A peeler	4. A grater
2. A steamer	5. A mixer
3. A beater	6. A slicer

Communicative Practice and Application II
15–20 minutes

 1. If students will use the Internet for this task, establish what device(s) they'll use: a class computer, tablets, or smartphones. Alternatively, print information from the Internet before class and distribute to groups.

2. Write the information types from 2C on the board. Explain that students will work in teams to research and report on this information. Ask: *Which search terms or questions can you use to find the information you need?* ["essential kitchen tools," "inexpensive/budget" + "kitchen tools" + city name] *How will you record the information you find?* [table, checklist, index cards] Remind students to bookmark or record sites so they can find or cite them in the future.

3. Group students and assign roles: manager, administrative assistant, IT support, and reporter. Verify students' understanding of the roles.

4. Give managers the time limit for researching the questions (ten minutes). Direct the IT support to begin the online research or pick up the printed materials for each team. Direct the recorder to record information for the team using a table, a checklist, or index cards.

5. Give a two-minute warning. Call "time."

6. Direct teams to help their administrative assistant record the team's findings. Direct the reporter to use the recorded information to report the team's findings to the class or another team.

TIP

When setting up task-based activities, verify that students understand their roles using physical commands. For example: *If you report on your team's work, stand up* [reporter]. *If you keep the team on task, point to the clock* [manager]. *If you write the team's responses, raise your hand* [administrative assistant]. *If you help the team research, hold up your smartphone/tablet* [IT support].

Evaluation
10–15 minutes

TEST YOURSELF

1. Read the instructions aloud and model the task with a volunteer.

2. Have pairs do the activity. Circulate and monitor.

Target the *Test Yourself* to the level of your students.

• **Pre-level** Have these students do the activity the first time with the option to look in their books as they guess. Then have them do the activity a second time without looking at their books as they guess.

• **Higher-level** Challenge these students to compete with each other to see who can guess ten of the words in the shortest period of time.

TIP

To provide further practice of the vocabulary:

1. Direct students to look up a recipe of something they want to make on the Internet and make a list of all the equipment that they will need to make the dish.

2. Ask volunteers to share with the class any new equipment words they learned.

EXTENSION ACTIVITY

More Kitchen Utensils

Learn more words for utensils.

1. Direct students to look at pictures of kitchen utensils in *The Oxford Picture Dictionary* or another picture dictionary. Ask them to make one list of utensils they have and another of utensils they don't have but want.

2. Elicit items from their "don't have but want" list. Ask students if there are any utensils in their kitchens that they never use.

Lesson Overview	Lesson Notes

MULTILEVEL OBJECTIVES

On- and Higher-level: Analyze, write, and edit the steps to cook a favorite recipe

Pre-level: Read and write about a favorite recipe

LANGUAGE FOCUS

Grammar: Past tense (*He cooked a big meal for everyone.*)

Vocabulary: Cooking, ingredients, and food words

For vocabulary support, see this **Oxford Picture Dictionary** topic: Food Preparation and Safety, pages 76–77

STRATEGY FOCUS

Use sequencing words to describe the order of events.

READINESS CONNECTION

In this lesson, students listen actively, read, and write about favorite dishes and recipes.

PACING

To compress this lesson: Assign the *Test Yourself* and/or 3C for homework.

To extend this lesson: Have students pantomime cooking a recipe. (See end of lesson.)

And/or have students complete **Workbook 3 page 38** and **Multilevel Activities 3 Unit 6 page 70**.

CORRELATIONS

CCRS: SL.1.B (d.) Explain their own ideas and understanding in light of the discussion.

SL.2.B Determine the main ideas and supporting details of a text read aloud or information presented in diverse media and formats, including visually, quantitatively, and orally.

R.1.B Ask and answer such questions as who, what, where, when, why, and how to demonstrate understanding of key details in a text.

R.2.A Identify the main topic and retell key details of a text.

R.7.B Use information gained from illustrations and the words in a text to demonstrate understanding of the text.

W.3.B Write narratives in which they recount a well-elaborated event or short sequence of events, include details to describe actions, thoughts, and feelings, use temporal words to signal event order, and provide a sense of closure.

W.4.B Produce writing in which the development and organization are appropriate to task and purpose.

W.5.B With guidance and support from peers and others, develop and strengthen writing as needed by planning, revising and editing.

W.6.B With guidance and support, use technology to produce and publish writing (using keyboarding skills) as well as to interact and collaborate with others.

L.1.B (c.) Form and use the past tense of frequently occurring irregular verbs. (l.) Produce simple, compound and complex sentences.

L.2.B (c.) use commas in greetings and closings of letters.

RF.4.B (a.) Read grade-level text with purpose and understanding.

ELPS: 6. An ELL can analyze and critique the arguments of others orally and in writing. 9. An ELL can create clear and coherent level-appropriate speech and text.

Warm-up and Review
10–15 minutes (books closed)

Review cooking words. Write cooking directions for particular food items on slips of paper and pass them out to volunteers. Have students use gestures and/or draw on the board to help the class guess what is on their slips. Ask the class member who guesses correctly to write the words on the board. Possible cooking directions: *Peel a carrot, steam broccoli, grate cheese, mix cookie dough, slice an onion, chop a tomato, pour a cup of tea.*

Introduction
5 minutes

1. Say: *In Lesson 1, we talked about cooking. Today we're going to talk about favorite dishes and recipes.* Write *Recipe* on the board and elicit a definition or an example from a volunteer. Have students repeat the word. Elicit the number of syllables. (You may need to distinguish *recipe* from *receipt*.)

2. State the objective: *Today we're going to read and write about our favorite dishes and recipes.*

1 Prepare to write

Presentation
20–25 minutes

A 1. Build students' schema by asking questions about the picture and the title. Ask: *Who is in the picture? Where are they? What are they going to do?*

2. Give students one minute to tell a partner their responses to questions 1 and 2. Elicit responses from the class. Encourage students to respond to each other's ideas. After one student speaks, ask other students their opinions. *Do you agree or disagree with what he/ she just said? Why?*

B 1. Ask: *When you were a child, who was the best cook in your home?* Read the title of the article. Point out that *dish* can mean prepared food as well as a plate or bowl. Introduce the model article and its purpose: *Now we're going to read an article about the writer's childhood. As you read, look for the purpose of the article: Why is he writing?* Have students read the article silently.

2. Check comprehension. Ask: *Who was the best cook in the writer's family?* [Papi] *What did the writer and Papi do together?* [cooked a big meal on Sundays]

3. Play the audio. Have students read along silently.

Guided Practice I
10 minutes

C 1. Have students work independently to underline the answers to the questions in the text.

2. Point out the *Writer's Note* and read the information aloud. Say: *When we explain how to do something, such as the steps in a recipe, it is good to use sequence words. They tell the order of when things happen.*

3. Ask students to annotate the information they underlined with the phrases "most important" for question 1 and "ending" for question 3. For question 2, they should annotate with numbers in the order the steps happen. Have pairs compare answers. Have volunteers call out answers and write them on the board for the class to check.

Answers
1. Answers will vary.
2. Steps
1. Cook the chicken with onions, garlic, and a few chilies.
2. Chop up tomatoes and vegetables and stir everything together.
3. Put in a tablespoon of lemon juice.
4. Add fruit juice.
5. Mix everything together.
6. Pour everything over rice.
3. By telling us that they'd like to make the recipe for their children someday.

MULTILEVEL STRATEGIES

Seat pre-level students together for 1C.

• **Pre-level** While other students are working on 1C, ask these students *yes/no* and *or* questions about the reading. *Was the writer's grandfather or grandmother the best cook in the house? Did the writer help him? Was his favorite dish chicken soup? Is the secret ingredient fruit juice?* Allow these students to copy the answers to 1C from the board.

2 Plan and write

Guided Practice II
15–20 minutes

A
1. Read question 1. Answer the question with your own ideas and have students share their ideas with the class.

2. Read question 2. Model creating a sequence diagram by saying your favorite dish and organizing the steps to make it on the board. Give students time to think of their own special dish and create their own sequence diagrams. Have students share their diagrams with partners.

B
Read through the template. Elicit ideas that could go in each paragraph. Have students write their texts individually.

> ### MULTILEVEL STRATEGIES
>
> Adapt 2B to the level of your students.
>
> • **Pre-level** Work with these students to go through the template sentence by sentence. Elicit students' ideas and write them on the board. Have students complete the text with the ideas from the board.
>
> • **Higher-level** Ask these students to include one or two additional sentences about if and when they make the dish now.

3 Get feedback and revise

Guided Practice III
5 minutes

A
Direct students to check their writing using the editing checklist. Tell them to read each item in the list and check their papers before moving on to the next item. Explain that students should not edit their writing at this stage. They should just use the checklist to check their work and mark any areas they want to revise.

Communicative Practice
15 minutes

B
1. Read the instructions and the sample sentences aloud. Emphasize to students that they are responding to their partners' work, not correcting it.

2. Use the article in 1B to model the exercise. *Your story about your Papi's chicken and rice made me miss my grandfather.*

3. Direct students to exchange papers with a partner and follow the instructions.

C
Allow students time to edit and revise their writing as necessary, using the editing checklist from 3A and their partner's feedback from 3B. If necessary, students could complete this task as homework.

> ### TIP
>
> After students have written and spoken about their favorite recipes, have them look up the recipes on the Internet. Tell students to type the names of the dishes and the word *recipe* into a search engine. Have them print out the recipes they find. Ask them to look for any differences between the online recipe ingredients and instructions and those of their families.
>
> If you don't have Internet access in class, elicit the names of several dishes that your students make at home. Bring in recipes for those dishes and have students compare them with their family recipes.

Application and Evaluation
10 minutes

TEST YOURSELF

1. Review the instructions aloud. Assign a time limit (five minutes) and have students work independently.

2. Before collecting student work, invite two or three volunteers to share their sentences. Ask students to raise their hands if they wrote similar answers.

> ### MULTILEVEL STRATEGIES
>
> Adapt the *Test Yourself* to the level of your students.
>
> • **Pre-level** Write questions for these students to answer in writing. *Was today's writing assignment difficult or easy? Do you enjoy writing stories about your own life and experiences?*

> ### EXTENSION ACTIVITY
>
> **Pantomime Cooking**
>
> Have students practice giving recipe directions. Review cooking verbs and write them on the board. Pair students. Tell Partner A to give instructions about how to cook something. Tell Partner B to pantomime these instructions. (You can simplify this by providing Partner A with a recipe to read aloud.) Circulate and monitor. Provide feedback as needed.

Lesson Overview	Lesson Notes

MULTILEVEL OBJECTIVES

On- and Higher-level: Use separable phrasal verbs to talk about food and cooking and listen for meaning in statements with phrasal verbs

Pre-level: Recognize and use phrasal verbs to write sentences

LANGUAGE FOCUS

Grammar: Phrasal verbs (*She put the eggs in the bowl.*)

Vocabulary: *Put in, figure out, write down, turn on, turn off, pick up, leave out, look for, come over, get on, get off, look after*

For vocabulary support, see this **Oxford Picture Dictionary** topic: Food Preparation and Safety, pages 76–77

STRATEGY FOCUS

Learn which phrasal verbs are separable and which are inseparable.

READINESS CONNECTION

In this lesson, students practice using phrasal verbs to talk about cooking and other activities.

PACING

To compress this lesson: Conduct 1B and/or 1C as a whole-class activity.

To extend this lesson: Have students ask and answer questions with phrasal verbs. (See end of lesson.)

And/or have students complete **Workbook 3 pages 39–40, Multilevel Activities 3 Unit 6 pages 71–72,** and **Multilevel Grammar Exercises 3 Unit 6.**

CORRELATIONS

CCRS: SL.2.B Determine the main ideas and supporting details of a text read aloud or information presented in diverse media and formats, including visually, quantitatively, and orally.

SL.6.B Speak in complete sentences when appropriate to task and situation in order to provide requested detail or clarification.

R.1.B Ask and answer such questions as who, what, where, when, why, and how to demonstrate understanding of key details in a text.

L.1.B (b.) Explain the function of nouns, pronouns, verbs, adjectives, and adverbs in general and their functions in particular sentences. (l.) Produce simple, compound and complex sentences.

RF.4.B (a.) Read grade-level text with purpose and understanding.

ELPS: 7. An ELL can adapt language choices to purpose, task, and audience when speaking and writing. 10. An ELL can demonstrate command of the conventions of standard English to communicate in level-appropriate speech and writing.

Warm-up and Review
10–15 minutes (books closed)

Play a "noun-verb" game with a light ball or a wadded-up piece of paper. Name a food as you toss the ball to someone. That person needs to add a cooking verb. For example, if you say *onion*, the student can say *chop the onion* or *fry the onion*. The student with the ball now names another food and tosses the ball to someone else. The rules of the game are: 1. The words must go together (not *pour the onion*). 2. No food or cooking words should be repeated.

Introduction
5–10 minutes

1. Say: *When I'm cooking, I chop up the vegetables, turn on the stove, and put away the dishes.* Chop up, turn on, *and* put away *are two-word verbs called phrasal verbs.*

2. State the objective: *Today we're going to use phrasal verbs to talk about cooking and other activities.*

1 Use separable phrasal verbs

Presentation I
20–25 minutes

 1. Direct students to look at the picture. Ask: *Where are the people? What are they doing? What is their reaction to the cake? Are they enjoying it?*

2. Read the instructions aloud. Before students read the story, ask them to call out any ingredients that usually go into a cake. Write the ingredients on the board for students to refer to for question 4. Ask students to read the story silently and answer the questions.

3. Read the first question aloud. Call on a volunteer for the answer. Ask the volunteer where in the story he or she found the answer. Read the rest of the questions aloud, calling on a different volunteer for each answer.

Answers
sugar
1. He wrote down the recipe.
2. She put eggs and flour in a bowl.
3. Ming turned the oven on.
4. They left the sugar out.

B 1. Demonstrate how to read the grammar chart.

2. Direct students to underline the six phrasal verbs in the story in 1A. Write them on the board.

3. Ask: *How many parts do these verbs have? What part of speech is the second word? What does* separable *mean? Do the phrasal verbs mean the same thing as just the verb: Does* left *mean the same as* left out*? What tense are the phrasal verbs in?* Ask students to give the present tense form of each phrasal verb.

4. Pair students and direct them to read the chart aloud to each other. Then read the chart aloud as students follow along.

5. Assess students' understanding of the chart. Write *sugar* on the board. Say: *Can I say* They left out the sugar*? Can I say* They left the sugar out*?* Write those sentences on the board. Ask: *What if I want to use the pronoun* it*? Where can I use* it*?* Write: *They left it out.* Say one of the other phrasal verbs in the chart and a noun, for example, *put in, milk.* Elicit three sentences. *They put in the milk. They put the milk in. They put it in.* Repeat with each of the phrasal verbs in the story.

Answers	
write down	turn on
put in	take out
pour in	figure out

Guided Practice I
10–15 minutes

 1. Tell students they will collaborate to complete the description of the grammar point. Model collaboration by working with the class to complete the first sentence. Encourage students to look at 1A and 1B to help them determine the correct words.

2. Pair students and have them work together to complete the description.

3. Project or write the completed definition on the board and have pairs verify the accuracy of their responses. Ask volunteers which sentences confused them and discuss.

Answers
verbs
can
object

Guided Practice II
10–15 minutes

 1. Read the instructions aloud. Model the questions and answers with a volunteer.

2. Ask students to practice the questions and answers with their partners using the information in the chart.

3. Have pairs merge to form teams of four and then take turns demonstrating questions and answers. Set a time limit (four minutes) and monitor the practice, identifying any issues.

4. Provide clarification or feedback to the whole class as needed.

MULTILEVEL STRATEGIES

For 1D, group same-level students together.

• **Pre-level** Sit with these students and elicit whether they will substitute *it* or *them* in each sentence in the chart. Then ask and answer the questions together.

• **Higher-level** Challenge these students to look at only the story and not the chart and ask and answer questions using separable phrasal verbs.

2 Use inseparable phrasal verbs

Presentation II
15–20 minutes

1. Introduce the new topic: *When I use the phrasal verb* turn on, *I can put the noun between the two words or at the end. For example:* I turn on the oven. I turn the oven on. *But some phrasal verbs are inseparable. I can't put any words between the verb and the preposition.*

2. Read the sentences in the chart aloud. Read the *Grammar Note.* Say and have students repeat the verbs listed there.

3. Direct students to look at the pictures. Ask a question about each picture. *What is he doing?* [He's getting on a bus.]

4. Have students work individually to complete the sentences. Go over the answers as a class.

Answers	
1. get over	3. get off
2. look after	4. get on

TIP

Write verbs on one side of the board: *pick, turn, put, leave, look, come, write, figure, get.* Write prepositions on the other side of the board: *in, on, off, after, up, over, out, down.* Call on volunteers to say a sentence combining two of the words to make a phrasal verb. As they say each verb, write it on the board. Continue until all of the combinations have been exhausted.

MULTILEVEL STRATEGIES

After 2A, provide more practice with phrasal verbs. Adapt the practice to the level of your students. Group same-level students together and provide each group with a sheet of butcher paper.

• **Pre-level** Tell these students to work together to write sentences with as many of the phrasal verbs from pages 88 and 89 as they can.

• **On-level** Tell these students to use five phrasal verbs from pages 88 and/or 89 in a story. Tell them that they will need to write more than five sentences so that their stories make sense and are not just a list of sentences.

• **Higher-level** Give these students the same instructions as the on-level students but tell them to incorporate eight phrasal verbs into their stories.

Have all groups post their papers on the wall when they finish. Ask a reporter from each group to read the group's writing aloud.

Guided Practice III
15–20 minutes

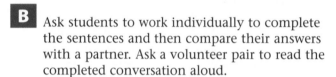

Ask students to work individually to complete the sentences and then compare their answers with a partner. Ask a volunteer pair to read the completed conversation aloud.

Answers
get on, Get off, Look for

C

1. Elicit the importance of accuracy. Tell students they will be building their accuracy in this task.

2. Organize students into groups. Demonstrate how to correct the sentence using the first example.

3. Have team members work together to correct the sentences. Circulate and monitor teamwork.

4. Project or write the corrected sentences on the board and have teams check their work.

5. Address questions and any issues you noted during your observation.

Answers
1. **Get off** the bus on Sixth Street.
2. The recipe was hard to **figure out**.
3. A babysitter will **look after my** children.
4. **Turn the oven** to 450 degrees.

3 Listen for phrasal verbs

Guided Practice IV
15–20 minutes

🔊 **2-15** 1. Say: *Now we're going to listen to people using phrasal verbs in sentences. Circle the sentence that has the same meaning as the sentence you hear.*

2. Direct students to read the first set of statements and then play the first sentence and have them circle the correct statement.

3. Elicit answers from the class. If students answered incorrectly, play the audio again, providing a listening clue (for example, *listen for the phrasal verb*).

4. Repeat for numbers 2–6.

Answers	
1. a	4. a
2. b	5. b
3. b	6. b

TIP
Have students listen to the sentences again and write down the phrasal verb in each sentence. Then have them write a new sentence using that phrasal verb. Have volunteers share their sentences with the class. Correct as needed.

4 Use phrasal verbs to talk about your life experience

Communicative Practice and Application
20–25 minutes

A 1. Group students and have them discuss dishes they can make.

2. Tell them to work individually to write the steps they take to prepare their recipe.

3. Have each group choose one recipe and send a volunteer to write the steps to make the recipe on the board.

B 1. Direct students to look at the chart. Elicit any questions about the verbs. Copy the chart onto the board.

2. Put students in groups of three. Read the instructions aloud. To model the exercise, call on volunteers to be Partner A and Partner B. Play the role of Partner C and work with the Partner B volunteer to check off the verbs in the chart.

3. Check comprehension of the exercise. Ask: *Who is Partner A? What are you going to do?*

4. Direct students to switch roles until all three students have played all three roles.

C 1. Provide students with a letter (*A*, *B*, or *C*) that corresponds to their individual roles and ask them to form a new group with students who have the same letter.

2. Have students tell their new groups about one of the recipes they heard about in their original groups.

3. Call on volunteers to share which recipes they thought sounded most delicious.

Evaluation
10–15 minutes

TEST YOURSELF

Ask students to write the sentences independently. Collect and correct their writing.

MULTILEVEL STRATEGIES

Target the *Test Yourself* to the level of your students.

• **Pre-level** Ask these students to write three sentences using their charts from 4B. *Put in the eggs. Chop up the nuts. Turn on the oven.*

• **Higher-level** Have these students write about three of the recipes they discussed.

EXTENSION ACTIVITY

Phrasal Verbs Q&A

1. Write all of the phrasal verbs from this unit on cards or slips of paper. Make enough slips so that each student in the class can have one.

2. Distribute the phrasal verbs. Direct the students to think of a question using the phrasal verbs. Elicit some sample questions.

3. Have the students stand up and find a partner from another part of the room. Tell them to take turns asking and answering their questions. Then have them switch papers and find a new partner. They can invent a new question or use the one their first partner asked them.

4. Participate in the game and provide feedback.

Lesson Overview

MULTILEVEL OBJECTIVES

Pre-, On-, and Higher-level: Describe a meal and listen for information about a restaurant order and tipping

LANGUAGE FOCUS

Grammar: Possessive pronouns (*How was yours?*)

Vocabulary: Menu and restaurant ordering words

For vocabulary support, see these **Oxford Picture Dictionary** topics: Food Preparation and Safety, pages 76–77; A Restaurant, pages 82–83

STRATEGY FOCUS

Use a possessive pronoun in place of a noun but not with another noun.

READINESS CONNECTION

In this lesson, students verbally communicate about and practice how to order a meal, ask for information in a restaurant, and use possessive pronouns to talk about meals.

PACING

To compress this lesson: Do 6A as a class activity and skip 6B.

To extend this lesson: Have students do a restaurant problem role-play. (See end of lesson.)

And/or have students complete **Workbook 3 page 41** and **Multilevel Activities 3 Unit 6 page 73**.

Lesson Notes

CORRELATIONS

CCRS: SL.1.B (d.) Explain their own ideas and understanding in light of the discussion.

SL.2.B Determine the main ideas and supporting details of a text read aloud or information presented in diverse media and formats, including visually, quantitatively, and orally.

SL.4.B Report on a topic or text, tell a story, or recount an experience with appropriate facts and relevant, descriptive details, speaking clearly at an understandable pace.

SL.6.B Speak in complete sentences when appropriate to task and situation in order to provide requested detail or clarification.

R.7.B Use information gained from illustrations (e.g., maps, photographs) and the words in a text to demonstrate understanding of the text (e.g., where, when, why, and how key events occur).

L.1.A (d.) Use personal, possessive, and indefinite pronouns.

L.1.B (h.) Form and use the simple verb tenses. (l.) Produce simple, compound and complex sentences.

L.3.B (b.) Recognize and observe differences between the conventions of spoken and written standard English.

RF.4.B (a.) Read grade-level text with purpose and understanding.

ELPS: 2. An ELL can participate in level-appropriate oral and written exchanges of information, ideas, and analyses, in various social and academic contexts, responding to peer, audience, or reader comments and questions. 9. An ELL can create clear and coherent level-appropriate speech and text.

Warm-up and Review
5–10 minutes (books closed)

Ask students what they like to order when they go to a restaurant. Tell them about your favorite restaurant and what you like to eat there.

Introduction
3 minutes

1. Say: *Sometimes when we order in a restaurant, we want to ask for more information about the food.*

2. State the objective: *Today we're going to learn how to order a meal, ask for information in a restaurant, and use possessive pronouns to talk about meals.*

1 Learn ways to order a meal

Presentation I
10 minutes

 A 🔊 **2-16** 1. Direct students to look at the picture. Ask: *Where are they?* [a restaurant]

2. Read the instructions aloud. Play the audio. Give students a minute to answer the question. Go over the answer as a class.

Answer
Four

Guided Practice I
20–25 minutes

B 🔊 **2-16** 1. Read the instructions and the questions aloud. Play the audio. Ask students to listen for the answer to each question.

2. Ask students to compare their answers with a partner. Circulate and monitor to ensure students understand the audio.

Answers
1. Spicy meat and tomato sauce
2. Salt. The customer is trying to eat less salt.
3. On the back of the menu

C 🔊 **2-17** Read the instructions aloud. Explain that students are going to hear the audio one more time. They should write the words they hear to complete the sentences. Play the audio. Call on volunteers to elicit the answers.

Answers
1. question about the
2. come with
3. I'd like to order

2 Practice your pronunciation

Pronunciation Extension
10–15 minutes

A 🔊 **2-18** 1. Write *First, chop up the nuts* on the board. Say the sentence and ask students to repeat it. Draw a line to connect the final *p* in *chop* with the *u* in *up*. Say: *Now we're going to focus on the way sounds link in phrasal verbs.*

2. Play the audio. Direct students to listen for the linking in *try out, turn over,* and *leave out.* Ask students to repeat the phrases.

B 🔊 **2-19** Play the audio. Have students work individually to complete the phrasal verbs.

Answers	
1. look for	4. turn on
2. turn off	5. go over
3. get off	6. get on

C 🔊 **2-19** 1. Play the audio again. Have students check their answers to 2B. Call on volunteers to read the completed verbs aloud.

2. Ask students to take turns reading the phrasal verbs in 2B with a partner. Monitor and provide feedback.

3 Use possessive pronouns

Presentation II and Guided Practice II
15–20 minutes

 A 1. Introduce the new topic: *Now we're going to talk about possessive pronouns. What is a pronoun?* Write: *Tom went to the restaurant. He ordered fish.* Underline *He.* Say: *Who is he?* [Tom] He *replaces* Tom *in this sentence. Pronouns replace nouns.*

2. Read the words in the chart and go over the *Grammar Notes.* Say: *Adjectives are used with nouns. They describe nouns. Pronouns replace nouns. Pronouns and nouns can't be used together.*

3. Read and have students repeat the adjectives and nouns in the chart.

4. Check comprehension. Say sentences with blanks. Clap to indicate the blanks. Elicit a choral response. *This is your lunch. This lunch is _____. Their order is ready. This order is _____. My plate is on the table. This plate is _____.*

5. Have students work in pairs to do the task. Circulate and monitor.

> **TIP**
>
> For more practice with possessives after 3A, put students in groups. Have students place items they own on the table. They can use anything recognizable—pencil cases, erasers, keys, glasses, candy, cell phone, etc. Have each group member pick up an item that doesn't belong to him/her and ask another student: *Is this yours?* or *Is this your pencil case?* The other student can respond with: *Yes, it's mine* or *No, it's not mine. I think it's his/hers.*

B
1. Read the instructions aloud. Have students do the task individually. Go over answers as a class.

2. Set a time limit (five minutes). Ask students to practice asking and answering the questions with several partners. Call on individuals to share their answers with the class.

Answers
1. Mine, yours
2. your
3. our
4. Mine, yours

4 Building conversation skills

Guided Practice III
15–20 minutes

A
Direct students to look at the picture and skim the conversation in 4B. Have them work with partners to identify where the people are. Elicit responses and ask: *How do you know?* or *Why do you say that?* to encourage students to state their reasoning.

Answers
In a restaurant; answers will vary.

B
🔊 **2-20** 1. Play the audio and have students read along silently.

2. Ask students to read the conversation with a partner. Circulate and monitor pronunciation. Model and have students repeat difficult words or phrases.

3. Ask: *In what other situations could you use this conversation?* Point out a few phrases that are not specific to ordering in a restaurant. Ask volunteers to point out others.

Communicative Practice and Application I
20–25 minutes

C
1. Pair students and have them read the instructions silently. Check their comprehension of the exercise. Ask: *What are the two roles? Where does the conversation take place?*

2. Model and have students repeat the expressions in the *In Other Words* box in 4B. Explain that they should use these expressions in their conversations.

3. Draw a T-chart on the board. Label the left column *Customer* and the right column *Server*. Elicit examples of what each person might say and make notes in the chart.

4. Set a time limit (three minutes). Have students act out the role-play. Call "time" and have students switch roles.

5. Ask three volunteer pairs to act out their role-play for the class. Tell students who are listening to make a simple table with four rows and two columns. Use the top row to label the columns *Suggestions* and *Orders*. Have students take notes in the chart for each role-play.

Seat same-level students together.

• **Pre-level** Work with these students and guide them in writing their new conversation, or provide a simplified conversation for these students to practice.

A: What is a chili dog?

B: It's a hot dog with a spicy meat sauce.

A: Do you recommend it?

B: Yes. I like it very much.

• **Higher-level** You can challenge students to add other menu items (use the menu from 4B if you did the *Tip* activity) to the conversation for the server to suggest.

5 Focus on listening for details

Presentation III and Guided Practice IV
20–25 minutes

A 1. Read the questions and statement aloud and model a discussion with a volunteer. Ask: *Do you think every server should get a tip? Why? / Why not? I agree because… / I disagree because…*

2. Pair students and tell them to discuss their own answers to the questions. Circulate and monitor.

TIP

To ensure that students are listening to each other, ask them to take brief notes of other students' responses and have them repeat back: *So, you said...*

B Direct students to read the sentences before they listen to the interview. Ask what kind of information they'll be writing in the blanks. Ask volunteers for predictions. If students struggle, start by offering your own prediction: *I think we will hear people's opinions about tipping.*

C ◄))2-21 1. Play the audio. Ask students to listen and write the correct answers.

2. Pair students and have them compare answers. If a pair has different answers, have the class vote on the correct answer with a show of hands.

Answers	
1. tip, much	4. low
2. percent	5. bad, leave
3. minimum, hour	

6 Discuss

Communicative Practice and Application II
15–20 minutes

A 1. Read the instructions aloud. Draw a sample chart on the board, with space for job titles on one side and skills on the other. Call on volunteers to read the sample conversation in 6A. Fill in the chart, writing *Server* on the left and *Be patient* and *Be polite* on the right. Explain that students will make a chart like this one based on their own discussions.

2. Put students into teams of three and assign roles: manager, administrative assistant, and reporter. Verify students' understanding of the roles. Encourage students to use the phrases in the *Speaking Note* during their discussions.

3. Set a time limit for the discussions (ten minutes). Write the sentence frame from 6B on the board. Then circulate and monitor.

B Call "time." Ask the reporter for each team to report the results of the team's discussion using the sentence frame on the board.

Evaluation
5 minutes

TEST YOURSELF

1. Ask students to complete the checkboxes individually.

2. Tell students that you are going to read each of the items in the checklist aloud. If they are not at all confident with that skill, they should hold up a closed fist. If they are not very confident, they should hold up one finger. If they are somewhat confident, two fingers; confident, three fingers; very confident, four fingers. If they think they could teach the skill, they should hold up five fingers. Read each item in the checklist and identify students who may need further support.

EXTENSION ACTIVITY

Restaurant Problem Role-play

Practice telling a restaurant server about a problem.

1. Have students brainstorm problems that sometimes occur with restaurant food— for example, food is cold, food is under/overcooked, part of order didn't arrive, wrong item. Write the problems on the board. Write something polite to say in each situation.

2. Have students role-play a customer telling a server about a problem with the food.

Lesson Overview

MULTILEVEL OBJECTIVES

Pre-, On-, and Higher-level: Read about and discuss safe food preparation

LANGUAGE FOCUS

Grammar: Imperatives

Vocabulary: *Bacteria, food poisoning, leftovers, throw out, expiration date, perishable, staple*

For vocabulary support, see this **Oxford Picture Dictionary** topic: Food Preparation and Safety, pages 76–77

STRATEGY FOCUS

Learn that imperatives communicate the importance of the information in a text and tone communicates the author's purpose.

READINESS CONNECTION

In this lesson, students verbally communicate information about food safety.

PACING

To compress this lesson: Assign 1F and/or 1G for homework.

To extend this lesson: Have students make food safety posters. (See end of lesson.)

And/or have students complete **Workbook 3 page 42** and **Multilevel Activities 3 Unit 6 pages 74–75**.

Lesson Notes

CORRELATIONS

CCRS: SL.1.B (a.) Come to discussions prepared, having read or studied required material; explicitly draw on that preparation and other information known about the topic to explore ideas under discussion. (b.) Follow agreed-upon rules for discussions. (c.) Ask questions to check understanding of information presented, stay on topic, and link their comments to the remarks of others. (d.) Explain their own ideas and understanding in light of the discussion.

SL.2.B Determine the main ideas and supporting details of a text read aloud or information presented in diverse media and formats, including visually, quantitatively, and orally.

R.1.B Ask and answer such questions as who, what, where, when, why, and how to demonstrate understanding of key details in a text.

R.2.A Identify the main topic and retell key details of a text.

R.5.B Know and use various text features to locate key facts or information in a text efficiently.

R.7.C Interpret information presented visually, orally, or quantitatively and explain how the information contributes to an understanding of the text in which it appears.

L.1.B (h.) Form and use the simple verb tenses. (l.) Produce simple, compound and complex sentences.

L.4.B (e.) Use glossaries and beginning dictionaries, both print and digital, to determine or clarify the meaning of words and phrases.

RF.4.B (a.) Read grade-level text with purpose and understanding.

ELPS: 1. An ELL can construct meaning from oral presentations and literary and informational text through level-appropriate listening, reading, and viewing. 3. An ELL can speak and write about level-appropriate complex literary and informational texts and topics.

Warm-up and Review
10–15 minutes (books closed)

Review food names. Write *Meat, Fish, Poultry*, and *Dairy* on the board. Ask volunteers to take turns writing food names in each category until the class runs out of ideas or you have several items in each category.

Introduction
10 minutes

1. Ask students about the food on the board from the *Warm-up. How often do you eat chicken? How do you prepare it? Why do you have to be careful when preparing chicken? What other foods do you need to be careful with how you handle and prepare them?*

2. State the objective: *We have been talking about how we prepare foods. Today we're going to talk about food safety.*

1 Read

Presentation
10–20 minutes

A Read the questions aloud. Ask students what is happening in the picture. Use ideas from the *Introduction* to help guide discussion.

B Read the words and definitions. Elicit sample sentences for each word, or supply them if the students can't. Ask students to identify how each of the words relates to food safety.

Pre-reading

C Read the instructions aloud and confirm that students understand where the headings are. Have students answer the question individually and then check answers as a class. If any students answer incorrectly, ask them to support their answer using the headings. Establish the correct answer.

Answer
b. Various ways to prevent food poisoning

Guided Practice: While Reading
20–30 minutes

D 1. Direct students' attention to the first *Reader's Note* and read the information aloud. Read the second *Reader's Note* aloud. Direct students to make annotations in the text as they read. Ask students to read the article silently and answer the question.

2. Check answers as a class. Ask volunteers to share what they annotated in the text.

3. Check comprehension. Ask: *What should you clean counters with?* [hot, soapy water] *Is the same temperature safe for every kind of food?* [no] *Why should you separate uncooked beef and chicken?* [bacteria can spread from food to food]

Possible Answers
Clean your hands, counters, and dishes. Cook food long enough to kill bacteria. Separate uncooked meat from fruits and vegetables. Refrigerate leftovers. Keep your refrigerator set at 40°F or less. Check the "use by" dates on food packages.

TIP

Print out the reading. Make sample annotations and hand out copies to students. Alternatively, if you have an overhead projector, project the reading and read the text aloud, stopping to make sample annotations as appropriate.

MULTILEVEL STRATEGIES

Adapt 1D to the level of your students.

• **Pre-level** Provide these students with a summary of the reading. *There are five important steps to safe eating. 1. Wash your hands and clean your dishes well. 2. Cook foods well. Look at a "safe temperatures" chart to see how long you need to cook them. 3. Separate uncooked meat from fruits and vegetables. 4. Keep food cold in the refrigerator. 5. Check the expiration dates on food. If the date has passed, throw the food away.* Direct these students to read the summary while other students are reading 1D.

Guided Practice: Rereading
20–25 minutes

 1. Provide an opportunity for students to extract evidence from the text. Have students reread the article and underline the action words the writer uses to give information about food safety.

2. Pair students and tell them to compare the words they underlined and report anything they disagree on. Discuss and clarify as needed.

Possible Answers
Wash, dry, clean, cook, separate, refrigerate, keep, check

F

1. Have students work individually to mark the answers *T* (true), *F* (false), and *NI* (no information). They should then write the line numbers where they found the true and false answers. Write the answers on the board.

2. Elicit and discuss any additional questions about the reading. You could introduce new questions for class discussion: *Have you followed any of the advice in the article? What is the hardest piece of advice to follow? What is the easiest?*

Answers
1. F, lines 3–8
2. T, lines 24–25
3. F, line 34
4. F, line 37
5. F, lines 40–42

G

Have students do the task individually and then compare answers with a partner. Go over answers as a class.

Answers	
1. soap, water	5. eggs
2. thermometer	6. throw away
3. 160° F	7. Expiration
4. Bacteria	

2 Talk it over

Guided Practice: Post-reading
15–20 minutes

 A

Have students look at the chart and read the information below it. Point out that they need to use the information from the chart and text to complete the sentences and answer the question. Set a time limit (ten minutes). Have students work in pairs to complete the task. Ask volunteers to share their answers with the class.

Answers
1. One week
2. 12–16
3. Four
4. 6–12 months

Communicative Practice
15–20 minutes

B Read the instructions aloud. Set a time limit (ten minutes). Allow students to think and then write their ideas in the chart in their books or draw a new chart in their notebooks.

C While students are doing the activity in 2B, write the chart on the board. Have pairs share their answers with the class and write them in the chart. Have students add any new ideas to their charts.

Application
15–20 minutes

BRING IT TO LIFE

Elicit items that the students might look at. Have students choose the three items they will look at in the market.

Warm-up and Review
10–15 minutes (books closed)

Begin the lesson by explaining that you work in a kitchen. The chef has left food on the stove and is talking to another cook, and the food has started to burn. Ask students for suggestions on how to get the chef's attention.

Introduction
5 minutes

1. Write *Excuse me* on the board. Ask volunteers to say situations when you need to interrupt someone and what other words and phrases they use.

2. State the objective: *Today we're going to talk about how to interrupt someone.*

Presentation
5 minutes

 2-22 Read the instructions aloud. Play the audio. Give students a minute to think about the question. Elicit responses from the class.

Answer
A customer at a restaurant is trying to order food, but the waiter is busy.

Guided Practice
10–15 minutes

 2-22 1. Read the instructions aloud. Play the audio and have students count how many times the customer tries to get the waiter's attention.

2. To check answers, play the audio again and have students raise their hands each time the customer interrupts.

Answer
Four

 2-22 Play the audio again. Direct students to listen for each time the customer interrupts and put a check next to any sentences or phrases that they hear mentioned.

Answers
Checked:
Excuse me, are you busy?
Do you have a moment?
Excuse me for interrupting, but...
Is this a good time?

Presentation and Communicative Practice
15–20 minutes

 1. Direct students' attention to the *Do/Say* chart and ask students to identify the lesson's soft skill [interrupting someone to ask a question]. Ask the class which column has examples of behaviors [left] and which has examples of language [right].

2. As a class, brainstorm ways to complete the second sentence in the right column. Write students' ideas on the board.

3. Model the sentences from the right column using authentic intonation. Have students practice imitating your inflection.

4. Put students in teams of four and assign each team a question. Assign roles: manager, administrative assistant, researcher, and reporter. Researchers will ask you questions on behalf of the team. Verify understanding of the roles. Set a time limit (five minutes) and monitor.

5. Write sentence frames on the board that teams can use to summarize their response. (*Our team discussed the following question: _____ We decided _____ because _____.*)

6. Call "time" and let reporters rehearse their report for one minute. Direct each reporter to present to three other teams.

Communicative Practice and Application
10–15 minutes

E 1. Tell students that they are going to work in pairs and practice interrupting using the sentences in D. Model the conversation with a volunteer.

2. Direct pairs to take turns doing each role.

3. As students carry out the conversation, circulate and monitor. Provide global feedback once the activity ends.

Lesson Overview

MULTILEVEL OBJECTIVES

Pre-, On-, and Higher-level: Review unit language

LANGUAGE FOCUS

Grammar: Phrasal verbs

Vocabulary: Words and phrases for ordering in a restaurant and interrupting

For vocabulary support, see this **Oxford Picture Dictionary** unit: A Restaurant, pages 82–83

READINESS CONNECTION

In this review, students work in a team to use phrasal verbs to talk about shopping and ordering in a restaurant.

PACING

To extend this review: Have students complete **Workbook 3 page 43**, **Multilevel Activities 3 page 76**, and **Multilevel Grammar Exercises 3 Unit 6**.

Lesson Notes

CORRELATIONS

CCRS: SL.1.B (d.) Explain their own ideas and understanding in light of the discussion.

SL.2.B Determine the main ideas and supporting details of a text read aloud or information presented in diverse media and formats, including visually, quantitatively, and orally.

SL.4.B Report on a topic or text, tell a story, or recount an experience with appropriate facts and relevant, descriptive details, speaking clearly at an understandable pace.

SL.6.B Speak in complete sentences when appropriate to task and situation in order to provide requested detail or clarification.

R.1.B Ask and answer such questions as who, what, where, when, why, and how to demonstrate understanding of key details in a text.

R.2.A Identify the main topic and retell key details of a text.

L.1.B (h.) Form and use the simple verb tenses. (l.) Produce simple, compound and complex sentences.

L.1.C (d.) Use modal auxiliaries to convey various conditions.

L.2.B (c.) Use commas in greetings and closings of letters.

RF.4.B (a.) Read grade-level text with purpose and understanding.

ELPS: 5. An ELL can conduct research and evaluate and communicate findings to answer questions or solve problems. 6. An ELL can analyze and critique the arguments of others orally and in writing.

Warm-up and Review
10–15 minutes (books closed)

1. Review *At Work* activity E.

2. Ask students to share the good, not-so-good, and interesting things that happened during the conversation. As students speak, write their responses in a chart on the board.

Introduction and Presentation
5 minutes

1. Pair students and direct them to look at the picture in their book. Ask them to describe what they see to their partner.

2. Ask volunteer pairs to share their ideas with the class.

Guided Practice
15–20 minutes

A 1. Read the instructions aloud and do the first item with the class.

2. Set a time limit (five minutes) for individuals to complete the task. Check answers as a class.

Answers	
1. Mira	5. Andy
2. Monica	6. Jose
3. Susan	7. Daniel
4. Greg	8. Nora

B 1. Read the instructions aloud and have students work in teams to complete the task. Circulate and monitor.

2. Check answers as a class.

Answers	
1. Check out	5. put in
2. pick out	6. pick up
3. get on	7. look into
4. call back	8. try on

Communicative Practice
30–45 minutes

C 1. Put students in groups of three or four and have them read the instructions silently. Check their comprehension of the exercise. Ask: *What are the roles? Where does the conversation take place?*

2. If necessary, review the expressions in the *In Other Words* box from Lesson 4, exercise 4B. Explain that they should use these expressions in their conversations. Model the sample conversation with a volunteer.

3. Draw a T-chart on the board. Label the left column *Customer* and the right column *Server.* Elicit examples of what each person might say and make notes in the chart.

4. Set a time limit (three minutes). Have students act out the role-play. Call "time" and have students switch roles.

D Have groups perform their role-plays from C for the class.

E 1. Read the instructions and have students copy the chart into their notebooks. Set a time limit (ten minutes) and have students do the task.

2. While students are interviewing their classmates, draw the chart on the board. Call on individuals to report what they learned about their classmates. Keep a running tally on the board for each statement, marking how many students agree or disagree with each one.

F 1. Use your tally for statement 1 to create a bar graph on the board. Instruct students to draw bar graphs for statements 2 and 3 in their notebooks. Circulate and answer any questions.

2. Ask volunteers to report the results of their interviews using the sentence frame.

PROBLEM SOLVING
10–15 minutes

A **2-23** 1. Ask: *Do you ever send food back in a restaurant? Is it easy or difficult to tell your server that you don't like the food?* Tell students they will read a story about a couple who had a bad meal in a restaurant. Direct students to read Dora and Jorge's story silently.

2. Ask: *What is the special occasion? Was everything about their meal bad?*

3. Play the audio and have students read along silently.

B 1. Elicit answers to question 1. Guide students to a class consensus on the answer.

2. As a class, brainstorm answers to question 2. Ask students if they know someone who has this problem and has overcome it or what they have done themselves to overcome the same problem.

Answers
1. Their meal was terrible, but their server was very nice. They don't know if they should leave a tip.
2. Answers will vary.

C Read the instructions and the note template. Have students do the task individually. Ask volunteers to read their notes to the class.

Evaluation
20–25 minutes

To test students' understanding of the unit language and content, have them take the Unit 6 Test, available on the Teacher Resource Center.

UNIT

7 Money Wise

Unit Overview

This unit explores banking and money management with a range of employability skills and contextualizes structures with real conditionals and time clauses to discuss future events.

KEY OBJECTIVES	
Lesson 1	Identify bank vocabulary
Lesson 2	Identify ways to reach your financial goals
Lesson 3	Use real conditionals to talk about ways to save money
Lesson 4	Ask about a problem
Lesson 5	Identify ways to protect yourself against identity theft
At Work	Disagree with someone
Teamwork & Language Review	Review unit language

UNIT FEATURES	
Academic Vocabulary	*financial, security, transfer, credit, identity, equipped, professional, removal*
Employability Skills	• Decide why it's important to save money • Decide how to avoid identity theft • Decide whether to get a credit card • Work independently • Understand teamwork • Locate information • Communicate verbally • Listen actively • Use writing skills • Comprehend written material • Analyze information

Resources	**Class Audio** CD2 Tracks 24–34
	Workbook Unit 7, pages 44–50
	Teacher Resource Center
	    Multilevel Activities 3 Unit 7
	    Multilevel Grammar Exercises 3 Unit 7
	    Unit 7 Test
	Oxford Picture Dictionary The Bank, Shopping, Crime

Lesson Overview	Lesson Notes

MULTILEVEL OBJECTIVES

On-level: Identify bank activities and employees and describe banking services

Pre-level: Identify bank activities, employees, and services

Higher-level: Talk and write about banking using words for activities, employees, and services

LANGUAGE FOCUS

Grammar: Questions with *can* (*How can I avoid bouncing checks?*)

Vocabulary: Bank employees and services, banking activities

For vocabulary support, see this **Oxford Picture Dictionary** topic: The Bank, page 134

STRATEGY FOCUS

Pool knowledge with team members to maximize vocabulary learning.

READINESS CONNECTION

In this lesson, students work in a team to learn words for bank activities, bank employees, and bank services.

PACING

To compress this lesson: Conduct 1B and 1C as a whole-class activity.

To extend this lesson: Have students compare banks. (See end of lesson.)

And/or have students complete **Workbook 3 page 44** and **Multilevel Activities 3 Unit 7 pages 78–79**.

CORRELATIONS

CCRS: SL.1.B (d.) Explain their own ideas and understanding in light of the discussion.

SL.2.B Determine the main ideas and supporting details of a text read aloud or information presented in diverse media and formats, including visually, quantitatively, and orally.

SL.4.B Report on a topic or text, tell a story, or recount an experience with appropriate facts and relevant, descriptive details, speaking clearly at an understandable pace.

R.1.B Ask and answer such questions as who, what, where, when, why, and how to demonstrate understanding of key details in a text.

R.5.B Know and use various text features to locate key facts or information in a text efficiently.

R.7.C Interpret information presented visually, orally, or quantitatively and explain how the information contributes to an understanding of the text in which it appears.

W.7.A Participate in shared research and writing projects.

L.1.B (l.) Produce simple, compound and complex sentences.

L.2.B (k.) Consult reference materials, including beginning dictionaries, as needed to check and correct spellings.

L.4.B (e.) Use glossaries and beginning dictionaries, both print and digital, to determine or clarify the meaning of words and phrases.

RF.4.B (a.) Read grade-level text with purpose and understanding.

ELPS: 8. An ELL can determine the meaning of words and phrases in oral presentations and literary and informational text.

Warm-up and Review
10–15 minutes (books closed)

Write *Money doesn't grow on trees, Money makes the world go around*, and *Time is money* on the board. Elicit students' ideas about what the expressions may mean. Ask if they have expressions in their languages with similar meanings. Explain that in this unit, they will be talking about money and banking.

Introduction
3 minutes

1. Ask: *Where do most people keep their money? From where do you borrow money when you want to buy a house?*

2. State the objective: *Today we're going to learn words for bank activities, bank employees, and bank services.*

1 Identify banking vocabulary

Presentation I
20–25 minutes

A 1. Write *Financial services* on the board and elicit one example from the whole class. Have students work together to brainstorm in a group. Make a list on the board of the services your students identify.

2. Have students identify the most essential service. Elicit ideas and put a checkmark next to the services students feel are essential, encouraging them to explain their reasons.

B 1. Direct students to look at the picture. Ask: *Where is this? Does it look the same as the one you use?*

2. Set a time limit (ten minutes). Have pairs do the task. Do not check the answers as a class yet.

Answers
10 accounts manager
7 accounts services desk
5 loan officer
9 make a deposit
2 desk teller
3 make a withdrawal
4 apply for a loan
1 get a cashier's check
8 open an account
6 cash a check

C 1. To prepare students for listening, say: *We're going to listen to information about banking. As you listen, look at the picture and check your answers.*

2. Play the audio and have students check their answers. Go over the answers as a class and answer any questions about vocabulary.

> To confirm students' understanding of the vocabulary, ask questions about their own banking experiences: *Do you use an ATM or talk to a desk teller? Have you ever applied for a loan? When do you need a cashier's check? How do you cash a check? When you make a withdrawal, do you put money in the bank or take money out? Who do you talk to when you need a car loan?*

Guided Practice I
10–15 minutes

D 1. Model the conversation with a volunteer. Model it again using other information from 1B.

2. Set a time limit (three minutes). Direct students to practice with a partner.

3. Call on volunteers to present one of their conversations for the class.

2 Learn about banking services

Presentation II
10–20 minutes

A 1. Direct students to look at the bank's website. Introduce the new topic: *Now we're going to talk about the services that a bank offers.*

2. Read the questions aloud and allow students to look through the website. Elicit any words, accounts, services, or tips that students do not know and write them on the board. Ask volunteers to explain any of the words they know.

3. Direct students to look up any remaining unknown words in their dictionaries. Discuss those words in relation to the lesson.

4. Go through each kind of account and service and elicit examples and definitions from students. *What's the difference between a savings account and a checking account? What is a joint account?*

5. Check comprehension of the website. Ask: *What happens if I write a check and I don't have enough money in my account?* [Your check bounces.] *What is it called when my employer sends my paycheck right to my bank account?* [direct deposit]

Guided Practice II
10–15 minutes

B 1. Read the instructions and the questions aloud.

2. Model a conversation with a volunteer. Model it again using a different question.

3. Set a time limit (three minutes). Direct students to practice with a partner.

4. Call on volunteers to present their conversations for each of the questions. Confirm answers as a class.

Answers
1. Click on "Direct Deposit"
2. Click on "Online Banking"
3. Click on "Transfer Money"
4. Click on "Bye-Bye Bounced Checks"

Communicative Practice and Application
25–30 minutes

C 1. If students will use the Internet for this task, establish what device(s) they'll use: a class computer, tablets, or smartphones. Alternatively, print information from the Internet before class and distribute to groups.

2. Explain that students will work in teams to research and report on this information. Ask: *Which search terms or questions can you use to find the information you need?* ["banking jobs" + "desk teller" + "responsibilities," "education," "salary"] *How will you record the information you find?* [table, checklist, index cards] Remind students to bookmark or record sites so they can find or cite them in the future.

3. Group students and assign roles: manager, administrative assistant, IT support, and reporter. Verify students' understanding of the roles.

4. Give managers the time limit for researching the question (ten minutes). Direct the IT support to begin the online research or pick up the printed materials for each team. Direct the recorder to record information for the team using a table, a checklist, or index cards.

5. Give a two-minute warning. Call "time."

D 1. Copy the sentence stems and frames on the board.

2. Direct teams to help their administrative assistant use the sentence stems and frames to record the team's findings. Direct the reporter to use the recorded information to report the team's findings to the class.

Evaluation
10–15 minutes (books closed)

TEST YOURSELF

1. Make a three-column chart on the board with the headings *Banking, Bank employees*, and *Bank services*. Have students close their books and give you an example for each column.

2. Have students copy the chart into their notebooks.

3. Give students five to ten minutes to test themselves by writing the words they recall from the lesson.

4. Call "time" and have students check their spelling in a dictionary. Circulate and monitor students' progress.

5. Direct students to share their work with a partner and add additional words to their charts.

EXTENSION ACTIVITY

Compare Banks

Bring in copies of two different bank brochures. Put students in groups and give each group the two brochures. Direct the students to look for differences between the two banks. Do they advertise different services? Do they have different operating hours? Do the brochures have the information you would want to know when choosing a bank? Have reporters share their groups' conclusions.

Lesson Overview	Lesson Notes
MULTILEVEL OBJECTIVES	
On- and Higher-level: Analyze, write, and edit a financial plan **Pre-level:** Read and write about financial planning	
LANGUAGE FOCUS	
Grammar: *I'm hoping, I'm going* (*I'm hoping to buy a new car. I'm going to save money.*) **Vocabulary:** Business-letter vocabulary, job-skills vocabulary, *colon* For vocabulary support, see this **Oxford Picture Dictionary** topic: The Bank, page 134	
STRATEGY FOCUS	
Use linking words *because* and *since* to connect statements and reasons.	
READINESS CONNECTION	
In this lesson, students listen actively, read, and write about financial planning and goals.	
PACING	
To compress this lesson: Assign the *Test Yourself* and/or 3C for homework. **To extend this lesson:** Have students talk about money mistakes. (See end of lesson.) And/or have students complete **Workbook 3 page 45** and **Multilevel Activities 3 Unit 7 page 80**.	

CORRELATIONS

CCRS: SL.1.B (d.) Explain their own ideas and understanding in light of the discussion.

SL.2.B Determine the main ideas and supporting details of a text read aloud or information presented in diverse media and formats, including visually, quantitatively, and orally.

R.1.B Ask and answer such questions as who, what, where, when, why, and how to demonstrate understanding of key details in a text.

R.2.A Identify the main topic and retell key details of a text.

R.7.B Use information gained from illustrations and the words in a text to demonstrate understanding of the text.

W.2.A Write informative/explanatory texts in which they name a topic, supply some facts about the topic, and provide some sense of closure.

W.4.B Produce writing in which the development and organization are appropriate to task and purpose.

W.5.B With guidance and support from peers and others, develop and strengthen writing as needed by planning, revising and editing.

L.1.B (l.) Produce simple, compound and complex sentences.

L.1.C (c.) Form and use the progressive verb tenses. (f.) Use verb tense to convey various times, sequences, states, and conditions.

L.2.C (a.) Use correct capitalization.

RF.4.B (a.) Read grade-level text with purpose and understanding.

ELPS: 6. An ELL can analyze and critique the arguments of others orally and in writing. 9. An ELL can create clear and coherent level-appropriate speech and text.

Warm-up and Review
10–15 minutes (books closed)

Ask: *What do you want to buy in the future?* As students give you ideas, write them on the board in categories: *Furniture, Appliances, Electronics, Transportation, Recreation.* Ask students to brainstorm other items that fit into each category. Leave these words on the board to help students with their 2B writing assignment.

Introduction
5 minutes

1. Ask: *When you want to buy something and you don't have enough money for it, what do you do?*

2. State the objective: *Today we're going to read and write about financial planning and goals.*

1 Prepare to write

Presentation
20–25 minutes

 1. Give students fifteen seconds to scan the blog post. Build students' schema by asking questions about the picture. Ask: *Where is the woman? Who is she talking to?*

2. Give students one minute to tell a partner their responses to questions 1 and 2. Elicit responses from the class. Encourage students to respond to each other's ideas. After one student speaks, ask other students their opinions. *Do you agree or disagree with what he/she just said? Why?*

Answers
1. A car
2. Learn to save money, don't buy unnecessary things, use coupons

B 1. Introduce the model blog post and its purpose: *Now we're going to read a blog post. As you read, look for the purpose of the blog post: Why is she writing?* Have students read the blog post silently.

2. Check comprehension. Ask: *What is Kim and her husband's problem?* [Their car is old, needs repairs, and uses too much gas.] *What are they doing now to solve the problem?* [saving money for a new car] *How is her husband getting to work?* [He is driving with a co-worker.] *How does Kim save money at the supermarket?* [She uses coupons.] *What is different about a new car?* [It is safer.]

3. Play the audio. Have students read along silently.

Guided Practice I
10 minutes

C 1. Have students work independently to answer the questions.

2. Point out the first *Writer's Note.* Have students find the sentences in the blog post that use *since* and *because.* Then have volunteers say which statements and reasons are being connected.

3. Point out the second *Writer's Note.* Ask students to identify the purpose of each paragraph of the blog post.

4. Have pairs compare answers. Have volunteers call out answers and write them on the board for the class to check answers.

Answers
1. A new car
2. Sharing rides to work, making lunch at home, using coupons at the grocery store
3. It won't be easy, but it's possible to reach her goal.

MULTILEVEL STRATEGIES

For 1C, challenge on- and higher-level students while working with pre-level students.

• **Pre-level** While other students are working on 1C, ask these students *yes/no* and *or* questions about the reading. *Does her husband drive to work alone? Do they buy lunch or bring it from home? Will they save money with a new car?* Give students time to copy the answers to 1C from the board.

• **On- and Higher-level** Write this question on the board for these students to answer after they finish 1C: *What are other ways that Kim and her husband could save money?* After allowing students to work individually to answer the question, have volunteers share their ideas. Write the ideas on the board for students to refer to for 2B.

2 Plan and write

Guided Practice II
15–20 minutes

 1. Read the questions aloud. Elicit students' answers.

2. Demonstrate how to create a cluster diagram by drawing a circle and writing *Save money to buy* in the center. Draw "spokes" with circles at the end and ask volunteers for one or two answers to fill them in. Have students create their own cluster diagram of things people want to buy and another one for ways to save money. Have students share their diagrams with partners.

3. Ask volunteers to share their diagrams with the class.

MULTILEVEL STRATEGIES

Adapt 2A to the level of your students.

• **Pre-level** Work with these students to brainstorm answers to the questions in 2A. Give students time to answer in complete sentences before moving on to the next question.

• **On- and Higher-level** Challenge these students to write actual estimates of how much they could save every week by doing each of their money-saving ideas.

B Read through the financial plan template in 2A. Elicit ideas that could go in each paragraph. Have students write their plans individually.

MULTILEVEL STRATEGIES

Adapt 2B to the level of your students.

• **Pre-level** Work with these students to write a group financial plan. Read through the template. At each blank, stop and elicit completions. Decide as a group what to write. Have these learners copy the group plan into their notebooks.

• **Higher-level** Ask these students to include one additional sentence that explains why they are saving for the item.

3 Get feedback and revise

Guided Practice III
5 minutes

 Direct students to check their writing using the editing checklist. Tell them to read each item in the list and check their papers before moving on to the next item. Explain that students should not edit their writing at this stage. They should just use the checklist to check their work and mark any areas they want to revise.

Communicative Practice
15 minutes

B 1. Read the instructions and the sample sentences aloud. Emphasize to students that they are responding to their partners' work, not correcting it.

2. Use the blog post in 1B to model the exercise. *Your money-saving ideas are clearly written, especially the first one.*

3. Direct students to exchange papers with a partner and follow the instructions.

C Allow students time to edit and revise their writing as necessary, using the editing checklist from 3A and their partner's feedback from 3B. If necessary, students could complete this task as homework.

TIP

Students may be interested in more information about saving money. Provide them with website addresses of free money-saving ideas.

Application and Evaluation
10 minutes

TEST YOURSELF

1. Review the instructions aloud. Assign a time limit (five minutes) and have students work independently.

2. Before collecting student work, invite two or three volunteers to share their sentences. Ask students to raise their hands if they wrote similar answers.

MULTILEVEL STRATEGIES

Adapt the *Test Yourself* to the level of your students.

• **Pre-level** Write questions for these students to answer in writing. *Was today's writing assignment difficult or easy? Did writing this plan help you organize your thoughts about saving money?*

EXTENSION ACTIVITY

Talk about Money Mistakes

1. Say: *Some people have trouble saving money because of bad spending habits. What do they do wrong?*

2. Ask students to brainstorm several answers to your question. Call on volunteers to share their ideas.

3. Have a class discussion about common bad-spending habits—for example, impulse buying, shopping for fun, borrowing on credit cards, always buying brand-name products.

Lesson Overview	Lesson Notes

MULTILEVEL OBJECTIVES

On- and Higher-level: Use real conditional statements and questions to talk about money and listen for the real conditional in conversations about spending and money

Pre-level: Use real conditional statements to talk about money and listen for the real conditional in conversations about spending and money

LANGUAGE FOCUS

Grammar: Real conditional (*If I buy the coat today, I'll save money.*)

Vocabulary: *If, until, clause*

For vocabulary support, see these **Oxford Picture Dictionary** topics: Shopping, page 27; The Bank, page 134

READINESS CONNECTION

In this lesson, students practice using real conditionals to talk about spending money in the future.

PACING

To compress this lesson: Conduct 1C and/or 1D as a whole-class activity.

To extend this lesson: Have students talk about possible future outcomes. (See end of lesson.)

And/or have students complete **Workbook 3 pages 46–47, Multilevel Activities 3 Unit 7 pages 81–82**, and **Multilevel Grammar Exercises 3 Unit 7**.

CORRELATIONS

CCRS: SL.2.B Determine the main ideas and supporting details of a text read aloud or information presented in diverse media and formats, including visually, quantitatively, and orally.

SL.6.B Speak in complete sentences when appropriate to task and situation in order to provide requested detail or clarification.

R.1.B Ask and answer such questions as who, what, where, when, why, and how to demonstrate understanding of key details in a text.

L.1.B (l.) Produce simple, compound and complex sentences.

L.1.D (h.) Form and use verbs in the indicative, imperative, interrogative, conditional and subjunctive mood.

RF.4.B (a.) Read grade-level text with purpose and understanding.

ELPS: 7. An ELL can adapt language choices to purpose, task, and audience when speaking and writing. 10. An ELL can demonstrate command of the conventions of standard English to communicate in level-appropriate speech and writing.

Warm-up and Review
10–15 minutes (books closed)

Review the future with *will*. Write *In the future, maybe I will* _____. on the board. Ask volunteers to take turns coming to the board to finish the sentence.

Introduction
5–10 minutes

1. Referring to the sentences on the board, say: *All of these are things we may do in the future. We're probably not sure because there is a condition attached.* Use several of the students' ideas to form real conditional sentences. For example, if the student wrote *Maybe I will buy a house*, say: *If I save enough money, I will buy a house.*

2. State the objective: *Today we'll learn how to use real conditionals to talk about spending money in the future.*

1 Use real conditionals

Presentation I
20–25 minutes

 1. Direct students to look at the picture. Ask: *Where are they? Who are they? What is happening?*

2. Read the instructions aloud. Ask students to read the conversation silently and answer the questions.

3. Read the first question aloud. Call on a volunteer for the answer. Ask the volunteer where in the conversation he or she found the answer. Read the rest of the questions aloud, calling on a different volunteer for each answer.

Answers
1. There's a big sale tomorrow and she'll save 20%.
2. Someone else might buy the coat today.
3. She'll save an extra 10%.

B 1. Demonstrate how to read the grammar chart.

2. Direct students to underline the *if* clauses in the conversation in 1A. Go over the answers as a class.

3. Write one of the sentences from the conversation on the board. Elicit the tense of the verb in the *if* clause [present]. Underline the main clause and elicit its verb tense [future]. Write the sentence with the time clause and main clause order reversed. Point out the change in punctuation.

4. Read the chart through sentence by sentence. Then read it again and have students repeat after you.

5. Assess students' understanding of the chart. Write *If it rains tomorrow,* on the board and elicit several main clauses. Write *I will be very excited* on the board and elicit several *if* clauses. As volunteers provide you with *if* clauses, write some before the main clause and some after.

Answers
If you wait until tomorrow, if I wait until tomorrow, if you come in before 9 a.m.

Guided Practice I
10–15 minutes

 1. Tell students they will collaborate to complete the description of the grammar point. Model collaboration by working with the class to complete the first sentence. Encourage students to look at 1A and 1B to help them determine the correct words.

2. Pair students and have them work together to complete the description.

3. Project or write the completed definition on the board and have pairs verify the accuracy of their responses. Ask volunteers which sentences confused them and discuss.

Answers
future
present
starts

Guided Practice II
10–15 minutes

 1. Ask students to work individually to complete the sentences. Make sure they understand to use the words in parentheses.

2. Have pairs compare answers. Have students read the sentences aloud for the class to check answers.

Answers
1. buys, will save
2. goes, will pay
3. will go, need
4. save, won't need
5. will speak, wants
6. transfer, won't bounce

For 1D, group same-level students together.

• **Pre-level** Sit with these students and complete the exercise together.

• **Higher-level** Challenge these students to rewrite each sentence by changing the order of the clauses. Make sure they still punctuate with a comma correctly if one is needed.

TIP

Show students that *may/might* and *should* can be used in the main clause. Say: *My sister is thinking about visiting me this weekend. If she visits me, we might go out to dinner. If we go out, we shouldn't spend too much money.* Write two sentence frames on the board and elicit completions from volunteers. *If _____ this weekend, I might _____. If _____ this weekend, I should _____.* Ask students about things they might do this weekend.

2 Use questions with real conditionals

Presentation II
30–45 minutes

1. Introduce the new topic. Say: *Now we're going to learn questions with real conditionals.*

2. Read the questions and answers in the chart aloud.

3. Direct students to work individually to match the questions and answers. Have them read the questions and answers with a partner.

Answers
1. e
2. c
3. a
4. b
5. d

Guided Practice III
10–15 minutes

B Read the example question in number 1 aloud. Direct students to work individually to complete the questions. Have them read the questions and answers with a partner. Ask volunteer pairs to read their questions and answers aloud for the class to check.

Answers
2. if he finds the right house
3. will they save if they take the bus
4. will they go if they need a new TV

After 2B, provide additional practice with real conditionals. Target the practice to the level of your students.

• **Pre-level** Provide these students with main clauses and *if* clauses and ask them to combine the sentences. *1. If I win the lottery, 2. If it rains tomorrow, 3. If I go to bed early tonight, 4. If I sleep late in the morning, 5. If I exercise every day, a. I'll feel good tomorrow, b. I won't go to the beach, c. I'll buy my mom a house, d. I'll be late to work, e. I'll be healthier.*

• **On- and Higher-level** Put these students in groups and direct them to write a chain story in the third person. Provide this example: *If she wakes up early tomorrow, she'll go downtown. If she goes downtown, she'll buy a jacket. If she buys a jacket, she'll wear it every day. If she wears it every day, it will get old. If it gets old, she'll throw it away. If she throws it away, she'll need a new jacket.* Provide each group with a "starter" clause: *If he moves to this city, if she falls asleep in class, if he stays up late, if she saves her money, if he buys a new car.* Ask a reporter from each group to read the group's story aloud.

C

1. Elicit the importance of accuracy. Tell students they will be building their accuracy in this task.

2. Organize students into groups. Demonstrate how to correct the sentence using the first example.

3. Have team members work together to correct the sentences. Circulate and monitor teamwork.

4. Project or write the corrected sentences on the board and have teams check their work.

5. Address questions and any issues you noted during your observation.

Answers
1. Where will you go **if you get** a vacation?
2. **If I get** a vacation, I will travel to the Grand Canyon.
3. What will Jason do **if he gets** a raise?
4. If Jason gets a raise, **he will buy** a new car.

3 Listen for real conditionals

Guided Practice IV
15–20 minutes

🔊 **2-26** 1. Say: *We're going to listen to questions about what people will do in the future. Circle the letter of the correct statement based on what you hear.*

2. Direct students to read the first set of statements. Then play the first question and have students circle the correct answer.

3. Elicit answers from the class. If students answered incorrectly, play the audio again, providing a listening clue (for example, *listen for the topic of the question*).

4. Repeat for numbers 2–6.

Answers	
1. b	4. b
2. a	5. a
3. b	6. a

4 Use real conditionals to talk about the future

Communicative Practice and Application
20–25 minutes

A Group students and direct them to talk about what they see in the picture. *Where are these people? What are they doing?*

B 1. Read the instructions aloud. Direct students to work in their groups from 4A to write five sentences.

2. Check comprehension of the exercise. Ask: *Who is going to write the sentences?* [everyone] *Is everyone going to write the same sentences or different sentences?* [the same] *What tense should the sentences be in?* [real conditional] Assign a time limit (five minutes).

3. Give each group member a letter *A–D*. Tell students to re-form into groups with other students who have the same letter. Have them read their sentences aloud to their new groups.

4. Call on a volunteer from each group to read one of the group's sentences.

Evaluation (books closed)
10–15 minutes

TEST YOURSELF

Ask students to write the sentences independently. Collect and correct their writing.

MULTILEVEL STRATEGIES

Target the *Test Yourself* to the level of your students.

• **Pre-level** Ask these students to follow this sentence frame: *If I _____, I will _____.*

• **Higher-level** Have these students write seven or eight sentences.

EXTENSION ACTIVITY

Talk about Possible Future Outcomes

Write possible results using real conditional sentences. Write a series of situations on the board. Have students work with a partner to write different possible outcomes for the situations. Do the first one as a class. *Tom left his ATM card in the machine.* Discuss possible results. *If he remembers the card, he'll come back for it. If he leaves the card there too long, the machine will swallow it. If someone finds it, they might steal his money.* Consider other situations. *Mary has only $10 in her checking account. Mark wants to apply for a loan. Sara charged $2,000 on her credit card, Joe has $1,000 under his mattress at home.* Call on volunteers to share their sentences with the class.

Lesson Overview	Lesson Notes
MULTILEVEL OBJECTIVES	
Pre-, On-, and Higher-level: Report a billing or banking error and listen for account information	
LANGUAGE FOCUS	
Grammar: Time clauses (*After we review your application, we'll call you.*) **Vocabulary:** Banking vocabulary For vocabulary support, see this **Oxford Picture Dictionary** topic: The Bank, page 134	
STRATEGY FOCUS	
Use time clauses to find information about when things happen.	
READINESS CONNECTION	
In this lesson, students verbally communicate about and practice how to report billing or banking errors and how to listen for account information over the phone.	
PACING	
To compress this lesson: Do 6A as a class activity and skip 6B. **To extend this lesson:** Have students write a letter of complaint. (See end of lesson.) And/or have students complete **Workbook 3 page 48** and **Multilevel Activities 3 Unit 7 page 83**.	

CORRELATIONS

CCRS: SL.1.B (d.) Explain their own ideas and understanding in light of the discussion.

SL.2.B Determine the main ideas and supporting details of a text read aloud or information presented in diverse media and formats, including visually, quantitatively, and orally.

SL.4.B Report on a topic or text, tell a story, or recount an experience with appropriate facts and relevant, descriptive details, speaking clearly at an understandable pace.

SL.6.B Speak in complete sentences when appropriate to task and situation in order to provide requested detail or clarification.

R.7.B Use information gained from illustrations and the words in a text to demonstrate understanding of the text.

L.1.B (l.) Produce simple, compound and complex sentences.

L.1.D (j.) Explain the function of phrases and clauses in general and their function in specific sentences.

L.3.B (b.) Recognize and observe differences between the conventions of spoken and written standard English.

L.6.B Acquire and use accurately level-appropriate conversational, general academic, and domain-specific words and phrases, including those that signal spatial and temporal relationships.

RF.4.B (a.) Read grade-level text with purpose and understanding.

ELPS: 2. An ELL can participate in level-appropriate oral and written exchanges of information, ideas, and analyses, in various social and academic contexts, responding to peer, audience, or reader comments and questions. 9. An ELL can create clear and coherent level-appropriate speech and text.

Warm-up and Review
10–15 minutes (books closed)

Write *Billing problem* on the board. Ask students to talk about any possible problems that can come up with a credit card, bank statement, or bill. Students can talk about their own experiences, or they can give ideas and not say anything too personal.

Introduction
3 minutes

1. Tell students about a time you experienced a billing or banking problem and how you handled it.

2. State the objective: *Today we're going to learn how to report problems on our bank statements and how to listen for account information over the phone.*

1 Learn ways to ask about a problem

Presentation I
10 minutes

 A 🔊 **2-27** 1. Direct students to look at the picture. Ask: *Are the two people in the same place?* [no] *Who is the customer?* [the woman, Min]

2. Read the instructions aloud. Play the audio. Give students a minute to answer the question. Go over the answer as a class.

Answer
There's a charge on it that she didn't make.

Guided Practice I
20–25 minutes

 B 🔊 **2-27** 1. Read the instructions and the questions aloud. Play the audio. Ask students to listen for the answer to each question.

2. Ask students to compare their answers with a partner. Circulate and monitor to ensure students understand the audio.

Answers
1. It says she spent $1,500 in a city she's never been to before.
2. No
3. Wait until her next bill arrives

C 🔊 **2-28** Read the instructions aloud. Explain that students are going to hear the audio one more time. They should write the words they hear to complete the sentences. Play the audio. Call on volunteers to elicit the answers.

Answers
1. the problem
2. What's the
3. How can I

2 Practice your pronunciation

Pronunciation Extension
10–15 minutes

 A 🔊 **2-29** 1. Write *He has a problem with his bill.* on the board. Say the sentence with relaxed pronunciation. Underline the *h* in *has* and *his*. Repeat the sentence and ask students to listen for how the /h/ sounds are dropped. Read the

Pronunciation Note aloud and say: *Now we're going to focus on linked words. We often don't pronounce the beginning* h *on the second word of two linked words.*

2. Play the audio. Direct students to notice how the /h/ sound is dropped.

 B 🔊 **2-30** Play the audio. Have students work individually to circle the linked words.

Answers
1. ask him
2. Will he
3. before he
4. When he

 C 🔊 **2-30** 1. Play the audio again. Have students check their answers to 2B. Call on volunteers to read the sentences aloud, making sure they link the sounds correctly.

2. Ask students to take turns reading the sentences in 2B with a partner. Monitor and provide feedback.

3 Use time clauses to discuss future events

Presentation II and Guided Practice II
15–20 minutes

 A 1. Introduce the new topic. Say: *Now we're going to look at time clauses using* before, when, *and* after. *They work just like future if clauses.*

2. Copy the sentences from the chart on the board. Read them aloud. Elicit the sequence of the action in each sentence. Ask: *Which will happen first—review the statement or send the next bill?* Write 1 and 2 above the correct clause to indicate the sequence of the action. Point out that *when* uses the same sequence as *after* and actually means immediately after.

3. Read the *Grammar Notes*. Reverse the clause order of one of the sentences on the board and elicit the comma placement.

4. Ask students to work individually to underline the first word in each time clause. Go over the answers as a class.

Answers
1. before
2. when
3. after

B Read the instructions aloud. Have students do the task individually. Have pairs compare answers before checking answers as a class.

Answers
1. b
2. c
3. d
4. a

TIP

For more practice with time clauses, call out a verb phrase: *eat dinner*. Have one volunteer say a sentence with *before*. *Before I eat dinner, I'll wash my hands.* Have another say a sentence with *after*. *After I eat dinner, I'll watch TV.* Have a third say a sentence with *when*. *When I eat dinner, I'll relax.* Switch to a new verb phrase and call on more volunteers. Possible phrases: *go home, go shopping, do my homework.*

4 Building conversational skills

Guided Practice III
15–20 minutes

A Direct students to look at the picture and skim the phone conversation in 4B. Have them work with partners to identify the purpose of the phone call. Elicit responses and ask: *How do you know?* or *Why do you say that?* to encourage students to state their reasoning.

Answers
There's an error on his checking statement; answers will vary.

B 🔊 **2-31** 1. Ask students to read the instructions and tell you what they are going to do [listen and read and respond to the question]. Play the audio and then elicit the answer to the question.

2. Ask students to read the conversation with a partner. Circulate and monitor pronunciation. Model and have students repeat difficult words or phrases.

3. Ask: *In what other situations could you use this conversation?* Point out a few phrases that are not specific to a phone call to a bank. Ask volunteers to point out others.

Answer
He deposited $500 cash at the bank, but his statement doesn't show that.

Communicative Practice and Application I
20–25 minutes

C 1. Pair students and have them read the instructions silently. Check their comprehension of the exercise. Ask: *What are the two roles? Are the people in the same room?*

2. Model and have students repeat the questions in the *In Other Words* box in 4B. Explain that they should use these questions in their conversations.

3. Draw a T-chart on the board. Label the left column *Bank employee* and the right column *Customer*. Elicit examples of what each person might say and make notes in the chart.

4. Set a time limit (three minutes). Have students act out the role-play. Call "time" and have students switch roles.

5. Ask three volunteer pairs to act out their role-play for the class. Tell students who are listening to jot down any time clauses they hear.

MULTILEVEL STRATEGIES

Seat same-level students together.

• **Pre-level** Work with these students and guide them in writing their new conversation based on the conversation in 4B.

• **Higher-level** You can challenge students to add another problem to talk about, such as a lost ATM card, forgotten PIN, credit card didn't arrive.

5 Focus on listening for details

Presentation III and Guided Practice IV
20–25 minutes

A 1. Read the question aloud and start a discussion with a volunteer. Ask: *Do you ever call your bank? What do you ask? What information does the bank need from you to give you information over the phone?*

2. Continue asking other students for their answers. Write the information you can get on the board. Suggest students copy it into their notebooks for future reference.

TIP

Make sure students know to be patient while other students are speaking and not interrupt or talk over each other. One way to ensure this is to make a habit of asking a student to repeat back what another student said.

B 🔊 **2-32** Direct students to read the sentences before they listen to the account information. Play the audio and have them mark the statements *T* (true) or *F* (false). Check answers as a class and have volunteers correct the false statements.

Answers
1. T
2. F
3. F

C 🔊 **2-32** 1. Play the audio. Ask students to listen and write the correct answers.

2. Pair students and have them compare answers. If a pair has different answers, have the class vote on the correct answer with a show of hands.

Answers		
1. 3/07	#266	$44.73
2. 3/07	#268	$106.50
3. 3/09	#267	$56.00
4. 3/09	#270	$27.61
5. 3/12	#271	$175.90

6 Discuss

Communicative Practice and Application II
15–20 minutes

A 1. Read the instructions aloud. Call on volunteers to read the examples in the chart. Confirm understanding of the task. Ask: *Where will you put good, positive things about using credit cards?* [the "pro" column] *What goes into the "con" column?* [things that are not good about using credit cards] Explain that students will make a chart like this one based on their own discussions.

2. Put students into teams of three and assign roles: manager, administrative assistant, and reporter. Verify students' understanding of the roles.

3. Set a time limit for the discussions (ten minutes). Write the sentence frame from 6B on the board. Then circulate and monitor.

B Call "time." Ask the reporter for each team to report the results of the team's discussion using the sentence frame on the board.

Evaluation
5 minutes

TEST YOURSELF

1. Ask students to complete the checkboxes individually.

2. Tell students that you are going to read each of the items in the checklist aloud. If they are not at all confident with that skill, they should hold up a closed fist. If they are not very confident, they should hold up one finger. If they are somewhat confident, two fingers; confident, three fingers; very confident, four fingers. If they think they could teach the skill, they should hold up five fingers. Read each item in the checklist and identify students who may need further support.

EXTENSION ACTIVITY

Write a Letter of Complaint

1. Tell students to imagine that the situation from the role-play in 4C was not resolved and that it is now necessary to put the complaint in a follow-up letter. Elicit the information you'll need to include in the letter: account number, description of problem, date and time of first complaint, request for action, and the name of the teller.

2. Compose the letter as a class and write it on the board. Ask students to copy it into their notebooks.

Lesson Overview	Lesson Notes

MULTILEVEL OBJECTIVES

Pre-, On-, and Higher-level: Read about and discuss identity theft

LANGUAGE FOCUS

Grammar: Gerunds (*dumpster diving*)

Vocabulary: *Crime, criminal, identify theft*

For vocabulary support, see this **Oxford Picture Dictionary** topic: Crime, page 145

STRATEGY FOCUS

Read the sentences around new words or phrases to understand their meaning.

READINESS CONNECTION

In this lesson, students verbally communicate information about identity theft.

PACING

To compress this lesson: Assign 1E and/or 1F for homework.

To extend this lesson: Have students make a poster. (See end of lesson.)

And/or have students complete **Workbook 3 page 49** and **Multilevel Activities 3 Unit 7 pages 84–85**.

CORRELATIONS

CCRS: SL.1.B (a.) Come to discussions prepared, having read or studied required material; explicitly draw on that preparation and other information known about the topic to explore ideas under discussion. (b.) Follow agreed-upon rules for discussions. (c.) Ask questions to check understanding of information presented, stay on topic, and link their comments to the remarks of others. (d.) Explain their own ideas and understanding in light of the discussion.

SL.2.B Determine the main ideas and supporting details of a text read aloud or information presented in diverse media and formats, including visually, quantitatively, and orally.

R.1.B Ask and answer such questions as who, what, where, when, why, and how to demonstrate understanding of key details in a text.

R.2.A Identify the main topic and retell key details of a text.

R.4.B Determine the meaning of general academic and domain-specific words and phrases in a text relevant to a topic or subject area.

R.5.B Know and use various text features to locate key facts or information in a text efficiently.

R.6.B Identify the main purpose of a text, including what the author wants to answer, explain, or describe.

R.7.C Interpret information presented visually, orally, or quantitatively and explain how the information contributes to an understanding of the text in which it appears.

L.1.B (l.) Produce simple, compound and complex sentences.

L.4.B (a.) Use sentence-level context as a clue to the meaning of a word or phrase. (c.) Use a known root word as a clue to the meaning of an unknown word with the same root. (e.) Use glossaries and beginning dictionaries, both print and digital, to determine or clarify the meaning of words and phrases.

RF.3.B (c.) Identify and know the meaning of the most common prefixes and derivational suffixes.

RF.4.B (a.) Read grade-level text with purpose and understanding.

ELPS: 1. An ELL can construct meaning from oral presentations and literary and informational text through level-appropriate listening, reading, and viewing. 3. An ELL can speak and write about level-appropriate complex literary and informational texts and topics.

Warm-up and Review
10–15 minutes (books closed)

Write the words *Thief* and *Theft* on the board and elicit definitions. Ask students how they protect themselves from theft at home and away from home. Ask them what kinds of things thieves usually steal. Write their ideas on the board.

Introduction
5 minutes

1. Go over the items on the board. Say: *We protect our houses by locking doors and windows. We protect our cars with alarms and electronic keys. But many people don't protect their personal information.*

2. State the objective: *Today we're going to read about and discuss identity theft.*

1 Read

Presentation
10–20 minutes

A Read the questions aloud. Call on volunteers to share their stories and tell students about any experiences you or someone you know has had with credit card theft. Discuss ways to prevent identity theft.

B Read the words and definitions. Elicit sample sentences from students using *crime* and *criminal*. Discuss identity theft: *Is it worse if someone steals your money or your credit card number? Why?*

Pre-reading

C Read the instructions aloud and confirm that students understand where the bolded headings are. Have students answer the question individually and then check answers as a class. If any students answer incorrectly, ask them to support their answer using the bolded headings. Establish the correct answer.

Answer
c. Ways criminals steal your identity.

Guided Practice: While Reading
20–30 minutes

D 1. Direct students' attention to the *Reader's Note* and read the information aloud. Ask students to read the article silently and answer the question.

2. Check answers as a class.

3. Check comprehension. Ask: *What is shoulder surfing?* [looking over someone's shoulder to steal their information] *What is a dumpster?* [a very large garbage bin] *What is an example of phishing?* [when someone emails you pretending to be your bank and asks for information]

Possible Answers
Be careful with your information in public places. Always cut up papers with your personal information before you throw them away. If you get an email with your bank's name on it and it asks you to send personal information, don't do it.

MULTILEVEL STRATEGIES
Adapt 1D to the level of your students. • **Pre-level** Provide these students with a summary of the reading. *Identity theft is a big problem in the U.S. There are three common ways that people steal personal information. 1. Shoulder surfing—a thief looks over your shoulder and copies your information. 2. Dumpster diving—a thief looks for personal information in your trash. 3. Phishing—a thief pretends to work for your bank or credit card company and sends email asking for your personal information.* Direct these students to read the summary while other students are reading 1D.

Guided Practice: Rereading
10–15 minutes

E 1. Provide an opportunity for students to extract evidence from the text. Have students reread the article and underline the words that support what the author thinks you can do to avoid identity theft.

2. Pair students and tell them to compare the words they underlined and report anything they disagree on. Discuss and clarify as needed.

Answers
Yes; underlines will vary.

F 1. Have students work individually to mark the answers *T* (true), *F* (false), and *NI* (no information). They should then write the line numbers where they found the true and false answers. Write the answers on the board.

2. Elicit and discuss any additional questions about the reading. You could introduce new questions for class discussion: *Have you followed any of the advice in the article? Do you know of any other ways thieves can steal your identity? What should you be careful of when you travel?*

Answers

1. F, line 2
2. F, lines 6–7
3. F, lines 23–24
4. T, lines 18–19
5. T, lines 37–39
6. NI

MULTILEVEL STRATEGIES

After 1F, adapt further comprehension questions to the level of your students.

• **Pre-level** Ask these students *yes/no* and *or* questions about their summaries from 1D while other students are completing 1F. *Is personal identity theft a big problem in the U.S.? Do you need to be careful when you give out personal information? Should you put your credit card statements in the trash whole, or should you tear them up?*

• **On-level and Higher-level** Have these students correct the false statements and write one more true statement based on the reading.

2 Word study

Guided Practice: Post-reading
10–15 minutes

A 1. Direct students to look at the chart and identify the topic (the suffix *-al*). Have students read the chart.

2. Read the sentence in the chart and the example for *personal*. Elicit sentences for the other words in the chart.

3. Have students repeat after you as you say each word with natural intonation, rhythm, and stress.

4. Direct students to complete the sentences and then compare answers with a partner. Read the correct answers and have students check their work.

Answers

1. national
2. professional
3. arrives
4. removal
5. arrival

B 1. Read the prompts aloud. Give students a few minutes to think of their answers.

2. Set a time limit (ten minutes). Have groups of three or four discuss the prompts. Circulate and help as needed.

3. Have students share their responses with the class.

3 Talk it over

Guided Practice
15–20 minutes

A Have students look at the graph and read the introduction and *Reader's Note*. Point out that they need to use the information from the graph and the note to complete the sentences and answer the question. Set a time limit (ten minutes). Have students work in pairs to complete the task. Ask volunteers to share their answers with the class.

Answers

1. 38
2. 8
3. Data breaches
4. Friends and people you know a little, shopping at a store or on the phone
5. Social Security card, credit cards that you don't use

Communicative Practice
15–20 minutes

B Read the question aloud. Set a time limit (one minute). Have students write as many ideas as they can.

C Read the instructions aloud. Put students in groups of six and have them compare lists.

D Have a class discussion. Have volunteers share their ideas. Write them on the board. Ask questions to guide discussion: *Which idea is the easiest to start doing today? Which idea is good but difficult/complicated to do?*

Application

15–20 minutes

BRING IT TO LIFE

Read the instructions aloud. As a class, brainstorm items that students might find.

EXTENSION ACTIVITY

Make a Poster

Review theft-prevention advice.

1. Put students in mixed-level groups of three or four. Tell them to close their books and make a poster giving advice on how to protect against identity theft. Ask them to include four or five pieces of advice.

2. Have a reporter from each group read the group's poster to the class. Display the posters around the room.

AT WORK

Warm-up and Review
10–15 minutes

1. Review the *Bring It to Life* assignment from Lesson 5. Have students who did the exercise share what they found. Write the names of the items on the board.

2. Say: *I don't think identity theft is a real problem.* Ask students to respond to your statement. Write any words for disagreement that they use on the board.

Introduction
10 minutes

1. Ask: *Do you have staff meetings at work? Do you speak during the meetings? Do you always agree with what people at meetings or in class say? Are you comfortable with expressing disagreement with others?*

2. State the objective: *Today we're going to talk about how to disagree with others.*

Presentation
5 minutes

 A **2-33** Read the instructions aloud. Play the audio. Give students a minute to think about the question. Elicit responses from the class.

Answer
Ways to attract good employees to their company

Guided Practice
10–15 minutes

 B **2-33** Play the audio again. Direct students to listen for each problem and put a check next to any that they hear mentioned.

Answers
Checked:
Raise salaries
Health benefits for part-time staff
Improve pension plan
More vacation days

 C **2-33** Read the instructions aloud. Play the audio again, encouraging students to take notes in their notebooks. Set a time limit (five minutes) for students to discuss their answers with a partner. Circulate to monitor.

Answers
Raise salaries—already offer very competitive wages compared to similar companies
Health benefits for part-time staff—cost too much
Improve pension plan—just increased it by 20% last year
More vacation days—no one cares about vacation days

Presentation and Communicative Practice
15–20 minutes

 D 1. Direct students' attention to the *Do/Say* chart and ask students to identify the lesson's soft skill [disagreeing with someone]. Ask the class which column has examples of language [right] and which has examples of activities [left].

2. Say a phrase from the left column and act it out. Say it again and have the class act it out with you. Say it a third time and have the class act it out for you. To confirm understanding, combine phrases: *Squint and shake your head.*

3. Model the sentences from the right column using authentic intonation. Have students practice imitating your inflection.

4. Put students in teams of four and assign each team a question. Assign roles: manager, administrative assistant, researcher, and reporter. Researchers will ask you questions on behalf of the team. Verify understanding of the roles. Set a time limit (five minutes) and monitor.

5. Write sentence frames on the board that teams can use to summarize their response. (*Our team discussed the following question: _____ We decided _____ because _____.*)

6. Call "time" and let reporters rehearse their report for one minute. Direct each reporter to present to three other teams.

Communicative Practice and Application
10–15 minutes

 E 1. Tell students that they are going to work in pairs and have a conversation about suggestions for improvements at their company or school. Read the *Suggestions* aloud. Model the conversation with a volunteer. Confirm understanding of the task. Ask: *Will*

you agree with your partner's suggestions? [no]
What will you say after "no"? [a reason for disagreeing]

2. Direct pairs to take turns giving a suggestion and disagreeing.

3. As students carry out the conversation, circulate and monitor. Provide global feedback once the activity ends.

MULTILEVEL STRATEGIES

Divide the class into same-level groups and have the discussion separately.

• **Pre- and On-level** Work with these students to write a conversation they can use for practice.

• **Higher-level** Challenge these students to use each of the situations in the *Suggestions* box.

Lesson Overview

MULTILEVEL OBJECTIVES

Pre-, On-, and Higher-level: Review unit language

LANGUAGE FOCUS

Grammar: Real conditional (*Before he buys a car, he will research ads online.*)

Vocabulary: Time words, identity theft vocabulary

For vocabulary support, see this **Oxford Picture Dictionary** topic: Crime, page 145

READINESS CONNECTION

In this review, students work in a team to use real conditionals to talk about making a purchase and identity theft.

PACING

To extend this review: Have students complete **Workbook 3 page 50**, **Multilevel Activities 3 Unit 7 page 86**, and **Multilevel Grammar Exercises 3 Unit 7**.

Lesson Notes

CORRELATIONS

CCRS: SL.1.B (a.) Come to discussions prepared, having read or studied required material; explicitly draw on that preparation and other information known about the topic to explore ideas under discussion. (b.) Follow agreed-upon rules for discussions. (c.) Ask questions to check understanding of information presented, stay on topic, and link their comments to the remarks of others. (d.) Explain their own ideas and understanding in light of the discussion.

SL.2.B Determine the main ideas and supporting details of a text read aloud or information presented in diverse media and formats, including visually, quantitatively, and orally.

SL.4.B Report on a topic or text, tell a story, or recount an experience with appropriate facts and relevant, descriptive details, speaking clearly at an understandable pace.

SL.6.B Speak in complete sentences when appropriate to task and situation in order to provide requested detail or clarification.

R.1.B Ask and answer such questions as who, what, where, when, why, and how to demonstrate understanding of key details in a text.

R.2.A Identify the main topic and retell key details of a text.

L.1.B (l.) Produce simple, compound and complex sentences.

L.1.C (d.) Use modal auxiliaries to convey various conditions.

L.1.D (h.) Form and use verbs in the indicative, imperative, interrogative, conditional and subjunctive mood.

RF.4.B (a.) Read grade-level text with purpose and understanding.

ELPS: 5. An ELL can conduct research and evaluate and communicate findings to answer questions or solve problems. 6. An ELL can analyze and critique the arguments of others orally and in writing.

Warm-up and Review
10–15 minutes (books closed)

1. Review *At Work* activity E.

2. Ask students to share the good, not-so-good, and interesting things that happened during the conversation. As students speak, write their responses in a chart on the board.

Introduction and Presentation
5 minutes

1. Review real conditionals. Ask questions and call on volunteers to answer. *What will you do before you eat dinner tonight? What will you do after I give a surprise test today? What will you do when you first come to class tomorrow?* Write students' answers on the board in complete sentences.

2. State the objective: *Today we're going to review real conditionals to talk about making a purchase and avoiding identity theft.*

Guided Practice
15–20 minutes

A 1. Direct students to work in groups of three or four to look at the pictures. Read the sample caption aloud.

2. Set a time limit (five minutes) for groups to complete the task. Have volunteers write one of their group's captions on the board for the class to check answers.

Communicative Practice
30–45 minutes

B 1. Group students and assign roles: manager, artists, and writers. Explain that students are going to work with their teams to make a poster about identity theft. Verify students' understanding of the roles.

2. Read steps 2–5 of the activity aloud. Check comprehension of the task. *What will you think about first?* [what to include in the poster] *What should the poster give information about?* [how to avoid identity theft] *Is it better to write paragraphs or short sentences/bullet points?* [short sentences/bullet points]

3. Set a time limit (fifteen minutes) to complete the exercise. Circulate and answer any questions.

4. Have managers from each team present their poster to the class.

C 1. Have students walk around the room to conduct the interviews. To get students moving, tell them to interview three people who were not on their team for B.

2. Set a time limit (five minutes) to complete the exercise.

3. Tell students to make a note of their classmates' answers but not to worry about writing complete sentences.

MULTILEVEL STRATEGIES

Adapt the mixer in C to the level of your students.

• **Pre- and On-level** Pair these students and have them interview other pairs together.

• **Higher-level** Have these students ask an additional question and write all answers in complete sentences.

D 1. Call on individuals to report what they learned about their classmates. Keep a running tally on the board for each question, marking if students or someone they know have been a victim of identity theft and if the problem was taken care of.

2. Use your tally for question 1 to create a chart on the board like the one on page 115. Instruct students to draw and complete the chart in their notebooks. Circulate and answer any questions.

PROBLEM SOLVING
10–15 minutes

A 1. Ask: *Do you think it's difficult to choose a credit card? Is the information from the credit card companies easy to understand?* Tell students they will read a story about a man who wants to choose a credit card. Direct students to read Li's story silently.

2. Ask: *How often does he receive credit card offers?* [every week] *How long does one card offer 0% interest?* [6 months] *What interest rate does one card offer all the time?* [7%] *One card offers 5% interest on what?* [balance transfers]

3. Play the audio and have students read along silently.

B 1. Elicit answers to question 1. Guide students to a class consensus on the answer.

2. As a class, brainstorm answers to question 2. Ask students if they know someone who has this problem and has overcome it or what they have done themselves to overcome the same problem.

Answers
1. Li doesn't know which credit card is best for him.
2. Answers will vary.

Evaluation
20–25 minutes

To test students' understanding of the unit language and content, have them take the Unit 7 Test, available on the Teacher Resource Center.

8 Living Well

Unit Overview

This unit explores health problems and hospitals with a range of employability skills and contextualizes structures with *used to* and the present perfect continuous.

KEY OBJECTIVES

Lesson 1	Identify organs and parts of the body and locate hospitals
Lesson 2	Identify ways to improve your health
Lesson 3	Use *used to*
Lesson 4	Learn ways to make and accept suggestions
Lesson 5	Learn about the information on prescription medication labels
At Work	Help teammates participate
Teamwork & Language Review	Review unit language

UNIT FEATURES

Academic Vocabulary	*relax, stress, injury, medical, benefit*
Employability Skills	• Think of alternatives to unhealthy habits • Match quotes and pictures • Decide what to do after an accident • Work independently • Understand teamwork • Locate information • Communicate verbally • Listen actively • Use writing skills • Comprehend written material • Analyze information
Resources	**Class Audio** CD2, Tracks 35–45 **Workbook** Unit 8, pages 51–57 **Teacher Resource Center** Multilevel Activities 3 Unit 8 Multilevel Grammar Exercises 3 Unit 8 Unit 8 Test **Oxford Picture Dictionary** Inside and Outside the Body, A Pharmacy, Taking Care of Your Health, Medical Care, A Hospital

Lesson Overview

MULTILEVEL OBJECTIVES

On-level: Identify organs and parts of the body, describe medical departments, and locate hospitals

Pre-level: Identify parts of the body and medical departments and locate hospitals

Higher-level: Talk and write about health using parts-of-the-body vocabulary and medical-department vocabulary and locate hospitals

LANGUAGE FOCUS

Grammar: Present perfect and *should* (*I've cut myself. Where should I go?*)

Vocabulary: Organs, parts of the body, medical departments

For vocabulary support, see these **Oxford Picture Dictionary** topics: Inside and Outside the Body, pages 106–107; Medical Care, page 111; A Hospital, pages 122–123

STRATEGY FOCUS

Pool knowledge with team members to maximize vocabulary learning.

READINESS CONNECTION

In this lesson, students explore and communicate information about body parts and talk about areas of the hospital where they go when they have trouble with them.

PACING

To compress this lesson: Conduct 1B and 1C as a whole-class activity.

To extend this lesson: Have students discuss health problems. (See end of lesson.)

And/or have students complete **Workbook 3 page 51** and **Multilevel Activities 3 Unit 8 pages 88–89**.

CORRELATIONS

CCRS: SL.1.B (d.) Explain their own ideas and understanding in light of the discussion.

SL.2.B Determine the main ideas and supporting details of a text read aloud or information presented in diverse media and formats, including visually, quantitatively, and orally.

SL.4.B Report on a topic or text, tell a story, or recount an experience with appropriate facts and relevant, descriptive details, speaking clearly at an understandable pace.

R.1.B Ask and answer such questions as who, what, where, when, why, and how to demonstrate understanding of key details in a text.

R.5.B Know and use various text features to locate key facts or information in a text efficiently.

R.7.C Interpret information presented visually, orally, or quantitatively and explain how the information contributes to an understanding of the text in which it appears.

W.7.A Participate in shared research and writing projects.

L.1.B (l.) Produce simple, compound and complex sentences.

L.1.C (d.) Use modal auxiliaries to convey various conditions.

L.4.B (e.) Use glossaries and beginning dictionaries, both print and digital, to determine or clarify the meaning of words and phrases.

RF.4.B (a.) Read grade-level text with purpose and understanding.

ELPS: 8. An ELL can determine the meaning of words and phrases in oral presentations and literary and informational text.

Warm-up and Review
10–15 minutes (books closed)

Review body parts. Have a volunteer come to the front of the room and call out body parts. Ask the rest of the class to stand and point to or touch the correct body part. Have another volunteer write the words on the board as the first volunteer says them. Ensure that students use classroom-appropriate body parts in this discussion (ears, feet, fingers, lungs, etc.).

Introduction
3 minutes

1. Ask: *Are any of these body parts on the inside of our bodies? Which ones?* Circle students' answers.

2. State the objective: *Today we're going to learn the names of more body parts and talk about areas of the hospital where we go when we have trouble with them.*

1 Identify organs and other parts of the body

Presentation I
20–25 minutes

A 1. Write *How to stay healthy* on the board and elicit one example from the whole class. Have students work together to brainstorm in a group. Make a list on the board of the ways your students identify.

2. Have students identify the most essential way to stay healthy. Elicit ideas and put a checkmark next to the ways students feel are the most important, encouraging them to explain their reasons.

B 1. Copy the first two rows of the chart onto the board.

2. Model the task by "thinking aloud" about the first word in the chart and marking the first column appropriately. Work with a volunteer to demonstrate completing the second and third columns.

3. Direct students to review the vocabulary independently, marking the first column of the chart in their books.

4. Pair students and ask them to complete the second and third columns of the chart together.

C 1. Elicit any words that pairs did not know and write them on the board. Ask volunteers to explain any of the words they know.

2. Direct students to look up any remaining unknown words in their dictionaries. Discuss those words in relation to the lesson. (Note: 1D and 1E will confirm students' understanding of the target vocabulary.)

Guided Practice I
15–20 minutes

D 1. Direct students to look at the first item. Then read question 2 aloud and elicit the answer.

2. Set a time limit (five minutes). Direct students to complete the activity individually. Do not check the answers as a class yet.

Answers		
1. h	4. g	7. b
2. f	5. a	8. i
3. d	6. c	9. e

E 🔊 **2-35** 1. Prepare students to listen by saying: *Now we're going to listen to speakers giving information about exercise and nutrition. While you listen, check your work in 1D.*

2. Play the audio. Ask students to circle any of their answers in 1D that don't match the audio. Elicit those items and play them again, focusing on clues to meaning in the 1D sentences.

3. Work with the pronunciation of any troublesome words.

2 Learn about medical departments

Presentation II
10–20 minutes

A 1. Direct students to look at the hospital directory. Introduce the new topic: *Now we're going to talk about places in the hospital.*

2. Elicit the names of the places students see on the directory. Read through the information in the chart and point out the parts that students need to fill in.

3. Ask students to work individually to complete the chart. Go over the answers as a class.

4. Check comprehension. Ask: *Where does a nine-year-old go when he or she is sick?* [Pediatrics] *Where does a woman go when she's pregnant?* [Maternity] *Where do you go if you break a bone?* [Emergency]

5. Direct students' attention to the directory key. Ask volunteers to explain why each symbol in the directory is used for each department.

Answers		
Sentence with Context	**Department Name**	**Department Function**
Zack might have a broken bone. He needs an X-ray.	Radiology	x-rays
Alan's mom is in the hospital. He wants to ask a nurse questions about his mother's condition.	Nurse's Station	Where nurses work
Rita is going to have a baby.	Maternity	Deliver and care for babies
Ted had a car accident. He came to the hospital in an ambulance.	Emergency Room	Emergency care
Ok Sook's 10-year-old daughter is in the hospital.	Pediatrics	Care for children
Habib needs to have some tests done on his heart.	Cardiology	Heart care

Guided Practice II
10–15 minutes

B 1. Model the conversation with a volunteer. Model it again using other information from 2A.

2. Set a time limit (three minutes). Direct students to practice with a partner.

3. Call on volunteers to present their version of the conversation for the class.

Communicative Practice and Application
25–30 minutes

C 1. If students will use the Internet for this task, establish what device(s) they'll use: a class computer, tablets, or smartphones. Alternatively, print information from the Internet before class and distribute to groups.

2. Write the questions from 2C on the board. Explain that students will work in teams to research and report on this information. Ask: *Which search terms or questions can you use to find the information you need?* ["hospital" + your city, "emergency services" + your city, "medical services" + your city] *How will you record the information you find?* [table, checklist, index

cards] Remind students to bookmark or record sites so they can find or cite them in the future.

3. Group students and assign roles: manager, administrative assistant, IT support, and reporter. Verify students' understanding of the roles.

4. Give managers the time limit for researching the question (ten minutes). Direct the IT support to begin the online research or pick up the printed materials for each team. Direct the recorder to record information for the team using a table, a checklist, or index cards.

5. Give a two-minute warning. Call "time."

TIP

When setting up task-based activities, verify that students understand their roles using physical commands. For example: *If you report on your team's work, stand up* [reporter]. *If you keep the team on task, point to the clock* [manager]. *If you write the team's responses, raise your hand* [administrative assistant]. *If you help the team research, hold up your smartphone/tablet* [IT support].

D 1. Copy the sentence frames on the board.

2. Direct teams to help their administrative assistant use the sentence frames to record the team's findings. Direct the reporter to use the recorded information to report the team's findings to the class or another team.

Evaluation
10–15 minutes

TEST YOURSELF

1. Direct Partner A to read prompts 1–4 from 1D on page 116 to Partner B. Partner B should close his or her book and write the answers in his or her notebook. When finished, students switch roles. Partner B reads prompts 5–9 from 1D.

2. Direct both partners to open their books and check their spelling when they finish.

EXTENSION ACTIVITY

Discuss Health Problems

Talk about health problems. Elicit the names of body parts discussed in this unit. Write the words on the board. As a class, discuss the most common ailments that are associated with particular organs/body parts—for example, *lungs and pneumonia, blood and leukemia, muscles and sprains or pulls.* Give students time to copy the ailment words and allow volunteers to share stories or ask questions about these illnesses.

Lesson Overview	Lesson Notes

MULTILEVEL OBJECTIVES

On- and Higher-level: Analyze, write, and edit a wellness plan

Pre-level: Read a wellness plan and write about health care and wellness

LANGUAGE FOCUS

Grammar: Imperatives (*Exercise every day.*)

Vocabulary: *Aerobics, weights, dental appointment, physical exam, wellness, cleaning, eye exam*

For vocabulary support, see this **Oxford Picture Dictionary** topic: Taking Care of Your Health, pages 116–117

STRATEGY FOCUS

Use an outline to make a plan for writing.

READINESS CONNECTION

In this lesson, students listen actively, read, and write about health care and staying well.

PACING

To compress this lesson: Assign the *Test Yourself* and/or 3C for homework.

To extend this lesson: Have students talk about health. (See end of lesson.)

And/or have students complete **Workbook 3 page 52** and **Multilevel Activities 3 Unit 8 page 90**.

CORRELATIONS

CCRS: SL.1.B (d.) Explain their own ideas and understanding in light of the discussion.

SL.2.B Determine the main ideas and supporting details of a text read aloud or information presented in diverse media and formats, including visually, quantitatively, and orally.

R.1.B Ask and answer such questions as who, what, where, when, why, and how to demonstrate understanding of key details in a text.

R.2.A Identify the main topic and retell key details of a text.

R.7.B Use information gained from illustrations and the words in a text to demonstrate understanding of the text.

W.2.B (a.) Introduce a topic and group related information together; include illustrations when useful to aiding comprehension.

W.4.B Produce writing in which the development and organization are appropriate to task and purpose.

W.5.B With guidance and support from peers and others, develop and strengthen writing as needed by planning, revising and editing.

L.1.B (l.) Produce simple, compound and complex sentences.

L.2.C (a.) Use correct capitalization.

RF.4.B (a.) Read grade-level text with purpose and understanding.

ELPS: 6. An ELL can analyze and critique the arguments of others orally and in writing. 9. An ELL can create clear and coherent level-appropriate speech and text.

Warm-up and Review
10–15 minutes (books closed)

Talk about health problems. Write *Health problems* on the board and elicit the most common health problems—for example, common cold, flu, cancer, heart disease, asthma, diabetes, depression, allergies, etc.

Introduction
5 minutes

1. Ask students which of the problems on the board can be avoided or made less likely by a person's behavior.

2. State the objective: *Today we're going to read and write about health care and staying well.*

1 Prepare to write

Presentation
20–25 minutes

 1. Build students' schema by asking questions about the pictures in the outline. Ask: *Does she look healthy?*

2. Give students one minute to tell a partner their responses to questions 1 and 2. Elicit responses from the class. Encourage students to respond to each other's ideas. After one student speaks, ask other students their opinions. *Do you agree or disagree with what he/she just said? Why?*

Answers
1. Possible answers: eat less fast food, eat low-fat ice cream, eat more vegetables, do aerobics, lift weights, make medical appointments, relax 2. Improve eating habits, get in shape, and stay well

B 🔊 2-36 1. Introduce the model outline and its purpose: *Now we're going to read the outline of a wellness plan. As you read, look for the purpose of the plan: Why is she writing?* Have students read the outline silently.

2. Check comprehension. Ask: *Why is Maria going to do aerobics and lift weights? How is she going to manage stress?* Elicit what Maria is doing in each of the pictures.

3. Play the audio. Have students read along silently.

Guided Practice I
10 minutes

 1. Have students work independently to underline the answers to the questions in the outline.

2. Point out the *Writer's Note* and check comprehension. Ask: *How many main ideas are there? What are they? Which main idea has three supporting ideas? Could "Manage Stress" change to be under "Get in Shape"? Why or why not? What is another supporting idea that can go under "Get in Shape"?*

3. Ask students to annotate the information they underlined with the phrases "eating habits" for question 1, "get in shape" for question 2, and "stay well" for question 3. Have pairs compare answers. Have volunteers call out answers and write them on the board for the class to check.

Answers
1. Eat less fast food, Eat low-fat ice cream, Eat more fresh vegetables at lunch and dinner 2. Do aerobics three times a week, Lift weights for strong bones and muscles 3. Make medical and dental appointments, Manage stress

MULTILEVEL STRATEGIES

For 1C, challenge on- and higher-level students while working with pre-level students.

• **Pre-level** While other students are working on 1C, ask these students *yes/no* and *or* questions about the reading. *Will Maria eat more or fewer vegetables? Will she do aerobics every day?* Give students time to copy the answers to 1C from the board.

• **On- and Higher-level** Write these questions on the board for these students to answer after they finish 1C: *What are other ways for Maria to manage stress? Why do you think Maria wrote a wellness plan? What things was she doing/not doing? How did she feel?* After allowing students to work individually to answer the questions, have volunteers share their ideas. Write the ideas on the board for students to refer to for 2B.

TIP

Teach students the expressions "stop and smell the roses" and "don't sweat the small stuff" as they relate to Maria's stress-management plan (and the accompanying pictures). Ask students if they know of any similar expressions in their own language.

2 Plan and write

Guided Practice II
15–20 minutes

 1. Read the questions aloud. Elicit students' answers.

2. Demonstrate how to create a cluster diagram by drawing a circle and writing *Healthy foods* in the center. Draw "spokes" with circles at the end and ask volunteers for one or two answers to fill them in. Have students create their own cluster diagram for *Manage stress*. Have students share their diagrams with partners.

3. Ask volunteers to share their diagrams with the class.

B Read through the outline template. Elicit ideas that could go in each section. Have students write their plans individually.

3 Get feedback and revise

Guided Practice III
5 minutes

A Direct students to check their writing using the editing checklist. Tell them to read each item in the list and check their papers before moving on to the next item. Explain that students should not edit their writing at this stage. They should just use the checklist to check their work and mark any areas they want to revise.

Communicative Practice
15 minutes

B 1. Read the instructions and the sample sentences aloud. Emphasize to students that they are responding to their partners' work, not correcting it.

2. Use the outline in 1B to model the exercise. *I like the idea* Don't worry about little things. *I'd like to ask this writer for an example of a little thing she's not going to worry about.*

3. Direct students to exchange papers with a partner and follow the instructions.

C Allow students time to edit and revise their writing as necessary, using the editing checklist from 3A and their partner's feedback from 3B. If necessary, students could complete this task as homework.

Application and Evaluation
10 minutes

TEST YOURSELF

1. Review the instructions aloud. Assign a time limit (five minutes) and have students work independently.

2. Before collecting student work, invite two or three volunteers to share their sentences. Ask students to raise their hands if they wrote similar answers.

Lesson Overview	Lesson Notes
MULTILEVEL OBJECTIVES	

MULTILEVEL OBJECTIVES

On- and Higher-level: Use *used to* to talk about health habits and listen for information about health habits

Pre-level: Recognize *used to* in conversations about health habits

LANGUAGE FOCUS

Grammar: *Used to (I used to exercise.)*

Vocabulary: *Junk food, take care of yourself, do yoga*

For vocabulary support, see this **Oxford Picture Dictionary** topic: Taking Care of Your Health, pages 116–117

READINESS CONNECTION

In this lesson, students practice using *used to* to talk about past habits.

PACING

To compress this lesson: Conduct 1C and/or 1D as a whole-class activity.

To extend this lesson: Have students make generalizations with *used to*. (See end of lesson.)

And/or have students complete **Workbook 3 pages 53–54, Multilevel Activities 3 Unit 8 pages 91–92,** and **Multilevel Grammar Exercises 3 Unit 8**.

CORRELATIONS

CCRS: SL.2.B Determine the main ideas and supporting details of a text read aloud or information presented in diverse media and formats, including visually, quantitatively, and orally.

SL.6.B Speak in complete sentences when appropriate to task and situation in order to provide requested detail or clarification.

R.1.B Ask and answer such questions as who, what, where, when, why, and how to demonstrate understanding of key details in a text.

L.1.B (b.) Explain the function of nouns, pronouns, verbs, adjectives, and adverbs in general and their functions in particular sentences. (k.) Use coordinating and subordinating conjunctions (l.) Produce simple, compound and complex sentences.

L.1.C (f.) Use verb tense to convey various times, sequences, states, and conditions.

RF.4.B (a.) Read grade-level text with purpose and understanding.

ELPS: 7. An ELL can adapt language choices to purpose, task, and audience when speaking and writing. 10. An ELL can demonstrate command of the conventions of standard English to communicate in level-appropriate speech and writing.

Warm-up and Review
10–15 minutes (books closed)

Write *Exercise* and *Eating habits* on the board. Ask students to share what they did for exercise when they were younger and what they do now. Write the ideas on the board. Ask what things they ate when they were younger that they don't eat now and vice versa. Write the foods on the board.

Introduction
5–10 minutes

1. Say: *Many people's eating and exercise habits change during their lives.* Restate the information on the board with *used to. Now I eat a lot of salad. I used to eat a lot of French fries.*

2. State the objective: *Today we're going to learn to use* used to *to talk about our past habits.*

1 Use *used to*

Presentation I
20–25 minutes

 1. Direct students to look at the pictures. Ask: *Did Sam have healthy habits before? Does he have healthy habits now?*

2. Read the instructions aloud. Ask students to read the paragraph silently and answer the questions.

3. Read the first question aloud. Call on a volunteer for the answer. Ask the volunteer where in the paragraph he or she found the answer. Read the rest of the questions aloud, calling on a different volunteer for each answer.

Answers
1. No
2. Healthy foods: fruits and vegetables
3. No
4. He walks every day and has more friends.

 1. Demonstrate how to read the grammar chart.

2. Direct students to underline the examples of *used to* in the paragraph in 1A. Go over the answers as a class.

3. Write one of the sentences with *used to* from the paragraph on the board. Ask: *Does Sam (eat junk food now)?* [no] *What words in the sentence tell you that?* [used to]. *What is the other verb in the sentence?* [eat] *What tense is it in?* [present]

4. Read the chart through sentence by sentence. Then read it again and have students repeat after you.

5. Assess students' understanding of the chart. Ask students to tell you which items from the *Warm-up* represent things they used to do or used to eat. Remind them that they can't use *used to* to describe things they still do. Ask a volunteer to say what is the small but important difference in the form of *used to* when it is negative [the -*d* is dropped].

Answers
used to eat, didn't use to eat, used to watch, didn't use to exercise, didn't use to have

Guided Practice I
10–15 minutes

 1. Tell students they will collaborate to complete the description of the grammar point. Model collaboration by working with the class to complete the first sentence. Encourage students to look at 1A and 1B to help them determine the correct words.

2. Pair students and have them work together to complete the description.

3. Project or write the completed definition on the board and have pairs verify the accuracy of their responses. Ask volunteers which sentences confused them and discuss.

Answers
verb
past
didn't

MULTILEVEL STRATEGIES

• **Pre-level** While other students are completing 1C, ask these students to use the charts in 1B to write two affirmative and two negative sentences. Give them time to copy the answers to 1C after they are written on the board.

• **On- and Higher-level** When these students finish 1C, have them write four original sentences using *used to*. Tell them to write two affirmative sentences and two negative sentences.

Guided Practice II
10–15 minutes

 1. Read the instructions and the sample sentence aloud. Have pairs do the task. Circulate and monitor.

2. Have students read their sentences aloud for the class to check answers.

MULTILEVEL STRATEGIES

For 1D, group same-level students together.

• **Pre-level** Sit with these students and complete the exercise together. Take turns with them to read each sentence.

• **Higher-level** Challenge these students to write two more sentences about Tara using their own ideas.

2 Use *used to* in questions and answers

Presentation II
30–45 minutes

 1. Introduce the new topic: *Now we're going to ask questions with* used to.

2. Read the questions and answers in the chart aloud.

3. Direct students to work individually to choose the correct words. Have them read the questions and answers with a partner.

Answers	
1. use to	4. use to
2. used to	5. used to
3. use to	6. use to

Guided Practice III
10–15 minutes

B Ask students to work individually to match the questions and answers and then compare their answers with a partner. Ask volunteer pairs to read their matching questions and answers aloud. Write the letter-number match on the board.

Answers	
1. b	4. a
2. c	5. f
3. d	6. e

C 1. Elicit the importance of accuracy. Tell students they will be building their accuracy in this task.

2. Organize students into groups. Demonstrate how to correct the sentence using the first example.

3. Have team members work together to correct the sentences. Circulate and monitor teamwork.

4. Project or write the corrected sentences on the board and have teams check their work.

5. Address questions and any issues you noted during your observation.

Answers
1. How often did Tom **use** to get a physical exam?
2. He **used** to get a physical exam once a year.
3. Did Mr. and Mrs. Diaz use **to** live in Mexico?
4. He didn't **use** to exercise, but now he does.

3 Listen for *used to* to determine the meaning

Guided Practice IV
15–20 minutes

◀))) 2-37 1. Say: *Now we're going to listen to some sentences about the health habits of the Martinez family.*

2. Direct students to read the first sentence and then play the audio for that sentence. Have them mark the sentence *T* (true) or *F* (false) and correct the statement if it is false.

3. Elicit answers from the class. If students answered incorrectly, play the audio again, providing a listening clue (for example, *listen for the words in the audio that are the same in the statement*).

4. Repeat for numbers 2–5.

Answers
1. F, Livia used to eat white bread.
2. T
3. F, Tomas used to spend a lot of money.
4. F, He used to only exercise on the weekend. OR He didn't use to exercise during the week.
5. T

4 Use *used to* to talk about your life experience

Communicative Practice and Application
20–25 minutes

 1. Direct students to work independently to complete the questions with *used to*.

2. Call on volunteers to share their sentences, correcting grammar as necessary.

Answers
1. use to
2. used to
3. use to
4. used to

B Direct students to work with a partner to write two more questions using *used to*.

C 1. Have pairs merge to form teams of four. Model the exercise by "joining" one of the teams. Each pair takes a turn asking and answering questions while the class listens.

2. Check comprehension of the exercise. Ask: *Who asks questions?* [everyone] *Who answers questions?* [everyone]

3. Ask volunteers to share something interesting they learned about their classmates.

> ### TIP
>
> Before students write the sentences for the *Test Yourself*, practice connecting clauses with *but*. Write several pairs of sentences and ask students to connect them with *but. Tom used to eat donuts for breakfast. Now he doesn't eat donuts. I didn't use to lift weights. Now I lift weights.*

TEST YOURSELF

Ask students to write the sentences independently. Collect and correct their writing.

EXTENSION ACTIVITY
Make Generalizations

As a follow-up to 4C, have students write generalizations about the class on the board: *Most of us used to exercise more often. Some of us used to smoke.* Read the sentences and ask for a show of hands to find out if the generalization is true.

LESSON **4** EVERYDAY CONVERSATION

Lesson Overview	Lesson Notes

MULTILEVEL OBJECTIVES

Pre-, On-, and Higher-level: Make and accept suggestions and listen for health information

LANGUAGE FOCUS

Grammar: Present perfect continuous (*I haven't been feeling well lately.*)

Vocabulary: Health and exercise vocabulary

For vocabulary support, see these **Oxford Picture Dictionary** topics: Taking Care of Your Health, pages 116–117; Medical Care, page 111

STRATEGY FOCUS

Use the present perfect continuous to talk about actions or situations that began in the past and are continuing now.

READINESS CONNECTION

In this lesson, students verbally communicate about and practice how to make and accept health-related suggestions.

PACING

To compress this lesson: Do 6A as a class activity and skip 6B.

To extend this lesson: Have students talk about activity levels. (See end of lesson.)

And/or have students complete **Workbook 3 page 55** and **Multilevel Activities 3 Unit 8 page 93**.

CORRELATIONS

CCRS: SL.1.B (d.) Explain their own ideas and understanding in light of the discussion.

SL.2.B Determine the main ideas and supporting details of a text read aloud or information presented in diverse media and formats, including visually, quantitatively, and orally.

SL.4.B Report on a topic or text, tell a story, or recount an experience with appropriate facts and relevant, descriptive details, speaking clearly at an understandable pace.

SL.6.B Speak in complete sentences when appropriate to task and situation in order to provide requested detail or clarification.

R.7.B Use information gained from illustrations and the words in a text to demonstrate understanding of the text.

L.1.B (l.) Produce simple, compound and complex sentences.

L.1.C (d.) Use modal auxiliaries to convey various conditions. (e.) Form and use the perfect verb tenses.

L.1.D (j.) Explain the function of phrases and clauses in general and their function in specific sentences.

L.6.B Acquire and use accurately level-appropriate conversational, general academic, and domain-specific words and phrases, including those that signal spatial and temporal relationships.

RF.2.A (g.) Isolate and pronounce initial, medial vowel, and final sounds (phonemes) in spoken single-syllable words.

RF.4.B (a.) Read grade-level text with purpose and understanding.

ELPS: 2. An ELL can participate in level-appropriate oral and written exchanges of information, ideas, and analyses, in various social and academic contexts, responding to peer, audience, or reader comments and questions. 9. An ELL can create clear and coherent level-appropriate speech and text.

Warm-up and Review
10–15 minutes (books closed)

Write some problems on the board. *I'm overweight. I'm under a lot of stress. I feel tired all the time. I can't sleep at night.* Elicit a suggestion for each problem and write it on the board.

Introduction
3 minutes

1. Point out that all of the problems on the board can be helped to some degree by exercise. Say: *That's why health experts often advise us to exercise.*

2. State the objective: *Today we're going to learn how to make and accept suggestions related to health.*

1 Learn ways to make and accept suggestions

Presentation I
10 minutes

 1. Direct students to look at the picture. Ask: *What is happening in the picture?* [a man is getting weighed/examined in a doctor's office]

2. Read the instructions aloud. Play the audio. Give students a minute to answer the question. Go over the answer as a class.

Answer
He's concerned about Leo's weight.

Guided Practice I
20–25 minutes

 1. Read the instructions and the questions aloud. Play the audio. Ask students to listen for the answer to each question.

2. Ask students to compare their answers with a partner. Circulate and monitor to ensure students understand the audio.

Answers
1. It's too cold outside.
2. Heart problems run in his family.
3. Walk in the mall, cook more

 Read the instructions aloud. Explain that students are going to hear the audio one more time. They should write the words they hear to complete the sentences. Play the audio. Call on volunteers to elicit the answers.

Answers
1. Why don't you
2. You might
3. You could
4. If I were you, I'd

2 Practice your pronunciation

Pronunciation Extension
10–15 minutes

 1. Write *She used to use too much salt* on the board. Say the sentence and ask students to repeat it. Underline the *s* in *used to* and *use* and repeat each word. Say: *Now we're going to focus on the pronunciation of* used to *and the verb* use.

2. Play the audio. Direct students to read the sentences.

3. Elicit the answers to the questions. Replay the audio or say the sentences and have students repeat.

Answers
z: I'll try to use your advice.
s: I used to jog every day.

B **2-41** **1.** Play the audio. Have students work individually to fill in the blanks.

Answers
1. What do most people use
2. These days, they use
3. Not long ago, people didn't use to
4. They didn't use microwaves
5. Long ago, they used to

C **2-41** **1.** Play the audio again. Have students check their answers to 2B. Call on volunteers to read the sentences aloud, making sure they link the sounds correctly.

2. Ask students to take turns reading the sentences in 2B with a partner. Monitor and provide feedback.

3 Use the present perfect continuous

Presentation II and Guided Practice II

15–20 minutes

A 1. Introduce the new topic: *Now we're going to learn a new tense, the present perfect continuous.* Direct students to look at the time line and read the sentence about Tomas.

2. Ask questions about the time line: *Is Tomas working at the restaurant now? Did he work there in the past?* Say: *When we talk about an action beginning in the past and continuing to the present, we use present perfect continuous.*

3. Write the sentence about Tomas on the board and elicit the three parts of the verb. [*have + be + -ing*]

4. Have students read the sentences in the chart with a partner. Point out the time expressions: *since April, recently, for two years, this week.* Read the *Grammar Note.*

TIP

Before students move on to 3B, provide more practice with the present perfect continuous. Write *What has he/she been doing?* on the board. Write several situations (or put up suitable pictures). *She's tired. His clothes are all wet. She's crying. He's sweating. Her shirt is dirty.* Tell students to answer the question about each situation using the present perfect continuous. Do one together as an example. *She's tired. What has she been doing? She's been exercising. She's been working hard lately. She's been getting up early lately. She's been staying up late every night.* Ask volunteers to write their ideas on the board.

B 1. Model the conversation with a volunteer. Set a time limit (five minutes) and have pairs do the task. Circulate and monitor. Have volunteers share some information about their partners with the class.

MULTILEVEL STRATEGIES

Target 3B to the level of your students.

- **Pre-level** Provide students with questions to ask and make sure they answer in complete sentences. *How long have you been living in your house/apartment? How long have you been living in this country? How long have you been working at your job? How long have you been exercising? How long have you been coming to this school?*
- **Higher-level** Challenge these students to ask their partner at least eight questions about their lives.

TIP

Point out that with some verbs, like *work* and *live,* we can use the present perfect to express the same idea, but with most actions, we use the present perfect continuous.

4 Building conversational skills

Guided Practice III

15–20 minutes

A Direct students to look at the picture and skim the conversation in 4B. Have them work with partners to identify the purpose of the conversation. Elicit responses and ask: *How do you know?* or *Why do you say that?* to encourage students to state their reasoning.

Answers
No; answers will vary.

B 2-42 1. Ask students to read the instructions and tell you what they are going to do. [listen and read and respond to the question] Play the audio and then elicit the answer to the question.

2. Ask students to read the conversation with a partner. Circulate and monitor pronunciation. Model and have students repeat difficult words or phrases.

3. Ask: *In what other situations could you use this conversation?* Point out a few phrases that are not specific to a conversation between a doctor and patient. Ask volunteers to point out others.

Answers
Walk around the neighborhood, invite a friend to join you, keep eating good food

Communicative Practice and Application I
20–25 minutes

C 1. Pair students and have them read the instructions silently. Check their comprehension of the exercise. Ask: *What are the two roles? Where does the conversation happen?*

2. Model and have students repeat the sentence stems and sentences in the *In Other Words* box in 4B. Explain that they should use these in their conversations.

3. Draw a T-chart on the board. Label the left column *Doctor* and the right column *Patient*. Elicit examples of what each person might say and make notes in the chart.

4. Set a time limit (three minutes). Have students act out the role-play. Call "time" and have students switch roles.

5. Ask three volunteer pairs to act out their role-play for the class. Tell students who are listening to make a simple table with four rows and two columns. Use the top row to label the columns *Problem* and *Advice*. Have students take notes in the chart for each role-play.

MULTILEVEL STRATEGIES

Seat same-level students together.

- **Pre-level** Provide a simplified conversation for these students. *A: I'm concerned about your heart. B: I'm always tired. A: Do you exercise? B: I used to ride my bike, but I don't have time now. A: You could ride your bike to work. B: OK, I'll start tomorrow.*

- **Higher-level** You can challenge students to add another problem to talk about, such as a painful knee, trouble sleeping, a headache.

---

5 Focus on listening for details

Presentation III and Guided Practice IV
20–25 minutes

A 1. Read the questions and statement aloud and model a discussion with a volunteer. Ask: *Is it easier for you to exercise or to have a healthy diet? Which is more important? Why? / Why not? I agree because… / I disagree because…*

2. Pair students and tell them to discuss their own answers to the questions. Circulate and monitor.

TIP

Remind students that they shouldn't be shy about asking another student to repeat what they said. Review phrases such as *Can you repeat that? Excuse me—what did you say? Can you say that first part again?* etc.

B Direct students to read the sentences before they listen to the radio show. Ask what kind of information they'll be writing in the blanks. Ask volunteers for predictions. If students struggle, start by offering your own prediction: *I think we will hear something about burning calories.*

C ◀))) 2-43 1. Play the audio. Ask students to listen and write the correct answers.

2. Pair students and have them compare answers. If a pair has different answers, have the class vote on the correct answer with a show of hands.

Answers
1. time
2. calories
3. 225
4. walking
5. swimming
6. exercise

TIP

If students are interested in learning more about calories per activity, have them type "calories" and "activity" into an Internet search engine. They can find the average number of calories burned for many activities. They can also find calculators to tell them how many calories they should consume every day based on their age, weight, and activity level.

---

6 Discuss

Communicative Practice and Application II
15–20 minutes

A 1. Read the instructions aloud. Call on volunteers to read the list. Model the conversation with a volunteer. Confirm understanding of the task. Ask: *What does alternative mean?* [something you can do instead] *What will you include on your poster?* [healthy habits]

2. Put students into teams of four and assign roles: manager, artist, administrative assistant, and reporter. Verify students' understanding of the roles. Encourage students to use the phrases in the *Speaking Note* during their discussions.

3. Set a time limit for teams to create their posters (ten minutes). Write the sentence frame from 6B on the board. Then circulate and monitor.

B Call "time." Ask the reporter for each team to present the team's poster to the class using the sentence frame on the board.

Evaluation

5 minutes

TEST YOURSELF

1. Ask students to complete the checkboxes individually.

2. Tell students that you are going to read each of the items in the checklist aloud. If they are not at all confident with that skill, they should hold up a closed fist. If they are not very confident, they should hold up one finger. If they are somewhat confident, two fingers; confident, three fingers; very confident, four fingers. If they think they could teach the skill, they should hold up five fingers. Read each item in the checklist and identify students who may need further support.

EXTENSION ACTIVITY

Talk about Activity Levels

1. Ask students to make a list of all of the activities they did over the last weekend.

2. Have students sit with a partner and together decide which activities and which partner probably burned the most calories over the weekend.

3. Ask if anyone's partner was exceptionally active. Ask those people to share what their partners did over the weekend.

Lesson Overview	Lesson Notes

MULTILEVEL OBJECTIVES

Pre-, On-, and Higher-level: Read about and discuss medication safety

LANGUAGE FOCUS

Grammar: Questions (*Does this medicine have any side effects?*)

Vocabulary: *Generic drug, side effect, dosage, quantity*

For vocabulary support, see these **Oxford Picture Dictionary** topics: A Pharmacy, pages 114–115; Taking Care of Your Health, pages 116–117; Medical Care, page 111

STRATEGY FOCUS

Read text near a chart to find a summary of the data and/or information the author thinks is most important.

READINESS CONNECTION

In this lesson, students verbally communicate information about using medication safely.

PACING

To compress this lesson: Assign 1E and/or 1F for homework.

To extend this lesson: Have students ask and answer questions about medicine labels. (See end of lesson.)

And/or have students complete **Workbook 3 page 56** and **Multilevel Activities 3 Unit 8 pages 94–95**.

CORRELATIONS

CCRS: SL.1.B (a.) Come to discussions prepared, having read or studied required material; explicitly draw on that preparation and other information known about the topic to explore ideas under discussion. (b.) Follow agreed-upon rules for discussions. (c.) Ask questions to check understanding of information presented, stay on topic, and link their comments to the remarks of others. (d.) Explain their own ideas and understanding in light of the discussion.

SL.2.B Determine the main ideas and supporting details of a text read aloud or information presented in diverse media and formats, including visually, quantitatively, and orally.

R.1.B Ask and answer such questions as who, what, where, when, why, and how to demonstrate understanding of key details in a text.

R.2.A Identify the main topic and retell key details of a text.

R.5.B Know and use various text features to locate key facts or information in a text efficiently.

R.7.C Interpret information presented visually, orally, or quantitatively and explain how the information contributes to an understanding of the text in which it appears.

L.1.B (l.) Produce simple, compound and complex sentences.

L.4.B (b.) Determine the meaning of the new word formed when a known prefix is added to a known word. (e.) Use glossaries and beginning dictionaries, both print and digital, to determine or clarify the meaning of words and phrases.

RF.3.B (c.) Identify and know the meaning of the most common prefixes and derivational suffixes.

RF.4.B (a.) Read grade-level text with purpose and understanding.

ELPS: 1. An ELL can construct meaning from oral presentations and literary and informational text through level-appropriate listening, reading, and viewing. 3. An ELL can speak and write about level-appropriate complex literary and informational texts and topics.

Warm-up and Review
10–15 minutes (books closed)

Bring in empty bottles of some familiar over-the-counter medications and prescriptions (with the patient's name blacked out). Pass the bottles around to different areas of the room. Ask volunteers to read the name of the medication and say what it's for. Ask them to find the adult dosage on the label. After students have spoken, have them pass the bottle so others can check the information.

Introduction
5 minutes

1. Say: *All of these medicines can be helpful when used correctly and dangerous when not used correctly.*

2. State the objective: *Today we're going to read about and discuss using medication safely.*

1 Read

Presentation
10–20 minutes

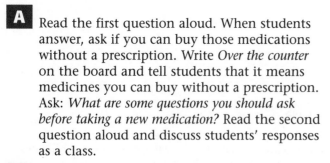 Read the first question aloud. When students answer, ask if you can buy those medications without a prescription. Write *Over the counter* on the board and tell students that it means medicines you can buy without a prescription. Ask: *What are some questions you should ask before taking a new medication?* Read the second question aloud and discuss students' responses as a class.

B Read the words and definitions. Tell students that *acetaminophen* and *ibuprofen* are generic names. Ask them if they know the popular brand names. Elicit other common side effects besides headaches.

Pre-reading

C Read the instructions aloud and confirm that students understand where the bolded headings are. Have students answer the question individually and then check answers as a class. If any students answer incorrectly, ask them to support their answer using the title and bolded headings. Establish the correct answer.

Answer
c. Advice on how to avoid problems with medications.

Guided Practice: While Reading
20–30 minutes

 1. Direct students' attention to the *Reader's Note* and read the information aloud. Ask students to read the article silently and answer the question.

2. Check answers as a class.

3. Check comprehension. Ask: *How long is the prescription good for?* [about five months] *How often should Joe take the medicine?* [three times a day] *Who can you ask about your medication?* [your doctor or pharmacist] *When should you read the label?* [each time you take the medicine]

Possible Answers
Ask the doctor or pharmacist questions about the medication, read and understand the label, follow the directions

MULTILEVEL STRATEGIES
Adapt 1D to the level of your students. • **Pre-level** While other students are reading 1D, direct these students to read the medicine label. Write these words on the board: *prescription, refill, expiration*. Ask students to copy the words and look them up in their dictionaries.

Guided Practice: Rereading
10–15 minutes

 1. Provide an opportunity for students to extract evidence from the text. Have students reread the article and underline the percentages and note what they learned from them.

2. Pair students and tell them to compare the percentages they underlined and what they learned from them and report anything they disagree on. Discuss and clarify as needed.

Answers
<u>63 percent</u> of Americans say they have taken vitamins in the last six months. <u>68 percent</u> say they have taken over-the-counter (OTC) medication. <u>54 percent</u> say they have taken a prescription medicine.

 1. Have students work individually to mark the answers *T* (true), *F* (false), and *NI* (no information). They should then write the line numbers where they found the true and false answers. Write the answers on the board.

2. Elicit and discuss any additional questions about the reading. You could introduce new questions for class discussion: *Have you followed any of the advice in the article? Do you ever have trouble following instructions on your medications? Have you ever experienced side effects? How do you feel about generic drugs?*

Answers
1. T, lines 1–2
2. NI
3. T, line 9
4. NI
5. F, line 18

MULTILEVEL STRATEGIES

After 1F, adapt further comprehension questions to the level of your students.

• **Pre-level** Ask these students *yes/no* and *or* questions about the medicine label from 1D while other students are completing 1F. *Whose prescription is it? When did he fill the prescription? How many capsules will he take in a day?*

• **On-level and Higher-level** Have these students correct the false statements and, if the Internet is available, find out if the NI answers are true or false.

2 Word study

Guided Practice: Post-reading
10–15 minutes

A 1. Direct students to look at the chart and identify the topic (the prefix *re-*). Have students read the chart.

2. Read the sentence in the chart and the example for *fill* and *refill*. Elicit sentences for the other words in the chart.

3. Have students repeat after you as you say each word with natural intonation, rhythm, and stress.

4. Direct students to complete the sentences and then compare answers with a partner. Read the correct answers and have students check their work.

Answers	
1. rewrite	4. refill
2. reread	5. take
3. reprint	6. reuse

B 1. Read the sentence stems aloud. Give students a few minutes to complete the sentences.

2. Set a time limit (ten minutes). Have groups of three or four discuss their sentences. Circulate and help as needed.

3. Have students share their responses with the class.

3 Talk it over

Guided Practice
15–20 minutes

A Have students look at the graph and read the note and the *Reader's Note*. Point out that they need to use the information from the graph and the note to answer the questions. Set a time limit (ten minutes). Have students work in pairs to complete the task. Ask volunteers to share their answers with the class.

Answers
1. Injuries
2. 3%
3. Pain, arm trouble, breathing issues
4. 44.5
6. 44.5% of Americans visit an emergency room each year. That equals 136.3 million ER visits every year.

Communicative Practice
15–20 minutes

B Read the questions aloud. Set a time limit (ten minutes). Tell students to copy the chart in their notebooks and complete it with their answers to the questions.

C Ask volunteers to share their ideas with the class.

Application
5–10 minutes

BRING IT TO LIFE

Ask students what common over-the-counter medicines they have in their houses. Have them choose one and write down the information to share with the class.

EXTENSION ACTIVITY

Ask about Medicine Labels

1. Use the label on page 126, or pass out empty medicine bottles. As a class, brainstorm the questions students can ask about the label. *How often do I need to take this? What's the dosage? How long should I take it? What's it for? What's the expiration date? Can my child take this medicine?*

2. Have students practice asking and answering the questions with a partner.

AT WORK

Warm-up and Review
5–10 minutes

Begin the lesson by asking students to think about the teamwork they did in Lesson 1, 2C. Ask volunteers to describe how they participated. *Did everyone on your team get a chance to participate?*

Introduction
10 minutes

1. Ask: *Do you like to participate in meetings at work or discussions in class? What do you like or not like about it?*

3. State the objective: *Today we're going to learn how to help all teammates participate in a discussion.*

Presentation
5 minutes

 A 2-44 Read the instructions aloud. Play the audio. Give students a minute to think about the question. Elicit responses from the class.

Answer
How to deal with the rising cost of medical insurance

Guided Practice
10–15 minutes

 B 2-44 Play the audio again. Direct students to listen for each solution and put a check next to any that they hear mentioned.

Answers
Checked: require employees to pay more have the company pay more offer less expensive health insurance

C 2-44 Read the instructions aloud. Play the audio again, encouraging students to take notes in their notebooks. Set a time limit (five minutes) for students to discuss their answers with a partner. Circulate to monitor.

Answers
1. Require employees to pay more: Many employees are already paying hundreds of dollars of their own money for medical bills. 2. Have the company pay more: The company can't afford extra expenses for higher insurance costs. 3. Offer less expensive health insurance: Cheaper plans will also require the patient to pay more of each medical expense.

Presentation and Communicative Practice
15–20 minutes

D 1. Direct students' attention to the *Do/Say* chart and ask students to identify the lesson's soft skill [helping teammates participate]. Ask the class which column has examples of language [right] and which has examples of activities [left].

2. Say a phrase from the left column and act it out. Say it again and have the class act it out with you. Say it a third time and have the class act it out for you. To confirm understanding, combine phrases: *Look at your teammate and tilt your head.*

3. Model the sentences from the right column using authentic intonation. Have students practice imitating your inflection.

4. Put students in teams of four and assign each team a question. Assign roles: manager, administrative assistant, researcher, and reporter. (Researchers will ask you questions on behalf of the team.) Verify understanding of the roles. Set a time limit (five minutes) and monitor.

5. Write sentence frames on the board that teams can use to summarize their response. (*Our team discussed the following question: _____ We decided _____ because _____.*)

6. Call "time" and let reporters rehearse their report for one minute. Direct each reporter to present to three other teams.

Communicative Practice and Application
10–15 minutes

 E 1. Tell students that they are going to work in pairs and have a conversation about what the company in A can do about higher medical insurance costs. Model the conversation with a volunteer. Confirm understanding of the task. Ask: *Will you talk only about the ideas in the audio?* [no] *How will you record your ideas?* [in a list]

2. Invite volunteers to share their suggestions.

Possible Answers
Offer a limited number of doctors and nurses people can see. Give insurance only to healthy people. Give insurance only to young people. Offer insurance only to employees after two years of employment.

 F 1. Have pairs merge to form teams of four. Tell students that they are going to be role-playing a staff meeting where they will suggest solutions to higher health-care costs at work.

2. Direct groups to think of more solutions that they did not talk about in E. Each group should select a manager to run the meeting. The other three members should each take turns bringing up solutions. Briefly review the ways to help everyone participate, if necessary.

3. As students carry out the role-play, circulate and monitor. Provide global feedback once the activity ends.

Lesson Overview

MULTILEVEL OBJECTIVES

Pre-, On-, and Higher-level: Review unit language

LANGUAGE FOCUS

Grammar: *Used to* (*I used to swim every day.*)

Present perfect continuous (*I've been swimming since I was five.*)

Vocabulary: Health habits vocabulary

For vocabulary support, see this **Oxford Picture Dictionary** topic: Taking Care of Your Health, pages 116–117

READINESS CONNECTION

In this review, students work in a team to use *used to* and the present perfect continuous to talk about living well.

PACING

To extend this review: Have students complete **Workbook 3 page 57**, **Multilevel Activities 3 Unit 8 page 96**, and **Multilevel Grammar Exercises 3 Unit 8**.

Lesson Notes

CORRELATIONS

CCRS: SL.1.B (a.) Come to discussions prepared, having read or studied required material; explicitly draw on that preparation and other information known about the topic to explore ideas under discussion. (b.) Follow agreed-upon rules for discussions. (c.) Ask questions to check understanding of information presented, stay on topic, and link their comments to the remarks of others. (d.) Explain their own ideas and understanding in light of the discussion.

SL.2.B Determine the main ideas and supporting details of a text read aloud or information presented in diverse media and formats, including visually, quantitatively, and orally.

SL.4.B Report on a topic or text, tell a story, or recount an experience with appropriate facts and relevant, descriptive details, speaking clearly at an understandable pace.

SL.6.B Speak in complete sentences when appropriate to task and situation in order to provide requested detail or clarification.

R.1.B Ask and answer such questions as who, what, where, when, why, and how to demonstrate understanding of key details in a text.

R.2.A Identify the main topic and retell key details of a text.

L.1.B (l.) Produce simple, compound and complex sentences.

L.1.C (d.) Use modal auxiliaries to convey various conditions. (f.) Use verb tense to convey various times, sequences, states, and conditions.

RF.4.B (a.) Read grade-level text with purpose and understanding.

ELPS: 5. An ELL can conduct research and evaluate and communicate findings to answer questions or solve problems. 6. An ELL can analyze and critique the arguments of others orally and in writing.

Warm-up and Review
10–15 minutes (books closed)

1. Review *At Work* activity F.

2. Ask students to share the good, not-so-good, and interesting things that happened during the conversation. As students speak, write their responses in a chart on the board.

Introduction and Presentation
5 minutes

1. Tell students something you used to do. *I used to live in Arizona.* Ask: *What did you use to do?* Write your question and some of their answers on the board.

2. Tell students about something you have been doing lately. *I've been waking up early lately.* Ask what they have been doing and write a few of their sentences on the board.

3. State the objective: *Today we're going to review* used to *and the present perfect continuous to talk about living well.*

Guided Practice
15–20 minutes

A Direct students to work in groups of three or four and look at the picture. Have students take turns reading the sentences aloud.

2. Set a time limit (five minutes) for groups to complete the task. Circulate and monitor.

3. Check answers as a class.

Answers	
1. b	5. e
2. c	6. f
3. a	7. g
4. d	

B Read the instructions aloud and have students work in the same teams from A to complete the task. Circulate and monitor.

Communicative Practice
30–45 minutes

C 1. Have students walk around the room to read their statements. To get students moving, tell them to talk to three people who were not on their team for B.

2. Set a time limit (five minutes) to complete the exercise. Circulate and answer any questions.

D 1. Direct students to look at the pictures and ask volunteers to describe what they see. Put students in groups of three or four. Read the instructions and the sample sentences.

2. Set a time limit (five minutes) and have groups complete the task. Have volunteers share their sentences with the class.

E 1. Have students walk around the room to conduct the interviews. To get students moving, tell them to interview three people who were not on their team for B or D.

2. Set a time limit (five minutes) to complete the exercise.

3. Tell students to make a note of their classmates' answers but not to worry about writing complete sentences.

MULTILEVEL STRATEGIES

Adapt the mixer in E to the level of your students.

• **Pre- and On-level** Pair these students and have them interview other pairs together.

• **Higher-level** Have these students ask an additional question and write all answers in complete sentences.

F 1. Call on individuals to report what they learned about their classmates. Keep a running tally on the board for each question, marking healthy meals, whether students think most people eat well or not, or whether it is easy or difficult for most people to exercise.

2. Use your tally for question 1 to create a pie chart on the board. Instruct students to draw pie charts for questions 2 and 3 in their notebooks. Circulate and answer any questions.

PROBLEM SOLVING
10–15 minutes

A 🔊 **2-45** 1. Ask: *Have you ever had a small accident? Were there people around to help?* Tell students they will read a story about a husband and wife who have a problem while riding their bikes. Direct students to read Juan and Anita's story silently.

2. Ask: *How did she hurt her ankle?* [She fell off her bike.] *Why do they think her ankle is broken?* [She can't move it.] *Why don't they go home?* [They don't know where they are in the park.]

3. Play the audio and have students read along silently.

B 1. Elicit answers to question 1. Guide students to a class consensus on the answer.

2. As a class, brainstorm answers to question 2. Ask students if they know someone who has this problem and has overcome it or what they have done themselves to overcome the same problem.

Answers
1. Anita fell off her bike while riding in a park and hurt her ankle. Juan has a cell phone but doesn't know where he is in the park.
2. Answers will vary.

Evaluation
20–25 minutes

To test students' understanding of the unit language and content, have them take the Unit 8 Test, available on the Teacher Resource Center.

Unit Overview

This unit explores car ownership with a range of employability skills and contextualizes time clauses to describe events and the structures *and...too, and...not either,* and *but.*

KEY OBJECTIVES	
Lesson 1	Identify automotive vocabulary
Lesson 2	Write a post about a memorable vacation
Lesson 3	Use time clauses to describe events
Lesson 4	Negotiate a price
Lesson 5	Learn about the lemon law
At Work	Build consensus
Teamwork & Language Review	Review unit language

UNIT FEATURES	
Academic Vocabulary	*maintenance, manual, consumer, reliable, features*
Employability Skills	• Compare time clauses • Determine pros and cons of owning a car • Analyze different types of car • Decide what to do if your car suddenly stops • Work independently • Understand teamwork • Locate information • Communicate verbally • Listen actively • Use writing skills • Comprehend written material • Analyze information

Resources	**Class Audio** CD3, Tracks 02–12
	Workbook Unit 9, pages 58–64
	Teacher Resource Center
	    Multilevel Activities 3 Unit 9
	    Multilevel Grammar Exercises 3 Unit 9
	    Unit 9 Test
	Oxford Picture Dictionary Basic Transportation, Buying and Maintaining a Car, Parts of a Car, A Road Trip

Lesson Overview	Lesson Notes

MULTILEVEL OBJECTIVES

On-level: Identify interior and exterior automobile parts and describe their functions

Pre-level: Identify interior and exterior automobile parts

Higher-level: Talk and write about automobiles

LANGUAGE FOCUS

Grammar: Simple present tense (*You use the rearview mirror to see behind you.*)

Vocabulary: Interior and exterior automobile parts

For vocabulary support, see this **Oxford Picture Dictionary** topic: Parts of a Car, pages 162–163

STRATEGY FOCUS

Pool knowledge with team members to maximize vocabulary learning.

READINESS CONNECTION

In this lesson, students communicate information about cars and car repair.

PACING

To compress this lesson: Conduct 1C and/or 2A as a whole-class activity.

To extend this lesson: Have students discuss cars. (See end of lesson.)

And/or have students complete **Workbook 3 page 58** and **Multilevel Activities 3 Unit 9 pages 98–99**.

CORRELATIONS

CCRS: SL.1.B (d.) Explain their own ideas and understanding in light of the discussion.

SL.2.B Determine the main ideas and supporting details of a text read aloud or information presented in diverse media and formats, including visually, quantitatively, and orally.

SL.4.B Report on a topic or text, tell a story, or recount an experience with appropriate facts and relevant, descriptive details, speaking clearly at an understandable pace.

R.1.B Ask and answer such questions as who, what, where, when, why, and how to demonstrate understanding of key details in a text.

R.4.B Determine the meaning of general academic and domain-specific words and phrases in a text relevant to a topic or subject area.

W.7.A Participate in shared research and writing projects.

L.1.B (l.) Produce simple, compound and complex sentences.

L.4.B (a.) Use sentence-level context as a clue to the meaning of a word or phrase. (e.) Use glossaries and beginning dictionaries, both print and digital, to determine or clarify the meaning of words and phrases.

RF.4.B (a.) Read grade-level text with purpose and understanding.

ELPS: 8. An ELL can determine the meaning of words and phrases in oral presentations and literary and informational text.

Warm-up and Review
10–15 minutes (books closed)

Find out how many car words students already know. Draw a simple car on the board and ask students to brainstorm words they associate with it. Write their ideas on the board.

Introduction
3 minutes

1. Ask how many of your students have a car. Ask if any of them can fix a car.

2. State the objective: *Today we're going to learn words for talking about cars.*

1 Identify automotive vocabulary

Presentation I
15–20 minutes

 1. Write *Parts of a car* on the board and elicit a few words that students remember from the *Warm-up*.

2. Read the instructions and the questions aloud. Put students in groups of three or four and have them take turns reading the sentences in the text to each other. Circulate and answer any questions about vocabulary. Have students work together to answer the questions based on the picture and the text.

3. If some students have changed their oil, ask them how they learned to do it and how often they do it.

Answers
1. Answers will vary.
2. Change your oil every 3,000 miles; answers will vary.

 1. Read the instructions aloud. Model the task by "thinking aloud" about the word *maintenance*: *I know that changing the oil is something you do to keep your car running well, and it's not a repair. So,* maintenance *must mean things you do regularly to make sure your car or something else works well.*

2. Set a time limit (three minutes) and direct students to do the task individually and then compare their answers with a partner.

3. Have students share their partner's answers with the class.

Guided Practice I
15–20 minutes

 (3-02) 1. Direct students to look at the words in the picture in 1A. Elicit any words that students do not know and write them on the board. Ask volunteers to explain any of the words they know.

2. Direct students to look up any remaining unknown words in their dictionaries. Discuss those words in relation to the lesson.

3. Set a time limit (five minutes) and have students do the task individually.

4. Play the audio for students to check their answers.

Answers	
1. windshield	5. turn signal
2. headlights	6. trunk
3. tires	7. license plate
4. hood	8. bumper

Communicative Practice and Application I
15–20 minutes

 1. Set a time limit (five minutes) and have pairs discuss the question.

2. Have students share their responses with the class. Write them on the board and tally which car repair the majority of the class thinks is the most common.

> **TIP**
> Give students the opportunity to share any experiences they have had with car repair.

2 Learn about the interior of a car

Presentation II
10–20 minutes

 1. Direct students to look at the picture of the car interior. Introduce the new topic: *Now we're going to look at the inside of a car.*

2. Read the words aloud and ask about each one. *What do you do with the steering wheel? What's the ignition for?* Have students repeat each word.

3. Ask students to work individually to complete the chart. Go over the answers as a class.

4. Check comprehension. Ask: *What tells you how fast the car is going?* [speedometer] *What do you use to see out the back window?* [rearview mirror]

5. Direct students to look at the picture again and identify any items that are not labeled (radio, vents, dashboard, gas gauge, etc.).

Answers	
Car part	**Function**
rearview mirror	Use this to check the road behind you.
speedometer	Use this to check your speed.
steering wheel	Use this to steer the car.
ignition	Use this to start the car.
glove compartment	Use this to keep the owner's manual safe.
horn	Use this to warn other drivers.

Guided Practice II
10–15 minutes

 B 1. Model the conversation with a volunteer. Model it again using other information from 2A.

2. Set a time limit (three minutes). Direct students to practice with a partner.

3. Call on volunteers to present their version of the conversation for the class.

Communicative Practice and Application II
20–25 minutes

C 1. If students will use the Internet for this task, establish what device(s) they'll use: a class computer, tablets, or smartphones. Alternatively, print information from the Internet before class and distribute to groups.

2. Write the information types from 2C on the board. Explain that students will work in teams to research and report on this information. Ask: *Which search terms or questions can you use to find the information you need?* ["Honda Accord" + "cost new," "Toyota Prius" + "cost of insurance," etc.] *How will you record the information you find?* [table, checklist, index cards] Remind students to bookmark or record sites so they can find or cite them in the future.

3. Group students and assign roles: manager, administrative assistant, IT support, and reporter. Verify students' understanding of the roles.

4. Give managers the time limit for researching the question (ten minutes). Direct the IT support to begin the online research or pick up the printed materials for each team. Direct the recorder to record information for the team using a table, a checklist, or index cards.

5. Give a two-minute warning. Call "time."

TIP

When setting up task-based activities, verify that students understand their roles using physical commands. For example: *If you report on your team's work, stand up* [reporter]. *If you keep the team on task, point to the clock* [manager]. *If you write the team's responses, raise your hand* [administrative assistant]. *If you help the team research, hold up your smartphone/tablet* [IT support].

 D 1. Copy the sentence frames on the board.

2. Direct teams to help their administrative assistant use the sentence frame to record the team's findings. Direct the reporter to use the recorded information to report the team's findings to the class or another team.

Evaluation
10–15 minutes

TEST YOURSELF

1. Direct Partner A to read prompts 1–4 from 1C on page 132 to Partner B. Partner B should close his or her book and write the answers in his or her notebook. When finished, students switch roles. Partner B reads prompts 5–8 from 1C.

2. Direct both partners to open their books and check their spelling when they finish.

MULTILEVEL STRATEGIES

Target the *Test Yourself* to the level of your students.

• **Pre-level** Have students do the task with their books open.

• **Higher-level** After these students have completed the task with the prompts from 1C, have them write additional sentences with the vocabulary words.

EXTENSION ACTIVITY
Discuss Cars

Discuss how cars have changed. Tell students that although cars have always had engines, steering wheels, and tires, they have changed in many ways in recent years. As a class, brainstorm a list of modern car features— for example, remote door locks, on-board navigation, side air bags, and hybrid engines. Write the list on the board. Ask students to rank these features from the one they would most like to have in their car to the ones they want the least.

Lesson Overview	Lesson Notes
MULTILEVEL OBJECTIVES	

On- and Higher-level: Analyze, write, and edit a post about a memorable vacation

Pre-level: Read a travel post and write about a memorable vacation

LANGUAGE FOCUS

Grammar: Past tense (*Last year I went to San Francisco.*)

Vocabulary: *Road trip, motel, scenic, lookout*

For vocabulary support, see this **Oxford Picture Dictionary** topic: A Road Trip, pages 166–167

STRATEGY FOCUS

Understand that the introduction of a text has two main purposes: it prepares readers for what they will read, and it creates reader interest with further details so that they will want to read more.

READINESS CONNECTION

In this lesson, students listen actively, read, and write about traveling.

PACING

To compress this lesson: Assign the *Test Yourself* and/or 3C for homework.

To extend this lesson: Have students talk about a "dream" vacation. (See end of lesson.)

And/or have students complete **Workbook 3 page 59** and **Multilevel Activities 3 Unit 9 page 100**.

CORRELATIONS

CCRS: SL.1.B (d.) Explain their own ideas and understanding in light of the discussion.

SL.2.B Determine the main ideas and supporting details of a text read aloud or information presented in diverse media and formats, including visually, quantitatively, and orally.

R.1.B Ask and answer such questions as who, what, where, when, why, and how to demonstrate understanding of key details in a text.

R.2.A Identify the main topic and retell key details of a text.

R.5.A Know and use various text features to locate key facts or information in a text.

R.7.B Use information gained from illustrations and the words in a text to demonstrate understanding of the text.

W.3.B Write narratives in which they recount a well-elaborated event or short sequence of events, include details to describe actions, thoughts, and feelings, use temporal words to signal event order, and provide a sense of closure.

W.4.B Produce writing in which the development and organization are appropriate to task and purpose.

W.5.B With guidance and support from peers and others, develop and strengthen writing as needed by planning, revising and editing.

L.1.B (l.) Produce simple, compound and complex sentences.

L.2.C (a.) Use correct capitalization. (d.) Use a comma to separate and introductory element from the rest of the sentence.

RF.4.B (a.) Read grade-level text with purpose and understanding.

ELPS: 6. An ELL can analyze and critique the arguments of others orally and in writing. 9. An ELL can create clear and coherent level-appropriate speech and text.

Warm-up and Review
10–15 minutes (books closed)

Write *Vacations* on the board. Underneath it, write *Where? How? Where do you sleep? What do you do?* Have volunteers come to the board and write the kinds of places people go on vacation (mountains, beaches, cities, landmarks, etc.), methods of travel, kinds of accommodations, and vacationing activities. Leave the list on the board.

Introduction
5 minutes

1. Tell students about a trip you have been on. Include the kinds of information listed on the board from the *Warm-up*.

2. State the objective: *Today we're going to read and write about traveling.*

1 Prepare to write

Presentation
20–25 minutes

 1. Build students' schema by asking questions about the title and pictures in the post. Ask: *Who do you think is writing the post? What does the title tell you about how the writer felt about the trip? Where did the family go? Where did they sleep?*

2. Give students one minute to tell a partner their responses to questions 1 and 2. Elicit responses from the class. Encourage students to respond to each other's ideas. After one student speaks, ask other students their opinions. *Do you agree or disagree with what he/she just said? Why?*

Answers
1. Answers will vary.
2. Camelback Mountain, Phoenix, Desert Botanical Garden, a motel, the Grand Canyon

B **3-03** 1. Introduce the model post and its purpose: *Now we're going to read a post from an online travel discussion board. As you read, look for the purpose of the post: Why is the writer writing?* Have students read the post silently.

2. Check comprehension. Ask: *How many days was the whole trip? What was the writer's favorite part of the trip?* Elicit what is happening in each of the pictures.

3. Play the audio. Have students read along silently.

Guided Practice I
10 minutes

C 1. Have students work independently to underline the answers to the questions in the post.

2. Point out the *Writer's Note* and read the information aloud. Ask: *How does the introduction in the post prepare readers for what they will read? Which details in the introduction create interest?*

3. Ask students to annotate the information they underlined with the phrases "places" for question 1, "Phoenix details" for question 2, and "Sonora Desert" and "Grand Canyon" for question 3. Have pairs compare answers. Have volunteers call out answers and write them on the board for the class to check.

Answers
1. Phoenix, the Sonora Desert, and the Grand Canyon
2. They stayed there for two days, visited the Desert Botanical Garden, and hiked up Camelback Mountain.
3. Possible answers: it's beautiful, there are few gas stations, it is hot

MULTILEVEL STRATEGIES

For 1C, challenge on- and higher-level students while working with pre-level students.

• **Pre-level** While other students are working on 1C, ask these students *yes/no* and *or* questions about the reading. *Did they take their trip in summer or spring? Was the Sonora Desert cold?* Give students time to copy the answers to 1C from the board.

• **On- and Higher-level** Write this question on the board for these students to answer after they finish 1C: *What is a scenic lookout? What advice does the writer give?* After allowing students to work individually to answer the questions, have volunteers share their ideas.

TIP

Have students work in small groups and ask: *What other places do you think this family would enjoy visiting?* Have groups share their ideas with the class and have the class vote on the best travel plan.

2 Plan and write

Guided Practice II
15–20 minutes

A 1. Read the questions. Demonstrate how to create a cluster diagram by drawing a circle and writing *My trip* in the center. Draw "spokes" with circles at the end and ask volunteers for one or two details to fill them in. Have students create their own cluster diagram for their trip. Have students share their diagrams with partners.

2. Ask volunteers to share their diagrams with the class.

> **MULTILEVEL STRATEGIES**
>
> Adapt 2A to the level of your students.
>
> • **Pre-level** Work with these students to respond to the questions in 2A. Give students time to answer in complete sentences before moving on to the next question.

B 1. Direct students to look back at the model in 1B. Focus their attention on the past and present tense verbs. Ask them to look through the post quickly and mark past and present verbs. Discuss the reasons for the tense choices.

2. Read through the trip review template. Elicit ideas that could go in each section. Have students write their trip reviews individually.

> **MULTILEVEL STRATEGIES**
>
> Adapt 2B to the level of your students.
>
> • **Pre-level** Sit with these students and help them write a simplified version of a trip review. Have them use the template and write one sentence per sentence stem.
>
> • **Higher-level** Tell these students to include some details about their favorite parts of the trip. *How was the weather? What did you see there? What did you do there?*

3 Get feedback and revise

Guided Practice III
5 minutes

A Direct students to check their writing using the editing checklist. Tell them to read each item in the list and check their papers before moving on to the next item. Explain that students should not edit their writing at this stage. They should just use the checklist to check their work and mark any areas they want to revise.

Communicative Practice
15 minutes

B 1. Read the instructions and the sample sentences aloud. Emphasize to students that they are responding to their partners' work, not correcting it.

2. Use the post in 1B to model the exercise. *I liked how the introduction made me want to read more. I'd like to ask this writer why the Grand Canyon is incredible.*

3. Direct students to exchange papers with a partner and follow the instructions.

C Allow students time to edit and revise their writing as necessary, using the editing checklist from 3A and their partner's feedback from 3B. If necessary, students could complete this task as homework.

> **TIP**
>
> If you have access to the Internet in class, have students look up pictures of their vacation spots. Encourage them to share the pictures with their partners when they exchange papers. Post their completed trip reviews with the pictures on a bulletin board.

Application and Evaluation
10 minutes

TEST YOURSELF

1. Review the instructions aloud. Assign a time limit (five minutes) and have students work independently.

2. Before collecting student work, invite two or three volunteers to share their sentences. Ask students to raise their hands if they wrote similar answers.

EXTENSION ACTIVITY

Talk about a Vacation

1. Pass out pictures of beautiful vacation spots or tell students to imagine a place they would love to go and have them quickly draw a "postcard" of it.

2. Tell students to imagine a "dream vacation." Write these questions on the board: *Where did you go? Who did you go with? How did you get there? How long did you stay? What did you do?* Elicit possible answers to these questions. Encourage students to use their imaginations.

3. Have students meet with several partners to show their "postcards" and ask and answer the questions.

Lesson Overview	Lesson Notes

MULTILEVEL OBJECTIVES

On- and Higher-level: Use past, present, and future time clauses to talk about driving and listen for the order of events

Pre-level: Recognize past, present, and future time clauses in conversations about driving

LANGUAGE FOCUS

Grammar: Past, present, and future time clauses (*When I start the car, it makes a strange noise. He put on his seat belt before he drove away. After I finish work. I'll call you.*)

Vocabulary: Automobile vocabulary

For vocabulary support, see these **Oxford Picture Dictionary** topics: Parts of a Car, pages 162–163; Buying and Maintaining a Car, page 161

STRATEGY FOCUS

Use time clauses to describe past, present, and future events.

READINESS CONNECTION

In this lesson, students practice using past, present, and future time clauses to talk about driving.

PACING

To compress this lesson: Conduct 1C and/or 2A as a whole-class activity.

To extend this lesson: Have students give travel advice. (See end of lesson.)

And/or have students complete **Workbook 3 pages 60–61, Multilevel Activities 3 Unit 9 pages 101–102,** and **Multilevel Grammar Exercises 3 Unit 9**.

CORRELATIONS

CCRS: SL.1.B (d.) Explain their own ideas and understanding in light of the discussion.

SL.2.B Determine the main ideas and supporting details of a text read aloud or information presented in diverse media and formats, including visually, quantitatively, and orally.

SL.6.B Speak in complete sentences when appropriate to task and situation in order to provide requested detail or clarification.

R.1.B Ask and answer such questions as who, what, where, when, why, and how to demonstrate understanding of key details in a text.

L.1.B (k.) Use coordinating and subordinating conjunctions. (l.) Produce simple, compound and complex sentences.

L.1.C (d.) Use modal auxiliaries to convey various conditions. (f.) Use verb tense to convey various times, sequences, states, and conditions.

L.1.D (j.) Explain the function of phrases and clauses in general and their function in specific sentences.

L.6.B Acquire and use accurately level-appropriate conversational, general academic, and domain-specific words and phrases, including those that signal spatial and temporal relationships.

RF.4.B (a.) Read grade-level text with purpose and understanding.

ELPS: 7. An ELL can adapt language choices to purpose, task, and audience when speaking and writing. 10. An ELL can demonstrate command of the conventions of standard English to communicate in level-appropriate speech and writing.

Warm-up and Review
10–15 minutes (books closed)

Ask for a show of hands of students who drove to school today. Choose a volunteer and use pantomime to coach him or her through a detailed description of driving away from home. *I put the keys in the ignition. I turned on the engine. I checked the rearview mirror. I backed out of the driveway.* Leave these sentences on the board.

Introduction
5–10 minutes

1. Say: *If we want to combine some of these sentences to show the sequence of events, we can use time words. After Jorge got in the car, he put the keys in the ignition.*

2. State the objective: *Today we're going to use past, present, and future time clauses to talk about driving.*

1 Learn to describe events with time clauses

Presentation I
20–25 minutes

1. Direct students to look at the picture. Ask: *Who are these men? Where are they?*

2. Read the instructions aloud. Ask students to read the introduction and the conversation silently and answer the questions.

3. Read the first question aloud. Call on a volunteer for the answer. Ask the volunteer where in the text he or she found the answer. Read the rest of the questions aloud, calling on a different volunteer for each answer.

Answers
1. This morning
2. Before he got to work
3. Before he drove to Denver last week
4. Call his mechanic

1. Demonstrate how to read the grammar chart. Copy the first sentence from the grammar chart on the board. Underline and label the main clause and the time clause. Elicit the verb tenses [present]. Read the other sentences in the chart. Ask students to identify the time clause in each sentence.

2. Direct students to underline the examples of time clauses in 1A. Go over the answers as a class.

3. For each underlined sentence in 1A, elicit which action came first. *Did he get to work first or did the red light next to the speedometer go on first?*

4. Assess students' understanding of the chart. *Can you use past tense verbs in time clauses? Can you use present tense verbs?*

5. Ask volunteers to combine some of the sentences from the *Warm-up* using *when*, *before*, and *after*.

Answers
When he started the car, Before he got to work, When I start the car, before I drove to Denver, after I finish work

Guided Practice I
10–15 minutes

1. Tell students they will collaborate to complete the description of the grammar point. Model collaboration by working with the class to complete the first sentence. Encourage students to look at 1A and 1B to help them determine the correct words.

2. Pair students and have them work together to complete the description.

3. Project or write the completed definition on the board and have pairs verify the accuracy of their responses. Ask volunteers which sentences confused them and discuss.

Answers
present
past
present
future

Guided Practice II
10–15 minutes

1. Read the instructions and the sample question and answers aloud. Have pairs do the task. Set a time limit (four minutes) and monitor the practice, identifying any issues.

2. Have volunteer pairs read their questions and answers aloud and have the class check answers.

2 Compare time clauses

Presentation II
30–45 minutes

A 1. Write this sentence frame on the board:
I usually _____ my car before I _____.
Elicit a present tense completion. Write
Yesterday, I _____ my car before I _____.
Elicit a past tense completion. Write *Tomorrow, I _____ my car before I _____.* Elicit a future tense completion. Say: *Now we're going to compare time clauses with* when, before, *and* after *in the past, present, and future.*

2. Underline each of the verbs. Draw students' attention to the use of the present tense verb in the future time clause. Reverse the order of the clauses to illustrate that the verb tenses don't change when the clauses are reversed.

3. Direct students to circle the correct words to complete the sentences. Ask volunteers to read the completed sentences aloud.

Answers
1. take
2. took
3. left
4. will buy

Guided Practice III
10–15 minutes

B 1. Read the instructions and the sample answer aloud. Have pairs take turns asking and answering the questions with time clauses. Circulate and monitor.

2. Have volunteers write their answers on the board for the class to check.

C 1. Elicit the importance of accuracy. Tell students they will be building their accuracy in this task.

2. Organize students into groups. Demonstrate how to correct the sentence using the first example.

3. Have team members work together to correct the sentences. Circulate and monitor teamwork.

4. Project or write the corrected sentences on the board and have teams check their work.

5. Address questions and any issues you noted during your observation.

Answers
1. Before they **left** on a road trip yesterday, my parents called us.
2. My mother usually **drives** first before she lets my dad take the wheel.
3. They drove south on the Interstate 5 before they **turned** east on Highway 79.
4. They'll find a place to sleep tonight before the sun **sets**.
5. Tomorrow morning my parents **will leave** after they eat a good breakfast.

3 Listen for time clauses to determine the meaning

Guided Practice IV
15–20 minutes

🔊 **3-04** 1. Tell students that they are going to hear a series of sentences with time clauses and that they'll need to decide which action happens first in each sentence.

2. Direct students to read the first set of statements. Then play the first sentence and have students circle the correct letter.

3. Elicit answers from the class. If students answered incorrectly, play the audio again, providing a listening clue (for example, *listen for the time clause*).

4. Repeat for numbers 2–8.

Answers	
1. a	5. b
2. a	6. a
3. a	7. a
4. b	8. a

4 Use time clauses to talk about your life experience

Communicative Practice and Application
20–25 minutes

A 1. Put students in pairs. Read the two assignment options.

2. Check comprehension of the exercise. Ask: *Should you write about vacations and moving?* [no—choose one] *How many things do you need to list?* [five] *Who needs to write?* [both partners]

B 1. Give each student a letter *A–D*. Tell students to form groups with other students who have the same letter.

2. Read the sample conversation aloud with a volunteer. Direct students to share their answers with their groups.

C 1. Copy the chart on the board.

2. Elicit students' ideas for both categories and then write them on the board. Have the class vote for the top five in each category.

Evaluation
10–15 minutes

TEST YOURSELF

Ask students to write the sentences independently. Collect and correct their writing.

MULTILEVEL STRATEGIES
Target the *Test Yourself* to the level of your students.
• **Pre-level** Allow these students to write first-person sentences. *I always _____ before I move to a new place. I always _____ after I move to a new place.*
• **Higher-level** Have these students write a paragraph in response to these questions: *How do you prepare for moving? What do you do afterward? How is what you do the same as or different from what your classmates do?*

EXTENSION ACTIVITY
Give Travel Advice
1. Give students several time clauses to get started with and then elicit completions.
Before you go overseas, you should _____.
When you travel in a foreign country, you should _____.
After you drive for several hours, you should _____.
2. Ask students to work with a partner to come up with more travel advice using *when, before,* and *after*. Call on volunteers to share their ideas with the class.

Lesson Overview

Lesson Notes

MULTILEVEL OBJECTIVES

Pre-, On-, and Higher-level: Negotiate prices and listen for information about car buying

LANGUAGE FOCUS

Grammar: Conjunctions (*I like that car, and he does too. I don't like it, and neither does he.*)

Vocabulary: *Negotiate, consider, accept, afford, flexible*

For vocabulary support, see these **Oxford Picture Dictionary** topics: Parts of a Car, pages 162–163; Buying and Maintaining a Car, page 161

STRATEGY FOCUS

Use the schwa sound to make speech sound natural.

READINESS CONNECTION

In this lesson, students verbally communicate about and practice how to negotiate prices and listen for information about buying a car.

PACING

To compress this lesson: Do 6A as a class activity and skip 6B.

To extend this lesson: Have students do a car-for-sale corners jigsaw. (See end of lesson.)

And/or have students complete **Workbook 3 page 62** and **Multilevel Activities 3 Unit 9 page 103**.

CORRELATIONS

CCRS: SL.1.B (d.) Explain their own ideas and understanding in light of the discussion.

SL.2.B Determine the main ideas and supporting details of a text read aloud or information presented in diverse media and formats, including visually, quantitatively, and orally.

SL.4.B Report on a topic or text, tell a story, or recount an experience with appropriate facts and relevant, descriptive details, speaking clearly at an understandable pace.

SL.6.B Speak in complete sentences when appropriate to task and situation in order to provide requested detail or clarification.

R.1.B Ask and answer such questions as who, what, where, when, why, and how to demonstrate understanding of key details in a text.

R.7.B Use information gained from illustrations and the words in a text to demonstrate understanding of the text.

L.1.B (k.) Use coordinating and subordinating conjunctions (l.) Produce simple, compound and complex sentences.

L.1.D (j.) Explain the function of phrases and clauses in general and their function in specific sentences.

RF.2.A (g.) Isolate and pronounce initial, medial vowel, and final sounds (phonemes) in spoken single-syllable words.

RF.4.B (a.) Read grade-level text with purpose and understanding.

ELPS: 2. An ELL can participate in level-appropriate oral and written exchanges of information, ideas, and analyses, in various social and academic contexts, responding to peer, audience, or reader comments and questions. 9. An ELL can create clear and coherent level-appropriate speech and text.

Warm-up and Review
10–15 minutes (books closed)

Say: *Buying a car is a big investment. What should you do before you buy a car? What should you do after?* Elicit students' answers and make sure students use time clauses in their responses.

Introduction
3 minutes

1. Tell students that usually when we buy things in a store in the U.S., we don't negotiate prices. One major exception to that rule is at car dealerships.

2. State the objective: *Today we're going to learn how to negotiate prices and listen for information about buying a car.*

1 Learn ways to negotiate price

Presentation I
10 minutes

A 🔊 3-05 1. Direct students to look at the picture. Ask: *What is happening in the picture?* [a woman is buying a car]

2. Read the instructions aloud. Play the audio. Give students a minute to answer the question. Go over the answer as a class.

Answers
It only has 30,000 miles on it, and it has a two-year warranty.

Guided Practice I
20–25 minutes

B 🔊 3-05 1. Read the instructions and the questions aloud. Play the audio. Ask students to listen for the answer to each question.

2. Ask students to compare their answers with a partner. Circulate and monitor to ensure students understand the audio.

Answers
1. $12,500
2. $8,900
3. The bumper is dented, and the windshield has a crack.

C 🔊 3-06 Read the instructions aloud. Explain that students are going to listen and should write the words they hear to complete the sentences. Play the audio. Call on volunteers to elicit the answers.

Answers
1. flexible
2. Would you accept
3. work something out

2 Practice your pronunciation

Pronunciation Extension
10–15 minutes

A 🔊 3-07 1. Write *He doesn't have a warranty* on the board. Say the sentence with relaxed pronunciation and ask students to repeat it. Underline the *oe* in *doesn't*, the word *a*, and the second *a* in *warranty*. Say: *Now we're going to focus on the most common sound in English, the "uh" sound. This sound can be spelled with any vowel and is very common in unstressed syllables.*

2. Read the *Pronunciation Note* aloud and confirm students' understanding.

3. Play the audio and have students repeat the words.

B 🔊 3-08 1. Play the audio and have students listen for the schwa sound in each word.

> **TIP**
>
> Play the audio again and have students underline the schwa sound in each word.

C 🔊 3-08 1. Play the audio again. Have students repeat the words in 2B. Call on volunteers to read the words aloud, making sure they pronounce the schwa sound correctly.

2. Ask students to take turns reading the words in 2B with a partner. Monitor and provide feedback.

D Read the instructions aloud and have students do the task. Have them compare answers with a partner and take turns pronouncing the words.

Possible Answers
ag<u>ai</u>n, fin<u>a</u>l, probl<u>e</u>m, n<u>e</u>gotiate, comm<u>o</u>n, c<u>o</u>mpare

> **TIP**
>
> Have students call out the words they found. Write them on the board. Point to each word and have volunteers say which letter(s) is the schwa sound.

3 Learn *and...too, and...not either, but*

Presentation II
10–15 minutes

 1. Introduce the new topic: *Now we're going to learn how to combine sentences with the conjunctions* and *and* but.

2. Direct students to look at the first set of sentences in the chart. Read them aloud. Ask: *Do Tom and I agree or disagree?* [agree] *Do we use* and *or* but *to show agreement?* [and] *Do we use* too *or* either*?* [too] Read the second set of sentences. *Are we saying the same thing about the radio and the CD player or something different?* [same] *Do we use* and *or* but *when the two parts of the sentence agree or say the same thing?* [and] *Both parts of the sentence are negative. Do we use* too *or* either *with negatives?* [either] Read the third set of sentences. *When do we use* but? [to show difference] *Do we use* too *or* either *with* but? [no]

Guided Practice II
10–15 minutes

 Have students work individually to circle the correct words in the sentences. Go over the answers as a class.

Answers
1. either
2. but
3. too
4. either

TIP

If you have access to the Internet in class, have your students look up information about two or three different cars and compare them using *and...too, and...not either,* and *but.* Tell them to choose a car year, make, and model. They can find safety test results, gas mileage, and reliability ratings. They can also find out where the car is being sold nearby and for how much. Have students share their information with each other or with the class.

4 Building conversational skills

Guided Practice III
15–20 minutes

 Direct students to look at the picture and skim the conversation in 4B. Have them work with partners to answer the questions. Elicit responses and ask: *How do you know?* or *Why do you say that?* to encourage students to state their reasoning.

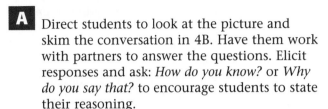 1. Ask students to read the instructions and tell you what they are going to do [listen and read and respond to the question]. Play the audio and then elicit the answer to the question.

Answer
$8,000

2. Ask students to read the conversation with a partner. Circulate and monitor pronunciation. Model and have students repeat difficult words or phrases.

3. Ask: *In what other situations could you use this conversation?* Point out a few phrases that are not specific to a conversation between a car dealer and a customer. Ask volunteers to point out others.

Communicative Practice and Application I
20–25 minutes

 1. Pair students and have them read the instructions silently. Check their comprehension of the exercise. Ask: *What are the two roles? Where does the conversation happen?*

2. Model and have students repeat the sentence stems and sentences in the *In Other Words* box in 4B. Explain that they should use these in their conversations.

3. Draw a T-chart on the board. Label the left column *Dealer* and the right column *Customer.* Elicit examples of what each person might say and make notes in the chart.

4. Set a time limit (three minutes). Have students act out the role-play. Call "time" and have students switch roles.

5. Ask three volunteer pairs to act out their role-play for the class. Tell students who are listening to make a simple table with four rows and two columns. Use the top row to label the columns *Car details* and *Problems with car.* Have students take notes in the chart for each role-play.

MULTILEVEL STRATEGIES

Seat same-level students together.

- **Pre-level** Provide a simplified conversation for these students. *A: This is a very stylish car. It has 17,000 miles on it and a two-year warranty. B: How much is it? A: It's $8,000. B: That's too expensive. The turn signals don't work. A: I'll talk to my manager.*
- **Higher-level** You can challenge students to add another problem to talk about, such as scratches in the paint, tear in the seat, headlight out.

5 Focus on listening for details

Presentation III and Guided Practice IV

20–25 minutes

A 1. Read the statement aloud and model a discussion with a volunteer. Say: *I think a new car is not worth the expense. We have lots of buses in town. Do you agree? Why? / Why not? I agree because… / I disagree because…*

2. Pair students and tell them to discuss their own opinions. Circulate and monitor.

TIP

Remind students that they shouldn't be shy about asking another student to repeat what he or she said. Review phrases such as *Can you repeat that? Excuse me—what did you say? Can you say that first part again?* and so on.

B Direct students to read the sentences before they listen to the interview. Ask what kind of information they'll be writing in the blanks. Ask volunteers for predictions. If students struggle, start by offering your own prediction: *I think we will hear something about buying a car.*

C 3-10 1. Play the audio. Ask students to listen and write the correct words.

2. Pair students and have them compare answers. If a pair has different answers, have the class vote on the correct answer with a show of hands.

Answers
1. planning 2. insurance 3. 15,000 4. states 5. change

6 Discuss

Communicative Practice and Application II

15–20 minutes

A 1. Read the instructions aloud. Draw a sample chart on the board, with space for pros on one side and cons on the other. Call on volunteers to read the sample sentences in 6A. Explain that students will make a chart like this one based on their own discussions.

2. Put students into teams of three and assign roles: manager, administrative assistant, and reporter. Verify students' understanding of the roles. Encourage students to use the phrases in the *Speaking Note* during their discussions.

3. Set a time limit for the discussions (ten minutes). Write the sentence frame from 6B on the board. Then circulate and monitor.

B Call "time." Ask the reporter for each team to present the team's results to the class using the sentence frame on the board.

Evaluation

5 minutes

TEST YOURSELF

1. Ask students to complete the checkboxes individually.

2. Tell students that you are going to read each of the items in the checklist aloud. If they are not at all confident with that skill, they should hold up a closed fist. If they are not very confident, they should hold up one finger. If they are somewhat confident, two fingers; confident, three fingers; very confident, four fingers. If they think they could teach the skill, they should hold up five fingers. Read each item in the checklist and identify students who may need further support.

EXTENSION ACTIVITY

Do a Car-for-sale Corners Jigsaw

1. In large letters, write four car descriptions on four separate poster boards as follows: Dealership A: 4-door sedan, 30,000 miles, interior like new, gets 25 mpg, cracked rearview mirror, $8,000. Dealership B: small 2-door sedan, 15,000 miles, gets 40 mpg, broken turn signal, $10,000. Dealership C: van, 10,000 miles; car seat torn, gets 20 mpg, exterior like new, $9,000. Dealership D: station wagon, 20,000 miles, exterior and interior like new, gets 25 mpg, $9,000. Hang each in a different corner of the room.

2. Put students in groups of four. Tell them that they are going to choose a car to buy and that each group member is going to a different dealership to look at cars. Assign each group member a letter *A–D* and explain which letters go to which corners.

3. Tell each student to memorize the information about the car at his or her dealership. Encourage students to talk to each other about the car. Say: *Ask the other customers at the dealership if they think the car is a good deal.*

4. Have students return to their original groups and describe their car. Tell the groups to discuss the pros and cons of each car and decide which one to buy. Call on a reporter from each group to share which car they chose and why.

5. As a follow-up, have the groups write sentences about the cars using *and* or *but*. The van costs $9,000, and the station wagon does, too.

Lesson Overview

| Lesson Notes |

MULTILEVEL OBJECTIVES

Pre-, On-, and Higher-level: Read about and discuss lemon laws

LANGUAGE FOCUS

Grammar: Time clauses (*When you buy a car from a friend, lemon laws don't protect you.*)

Vocabulary: *Consumers, defect, lemon*

For vocabulary support, see these **Oxford Picture Dictionary** topics: Parts of a Car, pages 162–163; Buying and Maintaining a Car, page 161

STRATEGY FOCUS

Use questions in an article to scan and locate information you want.

READINESS CONNECTION

In this lesson, students verbally communicate information about laws that protect car buyers.

PACING

To compress this lesson: Assign 1E and/or 1F for homework.

To extend this lesson: Have students role-play a conversation with a mechanic. (See end of lesson.)

And/or have students complete **Workbook 3 page 63** and **Multilevel Activities 3 Unit 9 pages 104–105**.

CORRELATIONS

CCRS: SL.1.B (a.) Come to discussions prepared, having read or studied required material; explicitly draw on that preparation and other information known about the topic to explore ideas under discussion. (b.) Follow agreed-upon rules for discussions. (c.) Ask questions to check understanding of information presented, stay on topic, and link their comments to the remarks of others. (d.) Explain their own ideas and understanding in light of the discussion.

SL.2.B Determine the main ideas and supporting details of a text read aloud or information presented in diverse media and formats, including visually, quantitatively, and orally.

R.1.B Ask and answer such questions as who, what, where, when, why, and how to demonstrate understanding of key details in a text.

R.2.A Identify the main topic and retell key details of a text.

R.5.B Know and use various text features to locate key facts or information in a text efficiently.

R.6.B Identify the main purpose of a text, including what the author wants to answer, explain, or describe.

R.7.C Interpret information presented visually, orally, or quantitatively and explain how the information contributes to an understanding of the text in which it appears.

L.1.B (l.) Produce simple, compound and complex sentences.

L.4.B (c.) Use a known root word as a clue to the meaning of an unknown word with the same root. (e.) Use glossaries and beginning dictionaries, both print and digital, to determine or clarify the meaning of words and phrases.

RF.3.B (c.) Identify and know the meaning of the most common prefixes and derivational suffixes.

RF.4.B (a.) Read grade-level text with purpose and understanding.

ELPS: 1. An ELL can construct meaning from oral presentations and literary and informational text through level-appropriate listening, reading, and viewing. 3. An ELL can speak and write about level-appropriate complex literary and informational texts and topics.

Warm-up and Review

10–15 minutes (books closed)

Write *Car problems* on the board. Ask students to brainstorm common problems that people have with their cars (brakes don't work, battery dies, hoses break, electrical system fails, air conditioner doesn't work, etc.). Help them with vocabulary and write their ideas on the board.

Introduction

5 minutes

1. Tell students that everyone expects these things to happen eventually, but sometimes they happen when we first buy a car.

2. State the objective: *Today we're going to read about and discuss laws that protect car buyers.*

1 Read

Presentation

10–20 minutes

A Read the questions aloud. Use ideas from the *Introduction* to help guide discussion. Encourage students to share their experiences with buying defective cars, appliances, or machines.

B 1. Read the words and definitions. Elicit sample sentences for the words or supply them if the students can't.

2. Ask: *Why do you think a product with many problems is called a "lemon"? What kind of face do you make when you bite into a lemon?*

Pre-reading

C Read the instructions aloud and confirm that students understand where the bolded questions are. Have students answer the question individually and then check answers as a class. If any students answer incorrectly, ask them to support their answer using the questions. Establish the correct answer.

Answer
b. When lemon laws can protect a consumer.

Guided Practice: While Reading

20–30 minutes

D 1. Direct students' attention to the *Reader's Note* and read the information aloud. Ask students to read the article silently and answer the question.

2. Check answers as a class.

3. Check comprehension. *How many times can the car be repaired for the same defect before it's a "lemon"?* [three or four] *Are used-car buyers protected?* [sometimes] *What can you do to be sure you're protected?* [keep a maintenance log] *How many times a year did the car in the maintenance log need service?* [once a year]

Answer
Laws that say that a car company has to fix a car that is under warranty. If the car cannot be fixed, then the company must give the customer another car or a refund.

MULTILEVEL STRATEGIES
Adapt 1D to the level of your students.   • **Pre-level** Ask these students to read only the portion of the article with the bolded headings. During the comprehension check, elicit questions about vocabulary. Write words and definitions on the board.

Guided Practice: Rereading

10–15 minutes

E 1. Provide an opportunity for students to extract evidence from the text. Have students reread the article and think about who wrote it and why.

2. Pair students and tell them to compare their answers and report anything they disagree on. Discuss and clarify as needed.

Possible Answers
consumer protection group, to educate people about their rights when buying a car

F 1. Have students work individually to mark the answers *T* (true), *F* (false), and *NI* (no information). They should then write the line numbers where they found the true and false answers. Write the answers on the board.

2. Elicit and discuss any additional questions about the reading. You could introduce new questions for class discussion: *Have you followed any of the advice in the article? Do you think all cars should be protected under the lemon law?*

Answers	
1. F, lines 6–7	4. T, lines 25–27
2. T, lines 10–12	5. T, lines 31–32
3. F, lines 15–16	

2 Word study

Guided Practice: Post-reading
10–15 minutes

1. Direct students to look at the chart and identify the topic (the suffixes *-er* and *-or*). Read the information in the chart and the example for *buy* and *buyer.* Elicit sentences for the other words in the chart.

2. Have students repeat after you as you say each word with natural intonation, rhythm, and stress.

3. Direct students to complete the sentences and then compare answers with a partner. Read the correct answers and have students check their work.

Answers
1. consume, consumer
2. sell, sellers
3. dealer, deal with
4. owners, own

3 Talk it over

Guided Practice
15–20 minutes

A Have students look at the table and read the note and the *Reader's Note.* Point out that they need to use the information from the table and the note to answer the questions. Set a time limit (ten minutes). Have students work in pairs to complete the task. Ask volunteers to share their answers with the class.

Answers
1. Yoyo Spark
2. Yoyo Spark, Tron Starflight, and Prince Utah
3. KCar Drone
4. Tron Starflight
5. Holden LeCar
6. Body and Interior Dependability

Communicative Practice
15–20 minutes

B Read the questions aloud. Set a time limit (five minutes) and have pairs discuss the questions. Ask volunteers to share their ideas with the class.

Application
15–20 minutes

BRING IT TO LIFE

Read the instructions aloud. Ask students what kind of car they will be looking for. Have them brainstorm kinds of cars (sedan, sports car, convertible, SUV, etc.) and adjectives to describe cars (*luxurious, sporty, sleek, fast, vintage,* etc.).

EXTENSION ACTIVITY
Role-play a Conversation with a Mechanic
1. Brainstorm car problems and write them on the board: *Brakes are squealing; engine is making a funny noise; car isn't starting; engine dies when I stop.*
2. Write a conversation frame on the board.
Mechanic: What seems to be the problem?
Customer: _____.
Mechanic: OK. I'll check it out.
Customer: Can you give me an estimate?
Mechanic: I'll let you know after I look at it.
3. Have students practice the conversation with a partner. Tell them to practice in both roles.

Warm-up and Review

10–15 minutes

Review the *Bring It to Life* assignment from Lesson 5. Have students who did the exercise show the picture of their dream car and describe it. Ask other students to describe the car of their dreams and explain their choices. Discuss if everyone had the same idea about what a "dream car" is.

Introduction

10 minutes

1. Ask: *Do you find it difficult to disagree with others? What does* consensus *mean? Why is it important for a group to reach a consensus?*

3. State the objective: *Today we're going to learn how to build consensus.*

Presentation

5 minutes

 A ◀)) **3-11** Read the instructions aloud. Play the audio. Give students a minute to think about the question. Elicit responses from the class.

Answer
Preparation for a big holiday car sale

Guided Practice

10–15 minutes

 B ◀)) **3-11** Play the audio again. Direct students to listen for each task someone is working on and put a check next to any that they hear mentioned.

Answers
Checked: put ads in the newspaper hire a face painter make signs buy flags

C ◀)) **3-11** Read the instructions aloud. Play the audio again, encouraging students to take notes in their notebooks. Set a time limit (five minutes) for students to discuss their answers with a partner. Circulate to monitor. Check answers as a class.

Answers
What day to place a newspaper ad "What do you guys think?" "Some of us think Wednesday, and some of us think Thursday." "What do we agree on?" Color of the flags "How can we make everyone happy?" To hire a face painter or not "What do we need to change?"

Presentation and Communicative Practice

15–20 minutes

D 1. Direct students' attention to the *Do/Say* chart and ask students to identify the lesson's soft skill [building consensus]. Ask the class which column has examples of language [right] and which has examples of activities [left].

2. Tell students to imagine that they are all part of a meeting. Say a sentence from the left column and act it out. Say it again and have the class act it out with you. Say it a third time and have the class act it out for you.

3. Model the sentences and sentence frames from the right column using authentic intonation. Have students practice imitating your inflection.

4. Put students in teams of four and assign each team a question. Assign roles: manager, administrative assistant, researcher, and reporter. Researchers will ask you questions on behalf of the team. Verify understanding of the roles. Set a time limit (five minutes) and monitor.

5. Write sentence frames on the board that teams can use to summarize their response. (*Our team discussed the following question: _____ We decided _____ because _____.*)

6. Call "time" and let reporters rehearse their report for one minute. Direct each reporter to present to three other teams.

Communicative Practice and Application
15–20 minutes

E 1. Tell students that they are going to work in groups to think of possible work disagreements and then build consensus about those problems. Model the conversation with two volunteers. Confirm understanding of the task. Ask: *What will you do first?* [make a list of three problems] *How many people will run the staff meeting?* [one] *What is the role-play setting?* [a staff meeting]

2. Set a time limit (five minutes) and direct groups to take turns saying ideas of problems and choose three.

3. Set another time limit (ten minutes) and have groups do the role-play. As students carry out the role-play, circulate and monitor. Provide global feedback once the activity ends.

TEAMWORK & LANGUAGE REVIEW

Lesson Overview	Lesson Notes
MULTILEVEL OBJECTIVES	
Pre-, On-, and Higher-level: Review unit language	
LANGUAGE FOCUS	
Grammar: Time clauses (*She'll call when she gets home.*); conjunctions (*Tom doesn't like to drive and Shirley doesn't either.*) **Vocabulary:** Transportation and car repair vocabulary For vocabulary support, see these **Oxford Picture Dictionary** topics: Basic Transportation, pages 154–155; Buying and Maintaining a Car, page 161; Parts of a Car, pages 162–163	
READINESS CONNECTION	
In this review, students work in a team to use time clauses and conjunctions to talk about driving and transportation.	
PACING	
To extend this review: Have students complete **Workbook 3 page 64**, **Multilevel Activities 3 Unit 9 page 106**, and **Multilevel Grammar Exercises 3 Unit 9**.	

CORRELATIONS

CCRS: SL.1.B (a.) Come to discussions prepared, having read or studied required material; explicitly draw on that preparation and other information known about the topic to explore ideas under discussion. (b.) Follow agreed-upon rules for discussions. (c.) Ask questions to check understanding of information presented, stay on topic, and link their comments to the remarks of others. (d.) Explain their own ideas and understanding in light of the discussion.

SL.2.B Determine the main ideas and supporting details of a text read aloud or information presented in diverse media and formats, including visually, quantitatively, and orally.

SL.4.B Report on a topic or text, tell a story, or recount an experience with appropriate facts and relevant, descriptive details, speaking clearly at an understandable pace.

SL.6.B Speak in complete sentences when appropriate to task and situation in order to provide requested detail or clarification.

R.1.B Ask and answer such questions as who, what, where, when, why, and how to demonstrate understanding of key details in a text.

R.2.A Identify the main topic and retell key details of a text.

L.1.B (l.) Produce simple, compound and complex sentences.

L.1.C (d.) Use modal auxiliaries to convey various conditions. (f.) Use verb tense to convey various times, sequences, states, and conditions.

L.1.D (j.) Explain the function of phrases and clauses in general and their function in specific sentences.

L.6.B Acquire and use accurately level-appropriate conversational, general academic, and domain-specific words and phrases, including those that signal spatial and temporal relationships.

RF.4.B (a.) Read grade-level text with purpose and understanding.

ELPS: 5. An ELL can conduct research and evaluate and communicate findings to answer questions or solve problems. 6. An ELL can analyze and critique the arguments of others orally and in writing.

Warm-up and Review
10–15 minutes (books closed)

1. Review *At Work* activity E.

2. Ask students to share the good, not-so-good, and interesting things that happened during the conversation. As students speak, write their responses in a chart on the board.

Introduction and Presentation
10 minutes

1. Ask a volunteer to describe his or her typical morning. Write the information on the board as a series of simple sentences. *Hugo gets up at 6:00. He walks his dog. He takes a shower. He eats eggs for breakfast.* After you have four or five sentences, call on another student to provide information about the same time of day. Write those sentences on the board as well.

2. Call on volunteers to combine some of the sentences on the board with *when, before,* and *after.* *Hugo walks his dog before he takes a shower. Hugo eats breakfast after he takes a shower.*

3. Call on other volunteers to compare the two students' stories using *and* and *but.* *Hugo gets up at 6:00, but Kate doesn't. She gets up at 7:00. Hugo takes a shower in the morning, and Kate does, too.*

4. State the objective: *Today we're going to review time clauses and conjunctions to talk about driving and transportation.*

Guided Practice
15–20 minutes

A   Direct students to work in groups of three or four and look at the picture. Have students take turns reading the sentences under the picture aloud.

2. Set a time limit (five minutes) for groups to complete the task. Circulate and monitor.

3. Have volunteers share their sentences with the class. Write their sentences on the board and correct any mistakes as a class.

Possible Answers
The family will cross the street after the light turns green.
After the bus stops, the family will cross the street.
The truck stopped before the train came by.
The woman paid the taxi driver after he dropped her off.
The couple will get on the bus after they climb the subway stairs.

B   1. Read the instructions aloud and have students work in the same teams from A to complete the task. Circulate and monitor. Have volunteers share their sentences as a class.

2. Have students write their sentences on the board and check answers as a class.

Communicative Practice
30–45 minutes

C   1. Pair teams and have them take turns reading their statements and saying if they are about the past, present, or future.

2. Set a time limit (five minutes) to complete the exercise.

D   Group students and assign roles: manager, writer, editor, and two presenters. Explain that students are going to work with their teams to write a dialogue for someone returning their lemon to a car dealer. Editors will review the dialogue and offer suggestions for changes. Verify students' understanding of the roles.

2. Read steps 2–4 of the activity aloud. Check comprehension of the task. *What is the first thing you should do?* [choose a problem from the list or make one up] *Who should be in the role-play?* [a customer and a car dealer] Model the sample dialogue with a volunteer.

3. Set a time limit (ten minutes) to complete the task. Circulate and answer any questions.

4. Have the two presenters from each team act out their role-play for the class.

E   1. Have students walk around the room to conduct the interviews. To get students moving, tell them to interview three people who were not on their team for A or D.

2. Set a time limit (five minutes) to complete the exercise.

3. Tell students to make a note of their classmates' answers but not to worry about writing complete sentences.

Adapt the mixer in E to the level of your students.

• **Pre- and On-level** Pair these students and have them interview other pairs together.

• **Higher-level** Have these students ask an additional question and write all answers as complete sentences.

Evaluation
20–25 minutes

To test students' understanding of the unit language and content, have them take the Unit 9 Test, available on the Teacher Resource Center.

F 1. Call on individuals to report what they learned about their classmates. Keep a running tally on the board for each question, marking lemons bought, whether students think lemon laws should protect used cars too, and whether it is better to buy a car from a dealer or a private individual.

2. Use your tally for question 1 to create a pie chart on the board. Instruct students to draw pie charts for questions 2 and 3 in their notebooks. Circulate and answer any questions.

PROBLEM SOLVING
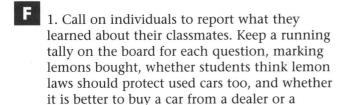
10–15 minutes

A **◀)) 3-12** 1. Ask: *Have you ever had something happen to your car in the middle of traffic?* Tell students they will read a story about a man who has a problem while driving to work. Direct students to read Frank's story silently.

2. Ask: *What does Frank do before work?* [He drives his kids to school.] *What did he hear?* [a strange noise from his car] *What is an intersection?* [a place where two roads cross each other]

3. Play the audio and have students read along silently.

B 1. Elicit answers to question 1. Guide students to a class consensus on the answer.

2. As a class, brainstorm answers and make a list for question 2. Ask students if they know someone who has this problem and has overcome it or what they have done themselves to overcome the same problem.

Answers
1. His car broke down in the middle of the street, and drivers of other cars are honking at him.
2. Answers will vary.

10 Crime Doesn't Pay

Unit Overview

This unit explores crime and community safety with a range of employability skills and contextualizes structures with gerunds and infinitives.

KEY OBJECTIVES	
Lesson 1	Identify safety vocabulary
Lesson 2	Identify home security features and write a letter asking for assistance
Lesson 3	Use gerunds as subjects to talk about home security
Lesson 4	Report a crime
Lesson 5	Identify careers in public safety
At Work	Show a positive attitude
Teamwork & Language Review	Review unit language

UNIT FEATURES	
Academic Vocabulary	*commit, areas, security, domestic, enforcement, options, inspector, investigate, federal, positive, attitude*
Employability Skills	• Determine the best way to avoid common crimes • Decide the similarities and differences between articles • Decide what to do if you think you see a crime • Listen actively • Understand teamwork • Communicate information • Work independently • Comprehend written material • Analyze information

Resources	**Class Audio** CD3, Tracks 13–23
	Workbook Unit 10, pages 65–71
	Teacher Resource Center
	    Multilevel Activities 3 Unit 10
	    Multilevel Grammar Exercises 3 Unit 10
	    Unit 10 Test
	Oxford Picture Dictionary The Legal System, Crime, Public Safety

Lesson Overview	Lesson Notes

MULTILEVEL OBJECTIVES

On-level: Identify safety vocabulary and describe the criminal justice system

Pre-level: Identify safety and criminal justice system vocabulary

Higher-level: Talk and write about safety and the criminal justice system

LANGUAGE FOCUS

Grammar: Present tense questions and answers (*What does a judge do? The judge listens to cases.*)

Vocabulary: Safety and criminal justice system vocabulary

For vocabulary support, see these **Oxford Picture Dictionary** topics: Public Safety, page 146; The Legal System, page 144

STRATEGY FOCUS

Pool knowledge with team members to maximize vocabulary learning.

READINESS CONNECTION

In this lesson, students explore and communicate information about safety and the criminal justice system.

PACING

To compress this lesson: Conduct 1D and/or 1E as a whole-class activity.

To extend this lesson: Have students listen for safety mistakes. (See end of lesson.)

And/or have students complete **Workbook 3 page 65** and **Multilevel Activities 3 Unit 10 pages 108–109**.

CORRELATIONS

CCRS: SL.1.B (d.) Explain their own ideas and understanding in light of the discussion.

SL.2.B Determine the main ideas and supporting details of a text read aloud or information presented in diverse media and formats, including visually, quantitatively, and orally.

SL.4.B Report on a topic or text, tell a story, or recount an experience with appropriate facts and relevant, descriptive details, speaking clearly at an understandable pace.

R.1.B Ask and answer such questions as who, what, where, when, why, and how to demonstrate understanding of key details in a text.

R.4.B Determine the meaning of general academic and domain-specific words and phrases in a text relevant to a topic or subject area.

R.7.C Interpret information presented visually, orally, or quantitatively and explain how the information contributes to an understanding of the text in which it appears.

W.7.A Participate in shared research and writing projects.

L.1.B (l.) Produce simple, compound and complex sentences.

L.4.B (a.) Use sentence-level context as a clue to the meaning of a word or phrase. (e.) Use glossaries and beginning dictionaries, both print and digital, to determine or clarify the meaning of words and phrases.

RF.4.B (a.) Read grade-level text with purpose and understanding.

ELPS: 8. An ELL can determine the meaning of words and phrases in oral presentations and literary and informational text.

Warm-up and Review
10–15 minutes (books closed)

Write *Crime* on the board. Elicit words students know for different kinds of crime: *car theft, mugging, bank robbery, murder, kidnapping, identity theft.* Write students' ideas on the board.

Introduction
3 minutes

1. Ask students how many of them worry about crime in their neighborhoods.

2. State the objective: *Today we're going to learn words for talking about safety and the criminal justice system.*

1 Identify safety vocabulary

Presentation I
15–20 minutes

A 1. Write *Staying safe* on the board and elicit one example from the whole class. Have students work together to brainstorm in a group. Make a list on the board of the ways to stay safe at home and the areas around town your students identify.

2. Have students identify the most effective ways of staying safe. Elicit ideas and put a checkmark next to the ways students feel are the most important, encouraging them to explain their reasons.

B 1. Copy the first two rows of the chart onto the board.

2. Model the task by "thinking aloud" about the first phrase in the chart and marking the first column appropriately. Work with a volunteer to demonstrate completing the second and third columns.

3. Direct students to review the vocabulary independently, marking the first column of the chart in their books.

4. Pair students and ask them to complete the second and third columns of the chart together.

C 1. Elicit any words that pairs did not know and write them on the board. Ask volunteers to explain any of the words they know.

2. Direct students to look up any remaining unknown words in their dictionaries. Discuss those words in relation to the lesson. (Note: 1D and 1E will confirm students' understanding of the target vocabulary.)

Guided Practice I
20–25 minutes

D 1. Read sentence 1 aloud. If students struggle to answer, direct their attention to the *Vocabulary Note*. Ask if there are any words in the question that are similar to the vocabulary from 1B. Elicit the answer.

2. Set a time limit (five minutes). Direct students to complete the activity individually. Do not check the answers as a class yet.

Answers	
1. d	5. b
2. e	6. h
3. c	7. f
4. g	8. a

E 1. Prepare students to listen by saying: *Now we're going to listen to speakers describe a time when they saw a crime. While you listen, check your work in 1D.*

2. Play the audio. Ask students to circle any of their answers in 1D that don't match the audio. Elicit those items and play them again, focusing on clues to meaning in the 1D sentences.

3. Work with the pronunciation of any troublesome words or phrases.

2 Learn about the criminal justice system

Presentation II
10–20 minutes

A 1. Direct students to look at the picture. Introduce the new topic: *Now we're going to talk about the criminal justice system.*

2. Say and have students repeat each of the words. Discuss what each person is doing in the courtroom.

3. Ask students to work individually to complete the article. Go over the answers as a class.

4. Check comprehension. Ask: *Who listens to the case?* [judge and jury] *Who is the person on trial?* [defendant]

5. Draw students' attention to the picture and ask students if they can name anything else in the picture or anything associated with a trial (*stand, judge's robes, jury box, flag, oath, swear, objection, verdict, sentence,* etc.). Students may know some of these words from watching TV courtroom dramas!

Answers

Everyone inside the courtroom was quiet. The <u>judge</u> listened to the case. Mary Gold (standing), an <u>attorney</u>, questioned the <u>witness</u>. All twelve people on the <u>jury</u> listened carefully too. The <u>defendant</u> sat quietly next to his attorney.

TIP

Show students a scene from a TV courtroom drama. Turn off the sound and play the show for a minute or two. Ask students to identify the attorney, defendant, judge, witness, and jury.

Guided Practice II
5–10 minutes

B 1. Model asking and answering the first question with a volunteer.

2. Set a time limit (three minutes). Direct students to do the task with a partner.

3. Call on volunteers to present their questions and answers for the class.

MULTILEVEL STRATEGIES

Adapt 2B to the level of your students.

• **Pre-level** Provide answers to the questions in mixed-up order and have students match the questions and answers.

• **Higher-level** Challenge these students to write two or three more questions about the picture to ask a partner.

Communicative Practice and Application
20–25 minutes

C 1. If students will use the Internet for this task, establish what device(s) they'll use: a class computer, tablets, or smartphones. Alternatively, print information from the Internet before class and distribute to groups.

2. Write the questions from 2C on the board. Explain that students will work in teams to research and report on this information. Ask: *Which search terms or questions can you use to find the information you need?* ["jury selection,"

"upcoming trials" + city name] *How will you record the information you find?* [table, checklist, index cards] Remind students to bookmark or record sites so they can find or cite them in the future.

3. Group students and assign roles: manager, administrative assistant, IT support, and reporter. Verify students' understanding of the roles.

TIP

When setting up task-based activities, verify that students understand their roles using physical commands. For example: *If you report on your team's work, stand up* [reporter]. *If you keep the team on task, point to the clock* [manager]. *If you write the team's responses, raise your hand* [administrative assistant]. *If you help the team research, hold up your smartphone/tablet* [IT support].

4. Give managers the time limit for researching the questions (ten minutes). Direct the IT support to begin the online research or pick up the printed materials for each team. Direct the administrative assistant to record information for the team using a table, a checklist, or index cards.

5. Give a two-minute warning. Call "time."

D 1. Copy the sentence frames on the board.

2. Direct teams to help their administrative assistant use the sentence frames to record the team's findings. Direct the reporter to use the recorded information to report the team's findings to the class or another team.

Evaluation
10–15 minutes (books closed)

TEST YOURSELF

1. Direct Partner A to read prompts 1–4 from 1D on page 148 to Partner B. Partner B should close his or her book and write the answers in his or her notebook. When finished, students switch roles. Partner B reads prompts 5–8 from 1D.

2. Direct both partners to open their books and check their spelling when they finish.

MULTILEVEL STRATEGIES

Target the *Test Yourself* to the level of your students.

• **Pre-level** Have these students do the activity the first time with the option to look in their books. Then have them do the activity a second time without looking at their books.

• **Higher-level** Direct these students to write a sentence defining each of the words their partner dictates.

EXTENSION ACTIVITY

Listen for Safety Mistakes

1. Read students this short story about someone who commits a number of safety "no-nos": *Tom overslept this morning, so he rushed out of the house without locking the doors and windows. He had to stop by the post office before work, so he left his car running to save time while he ran inside to mail the cash for his rent. After work, he walked down a dark alley to his favorite restaurant. He left his credit card on the table for the waitress while he went to the bathroom.*

2. Reread the story. Tell students to make a list of everything Tom did wrong. Call on volunteers to share the list.

Lesson Overview	Lesson Notes
MULTILEVEL OBJECTIVES	

On- and Higher-level: Analyze, write, and edit an essay about home and neighborhood security

Pre-level: Read and write about home and neighborhood security

LANGUAGE FOCUS

Grammar: Present tense (*I have a security alarm.*)

Vocabulary: *Deadbolt, peephole*

For vocabulary support, see this **Oxford Picture Dictionary** topic: Public Safety, page 146

STRATEGY FOCUS

Use connecting words like *even, though,* and *but* to show contrast.

READINESS CONNECTION

In this lesson, students listen actively, read, and write about home and neighborhood security.

PACING

To compress this lesson: Assign the *Test Yourself* and/or 3C for homework.

To extend this lesson: Have students do a neighborhood role-play. (See end of lesson.)

And/or have students complete **Workbook 3 page 66** and **Multilevel Activities 3 Unit 10 page 110**.

CORRELATIONS

CCRS: SL.1.B (d.) Explain their own ideas and understanding in light of the discussion.

SL.2.B Determine the main ideas and supporting details of a text read aloud or information presented in diverse media and formats, including visually, quantitatively, and orally.

R.1.B Ask and answer such questions as who, what, where, when, why, and how to demonstrate understanding of key details in a text.

R.2.A Identify the main topic and retell key details of a text.

R.5.A Know and use various text features to locate key facts or information in a text.

R.7.B Use information gained from illustrations and the words in a text to demonstrate understanding of the text.

W.3.A Write narratives in which they recount two or more appropriately sequenced events, include some details regarding what happened, use temporal words to signal event order, and provide some sense of closure.

W.4.B Produce writing in which the development and organization are appropriate to task and purpose.

W.5.B With guidance and support from peers and others, develop and strengthen writing as needed by planning, revising and editing.

W.6.B With guidance and support, use technology to produce and publish writing (using keyboarding skills) as well as to interact and collaborate with others.

L.1.B (l.) Produce simple, compound and complex sentences.

L.2.B (e.) Use commas and quotation marks in dialogue.

L.2.C (a.) Use correct capitalization. (d.) Use a comma to separate and introductory element from the rest of the sentence.

RF.4.B (a.) Read grade-level text with purpose and understanding.

ELPS: 6. An ELL can analyze and critique the arguments of others orally and in writing. 9. An ELL can create clear and coherent level-appropriate speech and text.

Warm-up and Review

10–15 minutes (books closed)

Write *Safe neighborhood* and *Unsafe neighborhood* on the board. Ask students what makes a neighborhood safe or unsafe. Write their ideas in the correct column.

Introduction

5 minutes

1. Looking at the "unsafe" column, ask students which of these things the neighbors themselves could take care of and which require the help of a building manager or city government.

2. State the objective: *Today we're going to read and write about home and neighborhood security.*

1 Prepare to write

Presentation

20–25 minutes

A 1. Build students' schema by asking questions about the pictures and the title. Ask: *Do you have any of these things in your home?*

2. Give students one minute to tell a partner their responses to questions 1 and 2. Elicit responses from the class. Write the names of the security features on the board.

Answers
1. Possible answers: Door chain, window bars, intercom
2. Home security

B 🔊 **3-14** 1. Introduce the model blog post and its purpose: *You're going to read a woman's description of the security at her apartment. As you read, look for the purpose of the model: Why is she writing?* Have students read the blog post silently.

2. Check comprehension. Ask: *What safety features does Sandi have at her apartment?* [deadbolt locks, chain lock, lights in hallways, neighborhood email group]

3. Play the audio. Have students read along silently.

Guided Practice I

10 minutes

C 1. Have students work independently to underline the answers to the questions in the text.

2. Point out the first *Writer's Note* and read the information aloud. Have students find the bolded words in the text and have volunteers read the sentences aloud. As a class, discuss what is being contrasted in each sentence. Read aloud the information in the second *Writer's Note* and ask a volunteer to read the exact words in the text.

3. Ask students to annotate the information they underlined with the phrases "reason for writing" for question 1, "additional feature" for question 2, and "communication" for question 3. Have pairs compare answers. Have volunteers call out answers and write them on the board for the class to check.

Answers
1. To discuss improving security in her apartment building
2. A peephole and better lighting
3. Email

MULTILEVEL STRATEGIES

Seat pre-level students together for 1C.

• **Pre-level** While other students are working on 1C, ask these students *yes/no* and *or* questions about the reading. *Does the writer have good locks on her doors? Does she have a peephole? Do they want new lights in the hallways or on the sides of the building?* Give students time to write the answers to 1C.

2 Plan and write

Guided Practice II

15–20 minutes

A 1. Read question 1. Elicit security problems and write them on the board. Choose one problem and demonstrate how to create a cluster diagram by drawing a circle and writing the problem in the center. Draw "spokes" with circles at the end and ask volunteers for one or two reasons to add to the diagram. Have students select one of the problems and create their own cluster diagram of reasons. Have students share their diagrams with partners.

2. Read question 2. Ask volunteers to report on what neighbors or the police should do about the problem.

B Read through the blog post template. Elicit ideas that could go in each paragraph. Have students write their blog post individually.

Adapt 2B to the level of your students.

• **Pre-level** Have these students write one paragraph in response to the sentence stems in the template.

• **Higher-level** Ask these students to include a fourth paragraph comparing the security of their current home to the security of a place where they used to live.

3 Get feedback and revise

Guided Practice III
5 minutes

A Direct students to check their writing using the editing checklist. Tell them to read each item in the list and check their papers before moving on to the next item. Explain that students should not edit their writing at this stage. They should just use the checklist to check their work and mark any areas they want to revise.

Communicative Practice
15 minutes

B 1. Read the instructions and the sample sentences aloud. Emphasize to students that they are responding to their partners' work, not correcting it.

2. Use the text in 1B to model the exercise. *I think the sentence about the neighborhood email group is interesting. I'd like to ask this writer how many emails she has received and what they said.*

3. Direct students to exchange papers with a partner and follow the instructions.

C Allow students time to edit and revise their writing as necessary, using the editing checklist from 3A and their partner's feedback from 3B. If necessary, students could complete this task as homework.

Application and Evaluation
10 minutes

TEST YOURSELF

1. Review the instructions aloud. Assign a time limit (five minutes) and have students work independently.

2. Before collecting student work, invite two or three volunteers to share their sentences. Ask students to raise their hands if they wrote similar answers.

Neighborhood Role-Play

1. With the class, brainstorm possible "suspicious" events in the neighborhood and appropriate responses to those events. Write them on the board.

2. Provide students with role-play instructions: Partner A: *Tell your partner you saw something suspicious—for example, a strange car parked with someone sitting in it.* Partner B: *Thank your neighbor for calling and tell him/her what you'll do. For example: Ask the police to drive down the street.*

3. Ask volunteer pairs to perform one of their role-plays for the class.

Lesson Overview

Lesson Notes

MULTILEVEL OBJECTIVES

On- and Higher-level: Use gerunds as subjects to talk about home security, distinguish gerunds from present continuous verbs, and listen for gerunds in sentences about crime

Pre-level: Identify gerunds in conversations about home security and crime

LANGUAGE FOCUS

Grammar: Gerunds as subjects (*Locking your doors is a good idea.*)

Vocabulary: *Break in, install*

For vocabulary support, see this **Oxford Picture Dictionary** topic: Public Safety, page 146

READINESS CONNECTION

In this lesson, students practice using gerunds as subjects to talk about home security.

PACING

To compress this lesson: Conduct 1B and/or 1C as a whole-class activity.

To extend this lesson: Have students have a class discussion about safety for children. (See end of lesson.)

And/or have students complete **Workbook 3 pages 67–68, Multilevel Activities 3 Unit 10 pages 111–112**, and **Multilevel Grammar Exercises 3 Unit 10**.

CORRELATIONS

CCRS: SL.1.B (d.) Explain their own ideas and understanding in light of the discussion.

SL.6.B Speak in complete sentences when appropriate to task and situation in order to provide requested detail or clarification.

R.1.B Ask and answer such questions as who, what, where, when, why, and how to demonstrate understanding of key details in a text.

L.1.B (l.) Produce simple, compound and complex sentences.

L.1.C (c.) Form and use the progressive verb tenses. (f.) Use verb tense to convey various times, sequences, states, and conditions.

L.1.D (f.) Explain the function of verbals (gerunds, participles, infinitives) in general and their function in particular sentences.

RF.4.B (a.) Read grade-level text with purpose and understanding.

ELPS: 7. An ELL can adapt language choices to purpose, task, and audience when speaking and writing. 10. An ELL can demonstrate command of the conventions of standard English to communicate in level-appropriate speech and writing.

Warm-up and Review
10–15 minutes (books closed)

Write *Safety habits* on the board and elicit as many as students recall from the previous lesson. Write expressions on the board beginning with a simple verb: *lock doors, call or email neighbors, report crimes, install window bars, have strong locks, close windows, leave lights on, install an alarm.*

Introduction
5–10 minutes

1. Use the expressions on the board to form sentences with gerunds as subjects. *Locking doors is a good idea. Installing an alarm can be expensive.*

2. State the objective: *Today we're going to learn how to use gerunds as subjects to talk about safety.*

1 Use gerunds as subjects

Presentation I
20–25 minutes

A 1. Direct students to look at the photo. Ask: *How old do you think the woman is?*

2. Read the instructions aloud. Ask students to read the article silently and answer the questions.

3. Read the first question aloud. Call on a volunteer for the answer. Ask the volunteer where in the article he or she found the answer. Read the rest of the questions aloud, calling on a different volunteer for each answer.

Answers
1. Locking doors
2. She called 911.
3. Thanking the police
4. Buying newer, stronger locks

B 1. Read the sentences in the chart aloud.

2. Direct students to underline the examples of gerunds as subjects in the article in 1A. Go over the answers as a class.

3. Copy one of the sentences from the article on the board. Ask students to identify the verb [*is* or *was*]. Ask students to identify the subject [the gerund].

4. Assess students' understanding of the charts. Ask: *Is* locking *the verb in the first sentence?* [no] *Can I use* lock *as the subject?* [no]

5. Assess students' understanding of the chart. Ask students to use the expressions on the board from the *Warm-up* to create sentences with gerunds as subjects.

Answers
locking, calling, thanking, buying

Guided Practice I
10–15 minutes

C 1. Tell students they will collaborate to complete the description of the grammar point. Model collaboration by working with the class to complete the first sentence. Encourage students to look at 1A and 1B to help them determine the correct words.

2. Pair students and have them work together to complete the description.

3. Project or write the completed definition on the board and have pairs verify the accuracy of their responses. Ask volunteers which sentences confused them and discuss.

Answers
verb
noun
-ing

Guided Practice II
10–15 minutes

D 1. Read the instructions and verbs aloud. Have a volunteer read the sample sentence.

2. Set a time limit (five minutes) and have pairs do the task.

3. Check answers as a class.

Answers	
1. Locking	4. Parking
2. Reporting	5. Calling
3. Walking	6. Protecting

MULTILEVEL STRATEGIES

For 1D, group same-level students together.

• **Pre-level** Sit with these students and answer any questions about vocabulary to help them choose the correct verb for the sentence.

• **Higher-level** Challenge these students to write three or four more sentences with gerunds as subjects using the verbs in the box.

2 Compare gerunds and the present continuous

Presentation II
15–20 minutes

A 1. Introduce the new topic. Say: *The* -ing *form can be used as a noun (a gerund), or it can be part of a verb (the present continuous). Now we're going to look at the difference between the gerund and the present continuous.*

2. Direct students to read the grammar chart. While they are reading, copy a gerund sentence and a present continuous sentence from the chart onto the board. Ask students to identify the subject and the verb in each sentence. Ask: *Is the present continuous verb complete with only the* -ing *form?* [No—it requires a form of *be*.]

3. Ask students to work individually to label the sentences *G* or *P*. Go over the answers as a class. Elicit the subject of each sentence.

Answers	
1. P	4. P
2. P	5. G
3. G	

TIP

For more practice with present continuous versus gerund, try the following activities:

1. Give each student an index card with *gerund* written on one side and *present continuous* on the other. Say sentences. Have students show the sides of their cards that indicate which forms they heard. *I'm reporting the accident.* [present continuous] *Reporting crimes to the police is important.* [gerund] *I think she's calling the police.* [present continuous] *Calling the police isn't necessary.* [gerund]

2. Have students line up in two teams at the board. Explain the rules: *The first team member writes a present continuous sentence. For example,* I'm looking for a new car. *The second team member writes a sentence using the same verb as a gerund subject. For example,* Looking for a new car isn't easy. *The third team member writes a sentence using the present continuous with a different verb. The fourth team member uses that verb as a gerund subject. Team members can call for assistance. Writers can finish and/or correct previous sentences, but only one person can write at a time.*

3. Call out *Switch!* every 20 seconds as a signal for the next team member to come to the board. The game ends after the last team member has written. The team with the most correct sentences at the end of the game wins.

Guided Practice III
15–20 minutes

B
1. Read the instructions aloud. Make sure students understand that they should use the bolded word and change it to the correct form to complete the sentence that follows.

2. Ask students to work individually to write the correct forms and then compare their answers with a partner. Ask volunteer pairs to read each set of exchanges aloud. Write the answers on the board.

Answers
A: My neighborhood is very safe. Why should I lock the door?
B: <u>Locking</u> the door protects you and your home.
A: OK, I'm locking the door right now.
B: And you should put your wallet in your purse.
A: I know, I know. <u>Putting</u> my wallet in my purse will keep it safe.
B: Right! Look, I'<u>m putting</u> my wallet in my purse.
A: And now, you're going to tell me how to walk.
B: Well, <u>walking</u> in the dark isn't smart.
A: Hah! I'<u>m</u> not <u>walking</u>. I plan to drive!
B: I guess <u>driving</u> in the dark is OK, but don't forget to turn your lights on.

MULTILEVEL STRATEGIES

While on- and higher-level students are completing 2B, go over the basics with pre-level students.

• **Pre-level** Provide these students with simple sentences and ask them to identify the subject and verb. *Running is good exercise. The suspect is running away. Walking in the dark isn't safe. She is walking on a well-lit street. Speaking English is fun. She is speaking in front of the class.*

• **On- and Higher-level** After these students finish 2B, ask them to work with their partners to write two additional sentences with gerund subjects and two with present continuous verbs. Have volunteers write their sentences on the board. Ask other students to identify the gerunds and present continuous verbs.

C
1. Elicit the importance of accuracy. Tell students they will be building their accuracy in this task.

2. Organize students into groups. Demonstrate how to correct the sentence using the first example.

3. Have team members work together to correct the sentences. Circulate and monitor teamwork.

4. Project or write the corrected sentences on the board and have teams check their work.

5. Address questions and any issues you noted during your observation.

Answers

1. **Walking** in well-lit areas is a good idea.
2. It's never safe **opening** your front door to a stranger.
3. No one enjoys **reporting** a crime to the police.
4. **Sleeping** with the windows open probably isn't too safe.

3 Listen for gerunds

Guided Practice IV
15–20 minutes

 1. Elicit some of the courtroom words students learned in the first lesson: *judge, jury, defendant*. Say: *Now we're going to listen to sentences that describe what's going on in a courtroom. Decide if each sentence uses a gerund subject or a present continuous verb.*

2. Direct students to look at the chart and then play the first sentence and have them check the correct column.

3. Copy the chart on the board while students are listening. Elicit the correct answers and check them off. If students answered incorrectly, play the audio again, providing a listening clue (for example, *listen for whether the -ing verb has the verb* be *in front of it*).

Answers

1. Present Continuous
2. Gerund
3. Gerund
4. Present Continuous
5. Present Continuous
6. Gerund

4 Use gerunds to talk about your life experience

Communicative Practice and Application
20–25 minutes

A 1. Direct students to look at the picture. Ask: *Is the man safe?*

2. Tell students to work individually to complete the survey.

B 1. Put students in groups of three. Read the sample conversation aloud with two volunteers. Point out that they may feel the situation is safe in some circumstances but not in others. For example, driving alone at night

may be safe sometimes and not safe other times.

2. Check comprehension of the exercise. Ask: *Are you talking to one partner or to the whole group?* [to the whole group] *Who is giving their opinions?* [everyone]

3. Direct students to compare their survey answers with others in their groups.

C Ask for a show of hands about each item on the survey. Encourage students to share their ideas about circumstances in which the activity would be safer or less safe.

Evaluation
10–15 minutes

TEST YOURSELF

Ask students to write the sentences independently. Collect and correct their writing.

MULTILEVEL STRATEGIES

Target the *Test Yourself* to the level of your students.

• **Pre-level** Ask these students to write four sentences. Provide this structure: _____ is dangerous; _____ is safe.

• **Higher-level** Have these students write a total of ten sentences.

EXTENSION ACTIVITY

Discuss Safety for Children

Have a class discussion about safety for children. Ask students what kind of advice they give their children to teach them about safety. Write their ideas on the board. Elicit categories for the advice: *Sports safety, Safety from crime, Safety for pedestrians*.

Lesson Overview

Lesson Notes

MULTILEVEL OBJECTIVES

Pre-, On-, and Higher-level: Report a crime and listen for a crime description

LANGUAGE FOCUS

Grammar: Gerunds and infinitives (*Locking the door is a good idea. It's a good idea to lock the door.*)

Vocabulary: All of a sudden, suddenly, hold on, witness, mugging

For vocabulary support, see these **Oxford Picture Dictionary** topics: Crime, page 145; Public Safety, page 146

STRATEGY FOCUS

Recognize that the infinitive form of a verb is formed by using *to* with the base form of the verb.

READINESS CONNECTION

In this lesson, students verbally communicate and practice how to report a crime and listen to a description of a crime.

PACING

To compress this lesson: Do 6A as a class activity and skip 6B.

To extend this lesson: Have students review crime and safety vocabulary. (See end of lesson.)

And/or have students complete **Workbook 3 page 69** and **Multilevel Activities 3 Unit 10 page 113**.

CORRELATIONS

CCRS: SL.1.B (d.) Explain their own ideas and understanding in light of the discussion.

SL.2.B Determine the main ideas and supporting details of a text read aloud or information presented in diverse media and formats, including visually, quantitatively, and orally.

SL.4.B Report on a topic or text, tell a story, or recount an experience with appropriate facts and relevant, descriptive details, speaking clearly at an understandable pace.

SL.6.B Speak in complete sentences when appropriate to task and situation in order to provide requested detail or clarification.

R.1.B Ask and answer such questions as who, what, where, when, why, and how to demonstrate understanding of key details in a text.

R.2.A Identify the main topic and retell key details of a text.

R.7.B Use information gained from illustrations and the words in a text to demonstrate understanding of the text.

L.1.B (l.) Produce simple, compound and complex sentences.

L.1.D (f.) Explain the function of verbals (gerunds, participles, infinitives) in general and their function in particular sentences.

L.3.B (b.) Recognize and observe differences between the conventions of spoken and written standard English.

L.6.B Acquire and use accurately level-appropriate conversational, general academic, and domain-specific words and phrases, including those that signal spatial and temporal relationships.

RF.4.B (a.) Read grade-level text with purpose and understanding.

ELPS: 2. An ELL can participate in level-appropriate oral and written exchanges of information, ideas, and analyses, in various social and academic contexts, responding to peer, audience, or reader comments and questions. 9. An ELL can create clear and coherent level-appropriate speech and text.

Warm-up and Review
5–10 minutes (books closed)

Write these words on the board: *a ran away hair man a student's the man had and thin long blond was laptop tall he he stole grabbed the laptop and.* Tell students someone saw a crime. The words make sentences that describe what the person saw. Ask them to create sentences with the scrambled words. Call on volunteers to write their sentences on the board. Praise all logical sentences.

Introduction
3 minutes

1. Write up the unscrambled version of the story: *A man stole a student's laptop. The man had long blond hair. He was tall and thin. He grabbed the laptop and ran away.* Say: *This is a statement from a witness who is reporting a crime.*

2. State the objective: *Today we're going to learn how to report a crime and listen to a description of a crime.*

1 Learn ways to report a crime

Presentation I
10 minutes

 A **3-16** 1. Direct students to look at the picture. Ask: *Who is on the phone?* [a police officer]

2. Read the question aloud. Play the audio. Give students a minute to answer the question. Go over the answer as a class.

Answer
He's reporting a crime to the police.

Guided Practice I
20–25 minutes

B **3-16** 1. Read the instructions and the questions aloud. Play the audio. Ask students to listen for the answer to each question.

2. Ask students to compare their answers with a partner. Circulate and monitor to ensure students understand the audio.

Answers
1. His local police
2. He broke into an apartment.
3. He ran away.

C **3-17** Read the instructions aloud. Explain that students are going to hear the audio one more time. They should write the words they hear to complete the sentences. Play the audio. Call on volunteers to elicit the answers.

Answers
1. First, he broke
2. Then he took a
3. all of a sudden

2 Practice your pronunciation

Pronunciation Extension
10–15 minutes

 A **3-18** 1. Write *I locked the door.* on the board. Say: *I locked the doors. You didn't lock them!* Ask students which word you stressed. Then say: *I locked the doors. I didn't just close them.* Ask students which word you stressed. Say: *I locked the doors. I didn't lock the windows.* Ask students which word you stressed. Say: *Now we're going to focus on using stress to show contrast.*

2. Play the audio. Direct students to listen for the stressed words as they read the sentences in the chart.

3. Elicit the stressed words. Ask students why those words were stressed [to emphasize contrast].

B **3-19** Have students look at the first set of sentences. Point out the bold type that indicates a stressed word. Ask them to listen to the audio and circle the sentences they hear.

Answers
1. a
2. b
3. a
4. b

C **3-19** 1. Play the audio again. Have students check their answers to 2B. Call on volunteers to read the sentences aloud.

2. Ask students to take turns reading the sentences in 2B with a partner. Monitor and provide feedback.

3 Review gerunds and infinitives

Presentation II and Guided Practice II
15–20 minutes

 1. Introduce the new topic. Write *Infinitive* and *Gerund* on the board. Elicit the infinitive and gerund forms of the verb *call*.

2. Read the sentences in the chart and the *Grammar Note*. Ask students to identify the subject of each sentence.

3. Check comprehension of the grammar in the chart. Ask: *Do we use the infinitive as a subject?*

4. Direct students to circle the correct words in the sentences below the chart. Ask volunteers to read the completed sentences aloud.

Answers
1. to listen
2. Going
3. Talking
4. to walk

B 1. Read question 1 and the example sentence aloud. Tell students to work individually to write new sentences with the same idea. Ask volunteers to write their sentences on the board.

2. Ask students to take turns reading their sentences with a partner.

Answers
1. <u>Walking</u> down a dark street is dangerous. <u>It's dangerous to walk down a dark street</u>.
2. It isn't safe <u>to leave</u> the garage door open at night. <u>Leaving the garage door open at night isn't safe</u>.
3. <u>Understanding</u> the criminal justice system is important. <u>It's important to understand the criminal justice system</u>.
4. It's important <u>to make</u> sure your home is safe. <u>Making sure your home is safe is important</u>.

MULTILEVEL STRATEGIES

Seat same-level students together for 3B.

• **Pre-level** Lead these students through the process of restating each idea with an infinitive or gerund.

• **On- and Higher-level** Have these students write two more pairs of infinitive/gerund sentences that express the same idea. Ask volunteers to write one of their sentence pairs on the board.

4 Building conversation skills

Guided Practice III
15–20 minutes

A Direct students to look at the picture and skim the conversation in 4B. Have them work with partners to identify where the people are. Elicit responses and ask: *How do you know?* or *Why do you say that?* to encourage students to state their reasoning.

Answers
The man is reporting a crime; answers will vary.

B 1. Ask students to read the instructions and tell you what they are going to do [listen and read and respond to the question]. Play the audio and then elicit the answer to the question.

Answer
He reported seeing a man break into a car and take some stuff.

2. Ask students to read the conversation with a partner. Circulate and monitor pronunciation. Model and have students repeat difficult words or phrases.

3. Ask: *In what other situations could you use this conversation?* Point out a few phrases that are not specific to reporting a crime. Ask volunteers to point out others.

Before moving on to 4C, provide more practice with reporting a crime by having students write a witness's statement.

1. Tell students they are going to witness a crime and they need to report it in writing. They should include what happened and what the suspect looked like. Allow them to work with a partner.

2. Show a short clip of a crime in progress from a TV show or movie. (Don't choose anything very violent or disturbing.) Have students work with their partners to describe what they saw. If you can't play a video in class, show pictures of the "criminals" for about 30 seconds. Have students invent the crime, but give descriptions of the people they saw.

3. Have volunteers share their statements with the class. Replay the video or show the pictures to check the accuracy of their descriptions.

Communicative Practice and Application I
20–25 minutes

C

1. Pair students and have them read the instructions silently. Check their comprehension of the exercise. Ask: *What are the two roles? Where does the conversation take place?*

2. Model and have students repeat the sequencing words in the *In Other Words* box in 4B. Explain that they should use these words in their conversations.

3. Draw a T-chart on the board. Label the left column *Witness* and the right column *Desk officer*. Elicit examples of what each person might say and make notes in the chart.

4. Set a time limit (three minutes). Have students act out the role-play. Call "time" and have students switch roles.

5. Ask three volunteer pairs to act out their role-play for the class. Tell students who are listening to make a simple table with four rows and two columns. Use the top row to label the columns: *Crime details* and *Questions*. Have students take notes in the chart for each role-play.

MULTILEVEL STRATEGIES

Seat same-level students together.

• **Pre-level** Work with these students and guide them in writing their new conversation or provide a simplified conversation for these students to practice.

A: I'd like to report a crime. B: What happened? A: I saw some teenagers spray-painting a building. B: What happened after that? A: They broke a few windows and ran away. B: Thank you for reporting the crime.

5 Focus on listening for details

Presentation III and Guided Practice IV
20–25 minutes

A

1. Read the questions and statement aloud and model a discussion with a volunteer. Ask: *Do you think every person should report a crime when they see it? Why? / Why not? I agree because… / I disagree because…*

2. Pair students and tell them to discuss their own answers to the questions. Circulate and monitor.

TIP

To ensure that students are listening to each other, ask them to take brief notes of other students' responses and have them repeat back: *So, you said…*

B

Direct students to read the sentences before they listen to the phone conversation. Ask what kind of information they'll be writing in the blanks. Ask volunteers for predictions. If students struggle, start by offering your own prediction: *I think we will hear someone report a crime.*

C ◀)) **3-21** 1. Play the audio. Ask students to listen and write the correct answers.

2. Pair students and have them compare answers. If a pair has different answers, have the class vote on the correct answer with a show of hands.

Answers
1. information
2. witnessed
3. carrying
4. woman
5. police

6 Discuss

Communicative Practice and Application II
15–20 minutes

A 1. Read the instructions aloud. Draw a sample chart on the board with five columns, one for each bullet point. Call on volunteers to read the sample conversation in 6A. Fill in the chart, writing *Carry wallet in front pocket* under the "Mugging" column. Ask: *What other columns can this go under?* ["Taking your wallet or purse from you" and "Identity theft"] Explain that students will make a chart like this one based on their own discussions.

2. Put students into teams of three and assign roles: manager, administrative assistant, and reporter. Verify students' understanding of the roles. Encourage students to use the questions in the *Speaking Note* during their discussions.

3. Set a time limit for the discussions (ten minutes). Write the sentence frame from 6B on the board. Then circulate and monitor.

B Call "time." Ask the reporter for each team to report the results of the team's discussion using the sentence frame on the board.

Evaluation
5 minutes

TEST YOURSELF

1. Ask students to complete the checkboxes individually.

2. Tell students that you are going to read each of the items in the checklist aloud. If they are not at all confident with that skill, they should hold up a closed fist. If they are not very confident, they should hold up one finger. If they are somewhat confident, two fingers;

confident, three fingers; very confident, four fingers. If they think they could teach the skill, they should hold up five fingers. Read each item in the checklist and identify students who may need further support.

Lesson Overview	Lesson Notes
MULTILEVEL OBJECTIVES	
Pre-, On-, and Higher-level: Read about and discuss careers in public safety	
LANGUAGE FOCUS	
Grammar: Simple present (*Health inspectors look for problems in restaurants.*) **Vocabulary:** *Options, law enforcement, rewarding, combination* For vocabulary support, see this **Oxford Picture Dictionary** topic: Public Safety, page 146	
STRATEGY FOCUS	
Look at more than one source to do effective research.	
READINESS CONNECTION	
In this lesson, students verbally communicate information about careers in public safety.	
PACING	
To compress this lesson: Assign 2A and/or 2B for homework. **To extend this lesson:** Have students do a "career counselor" role-play. (See end of lesson.) And/or have students complete **Workbook 3 page 70** and **Multilevel Activities 3 Unit 10 pages 114–115**.	

CORRELATIONS

CCRS: SL.1.B (a.) Come to discussions prepared, having read or studied required material; explicitly draw on that preparation and other information known about the topic to explore ideas under discussion. (b.) Follow agreed-upon rules for discussions. (c.) Ask questions to check understanding of information presented, stay on topic, and link their comments to the remarks of others. (d.) Explain their own ideas and understanding in light of the discussion.

SL.2.B Determine the main ideas and supporting details of a text read aloud or information presented in diverse media and formats, including visually, quantitatively, and orally.

R.1.B Ask and answer such questions as who, what, where, when, why, and how to demonstrate understanding of key details in a text.

R.2.A Identify the main topic and retell key details of a text.

R.5.B Know and use various text features to locate key facts or information in a text efficiently.

R.7.C Interpret information presented visually, orally, or quantitatively and explain how the information contributes to an understanding of the text in which it appears.

R.9.B Compare and contrast the most important points and key details presented in two texts on the same topic.

L.1.B (l.) Produce simple, compound and complex sentences.

L.1.C (d.) Use modal auxiliaries to convey various conditions.

L.4.B (e.) Use glossaries and beginning dictionaries, both print and digital, to determine or clarify the meaning of words and phrases.

RF.4.B (a.) Read grade-level text with purpose and understanding.

ELPS: 1. An ELL can construct meaning from oral presentations and literary and informational text through level-appropriate listening, reading, and viewing. 3. An ELL can speak and write about level-appropriate complex literary and informational texts and topics.

Warm-up and Review
10–15 minutes (books closed)

Review job titles. Write *Good jobs* on the board and ask students to brainstorm a list of jobs they would consider to be good jobs. Then elicit the reasons. *What makes a job good?* Write those ideas on the board. Ask how many of the jobs involve helping people.

Introduction
10 minutes

1. Ask students if any of the jobs on the board involve keeping people safe. Tell them that although most people might think of firefighters and police officers, there are many other jobs involved with public safety.

2. State the objective: *Today we're going read about and discuss careers in public safety.*

1 Read

Presentation
10–20 minutes

A Read the questions aloud. Use ideas from the *Introduction* to help guide discussion.

B Read the words and definitions. Elicit sample sentences for the words or supply them if the students can't.

Pre-reading

C Read the instructions aloud and confirm that students understand where the titles, chart, and headings are. Have students answer the question individually and then check answers as a class. If any students answer incorrectly, ask them to support their answer using the titles, chart, and headings. Establish the correct answer.

Answer
a. An overview of the jobs and people in public safety

Guided Practice: While Reading
20–30 minutes

D 1. Ask students to read the articles silently and answer the question.

2. Check answers as a class.

3. Direct students' attention to the *Reader's Note* and read the information aloud.

4. Check comprehension. Ask: *What are some advantages of a job in public safety?* [They're growing, have great benefits, and can be rewarding.]

Answer
They both talk about public safety jobs.

MULTILEVEL STRATEGIES

Adapt 1D to the level of your students.

• **Pre-level** Provide these students with definitions for the occupations in the chart and ask them to look at the chart. *Animal control workers pick up animals that are lost, sick, or dangerous. Fire inspectors look for problems that could cause fires. Paramedics go to accident sites and help people who may have been injured. Police officers enforce laws and protect the public.* Direct students to read this summary while other students are reading the articles in 1D.

Guided Practice: Rereading
10–15 minutes

E 1. Provide an opportunity for students to extract evidence from the text. Read the sentence stems in the sample chart aloud. Have students reread the articles.

2. Pair students and tell them to copy the chart in their notebooks and work together to complete it. While students are doing the task, write the chart on the board.

MULTILEVEL STRATEGIES

After 1E, adapt further comprehension questions to the level of your students.

• **Pre-level** Ask these students to identify public safety occupations. *Who picks up lost animals?* [animal control workers] Give students time to copy the answers to 1E from the board.

• **Higher-level** Ask these students to choose two of the jobs from the article and write three advantages and disadvantages of each job. After you go over the answers to 2F, call on volunteers to share their ideas with the class.

F 1. Have students share their answers with the class and write them in the chart on the board.

2. Elicit and discuss any additional questions about the reading. You could introduce new questions for class discussion: *Do any of the jobs sound interesting to you? Which job sounds the most difficult?*

2 Talk it over

Guided Practice: Post-reading
15–20 minutes

A Have students look at the graph and read the *Reader's Note*. Point out that they need to use the information from the graph to complete the sentences and answer the question. Reinforce the *Reader's Note*, which says it is helpful to read the comprehension questions first and then find the information in the graph. Set a time limit (ten minutes). Have students work in pairs to complete the task. Ask volunteers to share their answers with the class.

Answers	
1. Japan	5. 22–23
2. 9	6. 15
3. Two	
4. Australia or the United States	

Communicative Practice
15–20 minutes

B Read the questions aloud. Set a time limit (ten minutes). Tell students to copy the chart in their notebooks and complete it with their answers to the questions.

C While students are doing the activity in 2B, write the chart on the board. Have volunteers share their answers with the class and write them in the chart. Have students add any new ideas to their charts. Have a class discussion about whether students think it is good to live in a country that has many public employees.

> **TIP**
>
> For information about job training and education requirements, as well as average salaries and growth potential, direct students to look online for the Department of Labor's Occupational Outlook Handbook. The same kind of information can be found on many career information sites. If you have access to computers in class, have each student choose an occupation and write a list of questions to answer on the board: *What is the starting salary for this job? What education/training is required? What are the working conditions?* Direct students to scan through the information on the website looking for the answers to the questions.

Application
15–20 minutes

BRING IT TO LIFE

Find out if any of your students know people with public safety jobs. Have students decide in class which job they are going to research and how they are going to conduct their research.

> **EXTENSION ACTIVITY**
>
> **"Career Counselor" Role-play**
>
> 1. Write this role-play situation on the board. *Partner A: You are looking for a job. Tell the counselor what you are good at and what you like to do. Partner B: You are the counselor. Recommend a job for your partner. Say why it's a good match.*
>
> 2. Brainstorm things each person might say and write them on the board.
>
> 3. Have students practice the role-play in both roles. Call on volunteers to share whether or not their partners had good career matches.

Warm-up and Review
10–15 minutes

1. Review the *Bring It to Life* assignment from Lesson 5. Have students who did the exercise discuss what they learned. Have students who didn't do the exercise ask their classmates questions.

2. Find out if any students have changed their minds about a job based on their research. *Is the job better than you thought it was? Or not as good?*

Introduction
5 minutes

1. Explain that in the United States, showing that you have a positive attitude is very important in many situations. At work, even if you don't agree with someone, it is important to show that you still are planning on working together and moving forward.

2. State the objective: *Today we're going to talk about how to show you have a positive attitude.*

Presentation
5 minutes

 A 🔊 **3-22** Read the instructions aloud. Play the audio. Give students a minute to think about the question. Elicit responses from the class.

Answer
Preventing crime at work

Guided Practice
10–15 minutes

 B 🔊 **3-22** 1. Read the instructions aloud. Play the audio and have students check the police captain's suggestions.

2. To check answers, play the audio again and have students raise their hands each time the customer interrupts.

Answers
Checked:
Don't keep too much cash in the store
Try not to work alone
Have good lights
Greet all customers
Hire a security guard

 C 🔊 **3-22** Read the instructions aloud. Play the audio again, encouraging students to take notes in their notebooks. Set a time limit (five minutes) for students to discuss their answers with a partner. Circulate to monitor.

Answers
Don't make deposits when strangers are in the area, have good-quality locks and an alarm system, keep expensive items away from store entrances

Presentation and Communicative Practice
15–20 minutes

D 1. Direct students' attention to the *Do/Say* chart and ask students to identify the lesson's soft skill [showing a positive attitude]. Ask the class which column has examples of behaviors [left] and which has examples of language [right].

2. Model the sentences from the right column using authentic intonation. Have students practice imitating your inflection.

3. Put students in teams of four and assign each team a question. Assign roles: manager, administrative assistant, researcher, and reporter. Researchers will ask you questions on behalf of the team. Verify understanding of the roles. Set a time limit (five minutes) and monitor.

4. Write sentence frames on the board that teams can use to summarize their response. (*Our team discussed the following question: _____ We decided _____ because _____.*)

5. Call "time" and let reporters rehearse their report for one minute. Direct each reporter to present to three other teams.

Communicative Practice and Application
10–15 minutes

E Direct students to work in pairs to think of suggestions for preventing each of the work crimes in the box. Invite volunteers to share their suggestions. Tell students to make notes of their suggestions for possible use in the next exercise.

F 1. Have pairs merge to form teams of four. Tell students that they are going to be role-playing a staff meeting where they will suggest ways to prevent crime at work.

2. Direct groups to come up with three crimes and three solutions. Each group should select a manager to run the meeting. The other three members should each choose a crime to bring up.

3. As students carry out the role-play, circulate and monitor. Provide global feedback once the activity ends.

Lesson Overview

MULTILEVEL OBJECTIVES

Pre-, On-, and Higher-level: Review unit language

LANGUAGE FOCUS

Grammar: Gerunds and infinitives (*Calling the police was a good idea. It was a good idea to call the police.*)

Vocabulary: Personal safety vocabulary

For vocabulary support, see this **Oxford Picture Dictionary** topic: Public Safety, page 146

READINESS CONNECTION

In this review, students work in a team to use the present continuous, gerunds as subjects, and *it* + infinitive to talk about safety.

PACING

To extend this review: Have students complete **Workbook 3 page 71**, **Multilevel Activities 3 Unit 10 page 116**, and **Multilevel Grammar Exercises 3 Unit 10**.

Lesson Notes

CORRELATIONS

CCRS: SL.1.B (a.) Come to discussions prepared, having read or studied required material; explicitly draw on that preparation and other information known about the topic to explore ideas under discussion. (b.) Follow agreed-upon rules for discussions. (c.) Ask questions to check understanding of information presented, stay on topic, and link their comments to the remarks of others. (d.) Explain their own ideas and understanding in light of the discussion.

SL.2.B Determine the main ideas and supporting details of a text read aloud or information presented in diverse media and formats, including visually, quantitatively, and orally.

SL.4.B Report on a topic or text, tell a story, or recount an experience with appropriate facts and relevant, descriptive details, speaking clearly at an understandable pace.

SL.6.B Speak in complete sentences when appropriate to task and situation in order to provide requested detail or clarification.

R.1.B Ask and answer such questions as who, what, where, when, why, and how to demonstrate understanding of key details in a text.

R.2.A Identify the main topic and retell key details of a text.

L.1.B (l.) Produce simple, compound and complex sentences.

L.1.D (f.) Explain the function of verbals (gerunds, participles, infinitives) in general and their function in particular sentences.

RF.4.B (a.) Read grade-level text with purpose and understanding.

ELPS: 5. An ELL can conduct research and evaluate and communicate findings to answer questions or solve problems. 6. An ELL can analyze and critique the arguments of others orally and in writing.

Warm-up and Review
10–15 minutes (books closed)

1. Review *At Work* activity F.

2. Ask students to share the good, not-so-good, and interesting things that happened during the role-play. As students speak, write their responses in a chart on the board.

Introduction and Presentation
5 minutes

1. Write several familiar verbs on the board: *study, practice, speak*. Then write: *Present continuous, Gerund, Infinitive*. Elicit example sentences with the verbs for each category. *I am studying English. Studying English is fun. It's a good idea to study every day.*

2. State the objective: *Today we're going to review the present continuous, gerunds as subjects, and it + infinitive to talk about safety.*

Guided Practice
15–20 minutes

A 1. Read the instructions aloud. Point out the example.

2. Set a time limit (five minutes) for individuals to complete the task. Check answers as a class.

Answers	
1. d	4. a
2. e	5. f
3. c	6. b

B 1. Read the instructions and the sample sentence aloud. Have students work in teams to complete the task. Circulate and monitor.

2. Check answers as a class.

Answers
1. At night it's safer to walk with a friend.
2. It's a good idea to stay on well-lit streets.
3. It's important and easy to protect your purse and wallet.
4. One way to prevent crime is to lock your doors.
5. It is smart to shop on secure websites.
6. It's everyone's responsibility to report crimes.

C 1. Read the instructions and the sample sentence aloud. Have students write four more statements individually and then share them with their team. Circulate and monitor.

2. Have volunteers share their ideas with the class.

Communicative Practice
30–45 minutes

D 1. Group students and assign roles: manager, writer, editor, and presenter. Explain that students are going to work with their teams to write an email about a security concern in their neighborhood. Editors will review the email and offer suggestions for changes. Verify students' understanding of the roles.

2. Read steps 2–5 of the activity aloud. Check comprehension of the task. *What is the first thing you should do?* [choose a security concern from the box] *Who should your email be addressed to?* [the mayor]

3. Set a time limit (ten minutes) to complete the exercise. Circulate and answer any questions.

4. Have the presenter from each team read the team's email to the class.

E 1. Have students walk around the room to conduct the interviews. To get students moving, tell them to interview three people who were not on their team for D.

2. Set a time limit (five minutes) to complete the exercise.

3. Tell students to make a note of their classmates' answers but not to worry about writing complete sentences.

F 1. Call on individuals to report what they learned about their classmates. Keep a running tally on the board for each question, marking safety problems, public safety workers seen in the neighborhood, or the kind of safety worker students want to be.

2. Use your tally for question 1 to create a pie chart on the board. Instruct students to draw pie charts for questions 2 and 3 in their notebooks. Circulate and answer any questions.

PROBLEM SOLVING
10–15 minutes

A ◀)) **3-23** 1. Ask: *Do you know anyone whose house has been broken into?* Tell students they will read a story about a woman who sees something on her street that makes her nervous. Direct students to read Delia's story silently.

2. Ask: *Why is the truck suspicious?* [no license plates, driving slowly up and down the street, people sitting inside truck for 20 minutes]

3. Play the audio and have students read along silently.

B 1. Elicit answers to question 1. Guide students to a class consensus on the answer.

2. As a class, brainstorm answers to question 2. Ask students if they know someone who has this problem and has overcome it or what they have done themselves to overcome the same problem.

Answers
1. Delia is feeling nervous about a truck parked near her house. It was driving slowly down the street, and she doesn't think the people in the truck are neighbors.
2. Answers will vary.

Evaluation
20–25 minutes

To test students' understanding of the unit language and content, have them take the Unit 10 Test, available on the Teacher Resource Center.

11 That's Life

Unit Overview

This unit explores life events with a range of employability skills and contextualizes structures with the passive voice and *be able to* + verb for ability.

KEY OBJECTIVES

Lesson 1	Identify life-event vocabulary
Lesson 2	Write an email to reschedule a meeting
Lesson 3	Use the present passive to describe scheduled events at a retirement community
Lesson 4	Show excitement or concern when you respond to good or bad news
Lesson 5	Identify when and why people move
At Work	Praise someone
Teamwork & Language Review	Review unit language

UNIT FEATURES

Academic Vocabulary	*discrimination, promotion, reschedule, community, tradition, majority, security, utilities, indicate*
Employability Skills	• Ask for and give directions • Distinguish between emergencies and non-emergencies • Decide whether to accept an invitation • Work independently • Work with others • Locate information • Communicate verbally • Listen actively • Use writing skills • Comprehend written material • Analyze information

Resources	**Class Audio** CD3, Tracks 24–34
	Workbook Unit 11, pages 72–78
	Teacher Resource Center
	    Multilevel Activities 3 Unit 11
	    Multilevel Grammar Exercises 3 Unit 11
	    Unit 11 Test
	Oxford Picture Dictionary Everyday Conversation, Life Events and Documents, Finding a Home

LESSON **1** VOCABULARY

Lesson Overview	Lesson Notes

MULTILEVEL OBJECTIVES

On-level: Identify life events and describe special occasions

Pre-level: Identify life-event and special-occasion vocabulary

Higher-level: Talk and write about life events and special occasions

LANGUAGE FOCUS

Grammar: Past tense (*When was the wedding?*)

Vocabulary: Life events and special occasions

For vocabulary support, see this **Oxford Picture Dictionary** topic: Life Events and Documents, pages 40–41

STRATEGY FOCUS

Pool knowledge with team members to maximize vocabulary learning.

READINESS CONNECTION

In this lesson, students explore and communicate information about life events.

PACING

To compress this lesson: Conduct 1E as a whole-class activity.

To extend this lesson: Have students discuss their important life events. (See end of lesson.)

And/or have students complete **Workbook 3 page 72** and **Multilevel Activities 3 Unit 11 pages 118–119**.

CORRELATIONS

CCRS: SL.1.B (d.) Explain their own ideas and understanding in light of the discussion.

SL.2.B Determine the main ideas and supporting details of a text read aloud or information presented in diverse media and formats, including visually, quantitatively, and orally.

SL.6.B Speak in complete sentences when appropriate to task and situation in order to provide requested detail or clarification.

SL.4.B Report on a topic or text, tell a story, or recount an experience with appropriate facts and relevant, descriptive details, speaking clearly at an understandable pace.

R.1.B Ask and answer such questions as who, what, where, when, why, and how to demonstrate understanding of key details in a text.

R.4.B Determine the meaning of general academic and domain-specific words and phrases in a text relevant to a topic or subject area.

R.5.B Know and use various text features to locate key facts or information in a text efficiently.

R.7.C Interpret information presented visually, orally, or quantitatively and explain how the information contributes to an understanding of the text in which it appears.

W.7.A Participate in shared research and writing projects.

L.1.B (l.) Produce simple, compound and complex sentences.

L.4.B (a.) Use sentence-level context as a clue to the meaning of a word or phrase.

RF.4.B (a.) Read grade-level text with purpose and understanding.

ELPS: 8. An ELL can determine the meaning of words and phrases in oral presentations and literary and informational text.

Warm-up and Review
10–15 minutes (books closed)

Write a series of years on the board that represent events in your life—for example, the years you were born, graduated from high school/college, got married, had your first child, started working at this school. Ask students to guess what happened to you in each year. When someone gets it right, write the word next to the year—*born, married*, and so on.

Introduction
3 minutes

1. Have students tell you which of the items on the board would be considered major life events.

2. State the objective: *Today we're going to talk about life events and special occasions.*

1 Identify life-event vocabulary

Presentation I
15–20 minutes

A 1. Write *Life events* on the board. Have students work together to brainstorm in a group. Make a list on the board of the events your students identify.

2. Have students identify which life events are remembered forever. Elicit ideas and put a checkmark next to the events students feel are the most memorable, encouraging them to explain their reasons.

B Have students read the article. Suggest that they underline any words or phrases that are unfamiliar to go over later in D.

Guided Practice I
20–25 minutes

C 1. Have volunteers read the words and the definitions aloud.

2. Set a time limit (five minutes). Have pairs do the task. As students work, copy the wordlist on the board. Do not check the answers as a class yet.

Answers	
1. b	6. d
2. e	7. f
3. h	8. g
4. i	9. a
5. c	

D 1. To prepare students for listening, say: *Now we're going to listen to the life story of a man named Carlos Ortega. As you listen, check your answers to 1C.*

2. Play the audio. Have volunteers write the correct numbers on the board and have students make any corrections in their books. At this time, go over any other words from the article in 1B that students are unfamiliar with.

3. Pair students. Set a time limit (two minutes) and have students take turns pronouncing the words. Monitor pair practice to identify pronunciation issues.

4. Call "time" and work with the pronunciation of any troublesome words or phrases.

5. Replay the audio and challenge students to listen for more information. *When was Carlos born? What job was he promoted to? Where did he get engaged?* Call on volunteers for the answers.

MULTILEVEL STRATEGIES

After the group comprehension check in 1D, call on volunteers and tailor your questions to the level of your students.

• **Pre-level** Ask *or* questions. *What happens first, you are born or you have a baby?* [you are born]

• **On-level** Ask information questions. *Where do you get a promotion?* [at work]

• **Higher-level** Ask these students to say which life events usually involve a special ceremony.

Communicative Practice and Application I
10–15 minutes

E 1. Ask students to work in a team to brainstorm a list of life-event words.

2. Elicit words from the class. Write them on the board. Ask students to copy them into their vocabulary notes for the unit.

2 Learn vocabulary for life events and special occasions

Presentation II
10–20 minutes

 1. Direct students to look at the newspaper announcements and read the section titles. Ask: *Do you ever read this section of the newspaper?*

2. Have students complete the chart. Set a time limit (three minutes).

3. Write the chart on the board. Ask volunteers to share their answers with the class. Write their answers in the chart and have students check their answers.

Answers			
Date	**Event**	**Person or people**	**Location**
April 30	<u>Wedding</u>	<u>Lilly and Sam Rodriguez</u>	Valley Park
<u>May 9</u>	Birth	<u>George Allen, Joe, and Linda Lee</u>	
<u>May 10</u>	<u>Funeral</u>	Jerry Jones	<u>Valley Funeral Home</u>

TIP
Point out the image of the stork bringing the baby. The legend that storks bring babies began in Germany, where storks were a sign of good luck. Ask students if they know of other superstitions or customs associated with birth.

Guided Practice II
10–15 minutes

 1. Model the conversation with a volunteer. Model it again using different words from 2A.

2. Set a time limit (three minutes). Direct students to practice with a partner.

3. Call on volunteers to present one of their conversations for the class.

Communicative Practice and Application II
10–15 minutes

 1. If students will use the Internet for this task, establish what device(s) they'll use: a class computer, tablets, or smartphones. Alternatively, print information from the Internet before class and distribute to groups.

2. Write the information types from 2C on the board. Explain that students will work in teams to research and report on this information. Ask: *Which search terms or questions can you use to find the information you need?* ["obituary" + person's name, "wedding announcement" + person's name] *How will you record the information you find?* [table, checklist, index cards] Remind students to bookmark or record sites so they can find or cite them in the future.

3. Group students and assign roles: manager, administrative assistant, IT support, and reporter. Verify students' understanding of the roles.

4. Give managers the time limit for researching the questions (ten minutes). Direct the IT support to begin the online research or pick up the printed materials for each team. Direct the administrative assistant to record information for the team using a table, a checklist, or index cards.

5. Give a two-minute warning. Call "time."

6. Copy the sentence frames on the board.

7. Direct teams to help their administrative assistant use the sentence frames to record the team's findings. Direct the reporter to use the recorded information to report the team's findings to the class or another team.

TIP
When setting up task-based activities, verify that students understand their roles using physical commands. For example: *If you report on your team's work, stand up* [reporter]. *If you keep the team on task, point to the clock* [manager]. *If you write the team's responses, raise your hand* [administrative assistant]. *If you help the team research, hold up your smartphone/tablet* [IT support].

Evaluation
10–15 minutes

TEST YOURSELF

1. Pair students. Direct Partner B to close the book, listen to Partner A read definitions a–d from 1C, and write the vocabulary words. Then Partner B should read definitions e–i while Partner A writes the vocabulary words.

2. Direct both partners to open their books and check their spelling when they finish.

3. Circulate and monitor student work.

MULTILEVEL STRATEGIES

Target the *Test Yourself* to the level of your students.

• **Pre-level** Have these students read the words to each other and write them down.

• **Higher-level** Direct these students to write a sentence defining each of the words from the exercise.

EXTENSION ACTIVITY

Discuss Life Events

1. Have students write a series of years or dates representing important life events. Tell them not to write the events.

2. Direct them to sit with a partner and say one sentence about each date. *This is the year I was born. This is the year I got married. This is the year my son was born.* Instruct the partner to ask one question about that event. *Where were you born? Did you have a big wedding? What's your son's name?*

Lesson Overview

Lesson Notes

MULTILEVEL OBJECTIVES

On- and Higher-level: Analyze, write, and edit an email to reschedule a meeting

Pre-level: Read an email to reschedule a meeting

LANGUAGE FOCUS

Grammar: *Would like* (*I'd like to suggest a different date.*)

Vocabulary: *Reschedule, something's come up, fit, inconvenience*

For vocabulary support, see this **Oxford Picture Dictionary** topic: Everyday Conversation, page 12

STRATEGY FOCUS

Avoid "text" abbreviations and incomplete sentences when writing formal messages.

READINESS CONNECTION

In this lesson, students listen actively to, read, and write an email to reschedule a meeting.

PACING

To compress this lesson: Assign the *Test Yourself* and/or 3C for homework.

To extend this lesson: Have students respond to an email. (See end of lesson.)

And/or have students complete **Workbook 3 page 73** and **Multilevel Activities 3 Unit 11 page 120**.

CORRELATIONS

CCRS: SL.1.B (d.) Explain their own ideas and understanding in light of the discussion.

SL.2.B Determine the main ideas and supporting details of a text read aloud or information presented in diverse media and formats, including visually, quantitatively, and orally.

R.1.B Ask and answer such questions as who, what, where, when, why, and how to demonstrate understanding of key details in a text.

R.2.A Identify the main topic and retell key details of a text.

R.5.A Know and use various text features to locate key facts or information in a text.

R.6.B Identify the main purpose of a text, including what the author wants to answer, explain, or describe.

R.7.B Use information gained from illustrations and the words in a text to demonstrate understanding of the text.

R.9.B Compare and contrast the most important points and key details presented in two texts on the same topic.

W.2.A Write informative/explanatory texts in which they name a topic, supply some facts about the topic, and provide some sense of closure.

W.4.B Produce writing in which the development and organization are appropriate to task and purpose.

W.5.B With guidance and support from peers and others, develop and strengthen writing as needed by planning, revising and editing.

W.6.B With guidance and support, use technology to produce and publish writing (using keyboarding skills) as well as to interact and collaborate with others.

L.1.B (l.) Produce simple, compound and complex sentences.

L.2.A (e.) Use commas in dates and to separate single words in a series.

L.2.B Demonstrate command of the conventions of standard English capitalization, punctuation, and spelling when writing. (c.) Use commas in greetings and closings of letters.

L.2.C (a.) Use correct capitalization.

RF.4.B (a.) Read grade-level text with purpose and understanding.

ELPS: 6. An ELL can analyze and critique the arguments of others orally and in writing. 9. An ELL can create clear and coherent level-appropriate speech and text.

Warm-up and Review
10–15 minutes (books closed)

Write *Schedule a meeting* on the board. Elicit the meaning and find out if students have any experience with trying to schedule a meeting at work, at school, or for a club or community activity. *Is it easy to try to pick a date and time that are good for everyone? When is usually a good day and time to schedule different kinds of meetings? Do you keep a calendar in your house? Do you have one on your phone or computer?*

Introduction
3 minutes

1. Tell students: *In order to schedule meetings, it is important to be clear about the date and time. When you receive a request to meet, it's polite to respond, whether you can attend or not.*

2. State the objective: *Today we're going to read and write an email to reschedule a meeting.*

1 Prepare to write

Presentation
20–25 minutes

 1. Build students' schema by asking questions about the picture and the emails. Ask: *What is the picture of? Why is there a red X on one of the dates? Who are the emails from?*

2. Give students one minute to tell a partner their responses to questions 1 and 2. Elicit responses from the class.

Answers
1. Email 1
2. Possible answers: longer, no abbreviations, starts with "dear," more detail

 🔊 3-25 1. Introduce the model emails and their purpose: *You're going to read two emails from the same person. As you read, look for the purpose of the emails: Why is he writing?* Have students read the emails silently.

2. Check comprehension. Ask: *Who is each email to?* [Alicia Gomez] *What do* RU, thx, *and* L8R *mean?* [are you, thanks, later]

3. Play the audio. Have students read along silently.

Guided Practice I
10 minutes

 1. Point out the *Writer's Note* and read the information aloud. Say: *When someone sends you an email that is formal, particularly from work or an organization, it is important to respond in the same way. That means using a formal greeting, complete sentences, no "text" language, and a formal closing. Informal emails should only be written to friends or family.*

2. Have students work independently to underline and number the language in the text.

3. Have students check answers in pairs before checking answers as a class.

Answers
Formal:
David Gala
To: Alicia.gomez@cmail.com
Re: Need to Reschedule Meeting
Dear Ms. Gomez:
<u>I am writing you to request that we reschedule our meeting currently set for next Friday, April 10 at 3:30 (1)</u>. <u>A co-worker is ill and I've been asked to take some of his shifts (2)</u>.
<u>I'd like to suggest that we meet the following Friday, April 17, at 3:30 in your office (3)</u>. Please let me know if this new meeting time will fit into your schedule.
<u>I apologize for any inconvenience this schedule change may cause (4)</u>.
<u>Sincerely (5)</u>,
David Gala
5692 Turnpike
Houston, TX 77002
Informal:
David Gala
To: Alicia.gomez@cmail.com
Re: Need to Reschedule Meeting
Hey Alicia- How RU?
<u>I'm so sorry (4)</u> but <u>I need to change our meeting next Friday (1)</u>. <u>Something's come up and I can't make it (2)</u>. <u>How about the following week? Same time, same place (3)</u>?
Please let me know if this works—thx!
<u>L8R (5)</u>,
Dave

For 1C, challenge on- and higher-level students while working with pre-level students.

• **Pre-level** While other students are working on 1C, ask these students *yes/no* and *or* questions about the reading. *Is the meeting scheduled for April 10? Is the meeting scheduled for 3:30? Is David or his co-worker ill?*

• **On- and Higher-level** Ask these students to brainstorm possible excuses for not attending a meeting. After you go over the answers to 1C, have volunteers write their excuses on the board. Have the class decide if the excuses sound legitimate. Leave them on the board to help students with their 2B writing assignment.

2 Plan and write

Guided Practice II
15–20 minutes

A 1. Read question 1. Answer the question with your own ideas. Have the class brainstorm ideas and write them on the board.

2. As a class, discuss question 2. Tell students to take notes to use in their emails in 2B.

B 1. Direct students to look back at the formal email model in 1B. Focus their attention on what information and sentence structures are in each paragraph. Elicit ideas that could go in each paragraph.

2. Have students write their emails individually. Remind them to use their notes from the *Multilevel Strategy* and 2A.

MULTILEVEL STRATEGIES

Adapt 2B to the level of your students.

• **Pre-level** Work with these students to go through the template sentence by sentence. Elicit students' ideas for each sentence completion and write them on the board. Have students complete each sentence with the ideas from the board.

• **Higher-level** Ask these students to include a detailed excuse of why they need to reschedule.

3 Get feedback and revise

Guided Practice III
5 minutes

A Direct students to check their writing using the editing checklist. Tell them to read each item in the list and check their papers before moving on to the next item. Explain that students should not edit their writing at this stage. They should just use the checklist to check their work and mark any areas they want to revise.

Communicative Practice
15 minutes

B 1. Read the instructions and the sample sentences aloud. Emphasize to students that they are responding to their partners' work, not correcting it.

2. Use the emails in 1B to model the exercise. *The reason was very clear and was stated very politely.*

3. Direct students to exchange papers with a partner and follow the instructions.

C Allow students time to edit and revise their writing as necessary, using the editing checklist from 3A and their partner's feedback from 3B. If necessary, students could complete this task as homework.

Application and Evaluation
10 minutes

TEST YOURSELF

1. Review the instructions aloud. Assign a time limit (five minutes) and have students work independently.

2. Before collecting student work, invite two or three volunteers to share their sentences. Ask students to raise their hands if they wrote similar answers.

MULTILEVEL STRATEGIES

Adapt the *Test Yourself* to the level of your students.

• **Pre-level** Write questions for these students to answer in writing. *Was today's writing assignment difficult or easy? Which is harder to write: a formal or informal email?*

EXTENSION ACTIVITY

Respond to an Email

Have students use the emails they wrote in 2B and exchange them with a partner. Have students reply that they cannot meet that day, give a reason, and propose another day and time.

Lesson Overview

MULTILEVEL OBJECTIVES

On- and Higher-level: Use the present passive to describe scheduled events at a retirement community and listen for meaning in present passive in sentences about events

Pre-level: Recognize the present passive in sentences about events

LANGUAGE FOCUS

Grammar: Present passive (*Dinner is served at 6 p.m.*)

Vocabulary: *Retirement, serve, permit, invitation*

For vocabulary support, see this **Oxford Picture Dictionary** topic: Life Events and Documents, pages 40–41

STRATEGY FOCUS

Use *by* + person/thing when you want to say who performs the action in a passive sentence.

READINESS CONNECTION

In this lesson, students practice using the passive voice to talk about life events.

PACING

To compress this lesson: Conduct 1B and/or 1C as a whole-class activity.

To extend this lesson: Have students discuss cultural traditions. (See end of lesson.)

And/or have students complete **Workbook 3 pages 74–75, Multilevel Activities 3 Unit 11 pages 121–122**, and **Multilevel Grammar Exercises 3 Unit 11**.

Lesson Notes

CORRELATIONS

CCRS: SL.2.B Determine the main ideas and supporting details of a text read aloud or information presented in diverse media and formats, including visually, quantitatively, and orally.

SL.6.B Speak in complete sentences when appropriate to task and situation in order to provide requested detail or clarification.

R.1.B Ask and answer such questions as who, what, where, when, why, and how to demonstrate understanding of key details in a text.

R.5.B Know and use various text features to locate key facts or information in a text efficiently.

L.1.B (l.) Produce simple, compound and complex sentences.

L.1.D (g.) Form and use verbs in the active and passive voice.

RF.4.B (a.) Read grade-level text with purpose and understanding.

ELPS: 7. An ELL can adapt language choices to purpose, task, and audience when speaking and writing. 10. An ELL can demonstrate command of the conventions of standard English to communicate in level-appropriate speech and writing.

Warm-up and Review
10–15 minutes (books closed)

Say: *We've been talking in this unit about life events—growing up, getting married, getting a promotion—but let's think for a moment about when we were young. Life was easy then because we didn't have to do so many things for ourselves. For example, when you're a child, someone feeds you, someone buys you clothes, someone brushes your hair. What else?* Write a series of simple present sentences on the board. *Someone cleans your room. Someone washes your clothes. Someone takes you to school.*

Introduction
5–10 minutes

1. Point out that in all the sentences on the board, it's not important who did the actions. The main idea is that the child didn't have to do them. The point is not that *someone* cleaned the room but that *the room was cleaned.*

2. State the objective: *Today we're going to learn how to use the present passive to talk about daily life and events.*

1 Learn the present passive

Presentation I
20–25 minutes

  1. Direct students to look at the flyer. Ask: *What kind of community is this?* [retirement community]

2. Read the instructions aloud. Ask students to read the flyer silently and answer the questions.

3. Read the first question aloud. Call on a volunteer for the answer. Ask the volunteer where in the flyer he or she found the answer. Read the rest of the questions aloud, calling on a different volunteer for each answer.

Answers
1. Possible answers: meals are served, there is a calendar of events
2. No
3. Daily 5 p.m. to 7 p.m.
4. The time dinner is served

  1. Demonstrate how to read the grammar chart.

2. Direct students to underline the five examples of the present passive in the flyer in 1A. Write them on the board.

3. Check comprehension of sentences in the flyer. Ask: *Who picks up the trash? Who permits*

swimming? Point out that these sentences are passive because the emphasis is on what is done, not on who does it. Ask students to identify the forms of *be* and the past participles in the sentences in the chart and the flyer.

4. Pair students and direct them to read the chart aloud to each other. Then read the chart aloud as students follow along.

5. Assess students' understanding of the chart. Elicit passive versions of the sentences on the board from the *Warm-up. Your room is cleaned. Your clothes are washed.*

Answers
is served, is not permitted, is picked up, is picked up and delivered, is kept

Guided Practice I
10–15 minutes

  1. Tell students they will collaborate to complete the description of the grammar point. Model collaboration by working with the class to complete the first blank. Encourage students to look at 1A and 1B to help them determine the correct words.

2. Pair students and have them work together to complete the description.

3. Project or write the completed definition on the board and have pairs verify the accuracy of their responses. Ask volunteers which sentences confused them and discuss.

Answers
do not
is not
unclear

Guided Practice II
5–10 minutes

1. Read the instructions and verbs in parentheses aloud. Have a volunteer read the example sentence.

2. Set a time limit (five minutes) and have pairs do the task.

3. Check answers as a class.

Answers
1. is invited
2. is served
3. are mailed
4. is not provided

Communicative Practice
10–15 minutes

 E 1. Read the instructions aloud. Model the questions and answers with a volunteer.

2. Ask students to practice the questions and answers with their partners using the information in the checklist.

3. Have pairs merge to form teams of four and then take turns demonstrating questions and answers. Set a time limit (four minutes) and monitor the practice, identifying any issues.

4. Provide clarification or feedback to the whole class as needed.

> **MULTILEVEL STRATEGIES**
>
> For 1E, group same-level students together.
>
> • **Pre-level** Sit with these students and elicit the past participle for each verb in the checklist. Then ask and answer the questions together.
>
> • **Higher-level** Challenge these students to think of two more items to add to the checklist and ask and answer questions about those items.

2 Use the passive with *by*

Presentation II
15–20 minutes

 A 1. Introduce the new topic: *Sometimes we want to say who performed the action in a passive sentence. Then we use a* by *phrase.*

2. Read the active and passive voice sentences in the chart and the *Grammar Note* aloud. Have students work individually to match the parts of the sentences. Go over the answers as a class.

Answers	
1. b	4. c
2. e	5. a
3. d	

> **TIP**
>
> Most passive sentences have a *by* phrase. We often use the *by* phrase when we want to put known information at the beginning of the sentence. For example, in the sentence *Dinner is served by experienced servers*, the listener may already know that there is a dinner. The new information is who serves it.

Guided Practice III
15–20 minutes

 B 1. Have students work individually to answer the questions.

2. Direct students to take turns asking and answering the questions with a partner.

> **MULTILEVEL STRATEGIES**
>
> For 2B, adapt the exercise to the level of your students.
>
> • **Pre-level** Provide these students with more complete versions of the answers. Ask them to complete the sentences with time words. *1. In my neighborhood, mail is delivered _____. 2. Trash is picked up _____. 3. The streets are cleaned _____. 4. The classrooms are cleaned _____.*

> **TIP**
>
> Write *Baby shower* on the board and elicit what students know about baby showers. Read aloud this information: *In the U.S., when a woman is going to have a baby, her friends or family usually host a baby shower for her. It is traditional to invite only women to baby showers, but nowadays, they sometimes include men. Everyone brings a gift for the baby or the mother. Women usually play games at baby showers. You can find books of baby shower games at any bookstore.*
>
> After you read the information, write sentences on the board for students to complete: *The baby shower is usually hosted by _____. Traditionally, only women _____ to a baby shower. _____ are brought for the baby and the mother. Usually games _____ at the shower. Books about baby shower games can be bought at any _____.*
>
> Read the information again and ask students to work individually to complete the sentences on the board. Have volunteers come to the board to complete the sentences. Ask students if baby showers are traditional in their countries.

C 1. Elicit the importance of accuracy. Tell students they will be building their accuracy in this task.

2. Organize students into groups. Demonstrate how to correct the sentence using the first example.

3. Have team members work together to correct the sentences. Circulate and monitor teamwork.

4. Project or write the corrected sentences on the board and have teams check their work.

5. Address questions and any issues you noted during your observation.

Answers
1. The mail is always **delivered** before 12 p.m.
2. The Oak View Apartments **were** built in 1975.
3. Vince was **given** a watch when he retired.
4. Swimming **is permitted** between 10 a.m. and 6 p.m.

3 Listen for the present passive

Guided Practice IV
15–20 minutes

🔊 **3-26** 1. Say: *Now we're going to listen to people using the present passive in sentences. Circle the letter of the sentence with the same idea as the sentence you hear.*

2. Direct students to read the first set of sentences and then play the first sentence and have them circle the correct letter.

3. Elicit answers from the class. If students answered incorrectly, play the audio again, providing a listening clue (for example, *listen for the passive verb*).

4. Repeat for numbers 2–6.

Answers	
1. a	4. a
2. b	5. b
3. a	6. b

MULTILEVEL STRATEGIES

Replay the audio to challenge on- and higher-level students while allowing pre-level students to catch up.

• **Pre-level** Have these students listen again to circle the letters of the correct sentences.

• **On- and Higher-level** Have these students listen again and write down the verbs they hear. As you go over the answers, see if students can reconstruct the passive sentence they heard on the audio.

4 Use the present passive to talk about your life experience

Communicative Practice and Application
20–25 minutes

A 1. Direct students to look at the picture. Ask: *What's happening in this picture?*

2. Remind students of the life events discussed in Lesson 1. If necessary, brainstorm them again and write students' ideas on the board for their reference.

3. Have students work individually to complete the task.

B Read the instructions aloud and have pairs write their questions. Circulate and monitor.

C 1. Read the instructions aloud and model the sample conversation with a volunteer.

2. Put students in small groups. Set a time limit (ten minutes) and have students take turns asking and answering questions about the life event each one of them chose for 4A.

3. Have students share their answers with the class.

Evaluation
10–15 minutes

TEST YOURSELF

Ask students to write the sentences independently. Collect and correct their writing.

MULTILEVEL STRATEGIES

Target the *Test Yourself* to the level of your students.

• **Pre-level** Provide sentence frames for these students to complete about a type of party. *Presents are given at _____. Invitations are written for _____. A big meal is served at _____.*

• **Higher-level** Have these students write a paragraph in response to this question and prompt: *What was the best party you ever went to? Describe what happened at the party.*

EXTENSION ACTIVITY

Discuss Cultural Traditions

Compare cultures and discuss the use of the passive.

1. Brainstorm a list of life events and write them on the board—for example, *birth, important birthdays, graduation, wedding, retirement, moving.*

2. Put students in groups. Give each group a large sheet of paper. Tell them to list some differences between how these events are celebrated or recognized in their native countries and how they are celebrated here. Have each group write five sentences. Tell them it isn't necessary to write about all of the events.

3. Post students' sentences at the front of the room and use them as a springboard for discussing the passive voice. For most sentences, there is no reason to use the passive. *In Korea, pregnant women eat a special seaweed soup.* Other sentences may lend themselves to the passive. *In Mexico, a huge party is thrown on a girl's fifteenth birthday.*

Lesson Overview	Lesson Notes

MULTILEVEL OBJECTIVES

Pre-, On-, and Higher-level: Respond to good and bad news and listen for information about weddings

LANGUAGE FOCUS

Grammar: *Be able to* + verb for ability (*I will be able to drive next year.*)

Vocabulary: Menu and restaurant ordering words

For vocabulary support, see these **Oxford Picture Dictionary** topics: Everyday Conversation, page 12; Life Events and Documents, pages 40–41

STRATEGY FOCUS

Use an exclamation point (!) to show excitement when you write. Use rising intonation to show excitement when you speak.

READINESS CONNECTION

In this lesson, students verbally communicate and practice how to respond to good and bad news.

PACING

To compress this lesson: Do 6A as a class activity and skip 6B.

To extend this lesson: Have students talk about wedding traditions. (See end of lesson.)

And/or have students complete **Workbook 3 page 76** and **Multilevel Activities 3 Unit 11 page 123**.

CORRELATIONS

CCRS: SL.1.B (d.) Explain their own ideas and understanding in light of the discussion.

SL.2.B Determine the main ideas and supporting details of a text read aloud or information presented in diverse media and formats, including visually, quantitatively, and orally.

SL.4.B Report on a topic or text, tell a story, or recount an experience with appropriate facts and relevant, descriptive details, speaking clearly at an understandable pace.

SL.6.B Speak in complete sentences when appropriate to task and situation in order to provide requested detail or clarification.

R.1.B Ask and answer such questions as who, what, where, when, why, and how to demonstrate understanding of key details in a text.

R.2.A Identify the main topic and retell key details of a text.

R.6.B Identify the main purpose of a text, including what the author wants to answer, explain, or describe.

R.7.B Use information gained from illustrations and the words in a text to demonstrate understanding of the text.

L.1.B (l.) Produce simple, compound and complex sentences.

L.1.C (f.) Use verb tense to convey various times, sequences, states, and conditions.

L.3.B (b.) Recognize and observe differences between the conventions of spoken and written standard English.

RF.4.B (a.) Read grade-level text with purpose and understanding.

ELPS: 2. An ELL can participate in level-appropriate oral and written exchanges of information, ideas, and analyses, in various social and academic contexts, responding to peer, audience, or reader comments and questions. 9. An ELL can create clear and coherent level-appropriate speech and text.

Warm-up and Review
5–10 minutes (books closed)

Write *That's great!* and *That's too bad.* on the board. Say: *Which one do you say if I tell you I broke my leg? Which one do you say if I tell you my son just graduated from college?* Ask students for more examples of things people might say to elicit these responses. Write their ideas in the correct column.

Introduction
3 minutes

1. Say: *These are all examples of good news and bad news.*

2. State the objective: *Today we're going to practice responding to good and bad news, and we're going to listen for information about wedding traditions.*

1 Learn ways to talk about life events

Presentation I
10 minutes

 A **3-27** 1. Direct students to look at the picture. Ask: *Are they talking about good news or bad news?* [good news] *Why do you think so?* [because they are smiling and look happy]

2. Read the instructions aloud. Play the audio. Give students a minute to answer the question. Go over the answer as a class.

Answer
Four

Guided Practice I
20–25 minutes

 B **3-27** 1. Read the instructions and the questions aloud. Play the audio. Ask students to listen for the answer to each question.

2. Ask students to compare their answers with a partner. Circulate and monitor to ensure students understand the audio.

Answers
1. She had car trouble and was almost late to class.
2. She got an A on a test and will be able to take the advanced class. She was also accepted to State University.
3. They are going to a nice restaurant.

C **3-28** Read the instructions aloud. Explain that students are going to hear the audio one more time. They should write the words they hear to complete the sentences. Play the audio. Call on volunteers to elicit the answers.

Answers
1. fantastic
2. terrific
3. Congratulations

2 Practice your pronunciation

Pronunciation Extension
10–15 minutes

 A **3-29** 1. Write *That's wonderful* on the board. Read the sentence aloud in a bored tone of voice with falling intonation. Add an exclamation point and read the sentence again in an excited voice with rising intonation. Ask students how your voice changed the second time. Say: *Now we're going to focus on using rising intonation to show excitement.*

2. Read the *Pronunciation Note* aloud and confirm students' understanding.

3. Play the audio. Direct students to listen for rising intonation.

B **3-30** Play the audio. Direct students to check *yes* or *no* to indicate whether the speaker is excited or not.

Answers	
1. yes	4. yes
2. no	5. yes
3. no	6. no

C **3-30** Play the audio again. Have students check their answers to 2B. Ask for a show of hands about each number.

TIP

Write the audio script on the board. Have individual students take turns reading each sentence with the appropriate intonation. Play the audio again sentence by sentence and have students repeat.

3 Learn *be able to* + verb for ability

Presentation II and Guided Practice II
15–20 minutes

1. Introduce the new topic: *In the conversation in 1B, Min said:* Now I'll be able to take the advanced class. *What does that mean? Can she take an advanced class?* [yes]

2. Read the sentences in the chart. Elicit the correct forms of *be able to* and have students circle them in their books. Go over the *Grammar Note*.

3. Check comprehension. Write *I'm sorry I _____ to come to your party yesterday.* and *I'm sorry. I _____ to come to your party tomorrow.* on the board. Elicit the completions.

4. Have students complete the sentences. Check answers as a class.

Answers
will be able to attend
will be able to get married
won't be able to sing

1. Read the instructions aloud. Have students do the task individually. Go over answers as a class.

2. Set a time limit (five minutes). Ask students to practice asking and answering the questions with several partners. Call on individuals to share their answers with the class.

Answers
1. Will you be able to
2. Can you
3. could you

TIP

After 3B, try some oral practice with *will be able to* and *was able to*. Ask one student a question: *Will you be able to come to school tomorrow?* After that student answers, ask another student to say a sentence about the first student: *He/ She won't be able to come to class tomorrow.* Elicit other possible questions: *Were you able to find a good parking spot this morning? Were you able to get to school on time today? Will you be able to pass the test for this unit? Will you be able to attend school next summer?*

4 Building conversational skills

Guided Practice III
15–20 minutes

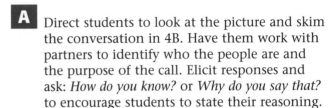

A Direct students to look at the picture and skim the conversation in 4B. Have them work with partners to identify who the people are and the purpose of the call. Elicit responses and ask: *How do you know?* or *Why do you say that?* to encourage students to state their reasoning.

Answers
A daughter calling her mother with good and bad news; answers will vary.

B **◀)) 3-31** **1.** Ask students to read the instructions and tell you what they are going to do [listen and read and respond to the question]. Play the audio and then elicit the answer to the question.

Answer
She passed her driving test and can get her license.

2. Ask students to read the conversation with a partner. Circulate and monitor pronunciation. Model and have students repeat difficult words or phrases.

3. Ask: *In what other situations could you use this conversation?* Point out a few phrases that are not specific to talking about good/bad news. Ask volunteers to point out others.

TIP

Make sure that students understand that *Terrific!* means good. They may be confused by its similarity to *terrible, terror,* and *terrify*.

Communicative Practice and Application I
20–25 minutes

C **1.** Pair students and have them read the instructions silently. Check their comprehension of the exercise. Ask: *What are the two roles? Are the speakers face-to-face?*

2. Model and have students repeat the expressions in the *In Other Words* box in 4B. Explain that they should use these expressions in their conversations.

3. Draw a T-chart on the board. Label the left column *Friend A* and the right column *Friend B*. Elicit examples of what each person might say and make notes in the chart.

4. Set a time limit (three minutes). Have students act out the role-play. Call "time" and have students switch roles.

5. Ask three volunteer pairs to act out their role-play for the class. Tell students who are listening to make a simple table with four rows and two columns. Use the top row to label the columns *News* and *Reaction*. Have students take notes in the chart for each role-play.

MULTILEVEL STRATEGIES

Seat same-level students together.

• **Pre-level** For these students, provide a simplified conversation. *A: I have some good news and bad news. B: What's the bad news? A: I got a huge credit-card bill this month. B: Oh, that's too bad. What's the good news? A: I got a promotion and a raise! I'll be able to pay off my bill next month. B: Congratulations! Let's celebrate tonight.*

• **Higher-level** You can challenge students to add a piece of good or bad news for Friend B and have Friend A react.

5 Focus on listening for details

Presentation III and Guided Practice IV
20–25 minutes

A 1. Read the questions and statement aloud and model a discussion with a volunteer. Ask: *Are there advantages to not being married? What are they? Should everyone get married? Why? / Why not? I agree because… / I disagree because…*

2. Pair students and tell them to discuss their own answers to the questions. Circulate and monitor.

B Direct students to read the sentences before they listen to the radio broadcast. Ask what kind of information they'll be writing in the blanks. Ask volunteers for predictions. If students struggle, start by offering your own prediction: *I think we will hear about wedding traditions.*

C 🔊 3-32 1. Play the audio. Ask students to listen and write the correct answers.

2. Pair students and have them compare answers. If a pair has different answers, have the class vote on the correct answer with a show of hands.

Answers
1. wedding
2. good-bye
3. dishes
4. brides
5. kiss

6 Discuss

Communicative Practice and Application II
15–20 minutes

A 1. Read the instructions aloud. Draw a sample chart on the board with space for country names on the right side and birthday events on the left side. Read the events in the bulleted list. Call on volunteers to read the sample conversation in 6A. Fill in the chart, writing *Argentina* on the left and *pull on ears for each year old* on the right. Explain that students will make a chart like this one based on their own discussions and that they should write the bulleted items in the chart next to any country that does them.

2. Put students into teams of three and assign roles: manager, administrative assistant, and reporter. Verify students' understanding of the roles. Encourage students to use the phrases in the *Speaking Note* during their discussions.

3. Set a time limit for the discussions (ten minutes). Write the sentence frame from 6B on the board. Then circulate and monitor.

TIP

To facilitate 6A, do one of the following:

Have students research birthday traditions as homework the night before doing 6A.

Provide each group with printouts of information about different birthday traditions around the world.

Allow students time during class to research birthday traditions on their smart phones, tablets, or computers.

B Call "time." Ask the reporter for each team to report the results of the team's discussion using the sentence frame on the board.

Evaluation

5 minutes

TEST YOURSELF

1. Ask students to complete the checkboxes individually.

2. Tell students that you are going to read each of the items in the checklist aloud. If they are not at all confident with that skill, they should hold up a closed fist. If they are not very confident, they should hold up one finger. If they are somewhat confident, two fingers; confident, three fingers; very confident, four fingers. If they think they could teach the skill, they should hold up five fingers. Read each item in the checklist and identify students who may need further support.

EXTENSION ACTIVITY

Talk about Wedding Traditions

1. Put students in groups. If possible, group them by country of origin. Give each group a large sheet of paper and ask the groups to write about wedding traditions in their native countries. Provide questions to help them get started: *Who pays for the reception? What are the before-wedding traditions? Where is the wedding held? Who participates in the wedding? What food is served? What are traditional gifts?*

2. Have a reporter from each group read the group's writing to the class.

Lesson Overview	**Lesson Notes**

MULTILEVEL OBJECTIVES

Pre-, On-, and Higher-level: Read about and discuss when and why people move

LANGUAGE FOCUS

Grammar: *It + infinitive (It's important to know your housing rights.)*

Vocabulary: *Disability, discrimination, fair, rights*

For vocabulary support, see this **Oxford Picture Dictionary** topic: Finding a Home, pages 48–49

STRATEGY FOCUS

Summarize what you read to help you understand and to share ideas with other people.

READINESS CONNECTION

In this lesson, students verbally communicate information about when and why people move.

PACING

To compress this lesson: Assign 1E and/or 1F for homework.

To extend this lesson: Have students practice asking questions to a landlord. (See end of lesson.)

And/or have students complete **Workbook 3 page 77** and **Multilevel Activities 3 Unit 11 page 124–125**.

CORRELATIONS

CCRS: SL.1.B (d.) Explain their own ideas and understanding in light of the discussion.

SL.2.B Determine the main ideas and supporting details of a text read aloud or information presented in diverse media and formats, including visually, quantitatively, and orally.

R.1.B Ask and answer such questions as who, what, where, when, why, and how to demonstrate understanding of key details in a text.

R.2.A Identify the main topic and retell key details of a text.

R.5.B Know and use various text features to locate key facts or information in a text efficiently.

R.6.B Identify the main purpose of a text, including what the author wants to answer, explain, or describe.

R.7.B Use information gained from illustrations and the words in a text to demonstrate understanding of the text.

R.7.C Interpret information presented visually, orally, or quantitatively and explain how the information contributes to an understanding of the text in which it appears.

L.1.B (l.) Produce simple, compound and complex sentences.

L.2.B (h.) Use conventional spelling for high-frequency and other studied words and for adding suffixes to base words.

L.4.B (c.) Use a known root word as a clue to the meaning of an unknown word with the same root (e.g., addition, additional). (e.) Use glossaries and beginning dictionaries, both print and digital, to determine or clarify the meaning of words and phrases.

RF.3.B (c.) Identify and know the meaning of the most common prefixes and derivational suffixes.

RF.4.B (a.) Read grade-level text with purpose and understanding.

ELPS: 1. An ELL can construct meaning from oral presentations and literary and informational text through level-appropriate listening, reading, and viewing. 3. An ELL can speak and write about level-appropriate complex literary and informational texts and topics.

Warm-up and Review
10–15 minutes (books closed)

Tell your students how many different homes you have lived in during your life. Give them a moment to think back on their lives and count how many places they have lived in. Have all students stand. Ask: *Has anybody lived in only two homes?* Have those students who have lived in only two homes sit down. Ask: *Has anybody lived in only three homes?* Then have those students sit down. Continue until you find the student who has moved the most times.

Introduction
10 minutes

1. Say: *Most people move several times in their lives. Moving is expensive and can be difficult, and it's important that we know our housing rights.*

2. State the objective: *Today we're going to read about and discuss when and why people move.*

1 Read

Presentation
10–20 minutes

A Read the questions aloud. Call on volunteers to answer the questions and share personal experiences with moving.

B Read the words and definitions. Elicit sample sentences for the words or supply them if the students can't. Ask students to identify how each of the words relates to housing and moving.

Pre-reading

C Read the instructions aloud and confirm that students understand where the headings are. Have students answer the question individually and then check answers as a class. If any students answer incorrectly, ask them to support their answer using the title, photo, and headings. Establish the correct answer.

Answer
b. People moving to a new home need to know their rights.

Guided Practice: While Reading
20–30 minutes

D 1. Ask students to read the article silently and answer the question.

2. Check answers as a class.

3. Check comprehension. Ask: *Why do people move?* [for their career, for retirement, or to be near family] *What laws protect people?* [Fair Housing Act, Equal Opportunity Credit Act] *You should never sign a lease when?* [if there is information missing]

Answer
A lease

MULTILEVEL STRATEGIES

Adapt 1D to the level of your students.

• **Pre-level** Ask these students *yes/no* questions. *Is it important to get a copy of the lease?* [yes]

• **On-level** Ask these students information questions. *Who should you contact if you experience discrimination?* [HUD]

• **Higher-level** Ask these students inference questions. Explain: *The article says that you might be in for a surprise if you sign an incomplete lease.* Ask: *What does that mean? What could the surprise be?*

Guided Practice: Rereading
10–15 minutes

E 1. Read the instructions aloud and have students read the article silently. Provide an opportunity for students to extract evidence from the text and have them underline the words that support their answer to the question.

2. Pair students and tell them to compare the words they underlined and report anything they disagree on. Discuss and clarify as needed.

3. Direct students' attention to the *Reader's Note* and read the information aloud. Set a time limit (three minutes) and have students write a summary of the article. Ask volunteers to read their summary to the class.

Answers
To give renters facts about how to protect themselves; underlines will vary.

TIP

Since this article has very important information, you can provide students with a brief summary and display it in the classroom.

F 1. Have students work individually to mark the answers *T* (true), *F* (false), and *NI* (no information). They should then write the line numbers where they found the true and false answers. Write the answers on the board.

2. Elicit and discuss any additional questions about the reading. You could introduce new questions for class discussion: *Have you followed any of the advice in the article? What is stressful about moving?*

Answers
1. F, lines 2–3
2. T, line 4
3. F, lines 11–12
4. NI
5. T, line 22

2 Word study

Guided Practice: Post-reading
15–20 minutes

A 1. Direct students to look at the chart and identify the topic (the suffix *-ment*). Have students read the information. Read the information in the chart and the example for *retire* and *retirement*. Elicit sentences for the other words in the chart.

2. Have students repeat after you as you say each word with natural intonation, rhythm, and stress.

B Direct students to work individually to write a sentence for each topic that includes the underlined word. Ask volunteers to write their sentences on the board. Have the rest of the class suggest grammar and spelling edits as needed.

3 Talk it over

Guided Practice
15–20 minutes

A 1. Have students look at the infographic and read the text. Point out that they need to use the information from the infographic and text to complete the sentences.

2. Read the *Reader's Note*. Ask volunteers to make statements about the infographic.

3. Set a time limit (ten minutes). Have students work in pairs to complete the task. Ask volunteers to share their answers with the class.

Answers
1. Tennessee
2. Oregon
3. South and west
4. Oregon
5. Florida

Communicative Practice
15–20 minutes

B Read the questions aloud. Set a time limit (ten minutes). Tell students to copy the chart in their notebooks and complete it with their answers to the questions.

C While students are doing the activity in 2B, write the chart on the board. Have pairs share their answers with the class and write them in the chart. Have students add any new ideas to their charts. Have a class discussion about reasons why students have moved and what places in the U.S. they would want to move to and why.

Application
15–20 minutes

BRING IT TO LIFE

Read the instructions aloud. Ask students whether they have leases or mortgage agreements at home. Check comprehension of the exercise. *Should you bring your lease to class?* [no] *How many rules are you going to copy?* [three]

EXTENSION ACTIVITY
Ask a Landlord
1. As a class, brainstorm a list of questions that a prospective tenant might want to ask about the lease agreement. *Are utilities included? Which ones? When can the landlord raise the rent? By how much? What are the rules about pets? What are the rules about visitors? Does the lease cover repairs?* Write the questions on the board.
2. Have the students practice the questions with a partner. Tell the "tenant" to ask the questions and the "landlord" to invent the answers.

Warm-up and Review
10–15 minutes

Begin the lesson by addressing one of the students and praising his or her work in the previous lesson. *Joe, thanks for your contributions to our discussion about moving to the U.S. Great work!* Ask students for suggestions about other ways to talk to a classmate about good work.

Introduction
5 minutes

1. Write *Praise* on the board. Confirm understanding of the word and ask volunteers to say situations where it is important to praise someone.

2. State the objective: *Today we're going to talk about how to praise someone.*

Presentation
5 minutes

 3-33 Read the instructions aloud. Play the audio. Give students a minute to think about the question. Elicit responses from the class.

Answer
Planning a wedding

Guided Practice
10–15 minutes

 3-33 1. Read the instructions aloud. Play the audio and have students put a check next to each part of the wedding preparation that has been taken care of.

2. To check answers, play the audio again and have students raise their hands each time they hear a part of the wedding preparation.

Answers
Checked:
photographer
florist
hotel

 3-33 Read the instructions aloud. Play the audio again, encouraging students to take notes in their notebooks. Set a time limit (five minutes) for students to discuss their answers with a partner. Circulate to monitor.

Answers
DJ, location, cake, food, invitations

Presentation and Communicative Practice
15–20 minutes

D 1. Direct students' attention to the *Do/Say* chart and ask students to identify the lesson's soft skill [praising someone]. Ask the class which column has examples of behaviors [left] and which has examples of language [right].

2. Model the sentences from the right column using authentic intonation. Have students practice imitating your inflection.

3. Put students in teams of four and assign each team a question. Assign roles: manager, administrative assistant, researcher, and reporter. Researchers will ask you questions on behalf of the team. Verify understanding of the roles. Set a time limit (five minutes) and monitor.

4. Write sentence frames on the board that teams can use to summarize their response. (*Our team discussed the following question: _____ We decided _____ because _____.)*

5. Call "time" and let reporters rehearse their report for one minute. Direct each reporter to present to three other teams.

Communicative Practice and Application
10–15 minutes

E 1. Tell students that they are going to work in pairs and practice praising each other using the sentences in D. Model the conversation with a volunteer.

2. Direct pairs to take turns sharing and praising.

3. As students carry out the conversation, circulate and monitor. Provide global feedback once the activity ends.

Lesson Overview

MULTILEVEL OBJECTIVES

Pre-, On-, and Higher-level: Review unit language

LANGUAGE FOCUS

Grammar: Present passive, *be able to*

Vocabulary: Words and phrases for discussing life events

For vocabulary support, see these **Oxford Picture Dictionary** topics: Everyday Conversation, page 12; Life Events and Documents, pages 40–41

READINESS CONNECTION

In this review, students work in a team to use present passive and *be able to* to talk about life events.

PACING

To extend this review: Have students complete **Workbook 3 page 78**, **Multilevel Activities 3 Unit 11 page 126**, and **Multilevel Grammar Exercises 3 Unit 11**.

Lesson Notes

CORRELATIONS

CCRS: SL.1.B (a.) Come to discussions prepared, having read or studied required material; explicitly draw on that preparation and other information known about the topic to explore ideas under discussion. (b.) Follow agreed-upon rules for discussions. (c.) Ask questions to check understanding of information presented, stay on topic, and link their comments to the remarks of others. (d.) Explain their own ideas and understanding in light of the discussion.

SL.2.B Determine the main ideas and supporting details of a text read aloud or information presented in diverse media and formats, including visually, quantitatively, and orally.

SL.4.B Report on a topic or text, tell a story, or recount an experience with appropriate facts and relevant, descriptive details, speaking clearly at an understandable pace.

SL.6.B Speak in complete sentences when appropriate to task and situation in order to provide requested detail or clarification.

R.1.B Ask and answer such questions as who, what, where, when, why, and how to demonstrate understanding of key details in a text.

R.2.A Identify the main topic and retell key details of a text.

L.1.B (l.) Produce simple, compound and complex sentences.

L.1.C (d.) Use modal auxiliaries to convey various conditions. (f.) Use verb tense to convey various times, sequences, states, and conditions.

L.1.D (g.) Form and use verbs in the active and passive voice.

L.4.B (c.) Use a known root word as a clue to the meaning of an unknown word with the same root.

RF.3.B (c.) Identify and know the meaning of the most common prefixes and derivational suffixes.

RF.4.B (a.) Read grade-level text with purpose and understanding.

ELPS: 5. An ELL can conduct research and evaluate and communicate findings to answer questions or solve problems. 6. An ELL can analyze and critique the arguments of others orally and in writing.

Warm-up and Review
10–15 minutes (books closed)

1. Review *At Work* activity E.

2. Ask students to share the good, not-so-good, and interesting things that happened during the conversation. As students speak, write their responses in a chart on the board.

Introduction and Presentation
5 minutes

1. Restate the rules from the lease and mortgage agreements using the present passive and *be able to.* Write examples on the board. *Pets are not permitted. Visitors are allowed for three days. Repairs are paid for by the landlord. If the rent is five days late, the landlord will be able to charge a fine. If the apartment is damaged, the landlord will be able to keep the security deposit.*

2. State the objective: *Today we're going to review the present passive and* be able to *to talk about life events.*

Guided Practice
15–20 minutes

A 1. Read the instructions aloud and have volunteers read the sample quotes. Do the first item with the class.

2. Put students in groups of three or four. Set a time limit (five minutes) for teams to complete the task. Check answers as a class.

B 1. Put pairs of teams together. Read the instructions aloud and have students complete the task. Circulate and monitor. As an extra challenge, have students identify who in the picture is saying the quote.

2. Check answers as a class.

Communicative Practice
30–45 minutes

C 1. Group students and assign roles: manager, writer, editor, and presenter. Explain that students are going to work with their teams to write an email to a co-worker to reschedule an important meeting. Editors will review the email and offer suggestions for changes. Verify students' understanding of the roles.

2. Read steps 2–5 of the activity aloud. Check comprehension of the task. *What is the first thing you should do?* [choose a reason from the box] *Who should your email be addressed to?* [the co-worker]

3. Set a time limit (ten minutes) to complete the exercise. Circulate and answer any questions.

4. Have the presenter from each team read the team's email to the class.

D 1. Have students walk around the room to conduct the interviews. To get students moving, tell them to interview three people who were not on their team for C.

2. Set a time limit (five minutes) to complete the exercise.

3. Tell students to make a note of their classmates' answers but not to worry about writing complete sentences.

E 1. Read the instructions and have students copy the chart into their notebooks. Set a time limit (ten minutes) and have students do the task.

2. Call on individuals to report what they learned about their classmates. Keep a running tally on the board for each response.

3. Use your tally for question 1 to create a pie chart on the board. Instruct students to draw a pie chart for responses to question 2 in their notebooks. Circulate and answer any questions.

4. Ask volunteers to report the results of their interviews.

PROBLEM SOLVING
10–15 minutes

A 1. Ask: *Do you ever have trouble getting vacation days? Is it sometimes difficult to choose between work and family events?* Direct students to read Soo's story silently.

2. Ask: *What is the special occasion? What did she have to ask her boss?*

3. Play the audio and have students read along silently.

B 1. Elicit answers to question 1. Guide students to a class consensus on the answer.

2. As a class, brainstorm answers to question 2. Ask students if they know someone who has this problem and has overcome it or what they have done themselves to overcome the same problem.

Answers
1. Soo forgot to tell her cousin that she couldn't attend her wedding. 2. Answers will vary.

Evaluation
20–25 minutes

To test students' understanding of the unit language and content, have them take the Unit 11 Test, available on the Teacher Resource Center.

Unit Overview

This unit explores civil rights and responsibilities with a range of employability skills and contextualizes structures with infinitives and gerunds.

KEY OBJECTIVES	
Lesson 1	Identify civic rights and responsibilities
Lesson 2	Identify a community problem and write an email asking for assistance
Lesson 3	Use verbs plus infinitives to plan an event
Lesson 4	Write and report requests
Lesson 5	Learn about the Civil Rights Movement
At Work	Help someone understand
Teamwork & Language Review	Review unit language

UNIT FEATURES	
Academic Vocabulary	*constitutional, contribution, immigrant, involvement, credit*
Employability Skills	• Decide when to talk about your achievements • Determine whether feedback is positive or negative • Analyze why young people do not vote • Decide what to do after a traffic accident • Work independently • Understand teamwork • Locate information • Communicate verbally • Listen actively • Use writing skills • Comprehend written material • Analyze information

Resources	**Class Audio** CD3, Tracks 35–45
	Workbook Unit 12, pages 79–85
	Teacher Resource Center
	    Multilevel Activities 3 Unit 12
	    Multilevel Grammar Exercises 3 Unit 12
	    Unit 12 Test
	Oxford Picture Dictionary Civic Engagement, Community Cleanup

Lesson Overview	Lesson Notes

MULTILEVEL OBJECTIVES

On-level: Discriminate between civic rights and responsibilities and use civics vocabulary

Pre-level: Identify civic rights and responsibilities

Higher-level: Talk and write about civic rights and responsibilities using civics vocabulary

LANGUAGE FOCUS

Grammar: *Can* and *have to* (*Can you vote? Do you have to vote?*)

Vocabulary: Civic rights and responsibilities

For vocabulary support, see this **Oxford Picture Dictionary** topic: Civic Engagement, pages 142–143

STRATEGY FOCUS

Pool knowledge with team members to maximize vocabulary learning.

READINESS CONNECTION

In this lesson, students explore and communicate information about civic rights and responsibilities.

PACING

To compress this lesson: Conduct 1C as a whole-class activity.

To extend this lesson: Have students use modals. (See end of lesson.)

And/or have students complete **Workbook 3 page 79** and **Multilevel Activities 3 Unit 12 pages 128–129**.

CORRELATIONS

CCRS: SL.1.B (d.) Explain their own ideas and understanding in light of the discussion.

SL.6.B Speak in complete sentences when appropriate to task and situation in order to provide requested detail or clarification.

SL.4.B Report on a topic or text, tell a story, or recount an experience with appropriate facts and relevant, descriptive details, speaking clearly at an understandable pace.

R.1.B Ask and answer such questions as who, what, where, when, why, and how to demonstrate understanding of key details in a text.

R.4.B Determine the meaning of general academic and domain-specific words and phrases in a text relevant to a topic or subject area.

R.5.B Know and use various text features to locate key facts or information in a text efficiently.

R.7.C Interpret information presented visually, orally, or quantitatively and explain how the information contributes to an understanding of the text in which it appears.

W.7.A Participate in shared research and writing projects.

L.1.B (l.) Produce simple, compound and complex sentences.

L.4.B (a.) Use sentence-level context as a clue to the meaning of a word or phrase. (e.) Use glossaries and beginning dictionaries, both print and digital, to determine or clarify the meaning of words and phrases.

RF.4.B (a.) Read grade-level text with purpose and understanding.

ELPS: 8. An ELL can determine the meaning of words and phrases in oral presentations and literary and informational text.

Warm-up and Review
10–15 minutes (books closed)

Write *Freedom* on the board. Ask students to brainstorm about freedom. *Do you have freedom in the U.S.? What are you free to do? Can you say negative things about the government? Can you write negative things about the government? Can you travel where you want to?*

Introduction
3 minutes

1. Say: *We have been talking about the things that we are allowed to do in this country. These are our rights. There are also things we have to do. These are our responsibilities.*

2. State the objective: *Today we're going to talk about civic rights and responsibilities.*

1 Identify civic vocabulary

Presentation I
15–20 minutes

A 1. Write *Rights* and *Freedoms* on the board. Discuss what the people are doing in each picture. *This man is speaking in the park.* Elicit students' answers to questions 1 and 2.

2. Have students identify the rights and freedoms they think are the most important. Elicit ideas and put a checkmark next to the rights and freedoms students feel are the most important, encouraging them to explain their reasons.

Answers
1. Freedom of peaceful assembly, freedom of speech, freedom of the press, the right to a fair trial
2. The right to vote, the right to carry a U.S. passport

B 1. Read the instructions aloud. Model the task by "thinking aloud" about the word *newcomers*: *I see the words* welcomed *and* from all over the world *before and after, so* newcomers *must mean people who are new to the U.S.*

2. Set a time limit (three minutes) and direct students to do the task individually and then compare their answers with a partner.

3. Have students share their partners' answers with the class.

Guided Practice I
20–25 minutes

C 1. Direct students to look at the words in the picture in 1A. Elicit any words that students do not know and write them on the board. Ask volunteers to explain any of the words they know.

2. Direct students to look up any remaining unknown words in their dictionaries. Discuss those words in relation to the lesson.

3. Set a time limit (five minutes) and have students do the task individually. Play the audio for students to check their answers.

4. Work with the pronunciation of any troublesome words or phrases.

Answers
1. right to vote
2. freedom of speech
3. Freedom of the press
4. right to a fair trial
5. freedom of assembly
6. carry a U.S. passport

D Replay the audio. Challenge students to listen for which rights and freedoms apply to all U.S. residents. Give students a minute to answer the question. Go over the answer as a class.

Communicative Practice and Application I
15–20 minutes

E 1. Direct a volunteer to ask you the questions. Model the answers.

2. Set a time limit (three minutes). Direct students to ask and answer the questions with a partner. Ask volunteers to share their ideas with the class.

2 Learn about civic responsibility

Presentation II
10–20 minutes

A 1. Direct students to look at the pamphlet. Introduce the new topic: *Now we're going to talk about civic responsibilities: the things that you have to do.*

2. Say and have students repeat the phrases. Read the definitions. Discuss the examples in the artwork. Elicit students' knowledge about each of the items. *What is a "no littering"*

law? When do you pay federal taxes? What does "respect the rights of others" mean? How do you know when it's time for you to serve on a jury? How can you get informed?

3. Ask students to work individually to complete the paragraph. Call on a volunteer to read the completed paragraph.

4. Check comprehension. Say sentences with missing words and have the class complete them. *If you are called to jury duty, you need to _____. [serve] You have to pay federal, state, and local _____. [taxes]*

Answers	
1. taxes	4. serve
2. laws	5. informed
3. respect	

MULTILEVEL STRATEGIES

While other students are completing 2A, provide pre-level students with an alternate activity.

• **Pre-level** Have these students match the verb to the rest of the phrase. *1. obey 2. pay 3. respect 4. serve 5. be a) the rights of others b) taxes c) the laws d) informed e) on a jury.* Ask volunteers to write the completed phrases on the board.

Guided Practice II
5–10 minutes

B

1. Model asking and answering the first question with a volunteer.

2. Set a time limit (three minutes). Direct students to do the task with a partner.

3. Call on volunteers to present their conversations for the class.

Communicative Practice and Application II
20–25 minutes

C

1. If students will use the Internet for this task, establish what device(s) they'll use: a class computer, tablets, or smartphones. Alternatively, print information from the Internet before class and distribute to groups.

TIP

This might be a good time to review/teach the titles of government officials on the local, state, and national level: congressman/woman, judge, alderman, mayor, state senator, senator, etc.

2. Write the questions from 2C on the board. Explain that students will work in teams to research and report on this information. Ask: *Which search terms or questions can you use to find the information you need?* ["candidates" + "election" + district/state name] *How will you record the information you find?* [table, checklist, index cards] Remind students to bookmark or record sites so they can find or cite them in the future.

3. Group students and assign roles: manager, administrative assistant, IT support, and reporter. Verify students' understanding of their roles.

4. Give managers the time limit for researching the questions (ten minutes). Direct the IT support to begin the online research or pick up the printed materials for each team. Direct the administrative assistant to record information for the team using a table, a checklist, or index cards.

5. Give a two-minute warning. Call "time."

TIP

When setting up task-based activities, verify that students understand their roles using physical commands. For example: *If you report on your team's work, stand up* [reporter]. *If you keep the team on task, point to the clock* [manager]. *If you write the team's responses, raise your hand* [administrative assistant]. *If you help the team research, hold up your smartphone/tablet* [IT support].

D

1. Copy the sentence frames on the board.

2. Direct teams to help their administrative assistant use the sentence frames to record the team's findings. Direct the reporter to use the recorded information to report the team's findings to the class or another team.

Evaluation
10–15 minutes (books closed)

TEST YOURSELF

1. Direct Partner A to read prompts 1–3 from 1C on page 180 to Partner B. Partner B should close his or her book and write the answers in his or her notebook. When finished, students switch roles. Partner B reads prompts 4–6 from 1C.

2. Direct both partners to check their spelling when they finish.

EXTENSION ACTIVITY

Use Modals

Have students use modals to write about rights and responsibilities. Write *can, can't, should,* and *have to* on the board. Ask students to work with a partner and use the words to write about the rights and responsibilities of U.S. residents. Have volunteers put their sentences on the board.

Lesson Overview	Lesson Notes
MULTILEVEL OBJECTIVES	

MULTILEVEL OBJECTIVES

On- and Higher-level: Analyze, write, and edit an email to a newspaper identifying a community problem and asking for assistance

Pre-level: Read an email to a newspaper asking for assistance with a community problem

LANGUAGE FOCUS

Grammar: Present tense (*When people get involved in their communities, good things happen.*)

Vocabulary: *Get involved, literacy, rewarding*

For vocabulary support, see this **Oxford Picture Dictionary** topic: Community Cleanup, pages 152–153

STRATEGY FOCUS

Use examples and details to make writing clear.

READINESS CONNECTION

In this lesson, students listen actively, read, and write about a community problem and how civic involvement can help.

PACING

To compress this lesson: Assign the *Test Yourself* and/or 3C for homework.

To extend this lesson: Have students discuss community involvement. (See end of lesson.)

And/or have students complete **Workbook 3 page 80** and **Multilevel Activities 3 Unit 12 page 130**.

CORRELATIONS

CCRS: SL.1.B (d.) Explain their own ideas and understanding in light of the discussion.

SL.2.B Determine the main ideas and supporting details of a text read aloud or information presented in diverse media and formats, including visually, quantitatively, and orally.

R.1.B Ask and answer such questions as who, what, where, when, why, and how to demonstrate understanding of key details in a text.

R.2.A Identify the main topic and retell key details of a text.

R.6.B Identify the main purpose of a text, including what the author wants to answer, explain, or describe.

R.7.B Use information gained from illustrations and the words in a text to demonstrate understanding of the text.

W.2.B (a.) Introduce a topic and group related information together; include illustrations when useful to aiding comprehension. (b.) Develop the topic with facts, definitions, and details. (c.) Use linking words and phrases to connect ideas within categories of information. (d.) Provide a concluding statement or section.

W.4.B Produce writing in which the development and organization are appropriate to task and purpose.

W.5.B With guidance and support from peers and others, develop and strengthen writing as needed by planning, revising and editing.

W.6.B With guidance and support, use technology to produce and publish writing (using keyboarding skills) as well as to interact and collaborate with others.

L.1.B (l.) Produce simple, compound and complex sentences.

L.2.B (c.) Use commas in greetings and closings of letters.

L.2.C (a.) Use correct capitalization.

RF.4.B (a.) Read grade-level text with purpose and understanding.

ELPS: 6. An ELL can analyze and critique the arguments of others orally and in writing. 9. An ELL can create clear and coherent level-appropriate speech and text.

Warm-up and Review
10–15 minutes (books closed)

Write *My neighborhood* on the board. Draw a smiley face and a frowning face. Ask students to think about what they like and don't like about their neighborhoods. *Are your neighbors friendly? How often do you talk to them? What do you talk about? Is there a nice park in your neighborhood? Good schools? Are the streets safe?* Ask volunteers to come to the board and write things they like and don't like about their neighborhoods.

Introduction
5 minutes

1. Point to the list of things that students don't like about their neighborhoods. Ask: *Can you do anything about these things? What can you do?*

2. State the objective: *Today we're going to read and write about asking for assistance with community problems.*

1 Prepare to write

Presentation
20–25 minutes

 1. Build students' schema by asking questions about the picture. Ask: *What is the man doing?* [writing a letter] *What is he imagining?* [getting involved in his community]

2. Give students one minute to tell a partner their responses to questions 1 and 2. Elicit responses from the class.

Answers
1. Planting a tree, protesting
2. The editor of a newspaper or online news site

B 🔊 3-36 1. Introduce the model email and confirm its purpose: *You're going to read a man's email to a newspaper about a literacy program at a library.* Have students read the email silently.

2. Check comprehension. Ask: *What can people who read and speak English do?* [participate in the community] *How much does the program cost?* [It's free.] *Who should students contact?* [Beverly Shultz, the program coordinator] *How often do tutors meet with students?* [once a week]

3. Play the audio. Have students read along silently.

Guided Practice I
10 minutes

C 1. Have students work independently to underline the answers to the questions in the text.

2. Point out the *Writer's Note* and read the information aloud. Ask: *What is a detail about the literacy program? What is an example of why the program is important? What is a detail about the problem with the program?* As a class, discuss what other examples or details are included in the email.

3. Ask students to annotate the information they underlined with the phrases "who" for paragraph 1, "offer" for paragraph 2, and "support" for paragraph 4. Have pairs compare answers. Have volunteers call out answers and write them on the board for the class to check.

Answers
Underlined:
1. immigrants and others who want to learn how to read
2. It offers 1:1 literacy tutors
3. the program needs more tutors

MULTILEVEL STRATEGIES
Seat pre-level students together for 1C.
• **Pre-level** While other students are working on 1C, provide these students with a summary of the email: *The library literacy program needs volunteer tutors to help people to learn to read and/or improve their English. The program offers one tutor for each student. It is free for all students. The program needs more tutors. Tutors meet once a week with a student. Training is provided for tutors.*
Direct students to complete 1C using this summary.

2 Plan and write

Guided Practice II
15–20 minutes

 1. Read question 1. Elicit types of civic involvement in the community and write them on the board.

2. Read question 2. Choose one type of civic involvement and demonstrate how to create a cluster diagram by drawing a circle and writing the type of involvement in the center. Draw "spokes" with circles at the end and ask

volunteers for one or two improvements to add to the diagram. Have students select one of the types of civic involvement and create their own cluster diagram of ways it will help the community. Have students share their diagrams with partners.

B Read through the email template. Elicit ideas that could go in each paragraph. Have students write their email individually.

> ### TIP
> Have students research which local newspaper they can write to and how and to whom they could send an email to appear in that newspaper.

> ### MULTILEVEL STRATEGIES
> Adapt 2B to the level of your students.
> • **Pre-level** Have these students complete each sentence in the template.
> • **Higher-level** Ask these students to include an additional paragraph that talks about why community involvement is a good thing in general.

3 Get feedback and revise

Guided Practice III
5 minutes

A Direct students to check their writing using the editing checklist. Tell them to read each item in the list and check their papers before moving on to the next item. Explain that students should not edit their writing at this stage. They should just use the checklist to check their work and mark any areas they want to revise.

Communicative Practice
15 minutes

B 1. Read the instructions and the sample sentences aloud. Emphasize to students that they are responding to their partners' work, not correcting it.

2. Use the text in 1B to model the exercise. *Your program sounds helpful to new immigrants.*

3. Direct students to exchange papers with a partner and follow the instructions.

C Allow students time to edit and revise their writing as necessary, using the editing checklist from 3A and their partner's feedback from 3B. If necessary, students could complete this task as homework.

Application and Evaluation
10 minutes

TEST YOURSELF

1. Review the instructions aloud. Assign a time limit (five minutes) and have students work independently.

2. Before collecting student work, invite two or three volunteers to share their sentences. Ask students to raise their hands if they wrote similar answers.

> ### EXTENSION ACTIVITY
> #### Discuss Community Involvement
> Have students ask and answer questions about community involvement.
>
> 1. Using the ideas from this lesson about community involvement, brainstorm a list of questions. *Have you ever or would you like to in the future work with your neighbors on a project? Have you ever gone to a city council meeting? Voted? Volunteered? Do you pay attention to politics? Do you talk to your neighbors?*
>
> 2. Direct students to ask and answer the questions in groups of three. Encourage them to supply additional information after they have given their *yes/no* answer.

Lesson Overview	Lesson Notes
MULTILEVEL OBJECTIVES	

On- and Higher-level: Use verbs plus infinitives or gerunds to plan an event and listen for information about community involvement

Pre-level: Recognize verbs plus infinitives or gerunds in conversations about community involvement and use the infinitive

LANGUAGE FOCUS

Grammar: Verb + infinitive or gerund (*I plan to walk. He enjoys working.*)

Vocabulary: *Pledge, volunteer*

For vocabulary support, see this **Oxford Picture Dictionary** topic: Community Cleanup, pages 152–153

STRATEGY FOCUS

Learn which verbs use gerunds or infinitives and which use only gerunds.

READINESS CONNECTION

In this lesson, students practice using verbs + infinitives and/or gerunds to communicate their ideas about community involvement.

PACING

To compress this lesson: Conduct 1B and/or 1C as a whole-class activity.

To extend this lesson: Have students practice gerunds and infinitives. (See end of lesson.)

And/or have students complete **Workbook 3 pages 81–82, Multilevel Activities 3 Unit 12 pages 131–132,** and **Multilevel Grammar Exercises 3 Unit 12.**

CORRELATIONS

CCRS: SL.6.B Speak in complete sentences when appropriate to task and situation in order to provide requested detail or clarification.

R.1.B Ask and answer such questions as who, what, where, when, why, and how to demonstrate understanding of key details in a text.

R.5.A Know and use various text features to locate key facts or information in a text.

R.7.C Interpret information presented visually, orally, or quantitatively and explain how the information contributes to an understanding of the text in which it appears.

L.1.B (l.) Produce simple, compound and complex sentences.

L.1.D (f.) Explain the function of verbals (gerunds, participles, infinitives) in general and their function in particular sentences.

RF.4.B (a.) Read grade-level text with purpose and understanding.

ELPS: 7. An ELL can adapt language choices to purpose, task, and audience when speaking and writing. 10. An ELL can demonstrate command of the conventions of standard English to communicate in level-appropriate speech and writing.

Warm-up and Review
10–15 minutes (books closed)

Write these words (including punctuation) on the board: *homework. I to volunteer enjoy children, school. I working with don't but I elementary at the like to correct want.* Ask students to unscramble the words and punctuation to make sentences. Have volunteers share their ideas. Accept any logical, correct sentence. Write the original order on the board: *I want to volunteer at the elementary school. I enjoy working with children, but I don't like to correct homework.*

Introduction
5–10 minutes

1. Underline *want to volunteer, enjoy working,* and *don't like to correct* in the example on the board. Say: *With* want, *we use a* to *form, or an infinitive. With* enjoy, *we use an* -ing *form, or a gerund. With* like *we can use either an infinitive or a gerund.*

2. State the objective: *Today we're going to learn some verbs that are followed by infinitives and some that are followed by gerunds, and we'll talk about planning an event.*

1 Use verbs + infinitives

Presentation I
20–25 minutes

 1. Direct students to look at the form. Elicit their answers to the question.

2. Ask: *What are they raising money for?* Ask students to read the form silently to find the answer. Call on a volunteer for the answer.

Possible Answers
walk, run, pledge money, volunteer to serve food, volunteer to clean up

B 1. Read the sentences in the chart aloud.

2. Direct students to underline the examples of infinitives in the form in 1A. Go over the answers as a class.

3. Copy one of the sentences from the form on the board. Ask students to identify which word is the verb and which is the infinitive.

4. Assess students' understanding of the chart. Call on volunteers to make new sentences using the verbs in the chart.

Answers
to walk, to run, to pledge, to serve, to clean up

Guided Practice I
10–15 minutes

 1. Tell students they will collaborate to complete the description of the grammar point. Encourage students to look at 1A and 1B to help them determine the correct words.

2. Pair students and have them work together to complete the description.

3. Project or write the completed definition on the board and have pairs verify the accuracy of their responses. Ask volunteers which sentences confused them and discuss.

Answers
verb
verbs

MULTILEVEL STRATEGIES

For 1C, seat same-level students together.

• **Pre-level** While other students are completing 1C, ask these students to write three sentences with infinitives. Provide these sentence frames: *I want to _____. I hope to _____. I need to _____.*

• **Higher-level** Have these students write four additional sentences using infinitives. Provide them with these verbs: *expect, promise, offer, seem.*

Guided Practice II
10–15 minutes

 1. Model the questions and answers with a volunteer. Go over the words in the *Event Planning Checklist.*

2. Ask students to practice the questions and answers with their partners using information from the *Event Planning Checklist* and their own ideas.

3. Have pairs merge to form teams of four and then take turns demonstrating questions and answers. Set a time limit (four minutes) and monitor the practice, identifying any issues.

4. Provide clarification or feedback to the whole class as needed.

Communicative Practice and Application I
10–15 minutes

D 1. Read each question aloud. Demonstrate answering with complete sentences by telling students your own answers.

2. Ask students to work individually to write answers to the questions.

3. Have students ask and answer the questions with a partner.

2 Use verbs + gerunds or infinitives

Presentation II
15–20 minutes

A 1. Introduce the new topic. Say: *Now we're going to look at some verbs that are followed by gerunds and infinitives.*

2. Direct students to read the charts. Ask: *Can every verb be followed by either an infinitive or a gerund?* [No, some can, but others can be followed only by a gerund.]

3. Ask students to work individually to choose the correct form(s) to complete the sentences. Call on volunteers to read the completed sentences aloud.

Answers
1. meeting / to meet
2. playing
3. listening
4. learning / to learn

TIP

After 2A, provide more practice with infinitives and gerunds. Put up the following incomplete story on the board and ask students to work with a partner to complete it: *My uncle Hal didn't like to get involved with the community. He never volunteered _____. His neighbors said, "Don't you like _____," and he said, "No, I have always disliked _____." His neighbor Mary continued _____, and finally, Hal began _____. Now, I think he even enjoys _____!* Tell students they need to use infinitives and gerunds, but they can add other things as well to make their stories clearer. Elicit possibilities for the first blank: *to do anything, to work on community cleanup days, to help with the neighborhood yard sale.* Have volunteers share their versions of the story with the class.

Guided Practice III
15–20 minutes

B 1. Read the first sentence aloud. Ask students to find *continue* in the grammar chart. Ask: *Can* continue *be followed by an infinitive?* [yes] Ask a volunteer to write a new sentence using the infinitive on the board.

2. Have students complete the task in teams. Set a time limit (five minutes). Have volunteers write their sentences on the board and go over answers as a class.

Answers
1. They continued to work last night.
2. I like to volunteer.
3. no change possible
4. He began to study at 8:00.
5. no change possible
6. We continued to work all night.

TIP

For additional practice, have students work with gerunds as subjects and gerunds or infinitives after verbs.

1. Provide this model conversation:

A: I want/plan/have decided to volunteer at my son's school.

B: Why?

A: Volunteering at the school is a good way to practice my English.

2. Elicit other possible completions for the conversation and write them on the board.

3. Set a time limit (five minutes). Have students walk around the room practicing the conversation with as many different people as possible.

3 Listen for gerunds and infinitives

Guided Practice IV
15–20 minutes

 1. Say: *Now we're going to listen to sentences about people getting involved with their communities. You will only hear the beginning of the sentence. You need to choose the correct ending.*

2. Play the audio. Direct students to read along silently without writing.

3. Replay the audio. Ask students to choose the correct endings.

4. Call on volunteers for the answers.

Answers	
1. a	4. b
2. a	5. b
3. b	6. a

MULTILEVEL STRATEGIES

Replay the audio to challenge on- and higher-level students while allowing pre-level students to catch up.

• **Pre-level** Have these students listen again to choose the correct answers.

• **On- and Higher-level** Ask these students to listen again and write the main verb they hear. Elicit the verbs and write them on the board.

4 Use gerunds and infinitives to talk about your life experience

Communicative Practice and Application II
20–25 minutes

A Read the instructions. Direct students to work individually to complete the chart.

B 1. Put students in groups of three. Read the sample conversation aloud with a volunteer.

2. Direct students to take turns asking and answering questions in their groups. Tell them to make notes of at least one of each person's answers.

3. Check comprehension of the exercise. Ask: *How many people are you going to talk to?* [two] *Do you need to write everything down?* [no]

C Ask volunteers to share something interesting they learned about their group members.

Evaluation
10–15 minutes

TEST YOURSELF

Ask students to write the sentences independently. Collect and correct their writing.

MULTILEVEL STRATEGIES

Target the *Test Yourself* to the level of your students.

• **Pre-level** Provide sentence frames for these students to complete:

_____ (classmate's name) likes _____.
_____ (classmate's name) dislikes _____.
_____ (classmate's name) plans _____.

• **Higher-level** Have these students write a paragraph in response to this prompt and questions: *Compare yourself to one of your classmates. How are your likes, dislikes, and plans the same? How are they different?*

EXTENSION ACTIVITY

Practice Gerunds and Infinitives

Provide more practice with gerunds and infinitives.

1. Show students pictures of famous people, or pass out magazines and ask students to find pictures of people involved in different activities.

2. Tell students to write sentences about the people using infinitives and gerunds. *He enjoys playing basketball. She likes working in the garden.*

Lesson Overview	Lesson Notes

MULTILEVEL OBJECTIVES

Pre-, On-, and Higher-level: Discuss legal problems and listen for information in a town meeting

LANGUAGE FOCUS

Grammar: Reported requests (*He told her to sit down.*)

Vocabulary: *Tenant, town meeting, express opinions*

For vocabulary support, see this **Oxford Picture Dictionary** topic: Civic Engagement, pages 142–143

STRATEGY FOCUS

Recognize homophones to avoid confusion.

READINESS CONNECTION

In this lesson, students verbally communicate and practice how to report requests and respond to others' ideas.

PACING

To compress this lesson: Do 6A as a class activity and skip 6B.

To extend this lesson: Have students write a letter. (See end of lesson.)

And/or have students complete **Workbook 3 page 83** and **Multilevel Activities 3 Unit 12 page 133**.

CORRELATIONS

CCRS: SL.1.B (a.) Come to discussions prepared, having read or studied required material; explicitly draw on that preparation and other information known about the topic to explore ideas under discussion. (b.) Follow agreed-upon rules for discussions. (c.) Ask questions to check understanding of information presented, stay on topic, and link their comments to the remarks of others. (d.) Explain their own ideas and understanding in light of the discussion.

SL.2.B Determine the main ideas and supporting details of a text read aloud or information presented in diverse media and formats, including visually, quantitatively, and orally.

SL.4.B Report on a topic or text, tell a story, or recount an experience with appropriate facts and relevant, descriptive details, speaking clearly at an understandable pace.

SL.6.B Speak in complete sentences when appropriate to task and situation in order to provide requested detail or clarification.

R.1.B Ask and answer such questions as who, what, where, when, why, and how to demonstrate understanding of key details in a text.

R.2.A Identify the main topic and retell key details of a text.

R.6.B Identify the main purpose of a text, including what the author wants to answer, explain, or describe.

R.7.B Use information gained from illustrations and the words in a text to demonstrate understanding of the text.

L.1.B (k.) Use coordinating and subordinating conjunctions (l.) Produce simple, compound and complex sentences.

L.1.C (d.) Use modal auxiliaries to convey various conditions. (e.) Form and use the perfect verb tenses. (f.) Use verb tense to convey various times, sequences, states, and conditions.

L.1.D (f.) Explain the function of verbals (gerunds, participles, infinitives) in general and their function in particular sentences.

L.3.B (b.) Recognize and observe differences between the conventions of spoken and written standard English.

RF.4.B (a.) Read grade-level text with purpose and understanding.

ELPS: 2. An ELL can participate in level-appropriate oral and written exchanges of information, ideas, and analyses, in various social and academic contexts, responding to peer, audience, or reader comments and questions. 9. An ELL can create clear and coherent level-appropriate speech and text.

Warm-up and Review
5–10 minutes (books closed)

Write *Neighbors*, *Work*, and *City* on the board. Tell students you want to brainstorm ideas about legal problems and put them in these categories. Ask: *What kinds of problems do people have with their neighbors?* Write them on the board. Do the same with *Work* and *City*.

Introduction
3 minutes

1. Ask if any of the problems on the board might cause you to ask for legal help.

2. State the objective: *Today we're going to learn how to ask for help at a legal clinic and listen for information at a town hall meeting.*

1 Learn to protect your rights

Presentation I
10 minutes

 A 🔊 **3-38** 1. Direct students to look at the flyer. Ask: *What kinds of legal services are offered at this clinic?*

2. Read the question aloud. Play the audio. Give students a minute to answer the question. Go over the answer as a class.

Answer
Her landlord asked her to move out of her apartment before her one-year lease was finished.

Guided Practice I
20–25 minutes

 B 🔊 **3-38** 1. Read the instructions and the questions aloud. Play the audio. Ask students to listen for the answer to each question.

2. Ask students to compare their answers with a partner. Circulate and monitor to ensure students understand the audio.

Answers
1. She was asked to bring in a copy of her lease.
2. His brother needs a place to live.
3. Yes

 C 🔊 **3-39** Read the instructions aloud. Explain that students are going to hear the audio one more time. They should write the words they hear to complete the sentences. Play the audio. Call on volunteers to elicit the answers.

Answers
1. I think it's because
2. It might be because
3. I suspect it's because

2 Practice your pronunciation

Pronunciation Extension
10–15 minutes

 A 🔊 **3-40** 1. Write *two*, *to*, and *too* on the board. Say a sentence with each one. *There are two council members. I drove to the meeting. I'm too tired to volunteer tonight.* Ask: *Do these words sound the same or different?* Tell students that words that sound the same are called *homophones*. Say: *Now we're going to focus on the pronunciation of common homophones.*

2. Play the audio. Direct students to listen for the words that sound the same.

3. Elicit the words. Read the *Pronunciation Note* about homophones aloud. Write *deer* on the board and elicit the homophone [*dear*].

B 🔊 **3-41** Play the audio. Direct students to underline the homophones.

Answers	

1. a. I get the <u>mail</u> every day.
   b. Pat is a 10-year-old <u>male</u>.
2. a. I need to <u>buy</u> some food.
   b. The market is <u>by</u> the bank.
	3. a. Tim is a <u>new</u> citizen.
	   b. He <u>knew</u> he could pass the exam.
	4. a. <u>I'll</u> go to the market.
	   b. Apples are in <u>aisle</u> six.

C 🔊 **3-41** 1. Play the audio again. Have students check their answers to 2B. Call on volunteers to read the sentences aloud and identify the homophones.

2. Ask students to take turns reading the sentences in 2B with a partner. Monitor and provide feedback.

3 Learn to report requests

Presentation II and Guided Practice II
15–20 minutes

A 1. Introduce the new topic. Say: *Now we're
going to learn how to report requests with the
verb* tell.

2. Direct students to look at the pictures. Ask:
*Who is the woman calling? Where do you think
the daughter is going?* Read the sentences below
each picture and the *Grammar Notes*.

3. Check comprehension. Write the sentences
below the pictures on the board. Have a
volunteer come to the board and label the
words in each sentence using the information
in the *Grammar Notes*.

4. Have students work individually to circle
the correct answers. Ask volunteers to read the
completed sentences aloud.

Answers
1. to call
2. to write
3. not to
4. her

B 1. Illustrate the transformation of quotation
to reported request by having students make
requests. Pass out slips of paper to several
students with requests on them. *Erase the
board. Turn off the light. Don't close the door.*
Have each student read the request. Respond
with the reported version. *Marcos told me to
erase the board.* Ask students to make new
requests. Respond with the reported versions.

2. Have students work individually to write the
reported version of each sentence.

3. Ask volunteers to write the reported requests
on the board.

Answers
1. The clerk told Sasha to sit down.
2. Then he told her to <u>fill out a form</u>.
3. Next <u>he told her not to leave the building</u>.

4 Building conversational skills

Guided Practice III
15–20 minutes

A Direct students to look at the picture and
skim the conversation in 4B. Have them
work with partners to identify the purpose
of the conversation. Elicit responses and ask:
How do you know? or *Why do you say that?* to
encourage students to state their reasoning.

Answers
The man was fired from his job yesterday, but he doesn't know why; answers will vary.

B   1. Ask students to read the
instructions and tell you what they are going
to do [listen and read and respond to the
question]. Play the audio and then elicit the
answer to the question.

Answer
He's thinks that it's because he is over 55 and makes more money than younger employees.

2. Ask students to read the conversation with a
partner. Circulate and monitor pronunciation.
Model and have students repeat difficult words
or phrases.

3. Ask: *In what other situations could you use
this conversation?* Point out a few phrases that
are not specific to speaking to a lawyer. Ask
volunteers to point out others.

Communicative Practice and Application I
20–25 minutes

C 1. Pair students and have them read the instructions silently. Check their comprehension of the exercise. Ask: *What are the two roles? Where does the conversation take place?*

2. Model and have students repeat the phrases in the *In Other Words* box in 4B. Explain that they should use these phrases in their conversations.

3. Draw a T-chart on the board. Label the left column *Client* and the right column *Law clerk*. Elicit examples of what each person might say and make notes in the chart.

4. Set a time limit (three minutes). Have students act out the role-play. Call "time" and have students switch roles.

5. Ask three volunteer pairs to act out their role-play for the class. Tell students who are listening to make a simple table with four rows and two columns. Use the top row to label the columns *Details of problem* and *Questions about problem*. Have students take notes in the chart for each role-play.

> **MULTILEVEL STRATEGIES**
>
> Seat same-level students together.
>
> • **Pre-level** Work with these students and guide them in writing their new conversation or provide a simplified conversation for these students to practice.
>
> *A: How can I help you? B: My landlord told me I have to move next month. A: Do you have a lease? B: Yes. It's for one year. B: OK. I think I can help you. Show me your lease.*

5 Focus on listening for details

Presentation III and Guided Practice IV
20–25 minutes

A 1. Read the questions and statement aloud and model a discussion with a volunteer. Ask: *Do you think everyone should go to every town meeting? Why? / Why not? I agree because… / I disagree because…*

2. Pair students and tell them to discuss their own answers to the questions. Circulate and monitor.

> **TIP**
>
> To ensure that students are listening to each other, ask them to repeat back what their partner said.

B Direct students to read the sentences before they listen to the meeting discussion. Ask what kind of information they'll be writing in the blanks. Ask volunteers for predictions. If students struggle, start by offering your own prediction: *I think we will hear someone talk about a new building in the neighborhood.*

C 1. Play the audio. Ask students to listen and write the correct answers.

2. Pair students and have them compare answers. If a pair has different answers, have the class vote on the correct answer with a show of hands.

Answers
1. school
2. parking
3. owned
4. taxes
5. opinion

> **MULTILEVEL STRATEGIES**
>
> Replay the conversation to challenge on- and higher-level students while allowing pre-level students to catch up.
>
> • **Pre-level** Have these students listen again to fill in the blanks.
>
> • **On- and Higher-level** Write questions on the board. *What's the problem with the street? What would be terrible? What would be cheaper?* After you have gone over the answers to 5C, have volunteers share their answers to the questions.

6 Discuss

Communicative Practice and Application II
15–20 minutes

A 1. Read the instructions aloud. Draw a sample pro/con chart on the board. Call on volunteers to read the sample conversation in 6A. Fill in the chart with the sample sentences. Explain that students will make a chart like this one based on their own discussions.

2. Put students into teams of three and assign roles: manager, administrative assistant, and reporter. Verify students' understanding of the roles. Encourage students to use the phrases in the *Speaking Note* during their discussions.

3. Set a time limit for the discussions (ten minutes). Write the sentence frame from 6B on the board. Then circulate and monitor.

B Call "time." Ask the reporter for each team to report the results of the team's discussion using the sentence frame on the board.

Evaluation
5 minutes

TEST YOURSELF

1. Ask students to complete the checkboxes individually.

2. Tell students that you are going to read each of the items in the checklist aloud. If they are not at all confident with that skill, they should hold up a closed fist. If they are not very confident, they should hold up one finger. If they are somewhat confident, two fingers; confident, three fingers; very confident, four fingers. If they think they could teach the skill, they should hold up five fingers. Read each item in the checklist and identify students who may need further support.

EXTENSION ACTIVITY

Write a Letter

Have students write a letter requesting legal help.

1. Put students in groups of three or four. Ask the groups to write a short letter explaining their legal trouble and asking for help.

2. Have a reporter from each group read the letter to the class. Ask the class to decide whether the problem could be dealt with by a legal clinic. In some cases, the person might be able to deal with it himself or herself, or police help might be needed.

Lesson Overview	Lesson Notes

MULTILEVEL OBJECTIVES

Pre-, On-, and Higher-level: Read about and discuss the Civil Rights Movement

LANGUAGE FOCUS

Grammar: Nouns and verbs (*The Montgomery Bus Boycott was the beginning of the Civil Rights Movement.*)

Vocabulary: *Movement, boycott, civil rights, discrimination, segregated*

For vocabulary support, see this **Oxford Picture Dictionary** topic: Civic Engagement, pages 142–143

STRATEGY FOCUS

Think about what is said and not said to identify an author's opinion.

READINESS CONNECTION

In this lesson, students verbally communicate information about voting.

PACING

To compress this lesson: Assign 1E and/or 1F for homework.

To extend this lesson: Have students talk about civil rights leaders. (See end of lesson.)

And/or have students complete **Workbook 3 page 84** and **Multilevel Activities 3 Unit 12 pages 134–135**.

CORRELATIONS

CCRS: SL.1.B (a.) Come to discussions prepared, having read or studied required material; explicitly draw on that preparation and other information known about the topic to explore ideas under discussion. (b.) Follow agreed-upon rules for discussions. (c.) Ask questions to check understanding of information presented, stay on topic, and link their comments to the remarks of others. (d.) Explain their own ideas and understanding in light of the discussion.

SL.2.B Determine the main ideas and supporting details of a text read aloud or information presented in diverse media and formats, including visually, quantitatively, and orally.

R.1.B Ask and answer such questions as who, what, where, when, why, and how to demonstrate understanding of key details in a text.

R.2.A Identify the main topic and retell key details of a text.

R.4.B Determine the meaning of general academic and domain-specific words and phrases in a text relevant to a topic or subject area.

R.5.A Know and use various text features to locate key facts or information in a text.

R.6.B Identify the main purpose of a text, including what the author wants to answer, explain, or describe.

R.7.B Use information gained from illustrations and the words in a text to demonstrate understanding of the text.

R.7.C Interpret information presented visually, orally, or quantitatively and explain how the information contributes to an understanding of the text in which it appears.

L.1.B (l.) Produce simple, compound and complex sentences.

L.4.B (a.) Use sentence-level context as a clue to the meaning of a word or phrase. (e.) Use glossaries and beginning dictionaries, both print and digital, to determine or clarify the meaning of words and phrases.

RF.4.B (a.) Read grade-level text with purpose and understanding.

ELPS: 1. An ELL can construct meaning from oral presentations and literary and informational text through level-appropriate listening, reading, and viewing. 3. An ELL can speak and write about level-appropriate complex literary and informational texts and topics.

Warm-up and Review
10–15 minutes (books closed)

Write *Segregation* on the board. Ask if anyone knows what segregation is. Find out what students know about the history of African Americans in this country. List ways in which African Americans and other minorities were segregated and discriminated against: separate schools and neighborhoods, separate areas of restaurants, job discrimination, laws against mixed marriage.

Introduction
10 minutes

1. Ask students if they know when the segregation and discrimination they have discussed became illegal.

2. State the objective: *Today we're going to read about the first important protest against segregation. After this protest, thousands of people fought against racial discrimination for years. We call it the Civil Rights Movement.*

1 Read

Presentation
10–20 minutes

A Read the questions aloud. Use ideas from the *Introduction* to help guide discussion.

B Read the words and definitions. Elicit sample sentences for the words or supply them if the students can't. Ask students if they can think of any examples of boycotts.

Pre-reading

C 1. Read the instructions aloud and confirm that students understand where the title and the photograph are. Have students answer the question individually and then check answers as a class. If any students answer incorrectly, ask them to support their answer using the title and photograph. Establish the correct answer.

2. Ask students to scan the article for dates. Elicit the dates and write them on the board.

Answer
a. How the civil rights movement started on a bus.

Guided Practice: While Reading
20–30 minutes

 1. Ask students to read the article silently and answer the question.

2. Check the answer with the class.

3. Direct students' attention to the *Reader's Note* and read the information aloud.

4. Direct students to underline unfamiliar words they would like to know. Elicit the words and encourage other students to provide definitions or examples.

5. Check comprehension. Elicit what happened on each of the dates on the board.

Answer
Rosa Parks, an African American woman, refused to give up her seat on a bus to a white man.

MULTILEVEL STRATEGIES

Adapt 2D to the level of your students.

• **Pre-level** Provide these students with a summary of the reading.

1. In 1955, buses were segregated. An African American woman named Rosa Parks refused to give her seat to a white man. She went to jail.

2. African Americans decided to boycott the buses. They didn't ride the buses for one year, so the city lost money. Martin Luther King, Jr. was their leader. On December 21, 1956, the Supreme Court told the city to change its bus laws. The boycott ended.

3. This was the beginning of the Civil Rights Movement. In 1964, the Civil Rights Act was passed. The Civil Rights Act made discrimination a crime.

Direct students to read this summary while other students are reading 2D.

Guided Practice: Rereading
10–15 minutes

 1. Provide an opportunity for students to extract evidence from the text. Have students reread the article and underline any words or phrases that indicate the author's attitude about the Civil Rights Movement.

2. Pair students and tell them to compare the words they underlined and report anything they disagree on. Discuss and clarify as needed.

Answers
Positive; underlines will vary.

F 1. Have students work individually to mark the answers *T* (true), *F* (false), and *NI* (no information). They should then write the line numbers where they found the true and false answers. Write the answers on the board.

2. Elicit and discuss any additional questions about the reading. You could introduce new questions for class discussion: *Are laws always needed to stop discrimination? Are boycotts an effective way to protest?*

Answers
1. T, lines 1–2
2. F, lines 6–8
3. NI
4. T, lines 24–27
5. F, lines 34–35

2 Word study

Guided Practice: Post-reading
10–15 minutes

A 1. Read the words in the chart aloud. For each of the first four words, write a sentence on the board using it in its noun and verb form. *They had a conflict about civil rights. Their ideas conflict with ours. He has a permit to drive. They won't permit you to park here. We should protest against injustice. The protest was very large. They object to discrimination. There's a strange object on the table.* Say each sentence and elicit the stressed syllable. Underline the stressed syllable. Then elicit whether the word is a noun or a verb.

2. Direct students to work individually to circle the correct word. Ask volunteers to read the completed sentences aloud.

Answers
1. pro̲tests
2. per̲mitted
3. obj̲ected
4. de̲crease
5. sus̲pect

B 1. Read the prompts aloud. Give students a few minutes to think of their answers.

2. Set a time limit (ten minutes). Have pairs discuss the prompts. Circulate and help as needed, confirming that students are using the underlined words in their discussions.

3. Have volunteers share their responses with the class.

3 Talk it over

Guided Practice
15–20 minutes

 Have students read the pie chart, the note, and the *Reader's Note*. Point out that they need to use the information from the pie chart and the note to complete the sentences and answer the question. Set a time limit (ten minutes). Have students work in pairs to complete the task. Ask volunteers to share their answers with the class.

Answers
1. 13
2. Lack of interest in politics
3. Lazy, believe that vote doesn't count, other
4. 13
5. 40
6. Answers will vary.

Communicative Practice
15–20 minutes

B Read the questions aloud. Set a time limit (ten minutes). Allow students to think about the questions and then write their answers in their notebooks.

C Ask volunteers to share their ideas with the class.

Application
15–20 minutes

BRING IT TO LIFE

Ask students whom they are going to tell Rosa Park's story to. Elicit any additional questions that they have about Rosa Parks. Write the questions on the board and ask them to look on the Internet or in the library for answers.

EXTENSION ACTIVITY

Talk about Civil Rights Leaders

Talk about people who led change in the students' native countries.

1. Say: *Rosa Parks is famous because her action started a movement that changed the whole country. Martin Luther King, Jr. is famous because he was the leader and the most important voice of that movement. Think of someone who is important in the history of your native country. How did that person change the country?* Call on volunteers for ideas and write the names on the board.

2. Have students sit in same-country groups. Tell them to choose one of the names and write about what he/she did. If you have too many different countries represented in your class to make same-country groups possible, have students sit in groups and tell each other about the leader from their country.

3. Have a reporter from each group read the group's story to the class. Or have volunteers share what they learned from their classmates.

AT WORK

Warm-up and Review
10–15 minutes

Begin the lesson by role-playing a student in an English class. The teacher is talking about the Civil Rights Movement, but you don't know what *civil rights* means. Ask students for their suggestions on how you can address this issue.

Introduction
5 minutes

1. Explain that at work, if you don't understand something, it is better to ask a question than to try to guess. Also, it is important to be able to clearly answer questions about what you say if a co-worker has a question.

2. State the objective: *Today we're going to talk about how to help someone understand.*

Presentation
5 minutes

 3-44 Read the instructions aloud. Play the audio. Give students a minute to think about the question. Elicit responses from the class.

Answer
Meeting of staff at a the Community Legal Clinic

Guided Practice
10–15 minutes

 3-44 1. Read the instructions aloud. Play the audio and have students check the kinds of problems that the legal clinic works with.

2. To check answers, play the audio again and have students raise their hands each time they hear one of the categories.

Answers
Checked: employee rights immigration tenant rights credit problems traffic accidents

Presentation and Communicative Practice
15–20 minutes

 1. Direct students' attention to the *Do/Say* chart and ask students to identify the lesson's soft skill [helping someone understand]. Ask the class which column has examples of behaviors [left] and which has examples of language [right].

2. Model the sentences from the right column using authentic intonation. Have students practice imitating your inflection.

3. Put students in teams of four and assign each team a question. Assign roles: manager, administrative assistant, researcher, and reporter. Researchers will ask you questions on behalf of the team. Verify understanding of the roles. Set a time limit (five minutes) and monitor.

4. Write sentence frames on the board that teams can use to summarize their response. (*Our team discussed the following question: _____ We decided _____ because _____.*)

5. Call "time" and let reporters rehearse their report for one minute. Direct each reporter to present to three other teams.

Communicative Practice and Application
10–15 minutes

D 1. Put students in teams of four. Read the instructions aloud. Have teams choose one student to run the staff meeting. Confirm understanding of the role-play. Ask: *What is the problem with the company?* [It is losing money.] *What is the only way to solve the problem?* [lay off an employee] *How many employees are in the department?* [four] *Are the employees part of the meeting?* [no] *How will you choose?* [read the information about each employee]

2. Elicit ways to complete the response in the sample conversation and write them on the board. Read the sample conversation with a volunteer.

3. As students carry out the role-play, circulate and monitor. Provide global feedback once the activity ends.

Lesson Overview

MULTILEVEL OBJECTIVES

Pre-, On-, and Higher-level: Review unit language

LANGUAGE FOCUS

Grammar: Infinitives and gerunds (*He wants to speak at the meeting. Next week I'll begin working.*)

Vocabulary: Verbs that are followed by infinitives and/or gerunds

For vocabulary support, see these **Oxford Picture Dictionary** topics: Civic Engagement, pages 142–143; Community Cleanup, pages 152–153

READINESS CONNECTION

In this review, students work in a team to use gerunds and infinitives and describe and complete a survey on community activities.

PACING

To extend this review: Have students complete **Workbook 3 page 85, Multilevel Activities 3 Unit 12 page 136, and Multilevel Grammar Exercises 3 Unit 12.**

Lesson Notes

CORRELATIONS

CCRS: SL.1.B (a.) Come to discussions prepared, having read or studied required material; explicitly draw on that preparation and other information known about the topic to explore ideas under discussion. (b.) Follow agreed-upon rules for discussions. (c.) Ask questions to check understanding of information presented, stay on topic, and link their comments to the remarks of others. (d.) Explain their own ideas and understanding in light of the discussion.

SL.2.B Determine the main ideas and supporting details of a text read aloud or information presented in diverse media and formats, including visually, quantitatively, and orally.

SL.4.B Report on a topic or text, tell a story, or recount an experience with appropriate facts and relevant, descriptive details, speaking clearly at an understandable pace.

SL.6.B Speak in complete sentences when appropriate to task and situation in order to provide requested detail or clarification.

R.1.B Ask and answer such questions as who, what, where, when, why, and how to demonstrate understanding of key details in a text.

R.2.A Identify the main topic and retell key details of a text.

L.1.B (l.) Produce simple, compound and complex sentences.

L.1.C (d.) Use modal auxiliaries to convey various conditions. (f.) Use verb tense to convey various times, sequences, states, and conditions.

L.1.D (f.) Explain the function of verbals (gerunds, participles, infinitives) in general and their function in particular sentences.

RF.4.B (a.) Read grade-level text with purpose and understanding.

ELPS: 5. An ELL can conduct research and evaluate and communicate findings to answer questions or solve problems. 6. An ELL can analyze and critique the arguments of others orally and in writing.

Warm-up and Review
10–15 minutes (books closed)

1. Review *At Work* activity D.

2. Ask students to share the good, not-so-good, and interesting things that happened during the conversation. As students speak, write their responses in a chart on the board.

Introduction and Presentation
5 minutes

1. Write sentences about Rosa Parks on the board using infinitives and gerunds. *She didn't want to give up her seat to a white man. She continued to fight against discrimination. On the day of her trial, African Americans began boycotting the buses in Montgomery.* Elicit the main verb of each sentence and the form of the second verb. Ask about each gerund/infinitive: *Can we change this to an infinitive/gerund?*

2. State the objective: *Today we're going to review infinitives and gerunds.*

Guided Practice
15–20 minutes

 1. Read the instructions aloud. Point out the example.

2. Set a time limit (ten minutes) for individuals to complete the task. Check answers as a class.

Possible Answers
1. Noah plans to put the recycling outside today.
2. Gloria likes dusting every month.
3. Ben enjoys taking all his toys off the shelf.
4. Moe wants to buy a dishwasher.
5. Elias begins to pour the trash into a bag.
6. Noah decides to recycle all the newspapers.
7. Beatriz will continue to clean the oven until it shines.
8. Emily needs to use a stepstool to reach the high windows.

B 1. Read the instructions and the sample answers aloud. Have students work individually to complete the task. Circulate and monitor.

2. Check answers as a class.

Possible Answers		
Infinitive	**Both**	**Gerund**
need	like	enjoy
decide	continue	
want	begin	
plan		

Communicative Practice
30–45 minutes

 1. Group students and assign roles: manager, writer, editor, and presenter. Explain that students are going to work with their teams to write an email to a community legal clinic about a problem. Editors will review the email and offer suggestions for changes. Verify students' understanding of the roles.

2. Read steps 2–4 of the activity aloud. Check comprehension of the task. *What is the first thing you should do?* [choose a reason from the box] *Who should your email be addressed to?* [the legal clinic] Answer any questions about vocabulary in the *Reasons* box.

3. Set a time limit (ten minutes) to complete the exercise. Circulate and answer any questions.

4. Have the presenter from each team read the team's email to the class.

 1. Have students walk around the room to conduct the interviews. To get students moving, tell them to interview three people who were not on their team for C.

2. Set a time limit (five minutes) to complete the exercise.

3. Tell students to make a note of their classmates' answers but not to worry about writing complete sentences.

MULTILEVEL STRATEGIES
Adapt the mixer in D to the level of your students.
• **Pre-and On-level** Pair these students and have them interview other pairs together.
• **Higher-level** Have these students ask an additional question and write all answers in complete sentences.

 1. Call on individuals to report what they learned about their classmates. Keep a list and running tally on the board for each question.

2. Have students work in their teams from C and make a poster of the responses from D. Circulate and answer any questions. Have teams present their posters to the class.

PROBLEM SOLVING

10–15 minutes

 A ◀)) **3-45** 1. Ask: *Have you or anyone you know had a small car accident?* Tell students they will read a story about a man who has a car accident and has to make a decision. Direct students to read Ruben's story silently.

2. Ask: *How did the accident happen?* [At a stoplight, another driver hit him from behind.] *What does the other driver want to do?* [pay Ruben for the damage]

3. Play the audio and have students read along silently.

B 1. Elicit answers to question 1. Guide students to a class consensus on the answer.

2. As a class, brainstorm answers to question 2. Ask students if they know someone who has this problem and has overcome it or what they have done themselves to overcome the same problem.

Answers
1. Ruben had a traffic accident and the other driver doesn't want to exchange insurance information. The other driver simply wants to give Ruben cash to repair his car. Ruben doesn't know what to do.
2. Answers will vary.

Evaluation

20–25 minutes

To test students' understanding of the unit language and content, have them take the Unit 12 Test, available on the Teacher Resource Center.